The Making of England
55 B.C. to 1399

A HISTORY OF ENGLAND
General Editor: Lacey Baldwin Smith

THE MAKING OF ENGLAND: 55 B.C. to 1399
C. Warren Hollister
University of California, Santa Barbara

THIS REALM OF ENGLAND: 1399 to 1688
Lacey Baldwin Smith
Northwestern University

THE AGE OF ARISTOCRACY: 1688 to 1830
William B. Willcox

Walter L. Arnstein
University of Illinois, Urbana-Champaign

BRITAIN YESTERDAY & TODAY:
1830 to the Present
Walter L. Arnstein
University of Illinois, Urbana-Champaign

The Making of England
55 B.C. to 1399

SIXTH EDITION

C. Warren Hollister
University of California, Santa Barbara

D. C. HEATH AND COMPANY
Lexington, Massachusetts   Toronto

Address editorial correspondence to:
D. C. Heath
125 Spring Street
Lexington, MA 02173

Cover Painting: Edward III (1312–1377) spares the lives of six notable citizens after the siege of Calais, 1346–1347. (The Granger Collection)

Published simultaneously in Canada.

Printed in the United States of America.

International Standard Book Number: 0-669-24457-0

Library of Congress Catalog Card Number: 91-73483

10 9 8 7 6 5 4 3 2 1

Foreword

Carl Becker once complained that everybody knows the job of the historian is "to discover and set forth the 'facts' of history." The facts, it is often said, speak for themselves. The businessman talks about hard facts, the statistician refers to cold facts, the lawyer is eloquent about the facts of the case, and the historian, who deals with the incontrovertible facts of life and death, is called a very lucky fellow. Those who speak so confidently about the historian's craft are generally not historians themselves; they are readers of textbooks that more often than not are mere recordings of vital information and listings of dull generalizations. It is not surprising, then, that historians' reputations have suffered; they have become known as peddlers of facts and chroniclers who say, "This is what happened." The shorter the historical survey, the more textbook writers are likely to assume godlike detachment, spurning the minor tragedies and daily comedies of humanity and immortalizing the rise and fall of civilizations, the clash of economic and social forces, and the deeds of titans. Anglo-Saxon warriors were sick with fear when Viking "swift sea-kings" swept down on England to plunder, rape, and kill, but historians dispassionately note that the Norse invasions were a good thing; they allowed the kingdom of Wessex to unite and "liberate" the island in the name of Saxon and Christian defense against heathen marauders. Nimbly the chronicler moves from the indisputable fact that Henry VIII annulled his marriage with Catherine of Aragon and wedded Anne Boleyn to the confident assertion that this helped produce the Reformation in England. The result is sublime but emasculated history. Her subjects wept when Good Queen Bess died, but historians merely comment that she had lived her alloted three score years and ten. British soldiers rotted by the thousands in the trenches of the First World War, but the terror and agony of that holocaust are lost in the dehumanized statistic that 750,000 British troops died in the four years of war.

In a brief history of even one "tight little island," the chronology of events must of necessity predominate; but if these four volumes are in any way fresh and new, it is because their authors have tried by artistry to step beyond the usual confines of a textbook and to conjure up something of the drama of politics, of the wealth of personalities, and even of the pettiness, as well as the greatness, of human motivation. The price paid will be obvious to anyone seeking total coverage. There is relatively little in these pages on literature, the fine arts, or philosophy, except as they throw light upon the uniqueness of English history. On the other hand, the complexities, the uncertainties, the endless variations, and above all the accidents that bedevil the design of human events—these are the very stuff of which history is made and the "truths" that this series seeks to elucidate and preserve. Moreover, the flavor of each volume varies according to the tastes of its author. Sometimes the emphasis is political, sometimes economic or social; but always the presentation is impressionistic—shading, underscoring, or highlighting to achieve an image that will be more than a bare outline and will recapture something of the smell and temper of the past.

Even though each book was conceived and executed as an entity capable of standing by itself, the four volumes were designed as a unit. They tell the story of how a small and insignificant outpost of the Roman Empire hesitantly, and not always heroically, evolved into the nation that has probably produced and disseminated more ideas and institutions, both good and bad, than any state since Athens. Our hope is that these volumes will appeal both individually, to those interested in a balanced portrait of particular segments of English history, and collectively, to those who seek the majestic sweep of the story of a people whose activities have been wonderfully rich, exciting, and varied. In this spirit this series was originally written and has now been revised for a fifth time, not only to keep pace with new scholarship but, equally important, to keep it fresh and thought-provoking to a world becoming both more nostalgic and more impatient of its past.

Lacey Baldwin Smith

Preface

Most authors, when revising their textbooks, are torn between introducing important changes, at the risk of irritating teachers who have grown accustomed to the materials in the book over a period of years, and making only cosmetic changes, at the risk of permitting the book to fade off into the sunset as exciting new archaeological evidence emerges and historical scholarship marches on. I have regularly chosen the first alternative, and I firmly believe that it is the wiser course. The sixth edition of *The Making of England* will not be altogether unfamiliar to users of previous editions, but they will find changes, stylistic or substantive, on virtually every page.

In recent years a great many pioneering books, articles, and archaeological reports on the subject of ancient and medieval Britain have been published. I have made every effort to incorporate the results of these new findings and interpretations into my revisions (often, necessarily, in simplified form). British archaeology, in particular, has been advancing by leaps and bounds. It has been of enormous help to me, as a historian lacking formal archaeological training, to have been privileged to explore the impressive excavations at the abandoned village of Wharram Percy, the hill forts of South Cadbury and Maiden Castle, the site of the Northumbrian royal hall at Yeavering, the early Anglo-Saxon abbeys of Jarrow and Wearmouth, and countless castle and abbey ruins. I am deeply grateful for the genial and astute guidance of Martin Biddle, who with such brilliance and originality directed excavations at the West Saxon capital of Winchester and the great Mercian religious center at Repton. I am also most thankful to Harold Taylor, who guided my wife Edith and me through his own fascinating excavation of the crypt of Repton Church.

More specifically, my revisions include the radically new picture that recent archaeology has provided of pre-Roman Britain—not as an untamed wilderness, as was previously believed, but as a heavily populated and developed land, intensively cultivated by farmers using heavy plows. This new understanding has sent reverberations through the entire history of Roman Britain and Anglo-Saxon England, depriving the Anglo-Saxons, for example, of the credit that they had so long enjoyed for taming the wilderness and for bringing the fertile clay soil of the lowlands under cultivation with the aid of the heavy plow (although some of the lands under cultivation during Roman times had become overgrown in the generations just following the Roman withdrawal and had to be retamed by the Anglo-Saxons).

Conversely, it is now possible to credit the people of Anglo-Saxon England with the development of nucleated villages, the characteristic agrarian centers of preindustrial England, once thought to have been part of the cultural luggage carried to Britain by the Germanic settlers of post-Roman times. The late development of the village, in turn, significantly erodes the long-standing conviction that the Anglo-Saxons wiped clean the Romano-British economic and cultural slate.

Recent scholarship has also reinterpreted the *Bretwaldaship* (much less important than formerly thought); King Arthur (if any such person ever existed); the wealth and power of the greater Anglo-Saxon kingdoms, as demonstrated by excavations of great royal halls in Northumbria, Mercia, and Wessex; the Irish Church and Celtic Christianity (less isolated than formerly believed); the structure and length of Offa's Dyke; the significance of the *burghs* of the West Saxon kings; the tenth-century monastic reform; the conquest and reign of Canute; Anglo-Norman castles; the English Investiture Controversy; St. Thomas Becket and the Becket controversy; and the personalities and politics of Kings Henry II, Henry III, Edward I, and Edward II (the latter, once thought to be a bad king, is now generally viewed as an absolutely atrocious king). This new edition incorporates recent reappraisals of John of Salisbury, Robert Grosseteste, John Wycliffe, the Cistercian Order, guilds, schools, Italian merchant bankers, late-medieval warfare, the Black Death, and the Peasants' Revolt.

The river of books and articles about medieval England flows ceaselessly on, and archaeologists continue their furious digging, providing new ideas and new evidence to challenge old certainties. I have made every effort to keep abreast of the historical and archaeological literature and to revise accordingly. I must admit, however, to having fallen a bit behind in my reading since our home burned to the ground in the great Santa Barbara fire of June 27, 1990, consuming my entire library.

There are those, I'm told, who can read everything; I cannot. (And I enjoy occasionally abandoning history to read a good novel or mystery story.) So, as in my previous editions, I ask for the help of my readers in correcting my lapses from good history or good style. As the early twelfth-century historian-archdeacon, Henry of Huntingdon, poetically expressed it,

> What I have well performed, in grace approve;
> Where I have erred, correct me in your love.

I invite your letters and promise prompt, cheerful replies.

A number of individuals contributed to the progress of this revision whom I take this opportunity to thank. James Given, University of California at Irvine, and Joseph Nigota, University of South Alabama, made many helpful suggestions. At D. C. Heath, I would like to acknowledge the assistance of James Miller, Senior Acquisitions Editor for History; Lauren Johnson, Developmental Editor for History; Sarah Doyle, Production Editor; Judy Miller, Designer; Martha Shethar, Photo Editor; and Susan Brown, Editorial Assistant.

C. W. H.

Contents

Illustrations

Maps

Genealogical Charts

The Making of England
55 B.C. to 1399

PART ONE

The Birth of the Realm

55 B.C. to A.D. 1066

HADRIAN'S WALL   *(The Granger Collection)*

1

Roman Britain and the Anglo-Saxon Settlements

History, as the recorded annals of human experience, began in England in the year 55 B.C., when Julius Caesar's troops waded ashore on the beaches north of Dover.[1] Caesar was a man of remarkable military skill and boundless confidence. He was an astute opportunist who rose to power amidst the political turmoil of the late Roman Republic, a great creative statesman who laid the groundwork for Rome's transformation from republic to empire. It was this man, this military adventurer and political genius, who first brought England into the orbit of classical civilization.

Caesar's invasion of Britain was almost an afterthought to his campaigns against the Gauls, which he chronicled in his *History of the Gallic Wars*. Between 58 and 50 B.C., prior to his rise to supreme power in Rome, he conquered an extensive territory roughly equivalent to modern France, a region then known as Gaul, which was inhabited by Celts. Although Caesar could not have realized it then, his conquest of Gaul was to have an incalculable influence on the development of Western civilization in later centuries. For Gaul extended far to the north of the Mediterranean Basin, and Caesar's victories brought Roman government and culture into the Western European heartland. The Romanization of Gaul proved to be a crucial factor in providing medieval and modern Europe with its enduring classical heritage.

The First Invasions

In the course of his campaigns, Caesar discovered that the Celts in Gaul were receiving support from their fellow Celts on the remote island of Britain. To teach them to respect the might of Rome, he undertook two military forays into Britain, the first in 55 B.C., the second a year later. Caesar's first raid was inconclusive, but in 54 B.C. he marched across Kent,

---

[1] An excellent general account of Roman Britain is Sheppard S. Frere, *Brittania: A History of Roman Britain* (rev. ed., London, 1978). The period of this chapter is treated in admirable historical and archaeological detail in the first two volumes of the new Oxford History of England series: Peter H. Salway, *Roman Britain* (Oxford, 1981), and J. N. L. Myres, *The English Settlements* (Oxford, 1986).

Contemporary Portrait Bust of Julius Caesar He was blessed not only with noble birth and acute intelligence but also with dashing good looks. (The Granger Collection)

forded the Thames River, and won a notable victory over a Celtic coalition. He demanded hostages from the defeated Britons, secured a promise of regular tribute payments, and then withdrew across the Channel. But the Britons never paid the promised tribute, and Caesar was too preoccupied with the consolidation of his Gallic conquest, and the advancement of his political fortunes in Rome, to return to Britain. The first encounter between classical Mediterranean civilization and the distant Celtic island was not followed up for nearly a century.

Nonetheless, Caesar's raids succeeded in bringing Britain to Rome's attention. And with the organization of Celtic Gaul into imperial provinces, the Britons began to feel the impact of Roman civilization. The close relations between Gaul and Britain continued much as before; the two lands remained tightly linked by bonds of commerce and kinship. A group of Celtic inhabitants of Yorkshire called the *Parisi*, for example, was related to a group in Gaul that gave its name to the future capital of France. The Romans, having subdued the Celts of Gaul, were almost bound to undertake the conquest of the Celts of Britain.

In A.D. 43 the conquest began in earnest: the emperor Claudius sent four Roman legions (perhaps 20,000 troops) across the Channel into Kent with the intention of bringing Britain under the authority of Rome. The Claudian invasion marks the real beginning of Roman Britain. Thenceforth the culture of the British Celts was reshaped by the well-trained legions of a huge cosmopolitan state and by the administrators and entrepreneurs who followed them.

By the time of Claudius's invasion, Rome had achieved a high degree of imperial stability. It had weathered the stormy decades of the late republic and had submitted to the rule of an emperor. In doing so, the Romans abandoned a tradition of self-determination for a new, authoritarian regime that promised order and political stability. With the coming of imperial government, the interior districts of the empire entered a prolonged, unprecedented epoch of security and peace. By Claudius's reign, the empire encompassed all the ancient lands around the Mediterranean and bulged northward across Gaul to the English Channel. Within its vast frontiers, guarded by well-trained legions, the cultures of Greece, Italy, and the ancient Near East drew together into one immense political and economic unit, unencumbered by national boundaries or tariff barriers, and spanned by a superb road system and the protected seaways of the Mediterranean.

Imperial unity brought to the upper classes of the ancient world a degree of prosperity hitherto unknown. But although Roman civilization was impressive, its chief beneficiaries constituted a small upper crust of the empire's population. The great majority—perhaps eighty to ninety percent—consisted of impoverished and undernourished slaves, half-free peasants, and townspeople. They benefited from the Roman Peace but from little else. Their living conditions were not regarded by Rome's leaders as an economic misfortune that might be alleviated but as the means necessary for the functioning of great estates, mines, and wealthy households. The leisured lives of the empire's elite, and the very survival of the imperial economy, depended on the muscles of slaves and poor laborers.

Roman women, even the wealthiest, were forbidden to hold any political office. By age-long tradition they were expected to stay home and obey their husbands, but many Roman wives declined to submit to these pressures. Indeed, in the empire's later centuries, women acquired considerable independence with respect to marriage, divorce, and the holding of property, and upper-class women were often well educated. The Roman father, however, was the master of the family and exercised what was virtually the power of life or death over his newborn children. If he liked their looks, he let them remain in his family; if they were scrawny or deformed, or if the father already had enough children (particularly female children), they were cast out and abandoned, sometimes to be taken in by another family, sometimes to die of exposure. This custom of selective infanticide was yet another brutal consequence of Rome's marginal economy: the empire could not afford to feed excess mouths.

Rome's harsh economic system provoked no general rebellion because the lower classes knew no better way of managing an empire. Nearly all ancient civilizations were afflicted by mass enslavement, widespread poverty, malnutrition, the suppression of women, and the abandonment of unwanted infants (although the religion of the Hebrews banned infanticide). In these respects Roman imperial civilization was no worse than the others, and in the larger cities, where public baths and free bread were available, it was significantly better.

The Roman economy, like almost all economies prior to the Industrial Revolution, was fundamentally agrarian, but the city was the focus of Roman politics and civilization. Surrounded by an extensive agrarian district, the city was the essential unit of local government throughout the empire, and it was on the cities that the Romans lavished most of their considerable architectural and engineering talents. Administrators, poets, scholars, even great landowners, made their homes in the cities. As Rome seized control of neighboring agrarian regions such as Gaul, old tribal centers evolved into cities, and new cities rose where none had existed before. Each city sought to adorn itself with impressive temples, baths, and public buildings on the model of Rome itself. Hence the paradox that the Roman empire was economically rural yet culturally urban.

These cities, scattered across the empire, were centers of cultural synthesis, where the various traditions of the Mediterranean world spread and intermingled. But above all, it was the Latin culture of Rome itself that inspired the architecture and literature of the Western European cities and dominated the curricula of their schools. Great Latin authors and poets such as Lucretius and Cicero, Virgil and Horace, set the canons of style for a Latin literary tradition that spread across the West. United politically by soldiers and administrators, the Roman Empire was united culturally—at least in its western provinces—by the power and magnetism of Roman literature and art.

The empire was united legally by Roman jurisprudence. It may well be that Rome made its most creative and enduring contribution in the field of law. As Rome won its empire, the narrow law code of the early republic evolved gradually into a broad, humane system of legal precedents and principles—a product of centuries of practical experience—designed to deal justly with conflicts among people of diverse cultures. Although essentially pragmatic in its development, Roman law was influenced by the Greek concept of natural law—the belief in universal and discoverable norms of human conduct, applicable not merely to certain civilized peoples but to all humanity. A concept of this sort was naturally attractive to Roman jurists, faced as they were with the task of bringing all the peoples of the empire under a single canopy of jurisprudence.

Such, in brief, was the civilization that Rome brought to Britain. Students of English history must never allow their preoccupation with the British Isles to obscure the fact that Claudius's invasion in A.D. 43 was an encroachment by a highly civilized empire on a remote island. In Roman times Britain could never be anything but an outwork—a distant frontier district of an age-old Mediterranean civilization.

The pre-Roman British were illiterate and therefore left no documents for historians to study. But archaeological investigations, which have gained growing momentum across the past generation, are providing an increasingly detailed picture of the material culture and the changing social and economic conditions of the British peoples before the Roman contact.

Until recently, scholars had viewed pre-Roman Britain as a virtually untamed wilderness, as an island that suffered "repeated incursions and invasions" (to quote from an earlier edition of this book). But scholars of prehistory have grown increasingly skeptical of employing great-invasion theories to explain social and cultural changes. Such developments might more reasonably be attributed to the importation or spread of new ideas, new technologies, or new religious cults—or to the political emergence of previously suppressed groups. This is not to deny that people had long been crossing from the Continent to Britain; Englanda's Kentish cliffs are clearly visible from France, and the two lands are separated by a channel only twenty-one miles wide at its narrowest point. But such crossings can more plausibly be viewed as migrations and colonizations (or as trading expeditions) than as amphibious military incursions.

The longstanding "untamed wilderness" picture of pre-Roman Britain has also been discarded. Recent archaeological excavations throughout much of Britain have demonstrated that human settlement was far more widespread—and more complex—than had previously been suspected. The Britain that the Romans encountered was a land of farms, fields, trackways, and hill forts sheltering permanent, well-organized communities. Caesar's Britain was the product of long ages of economic and cultural development from the Stone Age to the Bronze Age and finally, beginning in the fifth century B.C., to the Iron Age. The majestic stone trilithons at Stonehenge— a Bronze-Age religious center begun on a massive scale and completed on a scale still more grandiose—testify to the inhabitants' engineering skills, knowledge of astronomy, and sophisticated social organization nearly two millennia before the Roman invasion.

Stonehenge, in Wiltshire, North of Salisbury (Ronald Sheridan/The Ancient Art & Architecture Collection)

The pattern of pre-Roman settlements was governed by the island's geography. England is divided into two major districts: a lowland area, with rich, heavy soil broken by occasional ranges of hills, covers approximately the southeastern half of the country; and a highland zone dominates the northwestern half of the land, a mountainous district rich in mineral resources but with generally infertile soil (see the map on page 11). Cornwall and Devon at the southwestern tip of England, Wales in the west, and most of northern England and Scotland are hilly or mountainous, and England's chief mountain range, the Pennine chain, points southward like a great finger from the northern hill country into the heart of the midland plain.

The earlier prehistoric settlements tended to be concentrated in the southeast lowland zone, both in its hilly portions and in the lowlands themselves—where archaeological traces of prehistoric cultivation are more difficult to detect because of subsequent deposits of alluvial or drift soil and centuries of intensive plowing. The soil of the lowlands was both heavy and rich, and prehistoric plows proved equal to the task of cultivating it. A Celtic people called the Belgae, whom Julius Caesar describes as having migrated from the Continent to Britain in 75 B.C., appear to have brought with them heavy plows particularly suited to tilling these soils. With their plows, the Belgae advanced the cultivation of the lowlands still further. By the time of the Roman invasions, the Celtic settlement of lowland Britain was quite dense, and grain was being produced in such quantities that it became an important export commodity. A Roman author of the early first century A.D. mentions several other British exports that found regular markets in the empire: cattle, hides, dogs, iron, and slaves. And for centuries, traders of the Mediterranean world had known of the rich tin deposits in Cornwall. The considerable prosperity of pre-Roman Britain enabled a few of the island's chieftains, following the example of neighboring Roman provinces, to coin money.

As the first century progressed, everything pointed to a Roman invasion of Britain. The independence of the British Celts posed difficulties for the Roman administration of Celtic Gaul. The abundance of British resources suggested to the Romans that financially a conquest of the island would be well worth the effort. Finally, intertribal warfare among the Britons—and appeals by defeated British chieftains for Roman support—indicated that a conquest would not be unduly difficult. The invasion of A.D. 43 was a calculated act of imperial policy undertaken with every expectation of success.

Roman Britain

The British Celts, divided among themselves and inferior to the Romans in military organization, could offer only temporary resistance to the Claudian invasion. In the years following A.D. 43 the Roman legions repeatedly breached the Celtic defenses, storming hilltop fortresses and occupying first the southeastern lowland zone and finally, after some difficulty, the highland districts of the north and west. The administration of the able Roman governor Agricola (A.D. 78–84)—recorded in detail by his nephew, the Roman historian Tacitus—marks the essential completion of the conquest. By then, Roman authority extended over virtually all of modern England, Wales, and southern Scotland.

The Roman conquest of the lowland zone was relatively easy. It was challenged in A.D. 60, but only momentarily, by a rebellion of several British tribes who had as their figurehead leader a Celtic queen named Boudicca. Historians of earlier generations romanticized this uprising and pictured Boudicca, quite wrongly, as the first British patriot—a primitive Joan of Arc. The rebels, men and women alike, won some initial victories. They burned London and other newly established towns, but then fell before an army of well-trained legionaries. Boudicca died, perhaps from poison at her own hand. The rebels were massacred and the lowlands tamed. The consolidation of Roman authority in the highland zone was far more difficult, for the warlike hill peoples of Wales, the north, and the northeast could be controlled only by the continued presence of large Roman garrisons at strategic points.

Hence, Roman Britain was divided administratively into two districts, corresponding to the island's two geographic zones: a civil district in the southeast and a military district in the highlands. In the civil district, peace reigned and Roman culture flourished. But in the northwestern hill district, where Roman legions stood guard against uprisings and invasions, the new civilization could establish only the shallowest of roots. Altogether some 60,000 Roman soldiers, officials, and landholders settled in Britain, among a native population now estimated at some two to three million or more.

Originally four legions, each with several thousand men, guarded the highland zone. After about A.D. 100, the legions were reduced to three: one at Chester to keep watch on north Wales and northern Britain, another at Caerleon in south Wales, and a third at York as a strategic reserve for the northern frontier (see the map on page 11). These three legions succeeded more or less in upholding Roman authority and keeping the peace for considerable periods of time, but they were never able to safeguard their districts completely.

Britain's defense weighed heavily on Roman resources, requiring some ten percent of the entire imperial army. The emperor Hadrian (117–138), who inspected Britain personally in 122, determined to stabilize its northern frontier and reduce the drain on the military by constructing a wall, ten feet wide and fifteen feet high, across the entire seventy-three miles between Solway Firth and the mouth of the Tyne River. This great barrier, the largest in the Roman Empire, included fortresses at every mile (known, appropriately, as milecastles), a V-shaped ditch ten feet deep and nearly thirty feet wide along its northern side, and a more-or-less similar ditch along its southern side. The purpose of Hadrian's Wall was not to repel large

Queen Boudicca Leading Her Troops This nineteenth-century wood engraving depicts her, romantically and wrongly, as the first British patriot. (The Granger Collection)

assaults but to discourage small plundering expeditions and to serve as a base for attacks and counterattacks against hostile northern tribes.[2]

Later in the second century, during the reign of Emperor Antoninus Pius (138–161), the Romans constructed a second fortified line, the Antonine Wall, farther to the north across the narrows between the Firth of Clyde and the Firth of Forth. But eventually the legions found it impossible to hold this advanced position, and toward the end of the second century they withdrew to the Wall of Hadrian. In the third and fourth centuries, Roman punitive expeditions sometimes probed far north of Hadrian's Wall; at other times northern tribes crossed the wall and carried their devastation far to the south. But during most of the later age of Roman occupation, Hadrian's Wall marked the northern frontier.

After Boudicca's revolt, the lowland zone enjoyed unbroken peace and considerable prosperity. Here Roman institutions gradually penetrated the Celtic and pre-Celtic substructure, and wealthy Britons came to accept the peace, the thriving economy, the amenities—and the high taxes—that were customary throughout the Roman provinces. A network of Roman

---

[2] Elaborate modern excavations at various points along Hadrian's Wall have given rise to an entire subfield of British archaeology known as "Wall Studies."

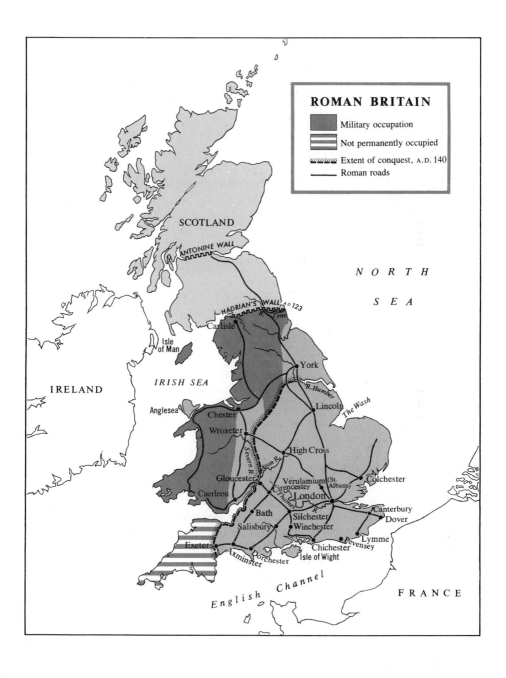

ROMAN BRITAIN

Military occupation
Not permanently occupied
Extent of conquest, A.D. 140
Roman roads

SCOTLAND

ANTONINE WALL

NORTH

SEA

HADRIAN'S WALL A.D. 123
R. Tyne
Carlisle

Isle
of Man

York

IRISH SEA

R. Humber

IRELAND

The Wash

Anglesea

Chester
Lincoln

Wroxeter

High Cross

Severn R.

Avon R.

Gloucester
Colchester
Vérulamium (St.
Cirencester   Albans)
Caerleon
London
R. Thames
Bath
Silchester   Canterbury
Salisbury   Winchester   Dover
Lymme
Exeter   Chichester Pevensey
Axminster Dorchester Isle of Wight

English Channel
FRANCE

roads linked Britain's military camps and commercial centers. Roman law courts brought with them a rational system of justice unknown to pre-Roman Britain. And with the coming of Roman civilization, towns and cities grew and flourished as never before.

In Britain, as elsewhere in the empire, the cities were of three basic types: (1) the *colonia*, usually a newly established urban center occupied by a colony of retired legionaries and their families; (2) the *municipium*, normally a previously existing town whose inhabitants received from the imperial government a charter conveying certain important privileges; and (3) the *civitas*, an older tribal center that developed urban institutions in imitation of the colonia and municipium. The inhabitants of coloniae and municipia were Roman citizens; those of the civitates were not. But all three enjoyed a degree of local self-government and exerted political control over surrounding lands. All were governed by local senates composed of wealthy townspeople, and by annually elected magistrates who supervised finances, the construction and upkeep of public buildings, and the courts. And all were adorned with public buildings, temples, and baths built of stone in the Roman style. Still, the civitates remained fundamentally Celtic tribal centers and were never as thoroughly Romanized as were the municipia and the coloniae.

Only four British cities are known to have possessed colonia status: Colchester, Gloucester, Lincoln, and York. And there is evidence of only one municipium: Verulamium (near the later St. Albans). Extant documents from the period do not state specifically that London was either a colonia or a municipium, but it was clearly the foremost city of Roman Britain. Indeed, it was the Romans who made London a significant center of trade. Whereas most of the chief British cities of the Roman era were between 100 and 200 acres in extent, London occupied some 325 acres. It was situated on the Thames at the crucial point where the river was broad enough to accommodate oceangoing ships and yet narrow enough to be bridged—a situation precisely analogous to Rome's position on the Tiber. Roman London thus assumed the dominant commercial position that it was destined to occupy in medieval and modern times. Then, as now, it was the commercial nexus of Britain.

It was natural, therefore, that London should be the focal point of the Roman road system. Stretching from London far and wide across the land, the Roman roads formed a vast, five-thousand-mile system of paved thoroughfares running in nearly straight lines over the countryside, enabling people and supplies to move across the island at speeds unmatched until the nineteenth century. Because the roads tended to be straight, they sometimes ascended hills without regard to the steepness of the grade. They were therefore more useful for the movement of legions and pack trains than for the transport of goods by horse- or ox-drawn wagons, such as became common many centuries later with the revival of commerce in the Middle Ages. Nevertheless, the Roman roads remained in use, though usually in ruinous condition, for many centuries after the Roman legions had departed.

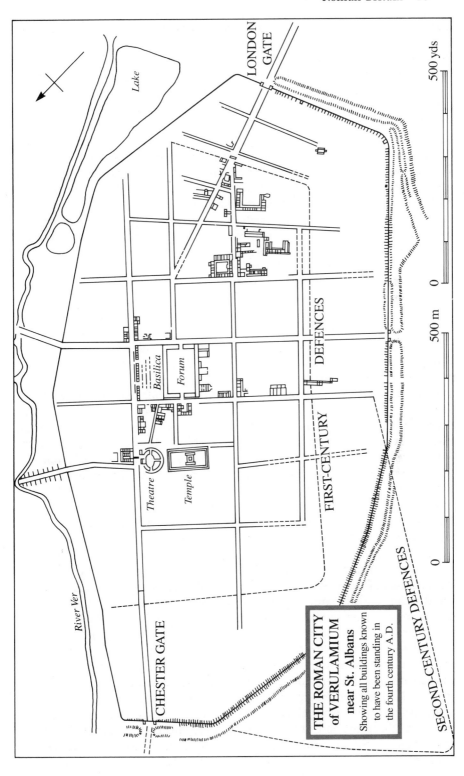

THE ROMAN CITY
of VERULAMIUM
near St. Albans
Showing all buildings known
to have been standing in
the fourth century A.D.

LONDON GATE

CHESTER GATE

River Ver

Lake

Theatre

Temple

Basilica

Forum

FIRST-CENTURY DEFENCES

SECOND-CENTURY DEFENCES

500 yds

500 m

0

In Roman Britain, as elsewhere in the empire, farming was the basic economic activity. Historians of former generations used to distinguish between two radically different agricultural communities: the village—pre-Roman in origin and little affected by the Roman occupation—and the villa—a typically Roman institution that consisted of a luxurious home surrounded by extensive fields. Recent research, based on more sophisticated archaeological techniques and on aerial photography, has modified this older view. We now realize that the buildings unearthed at a particular site often represent successive levels of development rather than one agrarian complex existing at a single moment in time. Consequently, scholars today doubt that the agricultural village played a particularly significant role in either Roman or pre-Roman Britain. Instead, the fundamental agrarian unit was the small family farm, a few acres in extent, consisting typically of a couple of houses, a number of pits for storing grain, and farmlands laid out in small, squarish fields. Farms of this type abounded in both Celtic and Roman times, and their inhabitants were little influenced by the coming of the Romans.

The older conception of the villa, with its gracious Roman provincial architecture, its mosaics and rich furnishings, glass windows and underfloor heating, also requires modification. Such villas did indeed exist, but they constituted only a small fraction of the total, and most of them achieved their grandeur only in the final century of the Roman occupation. Most villas were far more modest establishments, and some were actually squalid. Altogether, between six and seven hundred villas have been identified in Britain, most of them concentrated in small areas of the southeastern lowlands. Life in the villas, whether luxurious or not, was distinctly Roman in style and organization, and it was through the villas that Rome made its impact on the British countryside. The typical villa owner was a Roman or a Romanized Briton, who used hired laborers or slaves, sometimes in large numbers, to work the land. In the later years of the Roman settlement, much villa land, as elsewhere in the empire, was leased to tenant farmers. Peasant independence increased, but many of the advantages of large-scale farming were lost.

Notwithstanding the distinction between Celtic farm and Roman villa, the laborers on the villa's fields profited no more from Roman civilization than Celtic farmers did. In Britain as elsewhere, Rome's impact on the agrarian masses was slight. Rome had always lagged in agricultural technology, and it contributed little to Celtic farming practices because it had little to offer. Some further progress was made during the Roman occupation toward the clearing of forests and draining of swamps, but it was the achievements of the pre-Roman Celts and their predecessors that enabled Roman Britain to export agricultural products to the Continent.

The Romans did, however, contribute to the development of the British economy in areas other than agriculture. Britain had been exploiting its mines long before the Claudian invasion, but Rome introduced a far more efficient—and more ruthless—mining technology than was employed before. In particular, the Romans developed lead mines in Britain and made

**The Great Roman Villa at Chedworth, Gloucestershire, as Reconstructed by
A. Forestier** This villa, which seems to include two distinct residences with
shared workshop and storage facilities, probably was owned and operated by two
separate families in joint proprietorship. (The Mansell Collection)

that metal a major export commodity, along with copper, bronze, iron, and
tin.

Rome's greatest gift to Britain was peace. For more than three centuries,
Roman legions shielded lowland Britain from invaders and prevented intertribal warfare. As a frontier province, Britain fell under the direct authority
of the emperor. But apart from rare occasions when the emperor actually
visited the island, imperial control was exercised by an imperial legate who
was, in effect, a provincial governor. His responsibilities included both
administration of justice in the civil zone and command of the armies in the
military zone. Responsibility for the collection of imperial taxes and the
supervision of imperial estates fell to another official, the procurator, who
was administratively independent of the governor and subject to the emperor alone. It was up to the procurator to see that Britain paid its way and
that the occupation was financially worthwhile to Rome.

Such was the administrative structure of Britain in the era following the
Claudian invasion. In subsequent centuries, as the empire evolved steadily
toward military despotism, Roman administrative organization underwent
several major revisions, and the administration of Britain changed accordingly. Early in the third century the island was divided into two separate
provinces, which probably approximated its two zones: military and civil.
Toward the end of the same century, Emperor Diocletian designated Britain
as one of the twelve dioceses into which he divided the empire.

Throughout the epoch of the Roman occupation, cities remained the
key units of local government. The coloniae, municipia, and civitates managed their own affairs through their senates and magistrates, and supervised the surrounding countryside. In the final catastrophic years of Roman

Britain, it was the towns that took the lead in striving to defend the province against its enemies.

Decline and Fall

The Roman age of British history began and ended as a result of forces that transcended Britain itself. The fall of the Roman Empire in the West is an age-old historical problem for which numerous scholars have proposed numerous solutions—no less than 210 different reasons according to a fairly recent survey. They include such factors as sexual orgies, lead poisoning, climatic changes, bad ecological habits, and Christianity.[3] A few old-fashioned historians have even suggested that barbarian invasions had something to do with the problem. None of these explanations is satisfactory. The Eastern Empire, centered in Constantinople (the present Istanbul, Turkey), was more thoroughly Christianized than the Western, yet it survived for another thousand years. The most spectacular of the Roman orgies occurred during the earlier, pagan "Golden Age"; Christian conversion made them unstylish, and the invasions occurred long after the age of orgies had passed.

Many different factors contributed to the transformation from Roman to medieval Europe. For one thing, the educated classes of the empire underwent a profound change in outlook during the third and fourth centuries, turning from the humanism and rationalism of classical Greece, and the practical, worldly values of early Rome, to the mysticism and quest for eternal salvation that characterized late Antiquity and the Middle Ages. This change in mood marked the end of the viewpoint and value system of traditional Greco-Roman civilization. But one can never be certain whether the new transcendental spirit destroyed the old humanistic values, or whether the failure of those values gave rise to the new mysticism.

Historians have written endlessly about the political and economic problems that afflicted the Roman Empire. It has been said that the Roman political system never solved the problem of imperial succession, that the Roman economy was inefficient and parasitical, that the Roman bureaucracy was bloated and corrupt. One should be cautious, of course, in pointing out the "fatal flaws" of an empire that endured for some five hundred years in the West and a thousand years thereafter in the East. Nevertheless, certain of these criticisms stand. The economy of the early empire depended heavily on slave labor and on booty from conquered peoples. When,

---

[3] Gibbon's classic, *The Decline and Fall of the Roman Empire* (many editions), is majestic in style and fearlessly opinionated. Compare Lynn White, Jr., ed., *The Transformation of the Roman World: Gibbon's Problem after Two Centuries* (Berkeley, Calif., 1961), and Bryce Lyon, *The Origins of the Middle Ages: Pirenne's Challenge to Gibbon* (New York, 1972). And see, more recently, Walter Goffart, *Barbarians and Romans, A.D. 418–584: The Techniques of Accommodation* (Princeton, 1981); Richard Hodges and David Whitehouse, *Mohammed, Charlemagne and the Origins of Europe* (London, 1983); and Michael Grant, *The Fall of the Roman Empire: A Reappraisal* (New York, 1976).

in the course of the second century, imperial expansion ceased, the economic system in the West began to falter. Rome experienced no commercial or industrial revolution; its cities, particularly those in the West, tended to be military and administrative centers rather than centers of industrial production. Many of them harbored large masses of unemployed paupers and homeless people, and all of them teemed with soldiers and bureaucrats who consumed the wealth of the empire while producing nothing themselves. In the end, the largely agrarian imperial economy proved incapable of supporting the bureaucracy, the army, and the unproductive cities.

The economic breakdown brought widespread demoralization. So many overtaxed artisans, tenant farmers, and civic officials dropped out of their jobs and out of society that the emperors had to enact laws freezing people in their vocations and making vocations hereditary. By the early fourth century, a caste system had come into being. The Roman economy continued to function after a fashion, and the lightly taxed landed aristocracy remained prosperous. But the more productive classes of the empire—the workers in field and town, and the urban middle classes—were becoming impoverished and alienated.

Meanwhile, the Roman political structure was beginning to disintegrate. The emperors of the second century tended to be long-lived and dedicated, but as the third century dawned, the army came to exert increasing power in Roman politics. The middle decades of the century were marked by disputed successions, frequent assassinations of emperors or imperial claimants, and struggles between army units for control of the throne. In these years, barbarians breached the frontiers repeatedly, and large sections of the empire ignored the authority of the emperor in Rome. At length, as the third century closed, a series of determined warrior-emperors succeeded in restoring the frontiers and reestablishing imperial control over the Roman state. The most celebrated of these rulers, Diocletian (284–305), pulled the empire together by resorting to a military despotism of the most thoroughgoing sort and by enforcing strict controls over economic activity.

Diocletian's policy of law and order was carried on by Constantine (306–337) and his successors. Constantine's reign is marked by two epoch-making events: (1) his construction of Constantinople on the Bosporus—the great city that served as the capital of the Eastern or Byzantine Empire for more than 1,100 years thereafter—and (2) his conversion to the Christian faith.

Both of these events were responses to age-old trends. The center of gravity of the Roman Empire had been shifting eastward for many decades. The older eastern cities were more productive and more prosperous than those of the West, and the eastward movement reflected the new political order that abandoned the republican traditions of the city of Rome for the absolutism of the East. Diocletian had spent nearly all his reign in the eastern half of the empire, and now Constantine erected his new capital there.

Constantine I Colossal marble head of the Emperor Constantine. Rome, early fourth century. (The Granger Collection)

Constantine's conversion reflected not only the growing strength of Christianity within the empire but also a gradual drawing together of the classical and Christian traditions. The growth of a mystical spirit in Roman culture made the inhabitants of the empire ever more receptive to the doctrines of the Christian religion. The increasing emptiness and hopelessness of daily life in the empire created a growing need for the doctrines of human dignity before God and personal salvation that Christianity offered. The Christians, for their part, had incorporated into their theology many elements from classical philosophy—particularly the monotheistic philosophy of Plato—and had modeled their hierarchy on the administrative organization of the Roman Empire. The steadily closing chasm between church and empire was bridged by Constantine's conversion.

By the fourth century, Christianity had spread from its Near Eastern homeland across the entire empire. In Constantine's time it was still a minority religion, but its adherents were among the most vigorous and dedicated inhabitants of the Roman state. Previous emperors had persecuted Christians intermittently for their refusal to worship the official deities, but persecution only encouraged the Church to greater efforts. With Constantine's conversion, the persecutions gave way to a policy of toleration and encouragement, and before the fourth century had ended, Christian emperors were persecuting pagan and heterodox sects. Converts now flooded into the Church, and Roman intellectuals such as St. Ambrose, St. Jerome, and St. Augustine of Hippo devoted their lives to its service. The new religion, with its claim to universality, paralleled and reinforced the Roman Empire's similar claim. And Christianity harmonized perfectly with the otherworldly mood of the late empire. Well before the end of imperial rule in the West, the Christian faith had won the allegiance of the

Mediterranean world. By the fifth century, Greco-Roman civilization had virtually fused with the Judeo-Christian religious tradition.

The progress of Christianity in Roman Britain is difficult to trace. Christian archaeological remains from this period are scarce, and written references to the Romano-British Church occur only occasionally. Christian evangelism doubtless came late to remote Britain, but by the third century the process of conversion was under way. Early in the century, St. Alban and two fellow Christians were martyred at Verulamium (subsequently renamed after the martyr), and three British bishops, a priest, and a deacon are recorded as being present at an ecclesiastical council in Gaul during Constantine's reign.[4] Thus, fourth-century Britain possessed an ecclesiastical hierarchy and was active in the affairs of the imperial Church. Toward the end of the fourth century, Britain went so far as to produce a heresy all its own. The British priest Pelagius, who emphasized the importance of free will over divine grace, had the distinction of being attacked furiously by the noted theologian St. Augustine of Hippo. Pelagius left Britain as a young man and seems to have spent most of his life in Rome, but his teachings became popular among the British upper classes. Orthodox continental churchmen are recorded as preaching against Pelagianism in Britain in the fifth century. At about the same time, British evangelists such as St. Patrick (c. 389–461) were spreading the Gospel beyond the Roman frontiers into Ireland and southwestern Scotland.

Christianity was Rome's most enduring legacy in Britain. At a time when Roman civilization was losing its hold on the inhabitants of the empire, Christianity was reaching masses of people and affecting their lives in a way that Greco-Roman culture had failed to do even at its height. In later years, when Roman government was all but forgotten, when Germanic settlers had occupied the fertile lowland zone and driven British landowners into the western hills, the British held fast to their Christian faith and built an impressive new culture on it.

The ebbing of Roman authority in Britain was an inevitable consequence of Roman political and economic disintegration in the West. But because of its isolated location on the periphery of the empire, Britain was spared much of the agony and chaos of the third century, and its cities remained relatively prosperous throughout the fourth.

The history of Roman Britain is punctuated by occasional irruptions of semicivilized peoples from across its frontiers, most frequently the Scots and the Picts. The term *Scot* referred in this period to members of the various tribes of Ireland (not Scotland). These "Scots" undertook periodic attacks against Britain's western shore but met with no permanent success. *Pict* was the common term for the tribes across the northern frontier in what we would now call Scotland. With a few disastrous exceptions, Hadrian's Wall held firm against their incursions.

---

[4] At Arles in A.D. 314. The British delegates to the council represented the metropolitan churches of the four provinces into which Britain had been divided since Diocletian's time.

As the Roman period drew toward its end, Britain's security diminished. An intensification of sea raids by Germanic pirates from Saxony and elsewhere necessitated the building of fortifications and signal stations along the southeastern coast. In the fourth century these coastal defensive works were placed under the authority of a single military commander known, significantly, as the Count of the Saxon Shore. In 367 Britain suffered a furious combined attack of Picts from the north, Scots from the west, and Saxons from the Continent. Invaders flooded across Hadrian's Wall, killed the Count of the Saxon Shore, and besieged London. They were turned back only by the timely intervention of a large Roman army from the Continent led by Theodosius, a talented general and future emperor. By 370 Britain was secure once again, but only for a time.

As the fourth century closed, Britain remained Roman and its cities endured. But the Roman Empire as a whole was in desperate straits. An entire Germanic tribe, the Visigoths, had crossed the empire's Danube frontier in 376 and, by the first decade of the fifth century, was threatening Rome itself. As Roman troops withdrew from Britain and the Rhine frontier to strengthen the defenses of Italy, Gaul and Britain were left exposed. In the winter of 406 a mixed multitude of Germanic invaders poured across the frozen Rhine into defenseless Gaul, virtually cutting Britain loose from the empire. In the chaos that followed, an ambitious general, Constantine III, led what was left of the Roman-British troops southward across the Channel in an abortive attempt to save Gaul for the empire and win an imperial title for himself.

The year 410 marks the essential termination of Roman authority in Britain. In that year the Visigoths entered Rome and pillaged the city for three days. At about the same time Britain, stripped of its legions, was struck hard by barbarian raids. At this point our sources thin out and the sequence of events is clouded. One contemporary writer spoke of a native British uprising against the Roman administration—perhaps against the officials left behind by the usurper Constantine III rather than against Rome itself. A letter of A.D. 410 from Emperor Honorius to the civitates of Britain, evidently in response to their appeal for military help, commands them to see to their own defense. With Visigoths rampaging through Italy, there were no troops to be spared for a remote island outpost. The Roman legions and administrators were gone for good, leaving Britain "stripped of its armed men, its military supplies, and the whole flower of its active youth."[5]

The Germanic Settlements

As the fifth century progressed Britain became, from the standpoint of the civilized peoples of the Mediterranean Basin, the "land of legend," or the "Isle of the Dead." To the modern historian, the post-Roman epoch is almost equally obscure. There are a few oblique, secondhand references

---

[5] Bede, *Ecclesiastical History of the English People*, Bertram Colgrove and R. A. B. Mynors, eds. (Oxford, 1969), 1–10.

from contemporary writers from the Continent. A biography of St. Germanus of Auxerre reports that Germanus visited Britain in 429 and again in the 440s to contend against the Pelagian heresy, and that he succeeded not only in refuting the Pelagians at a conference at Verulamium but also in leading the Britons to military victory over an invading army of Picts and Saxons by teaching his followers to terrify the enemy by shouting out the Christian war cry, "Alleluia!"[6]

Apart from such isolated continental testimony, we are left to depend on a handful of unreliable Celtic sources and a few accounts written long afterwards by descendants of the Germanic conquerors. None of these sources is particularly revealing. The most valuable of them is a history of post-Roman Britain written by a Briton named Gildas sometime in the early or mid-sixth century.[7] Gildas's account is by no means an objective work of history; it is a bitter, emotional outcry against the moral shortcomings of contemporary British Christians. Yet its very existence bears witness to the survival of Latin letters among the Britons nearly 150 years after the departure of the Romans. On the Germanic or "English" side, the opening sections of the *Anglo-Saxon Chronicle*, which were first written in their present form in the late ninth century, contain information drawn from sources much closer to the invasion age and can therefore provide illumination if used with caution. The English historical genius Bede, writing in the early eighth century, gives an account of the Germanic conquests that also rests on earlier evidence, now lost, but there is much that Bede leaves out and much else that can be accepted only with reservations. For Bede, despite his remarkable historical skill, was centuries removed from the invasions themselves.

The few other written sources to which one can turn are fragmentary and even less trustworthy. Archaeological investigations have been enormously helpful in supplementing our patchy historical evidence: pagan grave sites containing ornaments, pottery, and weapons; the post holes of wooden buildings; even rubbish pits and cesspits can provide valuable clues to settlement patterns, diet, and cultural characteristics. The patterns of Celtic and Germanic settlement have been further illuminated through the study of place names. Scholars are able to identify particular names—and especially name endings—with particular peoples and thereby trace the advance of Germanic settlements and measure their density. A number of towns and settlements, for example, end in *-ing* or *-ingas*, which suggests that the settlers were dependents or followers of a particular leader. Hastings probably derived its name from a group of early settlers called Haestingas, that is, the followers of a person named Haesta, and we can conclude

---

[6] The account of the Alleluia Victory in the Life of St. Germanus has been dismissed as a piece of pious nonsense, but wrongly so. See Michael E. Jones, "The Historicity of the Alleluia Victory," *Albion*, 18 (1986): 363–373.

[7] See Gildas, *The Ruin of Britain and Other Works*, Michael Winterbottom, ed. and tr. (London, 1978); and *Gildas: New Approaches*, Michael Lapidge and David Dumville, eds. (Woodbridge, Suffolk, 1984).

tentatively that a Germanic leader of that name settled with his followers in the vicinity of the present town. But archaeological and place-name studies, valuable though they are, cannot produce an exact chronological framework. Scholarly investigations of fifth- and sixth-century Britain have been pushed forward with great ingenuity, yet much remains uncertain and much unknown. The epoch has become a battleground of conflicting theories, many of which may never be positively proven or discredited.[8]

Before entering this historical swamp it will be useful to establish, as far as we possibly can, the nature of the Germanic peoples as a whole and the significance of their invasions, not only of Britain but of the entire Western Roman Empire. Medieval European civilization was a synthesis of three distinct cultural traditions: the classical Greco-Roman, the Judeo-Christian, and the Germanic. We have seen how classical culture in the closing centuries of the Roman Empire began to move toward a mystical, otherworldly outlook, thereby drawing closer to the Judeo-Christian tradition. At the same time, Christian theologians were interpreting Christian doctrine in terms of Greek philosophy, and the Christian Church was developing a political and legal organization that drew heavily from Roman administrative and judicial practices. Well before the demise of Roman imperial authority in the West, these tendencies had progressed to the point where classical and Christian cultures had fused. The making of medieval civilization was in essence the product of a prolonged tension, interpenetration, and eventual fusion between the classical-Christian tradition, fostered by the early medieval Church, and the Germanic tradition of the barbarian kings and aristocracies that established themselves on the remains of the Western Roman Empire.

Because the early Germanic peoples were illiterate, our knowledge of their culture must be drawn chiefly from archaeology and from the often biased testimony of occasional Roman observers. In later generations Germanic writers, or Roman writers friendly toward Germanic kings, wrote histories of the origins and early conquests of various Germanic tribes, but these accounts tell us more about their later legends than about their early histories. Members of a Germanic tribe regarded themselves as a culturally and ethnically distinctive group—or, to use the common Latin term, as a *gens*, which can be translated roughly as "a people." Each Germanic gens had its own customs, its traditional allies and enemies, and its tribal legends. In reality, the tribes, or *gentes*, were by no means ethnically pure or

---

[8] On the Anglo-Saxon period, see James Campbell, ed., *The Anglo-Saxons* (Oxford, 1982); Peter Hunter Blair, *An Introduction to Anglo-Saxon England*, 2nd ed. (Cambridge, 1977); Henry R. Loyn, *Anglo-Saxon England and the Norman Conquest* (New York, 1962), and *The Governance of Anglo-Saxon England, 550–1087* (Stanford, 1984); and D. J. V. Fisher, *The Anglo-Saxon Age, c. 400–1042* (London, 1973). Technical studies of the period appear annually in the serial publication, *Anglo-Saxon England*. Leslie Alcock, *Arthur's Britain: History and Archaeology, A.D. 367–634* (New York, 1971), and John Morris, *The Age of Arthur: A History of the British Isles from 350 to 650* (rev. ed., New York, 1973), are good introductions to the early period. Both have been criticized for deducing too much from too little: see David Dumville, "Sub-Roman Britain: History and Legend," *History* 62 (1977): 173–192.

The Hornhauser Rider
A relief of a mounted
Germanic warrior from
the migration period. (Art
Resource)

constant in membership. Members might drop out, perhaps to join another tribe, and newcomers might be attracted in considerable number if the tribe were prosperous and winning its battles under a strong leader. The Germanic tribes differed most noticeably from one another in the extent to which they had been affected by contacts with Roman civilization. Some had long been settled along Roman frontiers, engaging in active commerce with the empire and often filling the ranks of Roman armies. In the course of the fourth century, several tribes were converted to Christianity.

Notwithstanding these actual or imagined differences, certain broad generalizations apply more or less to all the tribes. To the Romans, the Germanic peoples were scruffy blond giants. Their custom of grooming their hair with butter prompted the fifth-century Gallo-Roman country gentleman Sidonius Apollinaris to remark, "Happy the nose that cannot smell a barbarian." They devoted themselves chiefly to tending crops or herds, fighting wars, hunting, feuding, and drinking beer—in contrast to the favorite Roman pastime of drinking wine. Women played important roles in Germanic communities, performing much of the agricultural labor and sometimes joining in the traditionally male pursuits of hunting and warfare. The earliest Germanic law codes, however, treat women as perpetual minors under the guardianship of fathers, husbands, or, if widowed, male in-laws. The Germans possessed slaves—war prisoners for the most part, but on occasion free Germans might gamble themselves into slavery.

A tribe's success depended heavily on the ability, reputation and charisma of its leader, a chief or king. A successful king was one who led his warriors to victories that won them rich plunder, and who used his own war booty to reward his loyal followers with lavish generosity—with gold rings and other precious jewelry, with finely wrought swords and shields, with gold and silver bowls and cups. Because the king's ability was of such paramount importance to the tribe, its elders were permitted some latitude in selecting a royal successor. They chose a new king from among the sons and other close kinsmen of the former king. Kingship was hereditary, but there was no strict adherence to the custom of primogeniture; an able younger son of generous spirit who had proved his skill as a warrior was often chosen over a less competent elder son. The most honored profession was that of the warrior, and the warlike virtues of loyalty, courage, and military prowess were esteemed above all others.

The chief military unit within the tribe was the war band or *comitatus*, a group of warriors or "companions" bound together by their allegiance to the leader of their band. It was in the comitatus, above all, that military virtues were cherished. The chief of the band was bound to set an example of fearlessness and military skill, and his followers were obliged, should their leader fall in battle, to fight to the death in order to avenge him. The ethical foundations of the comitatus—honor, loyalty, courage—remained the norms of the English and continental warrior aristocracy for centuries thereafter.

Another, much older subdivision of the tribe was the kin group or clan. Members of a clan were duty-bound to protect the welfare of their kinfolk. Should anyone be killed or injured, all close relatives declared a blood feud against the wrongdoer's kin. Because murders and maimings were only too common in the violent, honor-ridden atmosphere of the Germanic tribe, blood feuds were a characteristic ingredient of Germanic society. To keep their tribes from being ripped apart by feuds, the Germanic peoples developed the legal concept of *wergelds* (literally, "man money")—sums of money that killers might pay to their victims' kin groups to appease their vengeance and avoid the feud.

Wergelds varied in size depending on the victim's sex, age, and social status—they tended to be highest for aristocratic male adults and women of childbearing age. In Anglo-Saxon England, the wergeld for a free, non-noble man or woman was 200 shillings, while that for a noble was 1,200 shillings. The Germanic laws established smaller payments (known as *bots*) for various nonfatal injuries—so much for the loss of a hand, less for a severed finger, still less for a fingernail, and so on.

Wergelds and bots mitigated the blood feud but by no means eliminated it, for there was no assurance that the alleged murderer would pay the required sum or even admit the deed. And early Germanic law was exceedingly limited in its jurisdiction. Many crimes of violence fell outside its scope. Its basic principle was the presumption of guilt: it was up to the accused to prove their innocence. Among the Franks, who settled in Roman Gaul, the custom had developed of requiring the accused to submit to an "ordeal." This procedure, which spread to the Anglo-Saxons and other Germanic peoples, was regarded as an appeal to divine judgment. The accused, for example, might be obliged to grasp a red-hot iron and carry it a prescribed distance, or to lift a stone from the bottom of a boiling cauldron. Several days thereafter the hand was examined carefully. If it was healing properly, the court concluded that the accused enjoyed divine favor and was innocent. But if the hand was infected, the accused was pronounced guilty. Similarly, the suspect might be lowered by rope into a pond to sink or float. Sinking was a proof of innocence and floating, a proof of guilt: pure water would not "accept" the guilty. Through such appeals to divine judgment, Germanic peoples sought to achieve community consensus—to heal the breaches in inter-family relationships created by acts of violence.

Throughout the early Middle Ages it was chiefly these Germanic customs, rather than the sophisticated, impersonal concepts of Roman law, that governed jurisprudence in England and across Western Europe. For Roman law depended not on local consensus but on the enforcement authority of a powerful state, and no such authority emerged in Western Europe until the twelfth century. Roman law survived the fall of the Western Empire in fragmentary or bastardized form, but only in the twelfth century did it undergo a fundamental revival in the West. Even then, England remained largely immune to its influence.

On the Continent, as we have seen, the fifth and sixth centuries witnessed the beginnings of a gradual fusion between the culture of the Germanic tribes and the classical-Christian tradition preserved and fostered by the Church. In Britain, on the other hand, the Germanic settlers remained immune to the Christian faith of the indigenous Britons. As British authority receded before the advance of the Anglo-Saxon conquerors, Christianity receded with it. The failure of the Britons to Christianize their conquerors may perhaps be attributed at least in part to the hostility that developed between the two peoples and the consequent unwillingness of British missionaries to evangelize among the hated newcomers. A century and a half elapsed between the first conquests and the beginnings of serious missionary work among the Germanic settlers in Britain.

The Anglo-Saxon Conquest

According to the eighth-century historian Bede, three distinct Germanic peoples invaded England: the Angles, the Saxons, and the Jutes. Bede's testimony is essentially correct, yet it oversimplifies the actual situation. It would be more precise to view the "invasions" as consisting of attacks—or often of peaceful settlements—by innumerable small Germanic groups coming from various points along the long coastline of the North Sea between southern Denmark and the mouth of the Rhine. These bands included many warriors from among the Angle and Saxon tribes that had long been settled in northern Europe, but they also included Frisians, Swabians, and other Germanic peoples. On the Continent the invaders came in large tribal groups; in Britain they came first as pirate bands hungry for booty and land, and then, more permanently, as groups of mercenaries hired to stiffen the island's defense against enemy incursions, including those of other Germanic war bands. Excavations of ancient cemeteries have disclosed Germanic mercenary settlements in the early fifth century in such widely separated locations as York, Lincoln, and Norwich (see the map on page 11). In time, the mercenaries turned against their masters and, once in power, encouraged the gradual settlement of thousands of their compatriots from the Continent.

The transition from Roman Britain to Anglo-Saxon England was gradual, complex, and prolonged. Roman Britain had long been subject to Germanic attacks, as the establishment of the Saxon Shore and the disaster of 367 make clear. And Rome had often invited Germanic warrior-mercenaries to settle within the empire—in Britain as elsewhere—to help defend the frontiers. This policy was continued in post-Roman times by a Romano-British aristocrat known as Vortigern,[9] who rose to political leadership in southeastern Britain sometime after 410 and took upon himself the responsibility of defending his lands against the sea raids of the Picts and Scots. By then the military situation was becoming desperate. The Britons again appealed to Rome, and again in vain: "The barbarians drive us to the sea; the sea drives us to the barbarians; between these two fatal threats we are either slain or drowned."[10]

In response to these calamities, Vortigern is said to have invited Germanic warriors to Britain, offering them lands in Kent in return for their military assistance. Gildas calls these warriors "Saxons," whereas Bede describes them as "Jutes" under the leadership of two chieftains named Hengist and Horsa. "How desperate and crass," Gildas lamented, "that the ferocious Saxons (name not to be spoken!), hated by man and God, should be let into the island like wolves into the sheepfold." But although many historians have followed Gildas in proclaiming Vortigern's decision an act of folly, this is scarcely a fair judgment. Vortigern was simply following Roman tradition.

Nevertheless, the Roman policy of settling Germanic peoples on imperial lands had disastrous consequences for the Western Empire in general and for Vortigern in particular. Once settled in Kent, the Germanic warriors rebelled against Vortigern's authority and spread devastation and terror across southeastern Britain. The rebellion can be dated to perhaps the mid-400s, and it appears to have been duplicated elsewhere. During the next century, Germanic colonists flooded into Britain, settling along the southern and eastern shores. They penetrated deep into the interior, chiefly by means of eastern Britain's three great estuaries—the Thames, the Wash, and the Humber—relegating British political authority to the far western districts of Devon, Cornwall, and Wales.

After about 470, however, the British defenses began to stiffen, and around the turn of the century the Britons won a major victory over the Germans at a site called Mount Badon. The inadequacies of our evidence are well illustrated by the fact that historians disagree heatedly as to both the site of this battle and its date. We know only that it was fought in southwestern England, probably in Dorset or Somerset, sometime between 491

---

[9] *Vortigern* is actually a title, not a name. It means, literally, "high king."

[10] The so-called Groans of the Britons, addressed to a Roman *magister militum*, usually identified as Aëtius, c. 446–451.

and 516. On the dubious authority of the anonymous ninth-century British author of the *Historia Brittonum*, the British victory at Mount Badon is associated with a leader named Arthur (described as a "general," not as a king), who became the inspiration for the richly elaborated Arthurian romances of later centuries. Perhaps the original Arthur was indeed a hero of the British resistance against the Anglo-Saxons, but this attractive conclusion is far from assured; the *Historia Brittonum* is a most untrustworthy authority, written a good three centuries after the event.

From time to time, people interested in King Arthur have speculated that his headquarters, the fabled Camelot, may have been located at a well-excavated hillfort in Somerset known today as South Cadbury. An important, well-populated political center in pre-Roman times, South Cadbury had been stormed, demolished, and abandoned by the conquering Romans. Centuries later, after the Romans had departed, the Britons reoccupied and refortified South Cadbury. Archaeologists have found a great embankment of rubble dating from about A.D. 500, strengthened by wooden beams and provided with two sizeable wood-and-timber gatehouses. Behind the embankment stood a great timber hall some sixty feet long. The entire fortress complex covers some eighteen acres and the site enjoys spectacular views of the surrounding countryside, including, off in the distance, the ancient Somerset monastery of Glastonbury whose monks, in the later Middle Ages, claimed to be in possession of Arthur's tomb. But the equating of South Cadbury with Camelot can be no more than a wild guess when some distinguished historians of today deny that King Arthur ever existed. Whatever the case, the glittering court at Camelot with its chivalrous, questing knights, as described in Arthurian literature many centuries later, was an idealization of the courtly society of the later Middle Ages. It had nothing to do with the shadowed, menacing world of sixth-century Britain.

For half a century after the victory at Mount Badon, so Gildas tells us, Britain enjoyed a period of relative peace and prosperity. British colonists crossed the Channel to settle on the peninsula of Armorica, appropriately known in later years as Brittany. British Christianity and culture were also spreading through Ireland, thanks to the intrepid evangelism of the Briton St. Patrick (d. c. 490) and his successors. Most of what we know of St. Patrick comes from his own Latin writings. And the existence of a flourishing Celtic, Latin-Christian culture in the lands surrounding the Irish Sea and western English Channel is further confirmed by the survival of some 200 Latin tombstone inscriptions from these regions dating between the fifth and seventh centuries.

The period of prosperity that Gildas describes can be dated roughly to the half-century between 500 and 550. Gildas himself, writing toward the end of that epoch, provides eyewitness testimony to the relative security of southwestern Britain in his own lifetime, even as he deplores the eagerness of his fellow Britons to exploit the prosperous times by engaging in various shameful depravities.

The era between about 550 and 600 was less fortunate for the Britons. A devastating pan-Eurasian plague struck in the mid-500s, and in the decades that followed, the Anglo-Saxons advanced significantly. We know extremely little about these decades: as James Campbell wisely said, "The natural vice of historians is to claim to know about the past." But with respect to fifth- and sixth-century Britain, "what really happened will never be known."

One must distinguish between the possibility of a regional Anglo-Saxon royal dynasty establishing its rule over both Germanic and Celtic subjects, and the alternative possibility of Anglo-Saxons settling a region in such great numbers as to drive the Britons out or to enslave them. Different regions seem to have followed different patterns. In Northumbria, Germanic kings ruled a people who, judging from the dearth of surviving Anglo-Saxon pottery, were more British than Germanic. Far to the south, in Kent and Wessex, Anglo-Saxon settlement was clearly much heavier, but whether the Britons were literally driven into the western mountains or were simply subordinated to Germanic lords cannot be determined from the surviving evidence.

A further complication is the fact that the dynasties of the various Anglo-Saxon kingdoms were not always descendants of the war chiefs who led their tribes to their original conquests. There is good archaeological evidence to suggest, for example, that the royal dynasty of the kingdom of Wessex—which would one day rule all England—came from the Continent to establish itself over a predominantly Anglo-Saxon population that had previously settled the region. To further complicate matters, the founder of the Wessex dynasty, Cerdic, bears a British name, suggesting the existence of some undiscoverable British family connection before Cerdic left the Continent. Whatever occurred in this particular case, there is evidence that Anglo-Saxon kings might occasionally take British wives. More generally, intermarriages between the two peoples, although impossible to document, may have been relatively common.

As a consequence of the near-total obscurity of the era, specialists have long been at odds over the issue of continuity or discontinuity between Roman Britain and Anglo-Saxon England. Traditionally, most investigators agreed that the Anglo-Saxons had almost totally eradicated Romano-British culture. The evidence for this conclusion once seemed compelling: unlike the conquered Roman provinces on the Continent—Italy, Gaul, Spain—Britain under the Anglo-Saxons experienced the loss of its language, its Latin culture, its Christian religion, its coinage, and, in time, its towns. The Latin and Celtic languages gave way to a Germanic tongue; Anglo-Saxon paganism engulfed Christianity. Saxon Britain, in short, lost its past.

Nevertheless, scholars today are skeptical of the notion that Anglo-Saxon England was an era without a past. They suspect, for example, that agrarian organization may have changed little between Roman and Saxon times, and that much of the Romano-British machinery of local governance may have continued under new management in some parts of Anglo-Saxon England. There is growing evidence, too, that town life continued and perhaps even flourished for a time after the departure of the Romans. Archaeological investigations have shown that certain towns were still constructing buildings in at least the early decades of the fifth century, and that workers at Verulamium laid down a water pipe around the mid- or late-fifth century.

But the fact that Verulamium and its surroundings are totally lacking in pagan cemeteries that date before the seventh century suggests the probability that the Britons were in control of the area throughout much of the sixth century, and that the new water pipe was installed under their management. Town life must have been drastically affected by the cutting off of coinage importation at the time of the Roman departure. No coins were minted and very few were imported into Britain after 410—until, more than two centuries later, Anglo-Saxon kings began minting their own coins. Meanwhile, although coins minted prior to 410 might have continued to circulate for a time, Britain was nevertheless drifting toward a moneyless economy—a Germanic economy of gift-giving and plunder—in which urban commercial life could not endure. Gildas declares that in his own time, midway through the fifth century, "The cities of our land are not populated now as they once were; right to the present they are deserted, in ruins, and unkempt."

In the course of the following century, the combination of bubonic plague, endemic warfare, and political and economic dislocation reduced the population severely and destroyed whatever remained of urban life. In the words of an early Anglo-Saxon poet, perhaps referring to the Roman town of Bath in Somerset:

> Fate has smashed those wonderful walls,
> This broken city, has crumbled the work
> Of giants. The roofs are gutted, the towers
> Fallen, the gates ripped off, frost
> In the mortar, everything molded, gaping,
> Collapsed. . . .

In a word Britain became the land of what Bede called the "gens Anglorum"—the English people. It became "Angleland"—England. And although the Anglo-Saxons had not cut themselves off completely from the Roman past, they were far less affected by it than other Germanic peoples of Western Europe, who had the Christian church to teach them the ways of Latin civilization.

England in A.D. 600

By the seventh century Anglo-Saxon England had resolved itself into about seven or eight major kingdoms and a number of less important ones—a political configuration that is traditionally called the *Heptarchy*. This term is misleading, because it implies the existence of precisely seven states, all more or less equal in power. In reality the number of kingdoms fluctuated constantly and tended to diminish as political consolidation advanced. Moreover, the kingdoms of the Heptarchy varied in wealth, prestige, and military might. Bede reports that as early as 600 it had become customary to

THE EARLY
ANGLO-SAXON KINGDOMS
ABOUT 600 A.D.

KENT: Kingdoms ruled by
Anglo-Saxons

DYFED: Kingdoms ruled by Celts

accord one king the honor of preeminence among all or most of his royal colleagues. Other contemporary evidence suggests that a king who enjoyed such preeminent status was sometimes called a *bretwalda* ("ruler of Britain"). This preeminence did not constitute a defined office, nor did it convey any powers that the king did not already possess. It was merely a status symbol. It was not permanently attached to a particular kingdom but shifted from one dynasty to another with the varying fortunes of politics and war. The earliest bretwaldas were kings whose military strength enabled them to dominate and perhaps collect tribute from a few weaker neighboring kingdoms and whose fame had spread over much of England. Other important monarchs might hold the bretwalda in respect, but the degree to which they deferred to his wishes depended on military and diplomatic circumstances. Among the more powerful Anglo-Saxon kings his primacy was merely honorary.

The preeminent Anglo-Saxon kingdom around the year 600 was Kent, in the southeast corner of the island. Although Bede singled out the Kentish king at this time as the greatest in England, the monarch seems to have exerted authority over only the two neighboring kingdoms of Essex and East Anglia. Kent was the sole Anglo-Saxon kingdom whose conquest Bede attributes to the Jutes—inhabitants of Jutland (Denmark). Kent did indeed exhibit a number of peculiar features not found elsewhere in Anglo-Saxon England: an entirely distinctive system of land measurement and assessment, and burial methods and legal customs unique to England. Yet for much of the twentieth century, scholars argued, chiefly on philological grounds, that Bede was mistaken in associating the settlers of Kent with the inhabitants of Jutland—thereby setting off a torrent of inquiries and scholarly skirmishes on the issue of where the Jutes might in fact have come from. A memorable symposium at the International Congress on Medieval Studies, entitled (if I recall correctly) "Whence the Jutes?," consisted entirely of papers playfully parodying the great Jute debate. More recently, however, an abundance of further archaeological investigations have resolved the issue by demonstrating strong connections between Kent and Jutland. Graves from the two regions have yielded similar pottery and jewelry, including distinctive decorated gold discs known as *bracteates*. Kentish grave sites disclose artifacts from other regions as well, revealing a brisk trade with the Franks whose kingdom lay just across the Channel, and reflecting the likelihood that the Germanic settlers of Kent were not an altogether homogeneous people. Nevertheless, there is no longer any doubt that most of them were Jutes. Bede was right.

To the west and northwest of Kent lay three kingdoms associated by name with the Saxon migrations: the kingdoms of the South Saxons, the West Saxons, and the East Saxons, known respectively as Sussex, Wessex, and Essex. Of these Saxon states, only Wessex had the potential for future expansion westward at British expense, and in the centuries following A.D. 600 Wessex grew to become one of the three leading kingdoms of the land. Ultimately, Wessex became the nucleus of a united England, and the West Saxon dynasty evolved into the English monarchy.

Replica of an Early Anglo-Saxon Helmet from Sutton Hoo (c. 650) (Reproduced by courtesy of the Trustees of the British Museum)

To the north of Kent lay the kingdom of East Anglia, whose inhabitants were divided into two separate groups—the North Folk and the South Folk—occupying the territories that would later become the shires of Norfolk and Suffolk. Subject to Kent in A.D. 600, the East Anglian monarchy became a dominating power in the following generation. The wealth of the East Anglian kings in this epoch is disclosed by the richly laden royal burial ship dating from the middle decades of the seventh century, discovered at Sutton Hoo in 1939. The ship contains an abundance of gold and silver jewelry, plate, coins, a lyre, dice, drinking horns, and weapons—some Frankish, some from distant Byzantium—and a marvelously well-preserved helmet and shield. The treasures of Sutton Hoo make it clear that the trappings of a seventh-century Anglo-Saxon monarch could be splendid indeed. Perhaps the most remarkable trapping of all is a hanging bowl with an enameled fish mounted to swivel on a pedestal inside it—a rudimentary version of a floating magnetic compass, perhaps included to provide the burial ship the latest navigational technology for its voyage to Valhalla.

The English midlands were dominated by the kingdom of Mercia, which first gained prominence with the accession of its great king, Penda, in 632. Like Wessex, Mercia could expand westward toward Wales at the expense of the Britons (or, as we should by now call them, the Welsh). Thus, in later years Mercia became one of the three dominant kingdoms of England. Indeed, throughout most of the eighth century the kings of Mercia were the most powerful monarchs in the land.

The third of these potentially dominant kingdoms was Northumbria—the land north of the Humber River. The kingdom of Northumbria took form shortly after A.D. 600 from the unification of two smaller kingdoms, Deira and Bernicia, under a single dynasty. In the later seventh and early eighth centuries, Northumbria became the setting of a splendid intellectual and artistic revival stimulated by a resurgence of Celtic culture and by the conversion of the Northumbrians to Christianity. Perhaps the greatest creative figure of this Northumbrian renaissance was the historian Bede, whose writings have done so much to illuminate the dark epoch when his own forebears were ravaging and subduing Britain.

By the early seventh century the chaos of the post-Roman age had given way to a more stable regime dominated by reasonably well-organized Anglo-Saxon kingdoms such as the seven described above: Kent, Sussex, Wessex, Essex, East Anglia, Mercia, and Northumbria. The splendor of Sutton Hoo demonstrates that the early Anglo-Saxons, though illiterate and untouched by Latin Christianity, were by no means lacking in culture or resources. By A.D. 600, however, Anglo-Saxon isolation was ending. The new century, an era of growing population and agricultural productivity, witnessed England's conversion to Christianity. The Church returned to England at last, gradually winning the allegiance of the Anglo-Saxons and profoundly shaping their historical development.

2

Conversion and Unification

By the time of the British victory at Mount Badon (c. 500), Roman political authority had collapsed in the West. But although the Western Roman Empire was a thing of the past, Roman political institutions survived, in altered but recognizable form, in the organization of the Roman Catholic Church. Indeed, some historians regard the Church as a kind of transfigured empire. Its administration paralleled the old Roman civil administration, with dioceses, provinces, parishes, and even a central authority in Rome. Where Roman emperors had once exerted political sway over the inhabitants of Western Europe, Roman popes now claimed responsibility for their immortal souls (although it was only centuries later that the papacy became a powerful international political force). And just as the emperor Constantine had established an imperial capital at Constantinople that rivaled Rome itself, so now an intense rivalry developed between the Roman pontiff and his eastern counterpart, the patriarch of Constantinople.

Accordingly, the Church has been termed the ghost of the Roman Empire. And although the ghost metaphor belies the very tangible and politically active organization of the early medieval Church, there is nevertheless some value in regarding the Church, in the political sense at least, as an institutional legacy of the defunct empire.

The Celtic Church

In England, however, Christianity was swamped by the Germanic migrations. A few churches may have continued to serve the Britons who remained in England, but Christianity as an organized institution receded into the mountains of Cornwall, Wales, and Cumberland (in northwest England).[1] In these barren lands the Britons found sanctuary against the

---

[1] For a good account of the early English Church, see John Godfrey, *The Church in Anglo-Saxon England* (Cambridge, 1962). Dorothy Whitelock, ed., *English Historical Documents*, I, 2nd ed. (London, 1979) provides a comprehensive selection of original documents in English translation from the period c. 500–c. 1042. On the process of conversion, see Henry Mayr-Harting, *The Coming of Christianity to Anglo-Saxon England*, 3rd ed., (State College, PA, 1991). See also the collection of eighteen interesting and rather technical studies in *The Anglo-Saxon Church: Papers on History, Architecture, and Archaeology in Honor of Dr. D. M. Taylor*, L. A. S. Butler and R. K. Morris, eds., Council For British Archaeology, Research Report 60 (London, 1986); and Nicholas Brooks, *The Early History of the Church of Canterbury: Christ Church from 597 to 1066* (Leicester, 1984).

**Muireadoch's Cross,
County Louth, Ireland
(c. 900)** (Courtesy of the
Irish Tourist Board)

military thrusts of the Anglo-Saxons, and here the British Church endured. Although several generations passed before Celtic Christianity made any headway against the Anglo-Saxons, Celtic missionaries were spreading their faith in other directions. In the fifth century, as we have seen, the fabled British missionary St. Patrick (d. 461) contributed much to the conversion of the Scots of Ireland, and other missionaries were winning new converts in Galloway (southwestern Scotland). Thus, although Christianity practically disappeared from England with the completion of the Anglo-

Saxon conquest, it continued to flourish in neighboring Celtic lands: Cornwall, Wales, Cumberland, Galloway, Ireland, and Brittany.

When St. Patrick established the Church in Ireland, he appears to have divided it into dioceses, each diocese ruled by a bishop. This was the standard pattern of church organization throughout the Christian West, but despite St. Patrick's original plan, the diocesan structure never took hold in Ireland. On the Continent, bishops governed their dioceses from towns or cities, neither of which existed in St. Patrick's Ireland. Lacking the urban substructure of Catholic episcopal organization, Irish Christianity developed its own distinctive organizational structure based on great, autonomous monasteries. The Celtic Church did have bishops, but they did not rule dioceses; their functions were spiritual and sacramental only. They had no administrative power and usually lived in monasteries under the authority of an abbot.

Celtic monasticism became one of the great energizing forces of the Church—in Ireland, on the Continent, and, eventually, among the English. Developing in relative isolation from the papacy, it originated a variety of customs and practices uniquely its own. During the sixth and seventh centuries Irish monks surpassed their continental counterparts in the rigor of their scholarship, the depth of their sanctity, the austerity of their lives, and the range of their missionary work. Irish monastic schools were perhaps the best in Western Europe at the time, and a rich Irish artistic tradition culminated in the illuminated manuscripts of the eighth century, which were the wonder of their age and continue to excite admiration in our own. Irish missionaries, striving to deepen and expand monastic life on the Continent, founded a number of important religious houses in the kingdom of the Franks and as far afield as northern Italy. Celtic monastic customs exerted a strong influence on the Franks, who often adapted Irish usages, usually in modified form, for the governance of their own monastic communities.

Some such modification was desirable because Irish monastic customs, in their pure form, were distinctly at variance with the customs of monastic movements emanating from Rome. The tonsure of Celtic monks (shaving the entire front half of the skull) differed from normal continental practice (bald spot on top). More significantly, the Celtic method of calculating the date of Easter varied from that of the Roman Church. In an age that set great store on the proper celebration of religious festivals, the Easter issue was of vital importance. Celtic monastic life was peculiar, too, by Roman standards. Irish monks led singularly harsh, simple, yet relatively unregulated lives. The unique combination of dedication and loose discipline does much to explain the wide-ranging and highly successful evangelical activities of the Irish monks. From the English perspective, the most significant of these Irish missionaries was St. Columba (d. 597), who worked with great success toward the conversion of the Picts. In about 565, Columba founded a monastery on the island of Iona, off the west coast of Scotland, and his monastery quickly became a fountainhead of missionary activity among the Picts of Scotland and the English of Northumbria.

With the founding of Iona, the Celtic Church at last turned in full force to the task of converting the Anglo-Saxons. But as it happened, the Celtic spiritual penetration of Anglo-Saxon England from the north began almost concurrently with an entirely distinct Christian missionary endeavor from the south. In 597, the very year of St. Columba's death, a large band of Christian missionaries sent to England by the Roman pope St. Gregory the Great and led by the monk St. Augustine made contact with King Ethelbert of Kent. So it was that the seventh century saw Anglo-Saxon paganism under spiritual assault from two historically distinct Christian traditions.

The Roman Church and Continental Monasticism

As England was developing from the chaos of the early Anglo-Saxon conquests to the somewhat more stable Heptarchy, much larger Germanic kingdoms were forming on the Continent. The Franks had established a kingdom in Gaul and the Rhinelands that came to be known as "Francia"; their first king, Clovis (d. 511), renounced paganism and adopted Catholic Christianity under the influence of his Christian wife. The Germanic Visigoths founded a loosely organized kingdom in Spain which also converted to Christianity and which was to be overwhelmed in the early eighth century by the advancing Muslims. Italy, after a series of upheavals, was ruled in part by the Byzantine Empire, in part by a Germanic tribe known as the "Long Beards" or Lombards. In Rome itself the papacy, under nominal Byzantine jurisdiction, maintained a precarious independence. Throughout these lands of Western Europe, scholarship languished, culture diminished, cities shrank, and political and economic organization became rudimentary (except in Byzantine Italy). Germanic culture and institutions were everywhere in the ascendancy. Among the rough aristocracy of this epoch, fighting skill and loyalty to one's lord and kinfolk were the appropriate virtues.

The taming of this violent society by the intellectual and cultural values of antiquity and the teachings of Christianity was yet to be accomplished. The Church of the later sixth century, throughout much of the Germanic West, suffered much the same widespread illiteracy and disorganization as the lay society that surrounded it and provided its leaders. Yet the continental Church of the sixth century found the strength to recover and to assume its mission in the world. Its reforming activities centered above all on two institutions: monasticism and the papacy.

Christian monasticism emerged in Egypt in the third century, but it did not become a significant factor in the life of the Church until the fourth. After the conversion of Constantine and his rise to power in 312, Christianity became a favored religion. Profession of the Christian faith was no longer the perilous and heroic act it had been in the days of the martyrs. As converts poured into the now respectable fold, men and women of unusual piety began to seek a more rigorously Christian way of life—one that would enable them to withdraw from the world and devote all their energies to communion with God. Many of them found what they were seeking in monasticism.

Traditionally, Christian monasticism was of two types: eremitic (hermit monasticism) and cenobitic (communal monasticism). During the fifth and sixth centuries increasing numbers of fervent believers became eremitic or cenobitic monks. The lives of the hermit monks were bewildering in their variety. Some established themselves atop pillars and remained there for many years—to be revered as wise and wonder-working "holy men" by their surrounding communities. Others retreated to the desert, living in a state of uncompromising austerity. And the monastic communities of the age tended to be equally diverse. Both hermit and communal monks often carried mortification of the flesh to extreme lengths, indulging in severe fasts, going without sleep for prolonged periods, wearing hairshirts, and whipping themselves.

In the course of the fifth century, much more ordered religious communities were emerging in which monks or nuns governed their lives by written rules of conduct, shared by all. In the West, the most influential of the monastic rules in subsequent centuries was framed by St. Benedict of Nursia (c. 480–c. 544), a well-born Italian who stressed the practical Roman virtues of discipline and organization. St. Benedict founded many monasteries in his lifetime, the most important of which was Monte Cassino, built on a mountaintop between Rome and Naples.

Benedict's rule was characterized by Pope Gregory the Great as "conspicuous for its discretion." The lives of Benedictine monks and nuns were austere, but not excessively so. They ate, slept, and dressed simply but adequately. Their day was divided into a regular sequence of activities: there was a time for eating, a time for sleeping, a time for prayer, and a time for work. The Benedictine order had no central organization. Each monastery and nunnery was autonomous (subject to the jurisdiction of the local bishop), and each was under the full and unquestioned authority of its abbot or abbess. On important matters, the heads of Benedictine houses were to consult with the whole community of the abbey, but they were not bound by the majority opinion. Still, St. Benedict cautioned his abbots to respect the views of their monks, not to "sadden" or "overdrive" them or give them cause for "just murmuring." Here, as elsewhere, is the element of discretion to which Pope Gregory alludes and which was doubtless the chief reason for the rule's success. St. Benedict tempered his sanctity with a keen knowledge of human nature. His monks had to submit to the discipline of their abbot and the authority of the rule; they had to practice poverty and chastity; they had to work as well as pray. Yet the life St. Benedict prescribed was not for spiritual superstars alone, but one any dedicated Christian might hope to follow.

Benedictine monasticism shaped the lives of countless English monks and nuns throughout the early Middle Ages and far beyond. Throughout the seventh and eighth centuries increasing numbers of monasteries and nunneries adopted the Benedictine Rule. They became islands of peace, security, and learning in a sea of barbarism. They operated the best (and often the only) schools of their day. Their extensive estates—the gifts of generations of pious donors—often served as models of the most efficient agricultural techniques known in their time. They were the supreme civilizers of early medieval Europe.

The other great invigorating institution in the early medieval Church was the papacy. For centuries the popes, as bishops of Rome and heirs of St. Peter, had claimed spiritual dominion over the Church, but they had seldom been able to exercise it until the pontificate of St. Gregory the Great (590–604). A man of humility and deep piety, St. Gregory was the most powerful pontiff of the early Middle Ages. He had been a monk before ascending the papal throne and had personally founded the Roman abbey of St. Andrews. Although neither Gregory nor his abbey were Benedictine, he was an enthusiastic admirer of St. Benedict and wrote his earliest biography.

The Mission to England

Gregory the Great was a man of many talents. Like St. Benedict, he possessed in full the practical genius of his aristocratic Roman forebears and was a gifted administrator as well as a sensitive pastor. He was a notable scholar, too, and is traditionally grouped with the great fourth-century intellectuals—St. Ambrose, St. Jerome, and St. Augustine of Hippo—as one of the "Doctors" of the early Latin Church. Much of his theological writing failed to rise far above the level of his day, but his *Pastoral Care*—a handbook on the duties of bishops and priests—is a work of extraordinary practical wisdom. It became one of the most admired and widely read books of the Middle Ages.

Paradoxically, Gregory never set foot in England and yet is one of the central figures of early English history. Bede relates that, prior to his elevation to the papacy, Gregory encountered a group of fair-haired young English boys who were being sold on the Roman slave market. Asking the name of their race, he was told that they were Angles. "That is appropriate," he replied, "for they have angelic faces, and it is right that they should become fellow heirs with the angels in heaven." The story is hard to believe; it seems unlikely that Gregory would risk his holy reputation by indulging in such a deplorable pun. Bede himself was suspicious of the tale, but he included it to illustrate "Gregory's deep desire for the salvation of our nation."

It was this desire that induced Pope Gregory to send a band of missionaries to work among the English. His devotion to the monastic ideal prompted him to entrust the hazardous task to a group of monks—indeed, a very sizeable group of forty monks from his own monastery of St. Andrews (they were probably the only missionaries readily available to him). They were led by a monk named Augustine, later St. Augustine (d. c. 604)—not to be confused with the great theologian, St. Augustine of Hippo (d. 430). The ultimate effect of Augustine's mission was not only to win England to the Christian faith but also to enlarge enormously the scope of monastic missionary activity and the authority of the papacy.

In 597 St. Augustine's army of monks arrived in Kent. This small kingdom was an ideal place to begin the work of conversion. It was the closest Anglo-Saxon kingdom to the Continent. Its king, Ethelbert, was momentarily the preeminent monarch of England. His queen, Bertha, was a Christian and a member of the Frankish royal family. As a condition of the marriage, a Frankish bishop accompanied Bertha to Kent and resided in King Ethelbert's household. Ethelbert had given him the abandoned Christian church of St. Martin in the royal capital of Canterbury ("Kent City"). The church of St. Martin still stands and is of great historical interest, but owing to modern Canterbury's diabolical one-way street system, it is much more difficult to find in the late twentieth century than it would have been in the sixth.

King Ethelbert received Augustine's mission courteously, permitted the monks to establish themselves in Canterbury (presumably at St. Martin's), and quickly became a convert to Christianity. Many of Ethelbert's Kentish subjects followed him into the new faith—10,000 were baptized at one time, so we are told—and Christianity began spreading into the client kingdoms of Essex and East Anglia. Returning briefly to the Continent, Augustine received consecration by papal order as "archbishop of the English peoples," thereby becoming the first in a line of archbishops of Canterbury that has continued unbroken up to the present day.

In the authority granted to Archbishop Augustine, the idea of an English people—a *gens Anglorum*—first saw the light of day. The concept may well have been the product of a misconception of Pope Gregory the Great, who viewed the Anglo-Saxons as being far more unified than they actually were. But if so, Pope Gregory's misconception, subsequently enshrined in the tradition of the archbishops of Canterbury, became a self-fulfilling prophecy. The authority of Canterbury over diverse kingdoms encouraged the notion of a single "English people."

In accordance with the sagacious instructions he received in letters from Pope Gregory, Augustine permitted his English converts to retain those aspects of their former heathen customs and rites that were not inconsistent with Christianity. Old temples were neither abandoned nor destroyed but were converted to Christian use. In general, Gregory and Augustine displayed a respect for the integrity of Anglo-Saxon folkways that would delight an anthropologist.

Almost from the beginning, St. Augustine was aware of the activities and potential rivalry of the Celtic Church. He attempted to secure its submission to his own archiepiscopal authority, but a series of unsuccessful summit conferences with leading Celtic ecclesiastics made it clear that the Celts would cling fast to their unique system of calculating Easter, their age-old independence, and their haircuts. The tension between Celtic and Roman Christianity was to continue for many decades.

It is no coincidence that Ethelbert of Kent, the first Anglo-Saxon monarch to become a Christian, was also the first to issue a series of written laws, or "dooms," for Christian conversion introduced literacy into Anglo-Saxon England. The Dooms of Ethelbert are the first in a long series of Anglo-Saxon vernacular law codes running down into the eleventh century.

They represent the first literary fruits of the encounter between Christianity and Anglo-Saxon culture. For although Ethelbert's Dooms are concerned largely with Germanic custom, they were committed to writing at the instigation of the Church, which was then the almost exclusive custodian of the written word. Indeed, the first doom in Ethelbert's list provides explicitly for the protection of ecclesiastical property. Other dooms deal with customary fines, wergelds, and injury rates. If a man cuts off another's ear he must pay twelve shillings; he must pay fifty shillings for an eye, six shillings for a front tooth, ten shillings for a big toe—rather along the lines of modern insurance schedules for accidental death or dismemberment.

The Conversion of Northumbria

At the death of Ethelbert in 616, Kent, Essex, and East Anglia underwent a pagan reaction. Political hegemony passed momentarily to East Anglia, whose king, Redwald, is said by Bede to have hedged his bets by keeping in the same temple "an altar to sacrifice to Christ and another, smaller one to sacrifice to devils." Redwald may well have been the king who was buried in heathen splendor at Sutton Hoo.

While paganism rallied in the southeast, the center of Christian missionary activity shifted to remote Northumbria. As we have seen, the kingdom of Northumbria came into being shortly after 600 through the unification of two northern kingdoms, Bernicia and Deira. The founder of Northumbria was a Bernician warrior-king named Ethelfrith (d. 616) who won a series of victories over the Celts, the Scots, and the Anglo-British inhabitants of Deira. Ethelfrith thereby established himself as the dominant power in the north and brought the kingdom of Deira under his sway. The Deiran heir, a young warrior named Edwin, went into exile for a time at the East Anglian court; but in 616 Edwin's forces defeated and killed Ethelfrith, and Edwin became king of Northumbria (616–633). Now it was the Bernician royal heirs who were driven into exile. They found refuge in Scotland where they fell under the influence of the Celtic monks of Iona.

Meanwhile, Edwin was proving himself a monarch of rare ability. He maintained a firm peace in Northumbria, led a highly successful military expedition against the Welsh, and even took his army on a triumphant campaign southward across the midlands into Wessex. Near his northern frontier he founded Edinburgh, which still bears his name. Another of his royal centers was located at Yeavering, high up in the Cheviot Hills, to the south of Edinburgh and some forty miles north of Hadrian's Wall. In 1949 an aerial photograph of the Yeavering site disclosed outlines in the earth of extensive ancient and early medieval buildings, which were afterwards subjected to meticulous archaeological investigations with dramatic results. These investigations revealed numerous graves from across many centuries, a large and well-defended cattle corral dating from the Iron Age, and several impressive plastered-timber structures that appear to date from the reign of Edwin. The most spectacular among Edwin's buildings is a great royal hall over eighty feet long and nearly forty feet wide. Its timber supports were set as much as eight feet into the ground, suggesting that the hall was of considerable height. It reminds one of the description in the celebrated Anglo-Saxon poem *Beowulf* of the hall of King Hrothgar, which was said to have been named "Heorot" and to have had a gilded roof. Perhaps King Edwin's hall at Yeavering was also named and gilded; there is no way of knowing. But that Edwin could hold court and feast in great splendor at Yeavering, there can be no doubt. Archaeology has even located a "constitutional" artifact at Yeavering—the outline of a grandstand with a seating capacity in Edwin's time of some 320, with a platform in front of it on which one can imagine Edwin standing as he addressed and consulted with his great men.

Yeavering was not King Edwin's capital, but only one of a number of royal vills, probably not the most elaborate of them. In conjunction with other evidence, the investigations at Yeavering make clear that Edwin was a monarch of unprecedented authority, dominating his Anglo-Saxon contemporaries as no king before him had done.

In the pages of Bede, Edwin's warlike prowess and successful statesmanship acquire a fundamental historical significance because of his conversion to Christianity. Like Clovis, king of the Franks, and Ethelbert of Kent, Edwin had a Christian wife. Indeed, he was wed to a daughter of Ethelbert himself, Ethelberga, who took with her to Northumbria a dedicated chaplain named Paulinus. King Edwin was subjected to Christian pressure from several quarters: from his devout wife, from Paulinus, and from the papacy. In one of his letters to Ethelberga, the pope gave this counsel: "Persist, therefore, illustrious daughter, and to the utmost of your power endeavor to soften the hardness of his [Edwin's] heart by insinuating the divine precepts, etc." To King Edwin, the pope wrote:

> Hear the words of your preachers, and the Gospel of God which they declare to you, to the end that believing . . . [in] the indivisible Trinity, having put to flight the sensualities of devils, and driven from you the suggestions of the venomous and deceitful enemy, and being born again by water and the Holy Spirit, you may, through His assistance and bounty, dwell in eternal glory with Him in whom you shall believe.

After a time Edwin succumbed. At a royal council of 627 he and his counselors accepted Christianity in its Roman form. Bede tells of an episode in this council which, whether authentic or not, provides insight into the mood of the age. It is one of the most famous anecdotes of early English history—as familiar to English school children as the story of George Washington and the cherry tree is to Americans, and considerably more credible. According to Bede, one of Edwin's Witan (a member of his council), on considering the question of Christian conversion, advised his monarch as follows:

> The present life of man, O king, in comparison to that time which is unknown to us, seems to me like the swift flight of a sparrow through the

hall wherein you sit at dinner in the winter, with your chieftains and ministers, and a good fire in the midst, while the storms of rain and snow rage without. The sparrow flies in at one door and immediately out at another. While he is within he is safe from the wintry storm, but after a brief interval of fair weather he immediately vanishes from sight into the dark winter from which he came. So this life of man appears for a brief interval, but we are utterly ignorant of what went before or what will follow. So if this new doctrine contains something more certain, it seems justly to deserve to be followed.

As the council concluded, the chief priest of the heathen gods is reported to have embraced the new religion and, with him, King Edwin himself. The Roman Church had won a notable triumph in a remote but powerful kingdom.

The chagrin of the Christian party must have been great when, six years after his conversion, Edwin was killed in battle (633). His adversary, the pagan King Penda of Mercia (c. 632–654), laid waste to Edwin's kingdom, Paulinus fled into exile, and Northumbria collapsed briefly into political and religious chaos. But with the fall of Edwin and the Deiran royal house, the two heirs of the Bernician dynasty, long in exile in Scotland, returned to claim their inheritance. These two princes, bearing the engaging names of Oswald and Oswy, brought with them the Celtic Christianity they had learned at Iona. Oswald, the older of the two, won the Northumbrian throne by defeating the Mercians and Welsh in 634. At this crucial encounter, known appropriately as the battle of Heavenfield, Oswald set up a wooden cross to symbolize his devotion to the new faith. But his victory must have evoked a mixed reaction among the Christians of Edwin's former court whose devotion to the Roman Easter made it difficult for them to accept the alien Celtic customs.

Under the patronage of King Oswald (634–642) and his successor Oswy (642–670), Celtic Christianity established itself firmly in Northumbria. The Celtic missionary, St. Aidan, founded a monastery on the "Holy Island" of Lindisfarne off the coast of northern Bernicia, which became a focal point of Celtic Christianity and culture. In the middle decades of the seventh century Celtic missionaries carried the Gospel south of the Humber into Mercia and other Anglo-Saxon kingdoms.

But it was Northumbria, above all, that witnessed the cross-fertilization of the Roman and Celtic traditions. The Celtic influence, radiating from Iona and Lindisfarne, was countered by the activities of Roman-Benedictine missionaries such as the fervent, uncompromising St. Wilfrid of Ripon (634–710), after whom our cat, Willie, is named. (Our feline Wilfrid is of a much sunnier disposition than the Anglo-Saxon saint.) And despite the Celtic leanings of Kings Oswald and Oswy, Roman Christianity, with its disciplined organization, its impressive ceremonial, and its majestic tradition, gradually expanded.

The final victory of Roman Christianity in Northumbria occurred in 664 at a synod held in King Oswy's presence at the abbey of Whitby, dramatically situated high atop a bluff overlooking the North Sea.[2] Present at the Synod of Whitby were leading clergy from all over England, representing both the Roman and the Celtic observances. The chief issue in question was the Easter date. Oswy, who had previously celebrated Easter according to the Celtic reckoning, was upset that his wife, who followed the Roman custom, should be keeping the Lenten fast while he was enjoying the Easter feast. But St. Wilfrid of Ripon placed the issue in a larger framework when he addressed the Celtic clergy at Whitby in these words:

> Although your fathers were holy men, do you imagine that they, a few men in a corner of a remote island, are to be preferred before the universal Church of Christ throughout the world? And even if your Columba—or may I say, ours also if he was a servant of Christ—was a saint of potent virtues, can he take precedence before the most blessed prince of the Apostles [St. Peter, whose vicar and representative the pope claimed to be] . . . ?

The Synod of Whitby closed on an almost comic note, as King Oswy, observing that Peter possessed the keys to the kingdom of heaven, agreed to follow Peter's vicar, the pope, in all matters: "Otherwise, when I come to the gates of heaven, he who holds the keys may not be willing to open them." Bede reports this statement in all seriousness, but another writer, possibly an eyewitness, reports that Oswy smiled as he uttered those words. Probably he had decided long before the synod opened to cast his lot with Rome.

Celtic Christianity by no means expired with the Synod of Whitby. It endured long thereafter, contributing much to Christian culture and the Christian life. But as time went on it blended more and more with Roman Christianity. In 716 Iona itself adopted the Roman Easter date (which the churches of southern Ireland had adopted long before Whitby), and in subsequent years the remaining Celtic churches did likewise.

The acceptance of Roman authority and customs at Whitby resulted in a thorough reorganization of the Anglo-Saxon Church along Roman lines. The architect of this great administrative undertaking was St. Theodore of Tarsus, a distinguished Greek-speaking scholar from Asia Minor who, having traveled to Rome, now journeyed on to England with a papal mandate to assume the archbishopric of Canterbury. Theodore arrived in England in 669 at the age of sixty-six. He set about at once to divide the land into dioceses and selected devout, energetic bishops to rule them. The rational episcopal structure that Archbishop Theodore imposed on the Anglo-Saxon Church was given unity and direction by a regular series of conciliar assemblies over which he presided. In the course of his twenty-one-year archiepiscopacy, Theodore succeeded in superimposing on the many Anglo-Saxon kingdoms a single, unified Church with clearly delineated territorial bishoprics and with ultimate administrative authority centered at Canter-

---

[2] Whitby, founded in 657, was a double monastery housing both nuns and monks and was ruled by an abbess—King Oswy's kinswoman, St. Hilda.

bury. Frowning on Celtic wanderlust, Theodore's Synod of Hertford (672) ruled that bishops should confine their activities to the people of their own dioceses and not interfere elsewhere, and that monks and clergy should not go wandering about without permission.

By these means and others, Theodore of Tarsus brought the English Church into line with the coherent political principles of the Roman papacy and, indirectly, the Roman empire. He gave the Church a degree of territorial organization and administrative centralization that contrasted sharply with the instability of the Anglo-Saxon states. As the political unity of the Roman Empire underlay the spiritual unity of the Roman Church, so the unity Theodore imposed on the English Church prefigured the political unity of England itself.

Theodore was a celebrated scholar who had earlier studied in Athens. He was accompanied on his journey to England by another scholar of eminence, a North African churchman named Hadrian. The Latin learning of Hadrian complemented the Greek scholarship of Theodore, and together they made Canterbury a distinguished intellectual center. Theodore established a school there which provided instruction in Greek and Latin letters and the principles of Roman law. The Roman legal tradition, which had virtually disappeared from Western Europe, was well known in Theodore's Byzantine homeland, and he was able to introduce it into England along with his native Greek tongue. Through their wide experience and broad cultural heritage, Theodore and Hadrian brought to seventh-century Canterbury the rich intellectual legacy of the Mediterranean world.

The Northumbrian Renaissance

Canterbury's distinction as an intellectual center did not long survive Archbishop Theodore. It was not at Canterbury but in Northumbria that Anglo-Saxon ecclesiastical culture reached its highest degree of creativity. There, at the northernmost edge of Christendom, the stimulating encounter between Celtic and Roman Christianity resulted in an intellectual and cultural achievement of the first order. In Northumbria during the later seventh and early eighth century, Anglo-Saxon culture—and perhaps the whole of Christian culture in the early Middle Ages—reached its zenith.

One of the great patrons of this renaissance was Benedict Biscop (628–690), a Northumbrian nobleman who assumed the name "Benedict" because of his deep admiration of St. Benedict of Nursia. A man of vigor and piety and a devoted monk, Benedict Biscop made several trips to Italy and southern Gaul and, indeed, was a companion of Archbishop Theodore and Hadrian on their journey from Rome in 668–669. In southern Europe Benedict encountered the ordered life of Benedictine monasteries and collected large quantities of books and precious works of art, which he brought back with him to his native Northumbria. He founded two neighboring Northumbrian monasteries of the strict Benedictine rule—Wearmouth (674) and Jarrow (681)—which he filled with his books and other treasures. These two houses, which stand to this day, became the foci of Roman-Benedictine

Illuminated Page from the Lindisfarne Gospels, Northumbrian Renaissance (c. 700) (Reproduced by courtesy of the Trustees of the British Museum)

culture in Northumbria, while the older establishment at Lindisfarne remained the center of Celtic culture.

Both cultures contributed to the renaissance in Northumbria. The impressive artistic achievements of the age were at once Celtic and Anglo-Saxon in inspiration. The magnificently illuminated Lindisfarne Gospels (c. 700) display a complex, curvilinear style reminiscent of Celtic art, but the illuminator was probably an Anglo-Saxon whose designs reflect the traditions of Germanic metalwork. The Latin literature of the period, on the other hand, is primarily Roman in inspiration; it has been suggested that the same impulse that gave rise to the Latin writings of the Northumbrian renaissance may also have inspired the written, vernacular version of the Germanic epic poem *Beowulf*.[3]

The achievements of the Northumbrian renaissance lay in many fields—art, architecture, poetry, palaeography, and manuscript illumination. But the supreme achievement of the age was the scholarship of the Venerable Bede (c. 673–735). In his writings, particularly the *History of the*

---

[3] The earliest extant version of *Beowulf* is from tenth- or early eleventh-century Wessex, but philological evidence suggests that the Wessex text may have been based on an earlier version from central or northern England. At present, however, the dating and placing of *Beowulf* are provoking war and mayhem among *Beowulf* scholars.

English Church and People, the intellectual tradition of Western Europe attained a level unequaled since the fall of Rome.[4]

Bede was a product of the Benedictine tradition. He spent his life under the Benedictine rule at Jarrow, where he was an exemplary monk. He was also a superb scholar whose investigations profited enormously from the fine library that Benedict Biscop had installed in the monastery in 681. Bede regarded his theological writings as his most important work, but his fame in later centuries rests primarily on his history. It was a pioneer effort, unprecedented in scope, and at the same time a work of remarkable maturity. Bede possessed a strong historical consciousness—an acute critical sense that caused him to use his sources with scrupulous care, evaluating their reliability and often quoting them in full. Bede was by no means a scientific historian in the modern sense. His history was embroidered with visions and other miraculous events, for as a Christian believer he accepted the possibility of miracles. But even in his miracle stories he demonstrated greater caution—more respect for the historical evidence—than was customary among his predecessors and contemporaries.

Bede's broad historical vision—his sense of historical structure—set his work apart from the annals and saints' lives that typified the historical writing of his day. And his miracle stories fit logically into the basic structure of his work. For it was Bede's purpose to narrate the miraculous rise of Christianity in Britain and its crucial role in imposing coherence and purpose on the chaos of human events. In Bede's hands the history of the Britons and Anglo-Saxons, and the rise of Christianity among them, acquired shape and direction. In effect, Bede was recording the developing synthesis between the Germanic and Christian cultures—the gradual softening of the martial traditions of the primitive Anglo-Saxons by the peace, love, and prayer that the Church urged upon its members.

It is characteristic of this man, who regarded Christianity as the supreme organizing force in history, that he should be the first major historian to use the Christian era as his chronological base—to date events not in terms of kings' reigns or lunar cycles but in terms of Christ's birth.[5] Thus Bede's sense of chronology and historical development prompted him to divide history into the two eras, B.C. and A.D. (*anno Domini*, "in the year of our Lord").

Finally, Bede powerfully reinforced in the minds of his contemporaries the concept of a *gens Anglorum*—an "English people." At a time when England was divided into numerous individual kingdoms, and loyalties were limited to one's clan or local lord, Bede conceived the notion of a single English people and made them the subject of his history. Thus, Bede accomplished at the conceptual level what Archbishop Theodore had

---

[4] Bede's masterpiece is most readily available in Leo Sherley-Price, tr., *A History of the English Church and People* (Baltimore, 1955). See also the excellent collection of other contemporary writings in *The Age of Bede*, J. F. Webb and D. H. Farmer, trs., rev. ed. (New York, 1983).

[5] Bede took the idea from a sixth-century scholar, the Roman monk Dionysius Exiguus.

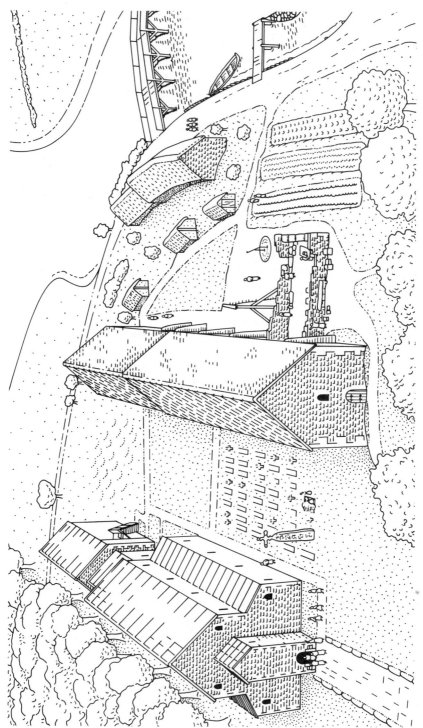

The Monastery at Jarrow as It Might Have Appeared in Bede's Time, Based on Current Excavations Two separate churches occupied the site, along with the monks' dormitory, refectory (dining hall), cemetery, garden, and workshops. (After reconstruction by R. J. Cramp; courtesy of The British Museum)

A Monk in His Study, Exactly Contemporary with Bede This illumination in the Gospel book of Ceolfrid, abbot of Bede's monastery of Jarrow, was done sometime before A.D. 716. (The Granger Collection)

accomplished at the level of ecclesiastical organization. In the face of the savage struggles of Anglo-Saxon kings, both men saw England as one.

Missions to the Continent

During the eighth century, the dynamic Christian culture of England made its impact on the continent of Europe, as Anglo-Saxon missionaries and scholars reinvigorated the Frankish Church and spread civilization and the Gospel among the pagan Germanic peoples east of the Rhine.

The most effective of these Anglo-Saxon missionaries was the Wessex monk, St. Boniface (d. 754). Working under the general direction of the papacy, and supplied with books and assistants by his Wessex compatriots, Boniface represented three dynamic forces of his day: the papacy, the Benedictine order, and the ecclesiastical culture of Anglo-Saxon England. During the 740s, with the cooperation of the Frankish kings, Boniface devoted himself to the regeneration of the Frankish Church, reforming monasteries and reconstructing Frankish diocesan organization on the disciplined pattern that Theodore of Tarsus had earlier established in England. It was this reformed Frankish Church that provided the necessary environment for the impressive cultural achievements of Charlemagne's reign a generation later.

St. Boniface also devoted himself to the immense undertaking of Christianizing the peoples of Germany. The task was far too great for a single person or a single generation to accomplish, but Boniface made a promising beginning. Among the several Benedictine houses he founded in Germany was the monastery of Fulda, which, like Wearmouth and Jarrow in Northumbria, became a major intellectual and evangelical center. Boniface devoted himself particularly to the conversion of the Saxons, Hessians, and Frisians, and it was at the hands of the Frisians that he died a martyr's death in 754.

Northumbria, too, participated in the work of evangelism on the Continent. The fiery Northumbrian Benedictine, Wilfrid of Ripon, had been active in missionary work across the Channel long before Boniface undertook his mission. Much later, in the reign of Charlemagne (768–814), the Northumbrian scholar Alcuin of York, a student of a student of Bede's, was a major counselor at Charlemagne's court and the foremost scholar in his realm. A product of the Northumbrian renaissance, Alcuin became the chief figure of the later and better known Carolingian renaissance.

In Northumbria itself, ecclesiastical culture declined from the summit attained in Bede's day, and in the ninth century it was virtually annihilated by the Vikings. Norse raiders sacked Lindisfarne in 793, Jarrow in 794, and Iona in 802. But before its demise in the north, this culture had spread its creative influence among the Franks and Germans. Having transformed the Anglo-Saxon world, the potent civilizing force of organized Christian evangelism now returned to the Continent to provide the intellectual and spiritual foundations for Charlemagne's empire.

The Movement Toward Political Consolidation: Mercia

During the 220 years following Bede's death in 735, the unity of England, foreshadowed in the ecclesiastical organization of Archbishop Theodore and in the historical work of Bede, was achieved at the level of secular politics. The chief historical theme of these years is the trend toward political consolidation and, at length, the genesis of the English monarchy.

During the seventh and eighth centuries, royal power was becoming consolidated in a handful of kingdoms. The smaller kingdoms of earlier years were gradually absorbed into the larger ones until, by the later seventh century, three kingdoms—Northumbria, Mercia, and Wessex—had come to overshadow the others. To speak very generally, Northumbria was the leading Anglo-Saxon kingdom in the seventh century, Mercia in the eighth, and Wessex in the ninth and tenth.

The epoch of Northumbrian hegemony is celebrated in the pages of Bede's history, and the great days of Wessex are recorded in the writings of King Alfred the Great's court and in the *Anglo-Saxon Chronicle*. Mercia left to posterity no impressive scholarly works and no history of its age of greatness. The power of Mercia's eighth-century kings cannot be denied, but local patriotism prevented both the Northumbrian Bede and the later Wessex authors of the *Anglo-Saxon Chronicle* from portraying the rival

Mercian state sympathetically. We must therefore use these sources with caution and be wary of underestimating the statesmanship of the Mercian kings or the creativity of Mercian culture.

Mercia's political and military power was impressive indeed. Even Northumbria in its greatest days lived under an almost constant Mercian threat. Mercia's powerful pagan monarch, Penda, had challenged the Northumbrian hegemony more than once in the seventh century, defeating and killing King Edwin in 633 and King Oswald in 642 before being killed himself in battle against King Oswy in 655. During much of his reign, Penda exerted an authority over the kingdoms south of the Humber exceeding that of all earlier southern kings. By the end of his reign, he had vastly increased the extent of his kingdom—by absorbing a number of small neighboring states—and had exerted his supremacy over both Wessex and East Anglia. A remarkably effective pagan warrior-king, he was portrayed by Christian writers of his day as something of a devil.

Penda's Christian son, King Wulfhere (658–675), resumed his father's drive for control of southern England, establishing dominion over Essex and the town of London, cowing Wessex, and winning the allegiance of Kent and Sussex. At his death he was endeavoring to subdue Northumbria itself. Had he succeeded, his authority over England would have been virtually uncontested.

The growth of Mercian power was interrupted for the half-century after Wulfhere's death by a resurgence of Wessex, particularly in the reign of its able king Ine (688–726), Sussex, Essex, and Kent passed for a time from Mercian into West Saxon control. It was obvious by now that these smaller states were too weak to maintain their independence. The only remaining question was which of the two "superpowers" would dominate them, Mercia or Wessex? During most of the eighth century Mercia not only successfully reasserted its dominion over these states but usually managed to dominate Wessex as well.

Mercian supremacy in the eighth century resulted from the intelligent exploitation of its strategic position and considerable resources by two adroit, long-lived kings: Ethelbald (716–757) and Offa (757–796). Under their leadership, Mercia dominated the midlands, exacting allegiance and probably tribute from the kingdoms to the south and east. Ethelbald described himself in a charter as "king of all Britain," and the royal boast was not far from the truth.

The reality of Mercian power is illustrated by a contemporary document known as the Tribal Hidage—a comprehensive assessment schedule that seems to have regulated tribute payments owed to the Mercian kings by various lesser kingdoms in southern and central England. In the early days of the Anglo-Saxon settlements the term *hide* had meant a unit of land sufficient to support the household of a single warrior. By the time of the Tribal Hidage, the hide had become an abstract unit of land assessment. In centuries to come, royal governments would exact taxes and military service from their subjects on the basis of the number of hides of land each subject held. The fact that the Mercian monarchy produced a document

**Offa's Dyke, South of
Chirk Castle, Clwyd,
Northeastern Wales**
(Aerofilms Library)

enumerating the hides of most of the Anglo-Saxon peoples south of the
Humber testifies to an administrative system and a central organization of
unprecedented scale.

The reigns of Ethelbald and Offa witnessed not only an unparalleled
degree of political power but also a resurgence of commercial activity. King
Offa's minters produced considerable quantities of the silver pennies that
would remain the basis of the English currency for centuries to come. And
the importance of commercial activities between the dominions of Offa and
the empire of his illustrious contemporary, Charlemagne, is demonstrated
by a remarkable treaty between these two monarchs. In it, Charlemagne
addresses Offa in these words:

> You wrote to us about merchants. We extend to them our personal protec-
> tion, as is the ancient custom for those engaged in trade. If treated wrong-
> fully, let them appeal to us or our judges, and we will see that they have full
> justice. Similarly, should any of our subjects suffer injustice in your king-
> dom, they shall appeal to you for a just remedy, so that no trouble may
> occur between our subjects.

It is significant that English merchants were sufficiently active on the
Continent at this time to require a formal arrangement between the two
rulers, and perhaps even more significant that Offa should take such a broad
view of his royal responsibilities as to intervene in behalf of English traders
abroad. In Offa's hands, Anglo-Saxon monarchy was assuming new and
larger dimensions.

Many details of Offa's reign are hidden from us by a lack of historical evidence. He has rightly been termed the most obscure great monarch of Anglo-Saxon England. As one historian wrote: "We can be sure that Offa was a crucial figure in the development of Anglo-Saxon institutions, without being able to find out exactly what he did."[6] Alcuin wrote to Offa from the Continent, praising him for being "intent on education, that the light of wisdom, which is now extinguished in many places, may shine in your kingdom,"[7] but we lack the details on Offa's educational reforms. Two centuries after Offa's death, King Alfred of Wessex spoke respectfully of his laws, but the laws themselves have perished. We have no contemporary history of his reign nor any celebration of his deeds. But we do know that Offa extended considerably the limits of the Mercian kingdom and the scope of Mercian royal authority. He advanced his power westward at Welsh expense by effectively sealing off Wales with an immense earthen embankment up to twenty-five feet in height known as Offa's Dyke. The earthwork was nearly 150 miles in length—longer than Hadrian's Wall and the Antonine Wall combined. It was paralleled on the Welsh side by a ditch six feet deep. Recent excavations suggest that at least parts of the earthwork were topped by a stone wall. Offa's Dyke would thus have been a formidable barrier against Welsh attacks. One scholar aptly described it as "the largest archaeological monument in Britain."[8]

Offa's Dyke was not, however, the only major monument erected during the Mercian hegemony. Excavations carried on between 1973 and 1986 at Repton, the site of a major Mercian religious center, have unearthed what seems to be a great eighth-century stone mausoleum for the Mercian kings and high nobility—later taken over by the Vikings for mass burials. And in the center of the modern industrial city of Northampton (in old Mercia) archaeologists have excavated the foundations of a vast timber hall of the eighth century, almost identical in scale to King Edwin's hall at Yeavering in northern Northumbria. Even more striking, the foundations of a second hall have been discovered on the same site, a massive structure of about the late eighth century—late in Offa's reign, perhaps—built entirely of stone. It would appear to be the first stone hall in Britain since Roman times; it measures some 123 feet long, 25 feet longer than the royal hall at Yeavering. Its vast dimensions, and its stone construction, make it an appropriate symbol of the Mercian monarchy at the height of its power.

In his quest for Mercian hegemony, Offa attempted to reshape the hierarchical pattern that Archbishop Theodore of Tarsus had earlier imposed on the English Church. Under Theodore, the archbishopric of Canterbury had stood unchallenged at the apex of the hierarchy; but in 735 the king of Northumbria founded a second bishopric at York, inferior in

---

[6] Eric John, *Orbis Britanniae and Other Studies* (Leicester, 1966), p. 35.

[7] *English Historical Documents* I, p. 846.

[8] Patrick Wormald, in *The Anglo-Saxons*, James Campbell, ed. (Oxford, 1982), p. 120.

prestige to Canterbury but nevertheless a potential rival. King Offa demanded a separate archbishopric for Mercia, and accordingly, in 787, a new archbishopric emerged at Lichfield. Shortly after Offa's death, however, the Lichfield archbishopric faded into oblivion, and thereafter the English Church was dominated by its two remaining archbishoprics of Canterbury and York.

The Church was active during Offa's reign. A papal legation came to England—the first since Augustine's time—and Offa himself contributed to poor relief in Rome. General councils continued to meet in Offa's realm and, at a lower level, country parishes were gradually taking shape. The development of an effective parish system was of immense importance to both church and society in the early Middle Ages. The Church had emerged from the highly urbanized Roman Empire with a diocesan organization based on the city. With the disintegration of Roman imperial society, the cities declined, but several centuries elapsed before the Church adjusted its organization to the needs of the rural society in which it worked. Peasants and small freeholders often were obliged to go many months without seeing a priest or attending Mass. The answer to this problem was the country parish, administered by a priest who was supported by the enforced tithes of his parishioners. Not until the twelfth century did the parish system reach full development in England, but in the eighth century, both in the empire of Charlemagne and in the kingdom of Offa, it was slowly developing.

In both ecclesiastical and secular affairs, Offa's regime marked a crucial stage in the development of the Anglo-Saxons. By the closing decade of his reign, he was issuing royal charters granting or confirming lands and privileges across much of England south of the Humber. The royal dynasties of Sussex, Essex, East Anglia, and Kent had succumbed to the expanding power of Mercia. The Mercian monarchy was transforming the vague overlordship exercised by earlier Anglo-Saxon kings into a direct control of subject kingdoms. With the Northumbrian monarchy in the doldrums and Mercian authority extending across all southwestern England, and with an astute monarch who could negotiate with Charlemagne on terms of equality, Offa's England attained a degree of political cohesion such as the Anglo-Saxons had never before experienced.

The Movement Toward Political Consolidation: Wessex

Notwithstanding their impressive achievement, the eighth-century Mercian kings fell short of giving England political unity. At Offa's death in 796, the Mercian crown passed to his able heir, Cenwulf (796–821), whose influence on Wessex and Northumbria diminished but who continued to dominate Kent and East Anglia and advanced against the Welsh. But after Cenwulf's successful reign the Mercian monarchy suffered from short-lived or inept kings and bitter dynastic rivalries. As a result, the leadership of southern England passed to Wessex.

There has been a tendency in modern historical writing to devote less attention to individual kings and battles and more to underlying historical forces and geographic determinants. There is much to be said for this approach, as long as it is not permitted to obscure the importance of individual human initiative. In the early medieval West, sophisticated bureaucratic government was unknown, and whatever the resources and physical environment of a kingdom, its success in the ruthless political competition of the era depended heavily on the military and administrative talents of its ruler, not to mention his good health and longevity. Thus, Mercia prospered mightily under Ethelbald and Offa but declined under their less able successors. On the Continent, the Carolingian Empire of the Franks declined similarly in the years following the death of Charlemagne in 814. Accordingly, the rise of Wessex in the early ninth century depended not merely on its wide extent and the relative abundance of its human and material resources, but also on the skill of its monarchs.

It was the gifted King Egbert of Wessex (802–839) who won for his kingdom the hegemony that Mercia had so long enjoyed. At the battle of Ellendon in 825 he routed the Mercian army and won control of the lesser states of southern England—Kent, Sussex, and Essex. Shortly afterward he received the submission and allegiance of East Anglia and, very grudgingly, Northumbria. For a brief time he ruled even in Mercia itself. Egbert's power was impressive, although less so than Offa's. But unlike Offa, Egbert had the good fortune to be succeeded by a series of able heirs. Egbert's reign was merely the beginning of a long epoch in which the Wessex monarchy, tempered by the fires of a terrifying Viking invasion, endured to become the sole royal power in the land. Egbert's descendants were to become the first kings of England.

The Viking Age and the Birth of the English Monarchy

The era of Mercian ascendancy corresponded approximately to the period in which Charlemagne and his predecessors expanded the power of the Frankish kingdom to such an extent that it absorbed almost all of continental Western Christendom. We have already noted the important intellectual upsurge at Charlemagne's court, and the role played by the Northumbrian Alcuin in the Carolingian renaissance. The hegemony of Wessex, on the other hand, was concurrent with the decline of the Carolingian Empire and the coming of the Viking Age.

Traveling from their Scandinavian homeland in long ships, the Vikings pillaged and conquered far and wide across northern Europe and the Atlantic. They subjected the Franks and Germans to fierce harassment, established a powerful dynasty in Russia, raided Islamic Spain, settled Iceland, and even touched the coast of North America.

Although the reasons for the Viking outburst are a matter of scholarly dispute, it is possible to suggest certain contributing factors. For one thing, a steady rise in population and political consolidation in Scandinavia may have prompted many adventurers (and exiled troublemakers) to seek their fortunes and satisfy their land hunger abroad. In addition, improvements in Viking shipbuilding seem to have added significantly to the mobility of these warriors. Charlemagne himself may have contributed unknowingly to the future debacle when he subdued and conquered the Frisians, a maritime people who lived along the northern shore of Europe east of the Rhine. The Frisians had previously functioned as a buffer between Western Europe and Scandinavia, and with their defeat the barrier was removed. After Charlemagne's death in 814, Europe's defensive posture grew slack. Three decades later, in 843, Charlemagne's grandsons divided his huge, unwieldy empire into three parts, creating thereby the nuclei of modern France, modern Germany, and the long strip of intermediate lands—Alsace, Lorraine, and Flanders—that France and Germany have contested ever since. Although Charlemagne's heirs were by no means incompetent, they represented a decline in leadership, owing in part to the greater problems that they faced. And the struggles among them created a political-military vacuum that proved irresistible to the Viking raiders.

Neither Charlemagne nor Offa had possessed a navy to speak of, and the English Channel had effectively separated the two powers. But to the seafaring Vikings, the Channel was less a barrier than a boulevard. They harried the lands on either side without partiality, plundering coastal settlements and sailing up rivers to bring havoc and terror deep into the interior of England and the Continent. Their first raids struck England, for they found it expedient to ignore continental Europe until the passing of Charlemagne. It is said that the great Frankish emperor wept on seeing Viking ships off the north Frankish coasts on their way to England, and Alcuin wrote a letter expressing profound sympathies when Norse seafarers sacked Lindisfarne in his native Northumbria in 793.

In the late 780s or 790s the Vikings struck the Dorset coast of Wessex. The *Anglo-Saxon Chronicle* reports that on the arrival of three Norse ships, the chief official of the region—the king's reeve—galloped to the coast "and tried to force them to the king's residence, for he did not know who they were. And they slew him." It was a portentous episode, for in subsequent years countless other raiders, first from Norway, then from Denmark, plundered and settled in England and the islands off its coasts.

Organized into small groups of ships' crews, with some thirty to sixty warriors per ship, the Vikings had the immense advantage of mobility and surprise over their more numerous, sedentary victims. At first confining themselves to plundering expeditions, they later turned to conquest and settlement. Norwegian Vikings attacked and overran Ireland, founded a state centering on Dublin, and remained in occupation of portions of Ireland for generations thereafter. Another Viking band established a permanent settlement in northern Francia (France) at the mouth of the Seine. Its ruler, a Viking chieftain named Rollo, adopted Christianity and received official recognition by the Frankish king, Charles the Simple, around 911. This Seine settlement evolved and expanded in later years into a powerful duchy known as Normandy (the land of the Northmen, or "Normans"), which gradually assimilated French culture, French institutions, and the French language. The establishment of the Norman duchy went unmarked in English annals, but Normandy was to play a crucial role in England's later history.

Midway through the ninth century, the Viking attacks on England began to change from plundering expeditions to campaigns of conquest. In 850 a large group of Danish Vikings spent the winter on the Isle of Thanet (off the eastern tip of Kent) rather than bothering to sail home at the close of the raiding season. In 865 a Danish host numbering in the thousands, known as the Great Army, transformed the character of the Viking wars. A series of bloody and highly successful campaigns won them virtually all of England outside Wessex.[9] Apart from an isolated section of northern Northumbria, the kingdoms and subkingdoms that had survived the eras of Mercian and Wessex hegemony were destroyed, and of the monarchies of the ancient Heptarchy, only Wessex endured.

In the wake of these conquests came Danish settlers in such numbers as to change permanently the social and institutional complexion of large areas of England. These areas of Danish settlement and occupation, later known as the Danelaw, included (1) Yorkshire (southern Northumbria) where the most intensive immigration occurred, (2) East Anglia, and (3) a large tract of central and eastern Mercia that came to be known as the Five Boroughs, after its five chief centers of settlement—Lincoln, Stamford, Nottingham, Leicester, and Derby. For centuries these three Danish districts differed sharply from the remainder of England in their traditions and customs.

Alfred the Great

In 870 the Danish attack against Wessex began in earnest, and with every hope of success. But Viking hopes were dashed when, in the following year, there came to the Wessex throne a man of extraordinary intellect and creative imagination, King Egbert's grandson, Alfred the Great (871–899).[10] Alfred was a monarch of many talents—a warrior, an administrator, a diplomat, a devotee of Christian learning, and a singularly persuasive leader. On one of the excellent silver pennies coined by Alfred's mints he is

---

[9] Some scholars have argued that contemporary Anglo-Saxon writers exaggerated the Viking terror—that Viking war bands were small in number and less predatory than their English enemies described them. See, for example, Peter Sawyer, *Kings and Vikings* (London, 1982). But as the late J. M. Wallace-Hadrill observed, the Vikings can hardly be dismissed as "long-haired tourists who occasionally roughed up the natives." Similarly, Alfred P. Smyth, in his *Warlords and Holy Men: Scotland, A.D. 80–1000* (London, 1984), p. 146, speaks of "the fury of these invaders who were instantly conspicuous to Scots, English, and Irish alike for their brutality and heathenism." On the sizes of Viking armies, see N. P. Brooks, "England in the Ninth Century: The Crucible of Defeat," *Transactions of the Royal Historical Society*, 5th series, 29 (1979): 1–20.

[10] A contemporary biography of Alfred is available in modern English translation: *Alfred the Great: Asser's Life of King Alfred and Other Contemporary Sources*, Simon Keynes and Michael Lapidge, eds./trs. (New York, 1983).

styled *rex Anglorum*, "king of the English," suggesting that Alfred and his contemporaries were aware of the political transformation to which his reign contributed so decisively: the evolution of the West Saxon monarchy into the English monarchy. Indeed, the legend on the coin obviously constituted a piece of royal propaganda contributing toward that evolution.

Alfred's accession occurred at a desperate moment in Anglo-Saxon history. In 872 he was obliged to purchase a truce from the Danes in order to gain the time necessary to put his defenses in order. During this brief intermission he took the initial steps toward a thorough reorganization of the West Saxon military forces, a process that he continued throughout his reign. His military reforms consisted of three major innovations. First, he divided his army—his fyrd, as it was called in Old English—into two halves, each serving for six months per year. Thus, when half of Alfred's fighting men were at home tending their lands and crops, the other half were under arms, ensuring that at no time would Wessex be defenseless. This reform strained West Saxon resources to the limit by dramatically increasing the customary term of military conscription, and it was abandoned once the Viking threat waned. But in Alfred's time it provided the sizeable and ever-alert force necessary to resist large, mobile Danish armies.

Secondly, recognizing that the Vikings must be challenged on the seas, Alfred established a fleet of sixty-oared ships. His biographer, the Welshman Asser, reports that Alfred built numerous ships, both large and swift, "neither after the Frisian design nor after the Danish, but as it seemed to him that they could be most serviceable." Faster, higher, and much longer than those of the Danes, these new ships reflect the creative intellect that Alfred applied to the problems of war.

Alfred's third and most significant military reform was the establishment throughout Wessex of a system of large walled and fortified settlements known as *burghs*. Asser wrote of "the cities and towns he restored and the others he constructed where none had been before." A remarkable early tenth-century document known as the Burghal Hidage—probably adapted from an Alfredian original—discloses a network of thirty large burghs scattered across the kingdom in such a way that virtually nobody in Wessex was more than a day's walk (twenty miles) from a burgh. The Burghal Hidage assigns responsibility for the maintenance and defense of each burgh to the occupants of a stipulated amount of surrounding countryside, reckoned in terms of hides of land. (We have already encountered the hide as the assessment unit of the Mercian Tribal Hidage; see page 51). Thus, the Burghal Hidage assigns 2,400 hides to Winchester, 1,500 to Cricklade, etc., to a grand total of some 27,000 hides. An intriguing appendix to the document explains: "If every hide is represented by one man, then every pole [5.5 yards] of wall can be manned by four men. Then for the maintenance of 20 poles of wall 80 hides are needed, and for a furlong [220 yards] 160 hides are needed by the same reckoning. . . ." The document thus records a carefully articulated, kingdom-wide burghal defense system involving a force totaling no less than 27,000 men—a sizeable number for a relatively small ninth-century kingdom.

The Burghal Hidage provides a unique opportunity to correlate written and archaeological measurements. And the dimensions of the surviving ramparts of Alfred's burghs that have been measured thus far match very closely the corresponding formulae in the Burghal Hidage. The 2,400 hides assigned by the Burghal Hidage to Winchester, for example, would provide for the manning of 9,900 feet of ramparts, which is within one percent of the circumference of the actual town wall (9,954 feet). Archaeological investigations have also shown that Alfred's burghs tended to be laid out on a standardized plan. Whether in the case of old Roman walled towns like Winchester, or reoccupied Iron Age or Roman fortifications like Portchester, or newly founded burghs like Wallingford and Shaftesbury, they had approximately square or rectangular walls, a single main street (or "High Street") with back streets running parallel to it and other streets running at right angles, intersecting with a street running around the inside of the wall. The similarity of these burgh layouts, combined with the evidence from Anglo-Saxon charters (establishing town markets) and laws (requiring that all trade take place in towns) and the subsequent use of burghs as the sites of mints, suggests that their purpose, even from the beginning, was commercial no less than military. Their effect was not only to serve as a formidable barrier to Danish incursions into Wessex and, later, as forward bases in the reconquest of the Danelaw, but also to provide a powerful stimulus to West Saxon commerce and, through rents and market tolls, a bonanza to the West Saxon royal treasury. The term *burgh* had originally meant "fortress," but in Alfred's age and thereafter its meaning was changing to "town." (In American colonial times, Pittsburgh was both a fortress and a commercial center.)

Alfred's military reforms were far reaching, but time was required to carry them out. And for Alfred, time was all too short. In 876 a Danish chieftain named Guthrum led a host against Wessex. Again early in 878, in the dead of winter, Guthrum led his army across the land, while another Viking army attacked Wessex from the northwest, threatening to trap Alfred in a pincers movement. Fleeing into the marsh country of Somerset, Alfred found refuge at a royal estate on the Isle of Athelney. Momentarily, almost all of England was at the mercy of the Danes.

Athelney was England's Valley Forge. Alfred held out with a small group of followers throughout the winter, and in the spring of 878 he was able to rally the Wessex fyrd. (The Danish army was much too small to occupy Wessex completely or to prevent Alfred from summoning his army.) The armies of Alfred and Guthrum met in pitched battle at Edington, and Alfred won a decisive victory. As a consequence, Guthrum agreed to Alfred's demands that he accept Christianity and abandon Wessex forever. These two demands were interrelated, for Christianity emphasized the importance of adhering to oaths, whereas the Viking ethos valued trickery and deception. As a Christian, Guthrum would be more likely to keep his promise not to invade Wessex again. And although Christian princes of the ninth and tenth centuries were known to have broken oaths, sometimes with careless abandon, the fact remains that Guthrum did keep out of

Wessex for the remainder of his life. Even more significantly, Guthrum was one of the first important Vikings to become a Christian. His baptism in 878, with Alfred as his godfather, foreshadowed the ultimate Christianization of the entire Viking world and its incorporation into the mainstream of Western European civilization.

In this age of warfare, skillful military leadership was essential to a king's survival. And Alfred, the ablest of the Anglo-Saxon kings, was a military commander of the first order. In the years after 878 he advanced the frontiers of his kingdom significantly. By 886 (at the latest) he had occupied London, and later in that year he entered into a new treaty with Guthrum which defined the boundary between English and Danish authority. The frontier ran approximately northwestward, along the old Roman road known as Watling Street, from London to Chester on the Irish Sea (see the map on page 61). This new agreement recognized West Saxon lordship over a large section of Mercia, and in that once powerful kingdom Alfred established a subking (ealdorman) named Ethelred. Alfred ensured the future allegiance of English Mercia by arranging a marriage between Ethelred and his own daughter Ethelfleda, known thereafter as the "Lady of the Mercians."

The struggle with the Danes continued to the close of Alfred's reign and well beyond. But by Alfred's death in 899 the crisis had clearly passed. He had made southwestern England secure, seized London, and established an effective policy of military organization and fortification. The authority of the West Saxon monarchy was supreme in non-Danish England.

Alfred's dynasty, like those of the Northumbrians and Mercians, built royal palaces on a lavish scale. Excavations at Cheddar in Somerset have disclosed traces of a long timber hall apparently dating from Alfred's time, along with smaller domestic buildings, in an architectural complex partially encompassed by a light fence and a drainage ditch. Later on, in the tenth century, a new timber hall was built on the same site at a right angle to the old one, and a chapel stood at its side. As in the case of Yeavering, we can by no means be certain that Cheddar was the primary residence of the royal dynasty—whose members, like all kings of the early Middle Ages, were constantly moving with their courts from one royal vill, palace, or hunting lodge to the next.

The creative intelligence that Alfred applied to military tactics and organization was equally effective in law and administration. Several of Alfred's predecessors had issued law codes or dooms. Ethelbert of Kent had been the first to do so, and he was followed by other monarchs such as Offa of Mercia (whose dooms are now lost) and Alfred's own distant ancestor, Ine of Wessex (688–726). But Alfred seems to have interpreted his lawmaking authority more broadly than his predecessors had. Although hesitant to create new laws, he exercised considerable latitude in his selection or rejection of old ones, thereby placing his own imprint on the legal structure of his day. In the preface to his dooms, Alfred expressed himself in these words:

ENGLAND
ABOUT 887 A.D.

> Then I, King Alfred, collected these [laws] together and ordered that many of them which our forefathers observed should be written down, namely, those that I liked; and, with the advice of my Witan [counselors], I rejected many of those that I didn't like and ordered that they be observed differently. I have not presumed to set in writing much of my own, because it was unknown to me what might please those who shall come after us. So I have collected here the dooms which seemed to me the most just, whether from the time of Ine, my kinsman, or of Offa, king of the Mercians, or of Ethelbert, the first of the English to receive baptism; I have thrown out the rest. Then I, Alfred, king of the West Saxons, showed these to all my Witan who declared that they were all pleased to observe them.

In this significant passage we can glimpse the king at work, surrounded by his advisers as Germanic monarchs had been since their earliest days, respectful of past custom as had always been the case, yet injecting into his traditional royal role a strong element of creative judgment.

Alfred was not only a talented warrior and statesman but a scholar as well. Like Charlemagne a century earlier, Alfred was a patron of learning who drew learned men to his court from far and wide—the Welshman Asser, a Frankish scholar from Rheims, several Mercians (including one with the intriguing name of Werwulf), and a number of others. And Alfred himself made a far greater personal contribution to scholarship than had the half-literate Charlemagne.

The contributions of Alfred's scholarly circle paralleled those of Charlemagne's in several ways. The renaissance of Charlemagne's era had been less an outburst of creative genius than a salvage operation designed to recover and preserve a classical-Christian heritage that was in danger of vanishing in the West. Charlemagne's scholars were not original philosophers but gifted schoolmasters who reformed the script, purged the Bible of scribal errors, established schools, copied manuscripts, and struggled to extend literacy and to preserve a correct liturgy. These were humble efforts, but they were desperately needed. The Anglo-Saxon renaissance of Alfred's time was almost certainly inspired by Charlemagne's example.

By the late ninth century the intellectual flowering of Bede's Northumbria had long passed. The widespread Viking destruction of monasteries and episcopal centers threatened the survival of classical Christian culture in England and, indeed, the survival of Christianity itself. Latin, the linguistic vehicle of classical Roman culture, was becoming virtually unknown in England. Priests could no longer understand the Latin Mass, much less study the works of Bede and the Church Fathers. And the Anglo-Saxon language, which everyone used, had only a very slender literary tradition behind it. Alfred himself described the decline of Latin in these words:

> So completely fallen away was learning now in the English race that there were very few on this side of the Humber who would know how to render their service book into English, and I doubt that there would be many on the other side of the Humber. There were so few of them that I cannot think of so much as a single one south of the Thames when I took the realm.

The king may have been exaggerating, but probably not by very much.

Alfred was determined to revive ecclesiastical culture in his land, and he did what he could to create a literate priesthood. The scholars he gathered around him developed a notable school at his court. He established a few monastic schools as well, but a general monastic revival was out of the question in those turbulent times. Alfred founded a nunnery at Shaftesbury with a strict Benedictine rule, and an abbey at the isle of Athelney in which he established monks from the Continent who were dedicated to monastic reform. But his most far-reaching contribution to learning rose from his conviction that lay aristocrats should be educated—that his administrators and military commanders should have some knowledge of the civilized heritage of Christendom. Such men were too preoccupied with the political and military hazards of their time to learn Latin, but Alfred hoped that they might be taught to read their native Anglo-Saxon, or at least to have works in Anglo-Saxon read aloud to them. Accordingly, he and his court scholars undertook to translate into the vernacular some of the important Latin masterpieces of the past—Boethius's *Consolation of Philosophy*, Bede's *History of the English Church*, and Pope Gregory's *Pastoral Care*. A copy of the Anglo-Saxon *Pastoral Care* was sent to every bishopric in England in the hope that Alfred's bishops might be instructed by Gregory's wisdom and common sense.

Alfred himself participated in the work of translation and sometimes added comments of his own to the original texts. In his translation of Boethius, Alfred injected the revealing observation, "In those days one never heard of ships armed for war," and in the preface to the *Pastoral Care* he spoke nostalgically of the time "before everything was ravaged and burned, when England's churches overflowed with treasures and books." In passages such as these, one is forcefully reminded of the enormous disadvantages against which Alfred worked.

Associated with Alfred's reign is another literary monument in the English vernacular, the *Anglo-Saxon Chronicle*.[11] This important historical project, which may possibly have been instigated by Alfred directly, was clearly inspired by the general surge of vernacular writing with which the king was associated. Its earliest compilers appear to have had some connections with Alfred's court circle. Around 892, an unknown West Saxon chronicler wrote a year-by-year account of English history and its Roman and British background, running from the birth of Christ to 891. The account was based on earlier sources, most of which are now lost. The identification and reconstruction of these forerunners have occupied several generations of scholars, and many aspects of the problem remain unresolved. In general, the early entries are characterized by extreme verbal economy:

634: In this year Bishop Birinus preached Christianity to the West Saxons.

---

[11] The *Anglo-Saxon Chronicle* is available in several modern English translations. The best is Dorothy Whitelock, David C. Douglas, and Susie I. Tucker, eds./trs., *The Anglo-Saxon Chronicle* (New Brunswick, N.J., 1961).

Penny Bearing the Effigy of King Alfred the Great. This contemporary portrait makes it clear that Alfred the Great was not only very talented but extremely good-looking as well. (The Granger Collection)

> 635: In this year King Cynegils [of Wessex] was baptized by Birinus, bishop of Dorchester, and Oswald [king of Northumbria] stood sponsor for him.

> 636: In this year Cwichelm [king of Wessex] was baptized at Dorchester, and the same year he passed away. And Bishop Felix preached the faith of Christ to the East Anglians.

> 639: In this year Birinus baptized Cuthred [king of Wessex] at Dorchester and stood sponsor for him.

Copies of the 892 chronicle were sent to a number of important ecclesiastical centers of the time, and in several instances these centers expanded the early entries to include facts and traditions available in other portions of England. One manuscript was sent to Northumbria, where the entry for 634, for example, was elaborated as follows:

> 634: In this year Osric, whom Paulinus had baptized, succeeded to the kingdom of the Deirans; he was the son of Elfric, Edwin's paternal uncle; and to Bernicia succeeded Ethelfrith's son, Eanfrith. Also in this year Birinus first preached Christianity to the West Saxons under King Cynegils. That Birinus came thither at the command of Pope Honorius, and was bishop there until his life's end. And also in this year Oswald succeeded to the kingdom of Northumbria, and he reigned nine years.

At several ecclesiastical centers the 892 chronicle was continued thereafter on a year-by-year basis. In subsequent years churchmen continued to exchange copies and take them from one monastery to another, with the result that the *Anglo-Saxon Chronicle* is a very complex document indeed. Strictly speaking, it is not a single chronicle but a series of related chronicles. Altogether, seven distinct manuscripts survive, representing four more or less separate accounts. Of these, three end in the later eleventh century—between 1066 and 1079—while the fourth continues to the accession of King Henry II in 1154.

The various versions of the *Anglo-Saxon Chronicle*, written by many different chroniclers in several religious houses over a number of generations, are exceedingly uneven. At times they fail to rise above the level of what one great English historian deplored as "our jejune annals"; at other times they provide fairly comprehensive accounts of the events of their day, sometimes even attempting a degree of historical interpretation. Like modern journalists, the chroniclers tended to pass over periods of peace and cultural creativity with a few bare allusions to royal deaths and accessions but became eloquent in times of upheaval and disaster. So little is made of the fruitful reigns of Alfred's successors, and so much is made of the second Danish invasions and the Norman Conquest, that readers of the chronicle are apt to be misled into regarding the Anglo-Saxon era as one vast, sterile bore relieved by occasional cataclysms. Whatever its shortcomings, the *Anglo-Saxon Chronicle* is unique in the European vernacular literature of its day and provides the modern student with an invaluable if sometimes aggravating narrative of later Anglo-Saxon history. It is appropriate that from the reign that marks the genesis of the English monarchy should come this remarkable national history in the Old English tongue.

In many respects, then, Alfred's reign is the watershed in the history of Anglo-Saxon England. It represents the turning point in the Danish invasions, the climax of the age-long trend toward political unification, and the first stage in the development of English royal government. Alfred once modestly described himself as one who works in a great forest collecting timber with which others can build. He was alluding to his efforts toward intellectual revival, but the metaphor is equally appropriate to his military, administrative, and political achievements. As architect of the English monarchy, he gathered the wood and also provided a preliminary blueprint that would guide his successors in constructing a durable political edifice.

3

Late-Saxon England

During the first three-quarters of the tenth century, King Alfred's talented successors vastly extended his work of reconquest and political consolidation.[1] At Alfred's death in 899, Wessex passed to his son Edward (899–924), whom later historians called Edward the Elder to distinguish him from subsequent monarchs of the same name. In his initial years, Edward the Elder faced a serious bid for his throne by an ambitious first cousin who allied with the Danes but who, fortunately for Edward, died in battle in 903. Afterwards, Edward and his sister Ethelfleda, Lady of the Mercians, pursued an aggressive military policy against the Danelaw, strengthening Alfred's burghs and founding a number of new ones in the midlands to consolidate their conquests. By 918, all of the Danish settlers south of the Humber had submitted to Edward the Elder's rule, and the death of Ethelfleda that year resulted in the permanent unification of Wessex and Mercia under Alfred's dynasty. Edward the Elder now bore the two titles King of the West Saxons and King of the Mercians.

Edward was succeeded by his son Athelstan (924–939), a skillful military leader who turned back a major invasion of Yorkshire by Norse Vikings from Ireland and extended his sway across Northumbria. By the time of Athelstan's death, nearly all England was under his control. His successors consolidated the conquest, put down revolts, and repulsed invasions until, by 954, England stood united under the Wessex dynasty of English kings.

The Consequences of Political Unification

Yet the word *united* is perhaps too strong to describe England's situation in 954. The kingdom was united politically (though with much regional and local autonomy remaining), but not socially or culturally. The inhabitants of northern Northumbria, who had managed to retain a precarious inde-

---

[1] The works cited in Chapter 1, note 8, and Chapter 2, note 1, are also relevant to Chapter 3. In addition, there are two very readable studies by Christopher Brooke: *The Saxon and Norman Kings* (London, 1963) and *From Alfred to Henry III, 871–1272* (New York, 1961). See also Lloyd Laing and Jennifer Laing, *Anglo-Saxon England* (New York, 1979); P. H. Sawyer, *From Roman Britain to Norman England* (New York, 1978); and Pauline Stafford, *Unification and Conquest: A Political and Social History of England in the Tenth and Eleventh Centuries* (London, 1989).

pendence during the age of Danish invasions, had long been isolated from their compatriots to the south and remained a people apart. And the numerous Danish settlers in Yorkshire, East Anglia, and the Five Boroughs remained socially and culturally distinct. The process of amalgamation between Danes and English required centuries to complete.

The immediate effect of reconquest and political unification was a generation of peace, well-being, and fruitful activity in the areas of royal administration and ecclesiastical reform. Anglo-Saxon England's happiest years coincided with the reign of King Edgar the Peaceable (959–975). In the words of the *Anglo-Saxon Chronicle,*

> His reign was marked by greatly improved conditions, and God granted that he lived his days in peace; he did his duty and labored zealously in performing it; he exalted God's praise far and wide and loved God's law; he improved the security of his people more than all the kings before him within human memory.

From another source we learn that Alfred's navy had developed by Edgar the Peaceable's time into a well-organized fleet that maintained constant coastal patrols, suggesting that Edgar was not only a serious Christian but also an intelligent military strategist who took strong measures to protect his land from Viking assaults.

Edgar's reign also witnessed an impressive movement of monastic reform that paralleled and drew inspiration from reform movements occurring on the Continent. Throughout its history, medieval monasticism followed a pattern of decline and renewal. Like other human institutions, it tended to decay with the passage of time from simplicity and fervor to luxury and complacency; yet over the centuries it proved capable of periodic revitalization through successive waves of reformist enthusiasm. By the tenth century, the reformation of continental monastic life brought about by the Carolingian renaissance had run its course, and many abbeys suffered neglect and abuse as they fell under the self-interested control of local aristocratic families. But the laxity of tenth-century monasticism was challenged by a religious movement centering on the new Burgundian monastery of Cluny. Founded in 909 by the duke of Burgundy, Cluny developed, under the leadership of talented and long-lived abbots, into a vital center of ecclesiastical reform. One important source of Cluny's success was the stipulation in its foundation charter that it would enjoy freedom from ducal or local aristocratic control. The Cluniac monks followed an elaborated version of the Benedictine rule, but they abandoned the traditional Benedictine principle of individual autonomous abbeys. Instead, Cluny became the mother house of an ever-growing congregation of reformed monasteries subject to the direction and discipline of a single abbot.

The most celebrated champion of monastic reform in King Edgar's England was St. Dunstan, a member of the royal family who became abbot of Glastonbury and, in 960, archbishop of Canterbury.[2] Dunstan had no formal connection with Cluny or with continental reform movements, and the reformed monasteries in England never became members of the congregation of Cluny. But other English reformers of Dunstan's day were deeply influenced by the example of Fleury, a Cluniac house on the Loire that rejoiced in possessing what purported to be the holy body of St. Benedict himself. The English reformers worked with much success toward ridding the abbeys of such traditional evils as drunkenness, licentiousness, wealth in the possession of individual monks or nuns, and control by local aristocratic families—many of which, understandably enough, resented this last reform. In place of such abuses the reformers, working closely with the monarchy, strove toward the strict enforcement of the Benedictine rule in all English monasteries and, indeed, in the cathedral chapters of several bishoprics. Some monk-reformers (including St. Dunstan) became bishops themselves, thereby adding considerably to the power and momentum of the movement. Throughout Britain old monasteries and nunneries were reformed and reorganized, or refounded after having been demolished by the Danes, and a number of entirely new ones were founded. In all of them the traditional Benedictine duties of individual poverty, chastity, obedience, and communal living were once again enforced, and the control of local aristocrats gave way to the overarching authority of the monarchy (the queen was formally granted the responsibility of being the protector of all English nunneries). Although individual Benedictine monks were forbidden to possess property, Benedictine abbeys could rightfully acquire considerable collective wealth, and most of them did. The landed endowment of a great Benedictine house—resulting from the accumulation of pious lay donations—could rival the landed wealth of a family in the upper aristocracy. Thus, whoever exercised authority over England's monasteries commanded immense power and riches.

In the course of the tenth century a vast amount of monastic land passed into the control of the West Saxon monarchy: first, during the process of reconquest when the kings took direct possession of estates formerly belonging to abbeys that the Danes had destroyed;[3] second, during the monastic reform movement when aristocratic control of many of the remaining abbeys gave way to royal control. The monarchy was generous in founding and refounding abbeys in formerly Danish lands; the effect was to establish across the Danelaw a network of royalist religious communities grateful and loyal to the West Saxon dynasty. The reform movement thus had the further effect of enhancing royal power significantly.

---

[2] See Eleanor S. Duckett, *Saint Dunstan of Canterbury: A Study of Monastic Reform in the Tenth Century* (London, 1955). See also, Eric John, *Orbis Britanniae and Other Studies* (Leicester, 1966), pp. 154–180; David Knowles, *The Monastic Order in England, 940–1216*, 2nd ed. (Cambridge, 1963), pp. 31–69; and C. H. Lawrence, *Medieval Monasticism: Forms of Religious Life in Western Europe in the Middle Ages*, 2nd ed. (New York, 1984), pp. 76–96.

[3] On this important point, much oversimplified here, see Robin Fleming, "Monastic Lands and England's Defence in the Viking Age," *English Historical Review*, 100 (1985), 247–265.

Nevertheless, it was piety, no less than ambition, that prompted King Edgar to cooperate fully with the monastic reformers. At their prompting he took steps to put the gradually developing system of local parishes on a sound footing by commanding his subjects to pay tithes (a tenth of one's income) to their parish churches. He recognized, as Alfred and Charlemagne had recognized long before, that a vigorous Church could contribute much to the political and social welfare of the realm and to the extension of royal authority. And he doubtless shared the belief of his times that the welfare of the Church was one of the chief responsibilities of a Christian king.

The Development of Anglo-Saxon Institutions

Edgar's peace was too good to last. His reign was followed by a second round of Danish invasions, the accession to the English throne of the Danish king, Canute (1016–1035), the reestablishment of the Wessex dynasty under Edward the Confessor (1042–1066), and, finally, the Norman Conquest of 1066. Before turning to these events, however, let us examine the development of political, social, and economic institutions in Anglo-Saxon England.

The kingdom of Wessex in Alfred's day was subdivided into large administrative regions called shires (or counties). As the West Saxon kings expanded their authority into Mercia and the Danelaw, these districts, too, were organized into shires on the Wessex model. Some of the new tenth-century shires corresponded to old kingdoms or subtribal districts—Norfolk, Suffolk, Kent, Sussex, and Essex, for example. Others—patterned after the Burghal Hidage districts—were organized around important towns, after which they were named: Bedfordshire, Northamptonshire, Cambridgeshire, Worcestershire, and others. Four of the Five Boroughs—Lincoln, Leicester, Derby, and Nottingham—became nuclei of new shires. The process of "shiring" the Danelaw progressed rapidly in the late ninth and early tenth centuries, and by Athelstan's reign it was virtually complete.

The shires of Alfred's time were governed by officials, drawn from the upper nobility, known as *ealdormen*. It was the ealdorman who led the warriors of his shire to join the royal army or to defend the shire against sudden Danish attack. The ealdorman was at once a royal official and a local aristocrat. He led the fyrd and governed the shire in the king's name, and only at times when the monarchy was weak did he assert a significant degree of independence. As time went on, a single ealdorman began to exert authority over several shires, and administrative and military command of an individual shire then passed to another royal official known as the *shire reeve* or sheriff.

The chief officer of the shire, whether sheriff or ealdorman, presided in the king's name over the shire court, which normally convened twice yearly to try important cases. The personnel of the shire court consisted of important freeholders of the district, who supplied evidence and declared ancient custom. Guilt or innocence, however, was determined neither by

THE ENGLISH SHIRES
Late Saxon England

SCOTLAND

NORTH
SEA

NORTHUMBERLAND

CUMBERLAND
WEST-
MORELAND

UNSHIRED LANDS
ANNEXED TO
YORKSHIRE

YORK

1 HUNTINGDON
2 BEDFORD
3 BUCKINGHAM
4 MIDDLESEX

IRISH SEA

IRELAND

BETWEEN RIBBLE
AND MERSEY

CHESHIRE

DERBY

NOTT-
INGHAM

LINCOLN

STAFFORD

LEICESTER

NORFOLK

SHROPSHIRE

NORTHAMPTON

CAMBRIDGE

1

SUFFOLK

WALES

WARWICK

WOR-
CESTER

2

HEREFORD

HERTFORD

ESSEX

GLOUCESTER

OXFORD

3

4

BERKS

KENT

WILTS

SURREY

SOMERSET

HANTS

SUSSEX

DEVON

DORSET

CORNWALL

English Channel

FRANCE

the members of the court nor by the presiding sheriff or ealdorman but rather by the process of compurgation—the solemn oath of the accused assisted by the sworn testimony of relatives or friends known as oath helpers—or by recourse to one of the ancient ordeals (see page 24). Run by local freeholders and presided over by an official of the king, the shire court was both a royal and a regional institution—an assembly in which monarchy and free subjects joined to provide justice.

The late-Saxon shire was divided into smaller territorial units called hundreds. Like the shires, the hundreds originated in Wessex and spread with the expansion of the Wessex monarchy. The hundred seems to have been patterned originally on a similar jurisdictional unit in the empire of Charlemagne. In tenth-century England, it was a territorial administrative district centering on a hundred court. Similar in purpose and organization to the shire court—and presided over by a royal reeve—the hundred court met more frequently, normally once a month, and played a more intimate role in the affairs of the average free subject. Originally the hundred court, like the shire court, represented a mixture of royal and popular justice; but in time jurisdiction over many hundred courts passed into the hands of great private lords, both lay and ecclesiastical. These powerful landholders received by royal charter the rights of jurisdiction in their districts (contemporary charters refer to these jurisdictional rights as *sac* and *soc*), and their representatives took the place of royal officials as presidents of the hundred courts they controlled. The abbot and monks of Bury St. Edmunds, for example, gained jurisdiction over more than a third of the hundreds of Suffolk, and by the late eleventh century, more than half the hundreds in Worcestershire were in the hands of three abbeys and a bishopric.

The hundred was typically (although by no means always) composed of one hundred hides. We have already seen that originally the hide was regarded as an estate sufficient to support the family of an individual warrior. The late-Saxon hide, however, was not a unit of standard size, but an assessment unit on which fiscal and military obligations were based. Of two estates of identical area, one might be more productive than the other and therefore be assessed at more hides than the other. Moreover, hidage assessment was often erratic and unfair, like the property tax in California. Some districts were assessed more severely than others, and sometimes, through royal generosity, an estate would have its hidage assessment diminished. A forty-hide estate owned by a royal crony might become a twenty-hide estate without being reduced by so much as a foot of land.

By the tenth century, and perhaps long before, the one-hide estate had come to be regarded as insufficient to provide the necessary economic support for a properly equipped warrior and was replaced by the estate of five hides. The profession of arms was the supreme aristocratic vocation in all Germanic societies, and the typical Anglo-Saxon aristocrat—the holder of an estate of five hides or more—was known as a *thegn* (rhyming with "brain"). In time of war, every five-hide unit was obligated to provide a fighting man for the army (or sometimes the navy), and although the owners of small estates within a five-hide unit might occasionally pool their resources to send a single well-equipped freeman as their representative to the fyrd, the normal five-hide warrior was a member of the thegnly aristocracy. The almost universally accepted relationship between status and arms in this violent age ensured that the society of Anglo-Saxon England—influenced so deeply by the hard necessities of war—would be profoundly aristocratic.

At times, the territorial five-hide fyrd proved insufficiently flexible or battle-ready and was augmented or replaced by full-time professional warriors. These might be simple mercenaries, or they might be landless household soldiers maintained on a permanent basis by the king or some great lord. In the course of the eleventh century these professionals became increasingly important. One such group, the "housecarles," who were instituted by Canute and retained by Edward the Confessor, formed the nucleus of the Anglo-Saxon army at Hastings in 1066.

Five-hide thegns or freemen, and professional warriors—these were the components of the Anglo-Saxon army. But a mere review of this organizational scheme fails to do justice to the powerful emotional factors that underlay the military structure of this age. In the tenth century, the ideology of the old Germanic comitatus was still very strong. Military prowess, absolute loyalty to lord, and honor among warriors remained the supreme aristocratic virtues. Indeed, in all Germanic literature the comitatus ideology is nowhere more powerfully illustrated than in a late-tenth-century Anglo-Saxon poem, the *Song of Maldon*; it describes a fierce battle in 991 in which an invading Danish host defeated the fyrd of Essex, led by its lord, the ealdorman Byrhtnoth.[4] Toward the battle's end, Byrhtnoth was killed and the English were on the verge of defeat. At this desperate moment, one of Byrhtnoth's sworn followers rallied the Anglo-Saxons:

> Then Byrhtwold spoke, he brandished his spear,
> raised up his shield; he was an old henchman;
> full boldly he taught the band of men:
> "Thought shall be the harder, heart the keener,
> mood shall be the more, as our might lessens.
> Here lies our earl, all hewn to earth,
> the good one, on the ground. He will regret it always,
> the one who thinks to turn from this war-play now.
> My life has been long. Leave I will not,
> but beside my lord I will sink to earth,
> I am minded to die by the man so dear."

Byrhtwold's speech is preceded by others in a similar vein. Inspired by these

---

[4] A modern English prose translation of the *Song of Maldon* is contained in Margaret Ashdown, tr., *English and Norse Documents Relating to the Reign of Ethelred the Unready* (Cambridge, 1930). See also the excellent translation by Stephen Pollington, *The Warrior's Way: England in the Viking Age* (London, 1989), pp. 39–68. The present excerpt is from the poetic translation by Kemp Malone: *Ten Old English Poems Put into Modern English Alliterative Verse* (Baltimore, 1941).

appeals to the traditional heroic ideal, the Anglo-Saxons attack the Danes, and in the midst of describing the fray the *Song of Maldon* manuscript breaks off abruptly. (We know from other evidence that the Danes won a decisive victory.) The author was doubtless embroidering his data and exaggerating Byrhtwold's eloquence. Nevertheless, the story reflects the highest aristocratic ideals of a people still tied to their bellicose past and dominated by the concept of lordship.

The development of Anglo-Saxon institutions can be understood as the gradual evolution of a Germanic warrior society toward territorial stabilization and administrative coherence. The fundamental element in this evolution was the rise of a centralized monarchy. Among a people to whom loyalty to one's lord was an almost holy virtue, the king endeavored to secure for himself the pledged allegiance not only of his ealdormen, sheriffs, and personal thegns, but of all his free subjects. In the dooms of King Edmund (939–946) it was commanded that "all, in the name of God . . . shall swear fealty to King Edmund, as a man should be faithful to his lord, without dispute or treachery, in public and in private, loving what he loves and shunning what he shuns." Thus the powerful bond of allegiance between an ealdorman and his thegns and household followers— reflected so vividly in the *Song of Maldon*—was subordinated to the still-higher duty of all free subjects to render loyalty to their monarch. The *Maldon* poet himself reports that Ealdorman Bryhtnoth defied the Danes with these words: "Here, with his troops, stands an earl of unstained renown who is ready to guard this realm, the home of Ethelred my lord. . . ."

This principle of universal allegiance to the king was essential to the maintenance and extension of royal control over England. The ealdormen had to be royal officers, not independent potentates; and when they led the fyrd of their shire they had to do so—as Byrhtnoth did—in the king's name and in the king's service. Indeed, when the fyrd was summoned on a regional or national scale, its normal leader was the king himself. As lord of the Anglo-Saxons, he was necessarily the supreme war leader of the people in arms.

In time of war the king was expected to be braver and fiercer than any of the warriors he led, but in time of peace he sought to temper the violence of his people. In his coronation oath, Edgar the Peaceable made these commitments:

> In the name of the Holy Trinity I promise three things to my Christian subjects: first, that God's Church and all the Christian people of my realm shall enjoy true peace; second, that I forbid robbery and wrongful deeds to all ranks of men; third, that I exhort and command justice and mercy in all my judgments, so that the gracious and compassionate God who lives and reigns may grant us all His everlasting mercy.

In effect, Edgar was blending the militarism of Germanic culture with the pacifism of the Christian tradition. The Germanic king must lead his people in war, but the Christian king must keep the peace. And in Edgar's time the two ideals had coalesced: a good king was both peacekeeper and

Christian warrior, protecting his realm from external attacks and internal violence.

The concept of the king's peace developed slowly. Anglo-Saxon England had no police force, no professional lawyers or judges, no comprehensive legal codes. Consequently, acts of private violence were more common than today—the rule, in fact, rather than the exception. Crimes of violence normally fell under the jurisdiction of the popular courts of shire and hundred, but almost from the beginning of Anglo-Saxon times there existed the concept that violations of the peace committed in certain places or at certain times were subject to a direct royal fine. At first the king's peace extended only to the limits of the royal household, but in time it came to cover the shire and hundred courts, major roads and rivers, and churches and abbeys. Since the royal household had no permanent headquarters but was constantly on the move, the king's peace moved too, protecting sometimes one area, sometimes another. Similarly, the king's peace gradually encompassed all crimes of violence committed during the holy seasons of Christmas, Lent, Easter, and Whitsuntide, and all murders, rapes, acts of arson, and other major felonies whenever and wherever committed. In the twelfth century, royal justice expanded significantly at the expense of regional and private justice and evolved ultimately into what the English call the common law. The gradual spread of the king's peace in Anglo-Saxon times was a first step toward the momentous legal concept of direct royal jurisdiction throughout the kingdom.

Anglo-Saxon law, like the law of most primitive societies, was far less precise, less logically constructed, and more obscure, varied, cumbersome, haphazard, and complex than the laws of modern states. It relied on the correct recitation of elaborate oaths and the intricate rituals of the various ordeals. It looked only at the criminal act, largely ignoring the question of intent. If a tree on your property was struck down by lightning and killed someone, you were in serious trouble. Anglo-Saxon law was a patchwork of many local customs, differing from region to region. Only through the gradual expansion of the royal government, long after the Norman Conquest, did English law achieve a degree of uniformity. Yet even in Anglo-Saxon times the monarchy endeavored, haltingly, to preserve and expand its area of jurisdiction. The power of the Anglo-Saxon kings made itself felt in the regional courts of hundred and shire, made up of local notables but presided over by the king's reeve. And the dooms, although far from comprehensive or consistently enforced, represented early efforts toward achieving at least some degree of legal uniformity through the exercise of royal authority.

As the scope and functions of the Anglo-Saxon monarchy expanded, the royal administrative machinery became steadily more elaborate. In the earliest days, the retinue of an Anglo-Saxon monarch normally included a number of military followers or "companions" and some servants to look after the stables, maintain the royal wardrobe and bedchamber, supervise the food and wine supply, and prepare the meals. The king's income was derived chiefly from the rents and harvests of his own vast and widely scattered estates—his demesne. Rather than having food transported to a central royal residence, the king and his entourage traveled from one royal estate to another, consuming as they went. In these circumstances, the minimal administrative duties of the royal household could easily be handled by the chief servants.

With time, the royal treasury grew larger, the royal military organization became more elaborate, and royal land gifts tended more and more to be committed to writing. Moreover, it became increasingly common for the king to communicate with his regional officers in writing rather than through verbal messages. One need not assume that lay officials were all illiterate and depended on their priests to decipher royal mandates. That literacy was not a priestly monopoly is suggested by the abundance of Old English inscriptions on rings, brooches, and the walls of churches; an important tenth-century ealdorman named Ethelweard wrote an imperfect but comprehensible Latin translation of the *Anglo-Saxon Chronicle*.

Nevertheless, the monarchy delegated its growing secretarial work to the royal chaplain and his priestly staff, which had been a part of every royal household since the conversion. In the eleventh century the king's chapel-secretariat came to be known as the *chancery* (from *chancel*, the space in a church reserved for officiating clergy), and its chief officer, the chancellor, became in later years one of the major officers of state.

The writing office of the late Anglo-Saxon kings was in some respects the most efficient royal chancery of its time in Western Europe. Like other chanceries, it prepared elaborate charters for the transfer of land and privileges—although often such charters were written by ecclesiastical beneficiaries and then presented to the king for his ratification. The unique contribution of the Anglo-Saxon royal writing office was its invention of a short document known as a *writ*—a direct, economical statement of a royal command to a subject, usually written in Old English rather than Latin and (by the eleventh century) bearing an imprint on wax of the king's Great Seal to prove its authenticity. The writ was sufficiently short and simple to serve as a highly effective instrument in the everyday business of government:

> King Canute sends friendly greetings to Bishop Eadsige and Abbot Alfstan and Aethelric and all my thegns in Kent. And I inform you that my will is that Archbishop Aethelnoth shall discharge the obligations on his landed property belonging to his episcopal see now at the same rate as he did before Aethelric was reeve and after he was reeve up to the present day. And I will not permit that any wrong be done the [arch]bishop whoever may be reeve.

> King Edward sends friendly greetings to Bishop Stigand and Earl Harold and all my thegns in East Anglia. And I inform you that I have granted to [the abbey of] St. Edmund, my kinsman, the land at Pakenham as fully and as completely as Osgot possessed it.[5]

---

[5] Translated from Old English by Florence E. Harmer, *Anglo-Saxon Writs* (Manchester, England, 1952), pp. 184, 185.

Writs became much more common after the Norman Conquest (and were normally in Latin rather than Old English), but the idea originated among nameless clerks in the chanceries of the Anglo-Saxon kings. The idea of a brief, written, authenticated command seems obvious enough, but in the largely illiterate society of Saxon England, it was a new and powerful means of bringing literacy and precision to royal government.

Other offices of the royal bureaucracy developed out of various branches of the household serving staff. The master or "count" of the stable—the constable of later times—supervised the royal hunt and eventually became a leading officer in the king's army. The chief servant of the royal bedchamber and wardrobe evolved into the later master chamberlain; and since the king customarily kept his treasure in his wardrobe (or sometimes under his bed), the chamberlain assumed important financial responsibilities. By the early eleventh century the monarchy had adopted the policy of leaving the bulk of its treasure at Winchester, the chief town of Wessex, and carrying on its travels only enough money to meet current expenses. The royal officer in charge of the Winchester treasure came to be known as the "treasury chamberlain" and eventually the "treasurer."

The chancellor, constable, master chamberlain, and other household officials such as the steward (in charge of food) and butler (wine)—although not known by those names until after the Norman Conquest—rose in importance with the growth of the Anglo-Saxon monarchy to become dominant figures in the royal administration. Besides performing their own special functions, they served the king collectively as a trusted and intimate group of advisers, accompanying him on his endless travels around the country. Together with such other magnates and important churchmen as might be present, they functioned as a pocket council, administering the king's justice and attending to the varied and ever-growing activities of royal government.

Occasionally, when unusually important business arose—such as the issuing of dooms or the undertaking of a major military campaign—an Anglo-Saxon monarch would call many of the great magnates of the realm, both lay and ecclesiastical, to join his normal household advisers in counseling him, giving their formal support to his policies, and attesting his charters. By analyzing the witness lists on royal charters, modern historians can identify the influential circle of friends and advisers surrounding various kings at various points in their reigns.

We have already encountered references to large councils—on the occasion of King Edwin's conversion in 627, and in King Alfred's statement that he had shown his laws "to all my Witan who declared that they were all pleased to observe them." The terms *Witan* or *Witenagemot* ("council") might apply to either the small household group or the larger and more formal assembly of magnates. The Witenagemot, both small and large, probably had its roots in the old Germanic tribal assemblies, but the limitations of our sources prevent us from tracing its evolution with any precision until the tenth and eleventh centuries. We know from occasional references that it existed in early Anglo-Saxon England, but we know very little about its normal size, composition, or functions.

The fuller sources of the late-Saxon period disclose that the Witenagemot, whether large or small, was a flexible and informal institution. It was in no sense, of course, a representative assembly. It possessed no formal right of veto over royal policy but was strictly advisory. It had no official members, as far as we can tell, but simply included whatever important household officers and great men happened to be available and, on the more significant occasions, a miscellaneous group of lords. Still, the sources make it clear that the Witenagemot played a crucial role in Anglo-Saxon government. Many historians today, in endeavoring to dispel the romantic myth of various nineteenth-century scholars that the Witenagemot was a proto-democratic national assembly, have tended to underestimate its importance. Although no Anglo-Saxon king was legally bound to follow his Witan's advice, few monarchs would have been so foolish as to flout it. In an age lacking precise definitions of constitutional relationships, the deeply ingrained custom that the king was to govern in consultation with his Witan, implicit in almost every important royal document of the period, is sufficient to make the Witenagemot one of Anglo-Saxon England's fundamental political institutions.

The expanding monarchy of late-Saxon England was able to draw on an increasing variety of financial resources. The royal demesne remained the chief source of income, and because most of the growing towns belonged to the king's demesne, exactions from townspeople poured into the royal treasury along with dues from the royal estates. The monarchy delegated responsibility for the fiscal exploitation of its demesne estates and towns to royal officials—reeves—who were assigned a fixed tax quota or "farm" to be collected from the districts they supervised. Any dues in excess of the quota belonged to them, and they had to make up any shortfall out of their own pockets. As commerce quickened, it became increasingly common for the monarchy to receive a portion of its demesne dues in coin rather than in kind, for during the last several decades before the Norman Conquest, Anglo-Saxon England enjoyed a circulation of currency that was unusually brisk by continental standards. In keeping with royal efforts toward unifying England, King Edgar ordered the minting of reformed, standardized silver pennies in 973, to circulate throughout the kingdom. Bearing Edgar's name and portrait, the kingdom-wide coinage was at once a stimulus to the economy and a subtle instrument of royal propaganda. Thenceforth the monarchy maintained tight control over its currency; every few years it commanded that all coins be brought to its mints for redemption and ordered the minting of a new coin type to supersede the previous issue. The managed currency of Saxon England's closing century contributed much to the monarchy's ability to collect and administer taxes.

Besides demesne revenues, the late-Saxon kings collected a kingdom-wide land tax. What began as a symptom of military weakness—the monarchy's endeavor to purchase security from Viking marauders—ultimately became an important source of royal income. In 991, King Ethelred "the Unready" imposed a tax known as danegeld to raise protection money for the Danes. Like military service, the danegeld was assessed on the basis of hides of land.[6] It was not restricted to the royal demesne but included all the lands of England. In time, as the Danish threat diminished, the monarchy collected danegelds for its own purposes—to hire soldiers and meet various other royal expenses. The taxing of lands and the bribing of Vikings were well known to the Carolingian Franks, but nowhere except in Anglo-Saxon England was there a land tax at once so comprehensive and so long-lived. The danegeld illustrates, perhaps more vividly than anything else, England's movement toward royal centralization and administrative sophistication.

Continental monarchs, like English monarchs, employed agents to collect dues from demesne estates. And on the Continent, as in England, central administrative bureaucracies were slowly evolving out of household staffs. But the late Anglo-Saxon royal administration was more coherent in organization and broader in scope than any other contemporary government in Western Christendom. In the centralization of its administrative structure, as in the relative efficiency of its coinage and taxation systems, England stood in the vanguard of a movement that, during the coming centuries, would transform the loosely structured Germanic monarchies of Western Europe into well-organized states.

Town and Field

The century and a half prior to the Norman Conquest was a period of accelerating commercial activity that paralleled the increasing political stability. With commerce came the growth of towns. They were smaller at first than those of Roman times—and dirtier—but they were the agents of a major economic transformation. Many Saxon towns, as we have seen, evolved out of the military burghs of Alfred and his successors. Their growth was both a cause and an effect of England's rising wealth and vigorous commerce. A vast amount of urban development lay in the future—in the decades and centuries following the Norman Conquest— but evidence suggests that the elaborate guild systems of future times were already in their formative stage in the late-Saxon period and that borough courts may have been functioning as early as the tenth century.

Typically, the town paid a regular tax to its lord, who in most instances was the king. In return the town received such privileges as the right to have its own court and to operate a market—a center of supervised buying and selling. The market became the commercial nexus not only of the town but of the neighboring countryside as well. Towns were a source of wealth to the monarchy, and the English kings favored them in many ways. Their emergence and growth were accompanied by slow but significant changes

---

[6] Often at the rate of two shillings per hide.

in the social and economic order. An economy based largely on barter gave way eventually to a money economy, and the localism of the early Middle Ages diminished with the growth of international commerce. In the High Middle Ages—the twelfth and thirteenth centuries—the towns would become the foci of a rich, vibrant culture. Two of the greatest glories of high medieval civilization, the cathedral and the university, were both characteristically urban.

In the tenth century, however, one could not know that the emerging towns had such a future before them or that they would one day be agents of momentous social change. They were still mere specks on an agrarian landscape—overgrown villages encircled by walls. Probably fewer than ten Anglo-Saxon towns had more than 3,500 inhabitants. Norwich, Winchester, and Lincoln may have had 6,000 or more; York had perhaps 8,000; only London—the chief commercial center—compared in size to a modern town. The townspeople went about their daily tasks; the aristocracy fought, trained, and dreamed of war; but the chief business of the Anglo-Saxons remained what it had been for generations past and what it would be for centuries to come: the raising of crops and tending of herds.

Among the myths of earlier historical scholarship was that of the stalwart Anglo-Saxon farmer, communing with the good earth, fighting against invaders like a Massachusetts Minuteman, and laying the foundations of democracy by participating fearlessly and intelligently in village councils and hundred courts. Historians have since concluded that most Anglo-Saxon peasants were inarticulate, semi-servile tenants known as "villeins." Such workers were not literally slaves, although some slaves did exist. Villeins could not be bought and sold or uprooted from their families, and they normally divided their labor between their own fields and their lords' demesne fields. But most villeins were bound to their lands. If they fled they could legally be hunted down (sometimes unsuccessfully). Such people as these were virtually ignored in contemporary documents, but without question they represented the vast majority in late-Saxon times and long afterward. They played no role in local or hundred administration; nor were they permitted to bear arms, for the possession of weapons was by tradition a mark of free status. Their influence on English constitutional development was minimal, but their contribution to the economy was vital. Their lives were hard beyond all imagining. An Anglo-Saxon writer of the late tenth century attributed these words to a fictional but not atypical peasant of his times:

> I work hard. I go out at daybreak, driving the oxen to the field, and then I yoke them to the plow. Be the winter ever so stark, I dare not linger at home for awe of my lord; but having yoked my oxen, and fastened plowshare and coulter, every day I must plow a full acre or more. I have a boy, driving the oxen with an iron goad, who is hoarse with cold and shouting. Mighty hard work it is, for I am not free.[7]

---

[7] *Aelfric's Colloquy*, G. N. Garmonsway, ed. (London, 1939), 11, 23–35.

From an Early-Eleventh-Century Anglo-Saxon Manuscript   *Top:* Peasants plowing with a heavy wheeled plow and four-ox team; *center:* cutting grain with scythes; *bottom:* threshing grain with flails, and winnowing the grain and chaff. (Reproduced with permission of the British Library)

Not all Anglo-Saxon peasants lacked personal freedom. At the top of the peasant hierarchy was a class of free farmers known as *ceorls*. It was this class that earlier scholars had in mind when they alluded to Anglo-Saxon grass-roots democracy. But the ceorls were neither as democratic nor as numerous as previously supposed. Rather than being "typical Anglo-Saxon peasants," the ceorls were a peasant elite. They bore arms and, on occasion, some of them fought in the fyrd alongside the aristocratic thegns. They usually possessed farms of their own, and many of them owned slaves. They enjoyed status before the law and were assigned a wergeld of 200 shillings. Beyond these few generalizations one cannot go, for the contemporary sources disclose very little about the free peasantry except to make it clear that the term *ceorl* was applied rather loosely to agrarian freeholders of widely differing economic and social levels.

At the next level up in the social hierarchy were the thegns, sharply differentiated by their 1,200-shilling wergeld but otherwise as heterogeneous as the ceorls. The thegns, as we have seen, constituted a warrior aristocracy; yet there is clear evidence that many of the lesser thegns were little better off economically than the wealthier ceorls. Some thegns seem to have labored in their own fields as a matter of course, but ordinarily their involvement in agriculture was limited to supervising the labor of their peasants.

Women of all classes tended to be treated in early Germanic law codes as perpetual minors, under the governance of their fathers or husbands. Gradually, however, the less restrictive traditions of the later Roman Empire and Christianity softened Germanic attitudes toward women.[8] By late-Anglo-Saxon times widows could be guardians of their children, daughters could inherit lands, and husbands could no longer divorce their wives at will. According to the Dooms of Ethelbert of Kent (c. 600), "If a freeman lies with the wife of another freeman, he shall pay the husband his wergeld and procure a second wife with his own money, and bring her to the other man's home." By the tenth century, however, Anglo-Saxon women were holding property on a sizeable scale and were willing it to their sons and daughters, sometimes in equal portions. By the closing decades of the century, as a consequence of generous royal endowments and the surge of monastic reform, wealthy Benedictine nunneries, ruled by aristocratic abbesses, functioned with a minimum of local aristocratic interference under the protection of the English queen.

The Anglo-Saxon peasantry—women and men, free and unfree—made an essential contribution to the realm by producing its food. Although we can no longer credit them with clearing the primeval forests (Roman Britain

---

[8] See Sheila C. Dietrich, "An Introduction to Women in Anglo-Saxon Society (c. 600–1066)," *The Women of England*, Barbara Kanner, ed. (Hamden, Conn., 1979), pp. 32–56; Marc A. Meyer, "Land Charters and the Legal Position of Anglo-Saxon Women," ibid., pp. 57–82; Marc A. Meyer, "Women in the Tenth-Century Monastic Reform," *Revue Bénédictine*, 87 (1977): 34–61; and Christine Fell, Cecily Clark, and Elizabeth Williams, *Women in Anglo-Saxon England and the Impact of 1066* (Oxford, 1986).

was far more intensely developed than was once believed), they were nevertheless confronted with considerable tracts of dense woodland that had regenerated on previously occupied land during the post-Roman era of invasions, plague, depopulation, and deurbanization. They set about clearing these newly afforested lands and recolonizing further abandoned lands that had reverted to wilderness.

At first the Anglo-Saxons, like the Romans and Britons before them, tended to live in agrarian settlements consisting of scattered individual farms or small clusters of them. It was only later, beginning in the eighth and ninth centuries, that these scattered settlements began to coalesce into villages of the later medieval and early modern type, with their houses set close together, often centered on a village green, or a well or pond, and surrounded by great fields. Agrarian communities of this sort are known as "nucleated villages"—i.e., a nucleus of houses encircled by fields. The causes underlying this process of village formation are not entirely clear. Perhaps a particularly large cluster of farms began to attract the inhabitants of the neighboring district through the power or initiative of a central lordship or through community consensus.

Village formation must have been further stimulated by the development of parishes. The social and religious life of villagers typically centered on their parish churches which, from the late-Saxon period onward, tended increasingly to be constructed of stone—thereby providing the community a sense of permanence. The formation of nucleated villages was a long, gradual process, but they do not date back to the coming of the Anglo-Saxons as was traditionally thought.

The fields encircling the villages were usually divided into long, narrow strips, like the stripes of an American flag. These strips of land were not held in common by the community but were apportioned among individual village households. Since the various strips comprised a single agrarian unit, however, it was necessary for a village council (perhaps dominated by the local thegn or the local steward of a great lord) to make decisions on such matters as crop rotation, boundary disputes, and the apportionment of plows and oxen.

The village thus became the fundamental agrarian unit of medieval England; but alongside it there often existed another, more artificial unit—the estate belonging to a thegn, churchman, or higher noble, known later as a *manor*. Normally a single village constituted a single manor. But occasionally a manor encompassed several villages and outlying farms, and a single village sometimes included parts of several manors. The village and the manor differed in that the village was an agrarian entity—a cluster of houses surrounded by fields—whereas the manor was a unit of lordship.

As the Anglo-Saxon era drew to a close, manorial lords exercised increasing political, judicial, and economic authority over the peasants on their manors. They often controlled the village water mill and charged peasants for its use. They were entitled by custom to tax their peasants in various ways and to collect a portion of their peasants' crops (later commuted in many cases to a payment of money—a rent). And lords usually had their own strips, their demesne lands, interspersed among their peasants' strips in the village fields. Peasants of villein status were normally obliged to labor on their lord's demesne for a certain number of days per week (the exact number depending on local custom and the season). The lord did not ordinarily do farm work himself but depended for his income on the taxes and labor of his peasants.

For the sake of coherence, the above discussion has depicted the manors of late-Saxon England as being considerably more uniform than in fact they were. The details of agrarian organization and class structure varied bewilderingly from one district to another. Kent remained throughout the Middle Ages a land apart, characterized by family farms. The same was true of Devonshire in the southwest. Throughout much of the Danelaw there were many more free peasants than elsewhere. In Northumbria the manor was slow in developing. And across large stretches of the north and northwest the land was given over to sheep raising rather than farming. Even in the grain-growing districts, field patterns varied according to soil fertility, split inheritances, climate, and above all, topography (American flags wrinkle badly when laid on hilly land). The ongoing studies of archaeologists, aerial photographers, pollen analysts, tree specialists, and kindred investigators are constantly adding to our understanding of the medieval English landscape, in all its variety, and providing swarms of exceptions to any generalizations. But when all is said, the achievements of Anglo-Saxon agriculture remain impressive.

Late-Saxon Art

In the arts, too, late-Saxon England demonstrated signs of a maturing civilization. No large Anglo-Saxon churches survive—most of them were torn down and replaced in the generation or two after the Norman Conquest—but descriptions by contemporary writers, confirmed by modern excavations, attest to the existence of spacious, well-designed cathedrals in episcopal centers such as Canterbury and Winchester. And there survive many village churches dating wholly or in part from Anglo-Saxon times. Although influenced to a degree by the styles of Carolingian Francia and, later on, of the Rhinelands, they show in their proportions and in the rhythm of their textured surfaces a strong native originality. The tower at Oxford, for example, is a bold, assured expression of a distinctive Anglo-Saxon style (page 84). The last great church of pre-Conquest England, Westminster Abbey, was built in the Norman Romanesque manner under the personal supervision of King Edward the Confessor (1042–1066). Although totally rebuilt by Henry III in the thirteenth century (again in the style of contemporary France), its original appearance can be imagined by looking at the majestic ruins of the Norman abbey of Jumièges, built at about the same time and in much the same style; vast and massive, its great round arches and heavy columns convey a feeling of solidity and permanence (page 85).

Tenth-century English monastic reform, associated with such figures as Dunstan and Edgar the Peaceable, produced an original body of religious

Tower, St. Michael's, Oxford   The rough rubble surface and double-splayed, double-arched windows are characteristic of Anglo-Saxon architecture. (Edwin Smith)

literature, written in the Anglo-Saxon language and intended for lay as well as ecclesiastical readers. A number of manuscripts of the period are illuminated in decorative styles that show the influence of both continental and earlier Northumbrian traditions. Tenth-century Winchester was the center of a highly original style of manuscript illumination that drew from Carolingian models and yet was thoroughly distinctive in its fluid outlines of human and animal figures, its fluttering draperies, and its soft pastel colors. In the eleventh century, the Winchester style developed a degree of emotional intensity unparalleled in Europe. The poignant crucifixion from the Gospel Book of Countess Judith (Winchester, c. 1050–1065) discloses a profound change in the mood of medieval piety—from the awesome to the human, from Christ in majesty to Christ suffering (page 86). Perhaps better than any other contemporary work of art, it shows the level of technical skill and emotional depth attained in the closing years of the Anglo-Saxon era.

Ruins of Jumièges Abbey (c. 1066) Edward the Confessor built the original Westminster Abbey in a similar style. (Bruce Norman/The Ancient Art & Architecture Collection)

The Reign of Ethelred "the Unready" (978–1016) and the New Invasions

A century after Alfred turned the Danish tide at the battle of Edington, disaster struck England. It was a disaster that few at the time could have foreseen, for in the year 978 England was apparently as prosperous and secure as it had been during the previous generation. Under Alfred and his descendants the monarchy and the kingdom had made notable progress. But in 978 a child-heir, Ethelred "the Unready," rose to the throne following the murder of his older half-brother, King Edward "the Martyr," apparently by men of Ethelred's own household.[9] Ethelred himself was blameless—he was only ten or eleven years old at the time—but the assassination produced a kingdom-wide shock that did not subside quickly. We know little about the luckless Edward "the Martyr" except that he was singularly ill-tempered, but a cult developed around his memory and his tomb, and Ethelred's reputation was darkened accordingly.

---

[9] "The Unready" is actually a mistranslation of Ethelred's nickname. The Old English term is *Unraed*, which means "no council" or "bad council," while *Ethelred* itself means "noble council." Thus, *Ethelred Unraed* makes a fine pun in Old English but a very obscure one in modern English. Some scholars have tried to compromise with "Ethelred the Redless," which has the disadvantage of being absolutely meaningless except to scholars trained in Old English. I will stick with "the Unready," which catches the original punning spirit and makes sense—even though not precisely the original sense.

Late-Anglo-Saxon Crucifixion Scene From the Gospel Book of Countess Judith, M. 709, f. lv. (The Pierpont Morgan Library)

To add to Ethelred's problems, a split had developed in the Anglo-Saxon aristocracy. Some favored continuing the monastic reforms of Archbishop Dunstan and King Edgar the Peaceable. Others urged the young king to oppose monastic reform. A number of thegns and ealdormen had lost wealth and influence as a result of the flood of land grants and privileges that royal monasteries had received under King Edgar and the trend toward transferring monastic lands from aristocratic to royal control. Because wealth and power were at stake, the pro- and antimonastic factions were prepared to carry their differences to the point of civil war. The child-king thus inherited an aristocratic power struggle and a tainted reputation—neither of his own making.

Ethelred has been portrayed, from the eleventh century to the twentieth, as a bumbler. The twelfth-century historian William of Malmesbury reported the rumor that Ethelred's troubles began early:

Archbishop Dunstan, indeed, had foretold his unworthiness, having discovered it by a filthy sign: for when Ethelred was a tiny infant, just as he was immersed in the baptismal font, with all the bishops standing around him, he defiled the sacrament with an abundant bowel movement. At this, Dunstan, being extremely angered, exclaimed, "By God and His mother, this will be a sorry fellow!"

The *Anglo-Saxon Chronicle* had earlier criticized the efforts of Ethelred's regime to repel the Danes:

> And when they were in the east, the English army was kept in the west, and when they were in the south, our army was in the north. Then all the counselors were summoned to the king, and it was decided how the country would be defended. But if anything was decided then, it did not last even a month. Finally there was no leader who would collect an army, but each fled as best he could, and in the end no shire would even help the next.

Despite such contemporary testimony, recent studies have demonstrated that Ethelred was the victim of nearly hopeless circumstances.[10] As a child he rose to a royal title clouded by his brother's murder; if Malmesbury can be trusted (and he probably cannot), an infant mishap aroused the anger of Archbishop Dunstan; and Ethelred had to deal with an aristocracy divided between Anglo-Saxons and Anglo-Danes, and between supporters and opponents of monastic reform. Worst of all, Ethelred's England was tormented by ceaseless Viking attacks of unprecedented force. Poor wretch! He held out against the Danes for a long generation—fighting them, bribing them, luring some to his service. Meanwhile he threaded his way between friends and enemies of monastic reform, attracting to his court strong aristocrats of differing persuasions (as his charter attestations disclose). He issued dooms on no less than ten occasions—more often than any of his predecessors. He maintained close control of the coinage, presided over great councils, and at them issued charters through a smoothly functioning royal chancery. In the end, some of his Anglo-Danish nobles betrayed him and the Vikings defeated him. And subsequent historians, judging his reign by its catastrophic end instead of its creative middle decades, labeled him a fool. He was, admittedly, not one of the towering intellects in the annals of the English monarchy, but he was betrayed by circumstances no less than by personal incapacity.

Ethelred had to cope with Danish raids of ever-greater intensity, and of a new sort. To an increasing degree, the Danish attacks were more than mere private-enterprise raiding parties; they were directed by the kings of Denmark themselves. But despite English divisiveness and Danish military superiority, the Anglo-Saxons managed to hold their own against the Danish attacks until 991, when a Viking band annihilated the East Anglian fyrd under Ealdorman Byrhtnoth at the Battle of Maldon—celebrated by the great heroic poem excerpted on page 72. Later in the same year, King Ethelred won a respite by paying the first danegeld. But in 994 the Danes

---

[10] See Eric John, "War and Society in the Tenth Century: The Maldon Campaign," *Transactions of the Royal Historical Society*, 5th series, 27 (1977): 173–195; Simon Keynes, *The Diplomas of King Ethelred the Unready: 978–1016* (Cambridge, England, 1980); and *Ethelred the Unready*, David Hill, ed., British Archaeological Reports, British Series, 59 (1978).

were back, this time led by King Swein of Denmark, son of Harold Blue-tooth.[11] Ethelred bought more intermissions by paying more danegelds, a tactic that won time but also made vividly clear to the Danes the extent of both England's weakness and its wealth.

In 1009, King Swein threw all his resources into a campaign of conquest. Three years later the Danes made peace in exchange for an immense danegeld of £48,000. Predictably enough, Swein led a renewed attack in 1013, convinced that any kingdom rich enough to pay such huge bribes was well worth conquering. And Anglo-Saxon England, now badly demoralized, fell into his hands. The old Danelaw gave Swein its firm support, and the English offered only mild resistance. Ethelred fled to his wife's homeland of Normandy, and most of the English accepted Swein as their new king.

But Swein enjoyed his triumph only briefly. He died in 1014, leaving the kingdom to his son Canute. Ethelred now returned to reassert his authority and succeeded in defeating Canute in battle. But in the spring of 1016 Ethelred died. As the *Anglo-Saxon Chronicle* understated it, "He had held his kingdom with great toil and difficulties as long as his life lasted." His son, a skillful warrior named Edmund "Ironside," fought on for a season but died later in 1016, whereupon the Witan concurred in the accession of the Danish king, Canute, to the throne of Alfred the Great.

The Reign of Canute (1016–1035)

King Canute was a more successful monarch than Ethelred the Unready. His contemporaries called him Canute the Wealthy; later generations knew him as Canute the Great.[12] A Norse saga writer provides a half-legendary description of him: he was tall and strong and had blond hair, keen eyes, and a long, narrow nose—slightly bent—that marred his good looks.

The new king was a product of civilizing forces that were just then transforming the Norse world. By 1016 Viking states from Iceland to Russia were embracing Christianity; and in Scandinavia itself the rise of royal power was bringing political coherence to the northern lands of Denmark, Norway, and Sweden. Accordingly, Canute ascended the Anglo-Saxon throne as a Christian. Alfred's dynasty was temporarily unseated, and the warfare of the previous generation had decimated the Old English aristoc-

---

[11] Harold Bluetooth was the first king of Denmark to convert to Christianity. Like him, many other characters from Viking history and sagas bear memorable nicknames: Eric Bloodaxe, Halfdan the Generous-with-Money-but-Stingy-with-Food, Ragnar Hairy-Breeches, Ivar the Boneless, etc. An Icelandic musician was called Einar Jingle-Scale; a Norwegian poet, Eyvind the Plagiarist.

[12] On the reign of Canute and his Anglo-Scandinavian "empire," Laurence M. Larson, *Canute the Great* (New York, 1912) is still useful. For a brief and more recent summary, see D. J. V. Fisher, *The Anglo-Saxon Age, c. 400–1042* (London, 1973), pp. 319–339. For an important reinterpretation, see Katharin Mack, "Changing Thegns: Cnut's Conquest and the Anglo-Saxon Aristocracy," *Albion*, 16 (1984), 375–387. See further Frank M. Stenton's classic study, "The Danes in England," *Preparatory to Anglo-Saxon England: Being the Collected Papers of Frank Merry Stenton*, Doris Mary Stenton, ed. (Oxford, 1970), pp. 136–165.

racy. But in Canute's reign, after an initial bloody purge and an enormous geld assessment, security and prosperity returned.

Canute's accession to the Old English throne made him master of two kingdoms: England and Denmark. A dozen years later, in 1128—by means of bribes, threats, soothing promises, and a show of naval force—he won control of the kingdom of Norway, and for a brief time he ruled a great empire girding the North Sea. But it was an ephemeral empire, held together by the fragile bonds of allegiance to a single man and backed by the riches of England. For a few years Canute was the dominant political figure in northern Europe, but at his death his dominions crumbled.

England was by far the wealthiest and most developed land in Canute's empire, and he spent much of his reign there. Aware of the achievements of his Anglo-Saxon predecessors, he ruled in the Old English tradition, respecting ancient customs, issuing dooms, and supporting the Church. He won the vigorous support of the clergy by granting them land and treasure and providing them with an environment of peace in which to work. In the

King Canute and Queen Aelfgifu The king and his first wife present a gift to the abbot and monks of the New Minster, Winchester, while Jesus, the Virgin Mary, and St. Peter look down approvingly. (Reproduced by courtesy of the Trustees of the British Museum)

words of one contemporary observer, "Merry sang the monks of Ely as Canute the king rowed by."

Canute succeeded better than his Anglo-Saxon predecessors in bringing unity to the land, for both the English and Anglo-Danes supported him. Indeed, perhaps only a Scandinavian king could have won for the English monarchy the unquestioned loyalty of the Danelaw. At a council at Oxford in 1018, Canute formally declared peace between the Danes and English and brought an end to their former strife. The king's Witan swore to uphold Christianity, to love Canute, and to observe the laws of King Edgar.

But as the master of a North Sea empire, Canute was obliged to delegate authority over England as none of his Anglo-Saxon predecessors had done. He divided the kingdom into four large districts—Northumbria, Mercia, East Anglia, and the former royal heartland, Wessex itself—and placed each of them under the jurisdiction of powerful new aristocrats of proven loyalty, known as *earls* (a name derived from the Old Norse *Jarl*). He brought to his court a bodyguard of Scandinavian housecarles—a sizeable group of trained infantrymen with their own elaborate regulations, their own judicial assembly, and an arsenal of terrifying two-handed battleaxes. But in most other respects Canute ruled much as an Anglo-Saxon might have done. Hundred courts and shire courts continued as before, towns grew even more rapidly through the stimulus of an increased North Sea commerce, and agrarian life proceeded unaffected. Canute sought to improve his royal credentials by marrying Ethelred's widow, a strong-minded Norman princess named Emma, who clearly preferred her second husband to her first.

On Canute's death in 1035, his empire was divided between his two sons, who ruled England in turn—briefly and badly. When the last of them died without heirs, the Witan chose as king a member of the old Wessex dynasty, the long-exiled son of Ethelred and Emma. In 1042 the dynasty of Alfred reestablished itself peacefully in the person of Edward the Confessor.

The Reign of Edward the Confessor (1042–1066)

Edward was no more an Englishman than Canute. Between the ages of twelve and thirty-six he had lived in exile in Normandy, the homeland of his mother, and had become deeply Normanized. A man of conventional piety and limited political talent, he spoke French by preference and installed Norman favorites in his court and kingdom. "When King Edward of holy memory returned from Francia," his biographer writes, "quite a number of men of that nation, and they not base-born, accompanied him. And these, since he was master of the whole kingdom, he kept with him, enriched them with many honors, and made them his privy counselors and administrators of the royal court."[13] Thus the Norman Conquest of Eng-

---

[13] *Vita Aedwardi Regis: The Life of King Edward*, Frank Barlow, ed. (London, 1962), p. 17. On the reign in general, see the excellent biography by Frank Barlow, *Edward the Confessor* (Berkeley, Calif., 1970).

land, although consummated on the field of Hastings in 1066, had its inception at Edward's accession in 1042. Such at least were the feelings of many of the English, who respected Edward but not his Norman favorites or his Norman customs.

The great earls were Canute's creations, and having been enriched by their king, they served him faithfully. But under Edward, who came from Normandy to rule a land of strangers, the earls began to assert their autonomy. Some of them became prime representatives of the growing Anglo-Saxon resentment against Norman infiltration into court and countryside. The most powerful of these magnates was Godwin, earl of Wessex, who managed to place his several sons in other earldoms and even engineered a marriage between his daughter Edith and Edward the Confessor. Godwin was the first magnate ever to receive jurisdiction over all Wessex—the ancestral homeland of King Edward's dynasty and the major source of its landed wealth. Indeed, Godwin's earldom included not only most of the old kingdom of Wessex but Cornwall, Sussex, and Kent as well. Canute's creation of the Wessex earldom was perhaps necessitated by his frequent absences from the kingdom to attend to his Scandinavian dominions, and the risk was minimized by his ability to direct Scandinavian military resources against any English earl contemplating rebellion. The result was that Edward, who had no resources outside England, inherited along with his crown an ambitious earl deeply entrenched in the home shires of the West Saxon kings. Within a few years of Edward's coronation, Godwin and his sons possessed considerably more land, in Wessex and throughout England, than the king himself.

The political tensions of the Confessor's reign reached their climax in 1051–1052 when Earl Godwin and his allies briefly turned against the king in open rebellion. The affair may have arisen from a dispute over the succession. The Norman sources (which are not entirely trustworthy in these matters) indicate that in 1051 Edward, who was childless, designated as his heir Duke William the Bastard of Normandy, his friend and kinsman.[14] It may be that Earl Godwin himself aspired to the throne and was driven to desperate measures by Edward's decision. Whatever the reasons, in 1051 Godwin rebelled against the king. The immediate cause was an incident that occurred at Dover, an important seaport in Godwin's Wessex earldom. A French lord, Eustace count of Boulogne, was returning home from a visit to the English royal court, perhaps as an envoy from Duke William. When Eustace came to Earl Godwin's town of Dover, the townspeople rioted and killed some of the knights in his retinue. King Edward may possibly have commissioned Eustace to seize Dover and hand it over to Duke William as a pledge for the future crown. Whatever the case, King Edward demanded that Godwin punish the townspeople. Godwin refused and assembled an army, perhaps hoping to force Edward to dismiss his

---

[14] Edward's mother, Emma of Normandy, was Duke William's great aunt.

Norman advisers and change his succession plans. But Godwin quickly discovered that Edward had the backing of most of the thegns and of the earls outside the Godwin clan. Consequently, Godwin and his sons had to flee the country. In 1052, however, they returned, rallied support to their cause, overawed Edward with a show of military force, and forced him to reinstate them.

The Godwin family had won an important bloodless victory. Edward was humiliated and, bowing to the wishes of the earl, sent home most of his Norman supporters. Among these was Robert of Jumièges, archbishop of Canterbury, who was forced to abandon his see. Archbishop Robert was replaced by a creature of the Godwins named Stigand—a vainglorious popinjay of a man who presided over the English Church with a singular lack of distinction. From then on, Edward became more and more a figurehead. The real power was exercised by Earl Godwin and, after Godwin's death in 1053, by his son Harold Godwinson, who succeeded to the earldom of Wessex.

Harold emerges from the writings of his age as a more attractive, less crassly ambitious figure than his father. Between 1053 and Edward's death in 1066, the king and the earl seem to have worked together on reasonably good terms. Harold behaved with proper deference toward Edward, did most of the necessary frontier campaigning, and left the monarch to his favorite pastimes—hunting, churchgoing, and directing the construction of the great Romanesque abbey at Westminster. Harold proved himself a leader of political talent and exceptional generalship, and in the years of his power the kingdom flourished.

By the standards of mid-eleventh-century Western Europe, England on the eve of the Norman Conquest was prosperous and well governed—although good governance had become dangerously dependent on the friendly relations between a submissive king and his over-mighty earl. The military organization was efficient, towns and commerce were growing, and money was circulating to a degree unmatched on the Continent. Despite diversities in law and custom between one region and another, Anglo-Saxon England had achieved a genuine sense of national unity, which contrasted sharply with the state of political chaos and endemic private warfare that plagued most of France. A vivid illustration of England's growing feeling of national cohesion is to be found in a passage from the *Anglo-Saxon Chronicle* under the year 1052. On Earl Godwin's return from exile, both he and King Edward had large military forces behind them, and for a time there seemed every possibility of open battle. But as the chronicle explains, the chief military leaders on both sides, still deeply apprehensive of the Viking threat, decided against a test of arms: "It was hateful to them that they should fight against men of their own race, because very few worthy men on either side were not Englishmen." As this passage makes clear, Bede's vision of the English as a single people was by now shared by the laity.

The Reign of Harold and the Norman Conquest (1066)

King Edward the Confessor died in January 1066. He is reputed to have remained chaste throughout his marriage to Godwin's daughter Edith. Whether this is true or merely a pious excuse for a childless marriage, his death brought to a head the problem of the royal succession—for the determination of which no clear, unambiguous principle existed in 1066.

There were three serious candidates for the Confessor's throne. Earl Harold Godwinson had been the most powerful man in England for the previous thirteen years and had proven his capacity as a military commander. Edward is alleged to have designated Harold his heir on his deathbed, and on the day after Edward's death the Witan chose the earl as king. In the absence of a royal son, Harold's position as heir designate of King Edward and his selection by the Witan and subsequent coronation gave him a strong claim. He also had a certain tenuous connection with the throne through his sister Edith, who was Edward's widow, although Harold was not himself of royal blood.

Duke William the Bastard of Normandy was distantly related to Edward through his great-aunt, Emma, the Norman wife of Ethelred the Unready and Canute. William also pressed his claim that Edward had earlier designated him heir to the English throne. It is quite possible, of course, that Edward had designated William in 1051 and Harold in 1066. Finally, William claimed priority over Harold Godwinson on the basis of a peculiar episode that occurred in 1064 or 1065. Harold, visiting the Continent, had fallen captive to a neighboring vassal of the duke of Normandy, who had then released him into Duke William's custody. William treated Harold as an honored guest, but it is by no means clear that the earl was free to leave the Norman court. At length, Harold took a public oath to support Duke William's claims to the English throne on Edward's death. Hence in 1066 William and his supporters regarded Harold as an oath breaker. And by both the Christian and the feudal ethics of the day, the violation of a pledge was regarded with profound contempt.

The third contender for the English throne was Harold Hardrada, king of Norway—an illustrious Norse warrior whose skill at arms had won him fame from Scandinavia to Byzantium. His claim to England, as a successor to Canute, was perhaps the weakest of the three, but his dazzling military reputation must have struck fear among the English. It was clear that Harold Godwinson would have to fight for his new crown.

Besides the claims of Harold Hardrada and William the Bastard, Harold Godwinson had two additional liabilities. In 1066 the Roman papacy was in the process of reasserting its authority over the European Church. As a strict guardian of proper canonical processes, the papacy could not accept the deposition of Robert of Jumièges as archbishop of Canterbury and the elevation of Stigand. The appointment of a new archbishop before the death of his predecessor was a flagrant violation of canon law. Hence the papacy was hostile toward Harold Godwinson, who had been crowned by Stigand and whose father had engineered the usurpation. Duke William exploited this hostility, winning full papal support for his projected conquest of England. William's invading army was privileged to carry the papal banner which, together with the Norman claim that Godwinson was a perjurer, placed the duke in a strong moral position and made his invasion a kind of holy war.

Harold Godwinson's other liability was his brother, Earl Tostig of Northumbria. Tostig, an unpopular lord, was overthrown by a Northumbrian revolt in 1065. The revolt appeared to have strong regional backing, and Harold made no effort to reinstate his brother in the earldom. Tostig was furious at Harold's "betrayal" and turned against him, forgetting the political maxim "the family that slays together stays together."[15] The Northumbrians chose as their new earl a magnate named Morcar, brother of Earl Edwin of Mercia and unrelated to the Godwin clan. Harold's passive role in this affair seems to have won him the gratitude of the two powerful brothers, Edwin and Morcar; but Tostig, now in exile, was bitterly hostile. In the months following his coronation Harold was reasonably secure at home, but he had more than his share of dangerous enemies abroad.

Normandy, on the eve of the battle of Hastings, was a well-organized principality whose duke controlled his vassals to a degree unmatched elsewhere in France.[16] During the century and a half since its establishment in 911, the Viking duchy of Normandy had embraced Christianity, absorbed French culture, adopted the French language, and built a military and political organization on the principles of French feudalism. Normandy in 1066 was a land of castles and of mounted knights whose tactics contrasted sharply with the infantry tradition of the Anglo-Saxon fyrd.

Evidence relating to pre-Conquest Norman history, although far from abundant, suggests that the high degree of ducal control and centralization Normandy enjoyed in 1066 was mostly a product of William the Bastard's own leadership. Winning a significant victory over rebellious barons in 1047, he spent the years thereafter founding and enriching grateful abbeys, working toward the elimination of private warfare, and reshaping the Norman nobility into a cohesive group of ducal kinsmen and supporters.

But strong as William was, he lacked the power to win for Normandy a position of hegemony in northern France that would provide him the necessary security to undertake a major invasion of England. He achieved this hegemony quite by accident when his two chief rivals, the count of neighboring Anjou and the king of France, both died in 1060. France passed to a child-king, and Anjou entered a period of disputed succession. In the mean-

---

[15] The quotation is from Eric John, "Edward the Confessor and the Norman Conquest," *English Historical Review* 94 (1979): 259.

[16] On the scope of Norman expansion in the eleventh century—into southern Italy, Sicily, and the Holy Land as well as England—see David C. Douglas, *The Norman Achievement, 1050–1100* (Berkeley, Calif., 1969). Two excellent, sharply differing books on pre-Conquest Normandy are David Bates, *Normandy Before 1066* (London, 1982), and Eleanor Searle, *Predatory Kinship and the Creation of Norman Power, 840–1066* (Berkeley, 1988).

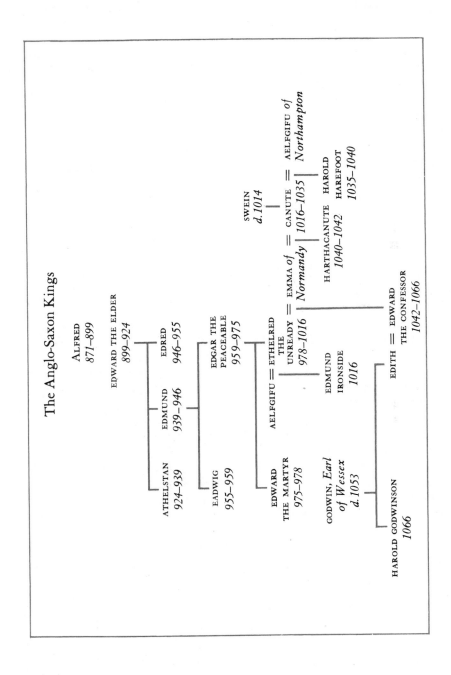

The Anglo-Saxon Kings

ALFRED
871–899

EDWARD THE ELDER
899–924

ATHELSTAN
924–939

EDMUND
939–946

EDRED
946–955

EADWIG
955–959

EDGAR THE PEACEABLE
959–975

EDWARD THE MARTYR
975–978

AELFGIFU = ETHELRED THE UNREADY
978–1016

EMMA of Normandy = ETHELRED THE UNREADY = CANUTE 1016–1035 = AELFGIFU of Northampton

SWEIN
d. 1014

EDMUND IRONSIDE
1016

HARTHACANUTE
1040–1042

HAROLD HAREFOOT
1035–1040

EDWARD THE CONFESSOR
1042–1066

EDITH = EDWARD THE CONFESSOR

GODWIN, Earl of Wessex
d. 1053

HAROLD GODWINSON
1066

time William had ensured the support of nearby Flanders by marrying the daughter of its count.

On Edward the Confessor's death, therefore, William was in a position to press his claim to the English throne. Good fortune provided the opportunity, and William had the courage, imagination, and greed to grasp it.[17] The barons of Normandy agreed to the daring enterprise at a council early in 1066, and William set about augmenting his Norman force with volunteers from all over Europe. Adventurous knights flocked to his banner from all quarters—from Brittany, Maine, Flanders, Aquitaine, central France, and even southern Italy—drawn by William's already formidable military reputation, by the generous wages he promised, and by the hope of treasure and estates in the conquered land. But despite the support of his duchy, the growing size of his army, and the moral backing of the papacy, William's projected invasion was an audacious gamble. England was far larger and wealthier than Normandy, and it was ruled by a warrior-king of ability and resolution.

Harold Godwinson, however, had a staggering task before him. Beset by enemies, he could not predict the place, the time, or the source of the first attacks against his kingdom. As it happened, the initial assault came from his brother Tostig. In May 1066, Tostig emerged from exile to begin harrying the coasts of southern and eastern England with a sizeable body of followers. But Tostig's men were turned back by local contingents of the fyrd, and he was obliged to retire to Scotland. Incapable of doing serious damage on his own, he entered into an alliance with Harold Hardrada and merged his forces with those of the Norse king.

By midsummer, Duke William's forces were on the Norman coast ready for the invasion, and only the persistence of contrary winds prevented their crossing the Channel. Harold Godwinson had meanwhile assembled the fyrd in southern England and had stationed a large fleet off the Channel shore. But week after week the winds remained contrary for William, and the English watched their coasts in vain.

Midway through September Harold Godwinson was forced to dismiss his army and fleet. There is some evidence that service in the fyrd was limited by custom to two months. By mid-September the term had expired, provisions were exhausted, and the warriors wished to return home for the harvest. The contrary winds had served William after all, for Harold now had only his housecarles to guard the shore.

Immediately after disbanding his army, Harold Godwinson received news that Harold Hardrada had invaded Yorkshire in northern England. Hardrada's army consisted of three hundred shiploads of Norse warriors, in

---

[17] Much has been written on the Norman Conquest. Sir Frank Stenton, *Anglo-Saxon England*, 3rd ed. (Oxford, 1971), provides a good summary. See also C. Warren Hollister, *Anglo-Saxon Military Institutions* (Oxford, 1962), especially pp. 147–152, and Henry R. Loyn, *The Norman Conquest* (London, 1965). On the background and aftermath of the Conquest, see R. Allen Brown, *The Normans and the Norman Conquest*, 2nd ed. (Woodbridge, Suffolk, 1986), and *The Normans* (Woodbridge, Suffolk, 1986: translated sources).

addition to Tostig and his considerable following. The combined force moved toward the key northern city of York. On September 20, 1066, Hardrada's host encountered the northern fyrd led by the two earls, Edwin and Morcar, at Fulford Gate, two miles south of York. The battle of Fulford raged for the better part of a day. In the end, after heavy mutual bloodshed, the northern fyrd broke before the invaders. Receiving the submission of York, Harold Hardrada then apparently conceived the idea of incorporating a number of Anglo-Danish Yorkshiremen into his army. He withdrew to the strategic crossroads at Stamford Bridge, seven miles east of York, to await hostages from the conquered city.

Harold Godwinson reassembled his army as best he could on short notice and dashed northward. Five days after Fulford, on September 25, his army arrived at Stamford Bridge, caught the Norwegian host by surprise, and crushed it after a long and savage battle. Tostig and Harold Hardrada both perished, and the battered survivors of the three-hundred-ship host returned to Norway in twenty-four ships. Stamford Bridge was perhaps the

The Bayeux Tapestry (Late Eleventh Century)   *Top:* The appearance of Halley's Comet alarms King Harold and his followers, whose fear of a Norman landing is depicted by the ships on the lower border. *Bottom:* A scene from the battle of Hastings, showing English foot soldiers repulsing Norman knights. (Giraudon)

greatest military triumph in Anglo-Saxon history. An ominous Scandinavian threat of twenty years' standing had been destroyed, and the mightiest Viking warrior of the age lay in his grave.

Two days after the battle of Stamford Bridge, the Channel winds changed at last and the Norman invasion began. At nine in the morning on Thursday, September 28, the Norman fleet entered Pevensey Bay in Sussex, and William's army disembarked at leisure on an undefended shore. The Normans immediately occupied the important port of Hastings and proceeded to build a castle there to protect their avenue of escape should the war turn against them. Modern historians, with the advantage of hindsight, have sometimes assumed that the Norman victory at the battle of Hastings was inevitable. But William, lacking the gift of foreknowledge, was far from certain of the outcome. Indeed, he could hardly have known at the time whether his enemy would be Harold Godwinson or Harold Hardrada.

On news of the Norman landing, Harold Godwinson acted with frenzied speed. Within thirteen days he settled affairs in Yorkshire, pulled together his tired and decimated army, and marched 240 miles from York to Hastings. From the standpoint of military strategy, Harold's haste was a serious error. There was no real reason for it, since William was too cautious to proceed far from the Sussex shore until he had done battle with the English. Perhaps Harold Godwinson was overconfident after his tremendous victory at Stamford Bridge or was hoping to surprise William as he had surprised Hardrada. Perhaps he was solicitous of the defenseless people of his former earldom of Wessex which was being ravaged by the Normans. Whatever his reasons, he chose to engage William with an exhausted army far below normal strength. Edwin and Morcar and their troops had been too severely mauled by the Norsemen at Fulford Gate to join Harold on his southward march, and there had been insufficient time to summon the full complement of the southern fyrd.

On Friday, October 13, William's scouts sighted King Harold's army, and on the following day there occurred the most decisive battle in English history. The battle of Hastings was fought on Saturday, October 14, from morning until dusk. For the English it was the third major battle in less than four weeks.

Harold's army, depending on the traditional infantry tactics of the Anglo-Saxons to turn back William's cavalry, took a strong defensive position on the crest of a low hill, the forward line standing shoulder to shoulder in the form of a shield wall.[18] In the course of the battle, the shield wall turned back repeated Norman cavalry charges. Although the arrows of Norman archers took many lives, the Anglo-Saxon line remained firm. At one point the Normans fled in panic until their duke rallied them and sent them back to slaughter a crowd of pursuing English. There is evidence that

---

[18] After the Conquest, William built Battle Abbey on this spot. The battle site is presently occupied by, among other things, a school, a modest convention center, and an excellent pub (called Chequers).

A "Motte and Bailey" Castle This model, based on archaeological excavations of the early post-Conquest castle of Abinger, Surrey, and evidence from the Bayeux Tapestry, shows the typical wooden tower encircled by a palisade atop an artificial mound surrounded by a moat (see p. 105). Such castles, new to England, were at once simple to build and difficult to storm, and the Normans consolidated their occupation of England by building hundreds of them. (Courtesy of The British Museum)

on one or two later occasions the Normans feigned flight in order to draw more of the English out of their positions. At length King Harold himself was slain, probably by an arrow fired on a high arc and falling at random. And with the king's death and the coming of dusk the shield wall broke at last. The English fyrd, now leaderless, fled into the Sussex forest.

William's triumph marks the end of Anglo-Saxon England and the beginning of the Anglo-Norman era. It remained only for William to consolidate his conquest and establish firm rule over the kingdom. Hastings left England kingless, disorganized, and all but defenseless against the Norman host. The great battle and its background have been described here in some detail in order to see beyond the traditional view that Hastings represented the inevitable victory of an up-to-date continental feudal state over an exhausted, insular culture with a cumbersome and outdated army. On the contrary, the Anglo-Saxon army gave a good account of itself under the most adverse conditions, and Anglo-Saxon civilization retained to the end its precocious political organization and rich cultural vitality. On the sturdy foundation constructed by Theodore of Tarsus, Alfred the Great, Edgar the Peaceable, and others like them, the Norman kings would build the most tightly organized Western European state since the days of the Romans.

PART TWO

The Growth of the Realm

1066 to 1216

CORONATION OF WILLIAM THE CONQUEROR ON CHRISTMAS DAY, 1066   A rather fanciful fifteenth-century depiction. *(The Granger Collection)*

4

The Impact of the Norman Conquest

William the Conqueror was a gifted warrior-statesman, tenacious in the pursuit of his goals, cruel or magnanimous as it suited his purposes, phenomenally energetic. A monk of the next generation described him in these words:

> He was tall and extremely fat, with a fierce look and a forehead bare of hair, with arms of such strength that nobody else could draw his bow, though he himself could bend it while his horse was at full gallop. He was majestic, whether sitting or standing—though the outward swell of his big belly deformed his royal person—of robust health, and addicted to the pleasures of hunting.[1]

Having won his audacious gamble at Hastings, William moved unerringly toward the completion of his conquest. He knew that London was the key to England, and shortly after the great battle he advanced northward toward it. Finding London Bridge too well defended to allow him to cross the Thames and assault the city directly, he led his army westward—devastating the countryside as he went—until he reached the town of Wallingford in Berkshire. There he crossed the Thames and advanced eastward on London. Before he reached the city, he was met by a number of London citizens and other notables—such as Archbishop Stigand and Earls Edwin and Morcar—who made their personal submissions to him and surrendered the city.

On Christmas Day, 1066, Duke William was crowned king of the English in the new Westminster Abbey, with all the pomp and ceremony that traditionally accompanied Anglo-Saxon coronations. All present, both Norman and English, promised their allegiance to the new king, and William, for his part, undertook to abide by the laws in effect during Edward the Confessor's reign and to rule in the tradition of the West Saxon kings.

---

[1] From William of Malmesbury, *Deeds of the Kings of the English*. The most complete biography is David C. Douglas, *William the Conqueror* (Berkeley, Calif., 1964), which also provides an excellent account of pre-Conquest Normandy. Frank Barlow, *William I and the Norman Conquest* (London, 1965), is a good summary that presents William as a man with the values and talents of an able but essentially ordinary baron. See also the outstanding biography by David Bates, *William the Conqueror* (London, 1989).

William the Conqueror, Depicted on a Silver Penny of His Reign, c. 1068 (The Granger Collection)

Normans and English alike acclaimed William so loudly that the Norman soldiers on guard outside the abbey, fearing a riot, began to set fire to some nearby houses.

The Conquest Consolidated

To an extent, William abided by his promises, but it soon became clear that more than words would be required to pacify his new kingdom. In the months and years following the coronation, many English refused to submit to him or revolted against his rule. The Scandinavians too, despite their calamitous defeat at Stamford Bridge, continued to attempt new invasions of England. To complicate matters, the kingdom of France and the county of Anjou were gradually recovering their former strength, and William had to devote much of his energy to continental campaigning to protect his Norman duchy. In short, William's new Anglo-Norman state was threatened by many hostile forces, both internal and external, and his energy was taxed to the limit in the defense of his far-flung dominions.

During the five years following the Conquest, William and his magnates had to cope with a series of English rebellions, some of them coordinated with amphibious attacks from Scandinavia. William of Malmesbury, writing several decades later, comments on the savage measures the Conqueror took in defense of his crown:

> Perhaps the king's behavior can be excused if he was at times quite severe with the English, for he found scarcely any of them faithful. This fact so irritated his fierce mind that he took from the greater of them first their wealth, then their land, and finally, in some instances, their lives.

In the course of these revolts Edwin and Morcar turned against the Conqueror, and both lost their lives. A hoodlum named Hereward entrenched himself against William on the Isle of Ely and plundered the surrounding East Anglian countryside but eventually succumbed to the might of the Normans. Despite his brutal sack of Peterborough Abbey, Hereward later became a glamorous figure in English patriotic legend.

William used both kindness and cruelty in consolidating his new realm, but his cruelty predominated. Obliged to besiege the town of Exeter, he allowed its citizens to surrender on generous terms. But he replied to a major revolt in Yorkshire with a campaign of ruthless devastation, reducing vast areas of that once-prosperous county to wasteland in order to break northern England's will to resist. Contemporary writers speak of hundreds of rotting corpses in the Yorkshire countryside and thousands of starving refugees.

During these bitter years William's task was rendered all the more difficult by the fact that he had to divide his time between England and Normandy. His ultimate success in subduing England was due to several interrelated factors: (1) English opposition was never properly coordinated; almost from the beginning William was able to summon substantial portions of the English fyrd to fight in his behalf against English rebels. (2) While William was gaining power in pre-Conquest Normandy, he had won the firm support of a rising new aristocracy; after the Conquest he could usually depend on these powerful Norman aristocrats, many of whom were his kinsmen, to defend his interests in both Normandy and England. As holders of vast estates in the conquered land, they had both the power and the motivation to support the Norman regime. (3) William himself exhibited remarkable energy and resourcefulness in these years and demonstrated an almost uncanny ability to buy off his enemies, win their loyalty through generous terms, or terrorize them with his cruelty, as the occasion might demand. (4) Both William and his aristocratic followers built numerous castles in England. These fortresses, which had long been a characteristic feature of the Norman landscape, were smaller, tougher, and far more abundant than the earlier English burghs. Unlike the burghs, the Norman castles were designed to house only a garrison of knights (and in some instances a noble household), not an urban population. Indeed, the Normans often erected their castles within the walls of Anglo-Saxon burghs. Most of the castles built immediately after the Conquest were crude by later standards, often consisting of an earthen mound encircled by a moat and surmounted by a square wooden tower within a palisade (see page 99). But they were nevertheless exceedingly difficult to capture by assault. They became bastions of Norman power and stark symbols of Norman authority in the conquered realm.

The Anglo-Saxon revolts ended around 1071. Thereafter the English were loyal to William and his successors, and in later years the Norman kings often employed Englishmen to help suppress rebellions by Norman barons. Nevertheless, even if the Conqueror did intend in 1066 to allow members of the Anglo-Saxon aristocracy to share the wealth and governance of England with his Norman followers, the revolts of 1066–1071

IRELAND

IRISH SEA

SCOTLAND
Melrose •
Jedburgh •
Tyne R.
• Tynemouth
Newcastle
Durham •
Tees R.
Richmond •
• Whitby
Oure R.
• York
Gt. • Stamford
Fulford • Bridge
Ribble R.
Pontefract •
E N G L A N D
Chester •
Rhuddlan •
Degannwy •
Nottingham •
Trent R.
• Lincoln
W A L E S
Shrewsbury •
Montgomery •
• Crowland
Lichfield • • Thorney
Peterborough • • Thetford
• Elmham
• Norwich
Severn R.
Warwick •
Huntingdon • • Ely
Northampton • • Eye
• Pakenham
Hereford •
Worcester •
• Evesham
Winchcomb •
Gloucester •
• Cambridge
• Clare
Usk R.
St.David's •
Berkhamsted •
• St.Albans
Thames R.
Bristol •
Malmesbury •
Wallingford •
Dorchester •
West-
minster
London •
Rochester •
• Canterbury
Glastonbury •
Montacute •
Wells •
Salisbury •
Winchester •
Ramsey •
Battle •
• Dover
• Romney
Exeter •
Sherborne •
Bosham •
Chichester •
Selsey
• Hastings
Pevensey •
Isle of Wight

NORTH
SEA

Bruges •
F L A N D E R S
• Ghent
Wissant •
• St.Bertin's
Boulogne •

ARTOIS

St.Valéry •
PONTHIEU

English Channel

Rouen •
• Gisors
Bayeux • • Dives
Coutances • • Caen
Avranches • Falaise •
Dinan • • Dol
• Domfront
Gael • • Rennes
B R I T T A N Y
N O R M A N D Y
• Evreux
Mantes • • Paris
Alençon •
• Bellême
• Chartres
M A I N E
LeMans •
• Blois
BLOIS
Angers • • Tours
A N J O U
T O U R A I N E
P O I T O U
• Poitiers
A Q U I T A I N E

Rhine R.

Meuse R.

Oise R.

Seine R.

FRENCH

ROYAL

DEMESNE

F R A N C E

Loire R.

ENGLAND
AND NORMANDY
AFTER 1066

forced him to adopt a thoroughgoing policy of Normanization. As a consequence of this royal policy, and of a vast amount of Norman baronial bullying and landgrabbing, the Anglo-Saxon aristocracy was virtually disinherited. The spoils of the Conquest passed almost entirely to the king, his great Norman nobles, and other continental lords who had supported the invasion. Not only was the Anglo-Saxon secular aristocracy dispossessed; the great abbeys and bishoprics of England also passed, with few exceptions, into the hands of Norman prelates. Never again in its history would England experience such a revolutionary change in its power structure.

The effect of the Norman Conquest on England has long been one of the most hotly contested issues in English medieval scholarship. That it resulted in a transformation of aristocratic society there can be no question, for it brought to power a French-speaking nobility accustomed to knightly cavalry warfare and castle building, different in many respects from the aristocracy of Anglo-Saxon times. But the new aristocracy, powerful though it was, constituted only a tiny fraction of the population. What of the rest?

English towns were growing in size and economic importance before the Conquest and continued to grow after it. On the whole they seem to have been little affected by the dynastic and aristocratic revolution, except for a heavy migration of Norman merchants and artisans into English towns and a large influx of Jews from Rouen into the city of London. If commerce with Scandinavia declined, commerce with the Continent increased. So although the century or two following William's invasion witnessed an extensive growth in towns and commerce, this expansion was a product not of the Norman Conquest but of the vast economic upsurge that was affecting all Europe.

Peasant life, too, went on much as before. In the long run, the Norman Conquest tended to make the peasantry more uniform than in Anglo-Saxon times, raising the status of slaves and lowering that of freeholders. Gradually, both were absorbed into the middle range of villeins (dependent farmers) and were brought increasingly under the jurisdiction of manorial lords. More and more peasants were tied to their land and obliged to give a portion of their produce to their lord and to work certain days of the week on his demesne. But such changes occurred slowly and are difficult to trace with certainty. Eventually the buoyant economy of twelfth-century Europe brought a gradual rise in the wealth and status of peasants, both in England and on the Continent.

Architecturally, the Norman Conquest brought visible and impressive changes to the face of the land. Besides the numerous small wooden castles on artificial mounds, the Normans erected castles of monumental proportions—great square keeps with heavy stone walls, such as the Conqueror's Tower of London, Henry I's huge tower within the ancient Roman fortification at Portchester (page 108), and Castle Hedingham, erected in the twelfth century by the de Vere earls of Oxford (page 108).

Under the Conqueror and his sons, countless churches rose in the Norman Romanesque style, which had already been introduced into England in Edward the Confessor's Westminster Abbey. Almost every English

Castle Hedingham, Essex A great baronial castle built in the 1140s by the de Vere earls of Oxford. (A. F. Kersting)

Portchester Castle A great stone keep of the early twelfth century (bottom right) stands at a corner of a larger defensive work built by the Romans some 800 years earlier to protect the "Saxon Shore." (Aerofilms Ltd.)

Gloucester Cathedral A view of the Norman cathedral's arcade arches. (Dr. Martin Hürlimann)

cathedral[2] was rebuilt after 1066 in the new fashion, along with a great many village and abbey churches. In the early post-Conquest days the style was heavy and stark, but by the opening years of the twelfth century it was becoming more decorative. Stonemasons carved complex geometrical designs around portals and arches. Interiors were dark but painted in bright colors and often decorated with frescoes, some of which survive to this day. As architects grew in skill and daring, wooden roofs gave way to stone vaulting. Much of this Norman construction still stands: in small churches such as Iffley and Tickencote (page 111), and in large ones such as Norwich, Durham, Tewkesbury, and Gloucester (above). Their thick walls, columns, and round-arched arcades, their solid towers and dominating proportions, evoke a feeling of strength unique in English architecture, bearing witness even now to the power of the Normans.

Yet in architecture, as in so many other areas, major changes would surely have come to England even if Harold had won at Hastings. The Romanesque style was spreading across Western Europe in the later eleventh century, although not always with the massive proportions favored by the Normans. The Norman Conquest occurred toward the beginning of a notable epoch of European expansion—economic, political, military, reli-

---

[2] Technically, a cathedral is the headquarters of a bishop and his diocese, not simply a big church.

gious, cultural, and intellectual.[3] This creative surge has been termed "the renaissance of the twelfth century," but in fact it affected the entire period between the mid-eleventh century and the late thirteenth—the period conventionally called the High Middle Ages. France was the core of this remarkable cultural development—the source of Gothic architecture, the site of the great University of Paris, the home of many of medieval Europe's most distinguished scholars and writers, and the birthplace of the Crusades and related military adventures that expanded the frontiers of Western Christendom. It has been suggested that because the culture of the High Middle Ages was preeminently French, the conquest of England by a French duchy had the effect of making England much more susceptible to the creative trends of the era. This is an attractive theory, but it should not be pressed too far. Ties with the Continent had been strong ever since the conversion of England to Christianity. With or without the Norman connection, England would have been deeply influenced by the culture of high-medieval Europe.

One must keep this fact in mind when turning to the problem of Norman influence on the English Church. William came to England with the blessing of the reform papacy on his head and holy relics around his neck. The papacy objected to Harold's archbishop, the usurper Stigand, and in time William had him deposed. Stigand's successor was a skillful ecclesiastical statesman named Lanfranc—a noted scholar, abbot of the newly founded Norman ducal abbey of St. Etienne in Caen, and one of William's most trusted advisers. Under Archbishop Lanfranc the English Church began a thoroughgoing reform in keeping with recent policies of the papal court. Lanfranc and his kingdom-wide synods banned simony—the buying or selling of church offices—and prohibited the marriage of clergymen, a practice long uncanonical but widespread nevertheless (the custom of clerical marriage proved exceedingly difficult to uproot). New monasteries were founded, old ones were reformed, and cathedral clergy began to follow more stringent rules. Finally, William issued an ordinance that expanded the judicial authority of bishops in England, thereby contributing to the development in the following century of a highly organized system of ecclesiastical courts separate from the courts of shire and hundred.

One might well conclude that the Norman Conquest had a momentous effect on the English Church, bringing its practices closely into line with the notions of continental reformers. But it could be argued, on the other hand, that church reform would soon have come to England even without

---

[3] The bibliography on the High Middle Ages is immense. See in particular Charles H. Haskins, *The Renaissance of the Twelfth Century* (Cambridge, Mass., 1927); Sir Richard Southern, *The Making of the Middle Ages* (New Haven, 1953); Christopher Brooke, *The Twelfth Century Renaissance* (London, 1969); C. Warren Hollister, *The Twelfth-Century Renaissance* (New York, 1969); Robert L. Benson and Giles Constable, eds., *Renaissance and Renewal in the Twelfth Century* (Cambridge, Mass., 1982); Robert S. Lopez, *The Commercial Revolution of the Middle Ages* (Englewood Cliffs, N.J., 1971); M.-D. Chenu, *Nature, Man and Society in the Twelfth Century* (Chicago, 1968); and Alexander Murray, *Reason and Society in the Middle Ages* (Oxford, 1978).

Chancel Arch, Tickencote Church, Rutland The arch exemplifies the exuberant decoration of late-Norman Romanesque architecture. (The Ancient Art & Architecture Collection)

the Norman Conquest. The greatest of the eleventh-century reformers, Pope Gregory VII, rose to the papal throne only in 1073; it was not until his pontificate that the reform movement attained its full momentum. Gregory VII's reform policies were bound to affect England, and the most that can be said of the Norman Conquest in this respect is that it hastened the process.

King William and Archbishop Lanfranc were by no means as extreme in their advocacy of church reform as Gregory VII. He and many of the reform cardinals who surrounded him in Rome were convinced that such evils as simony and clerical wives or girlfriends reflected a more basic flaw in Christian society. To these reformers it was profoundly wrong that the appointment of clergy should be in the hands of lay lords, as had long been the case in Western Europe. In the tenth and eleventh centuries it was customary for kings and dukes to select their archbishops, for counts to select their bishops, and for manorial lords to select their parish priests. Indeed, until the 1050s it was by no means uncommon for the Holy Roman emperors to appoint popes. To lay lords, control of the Church seemed essential to their power, for the Church held vast tracts of land and church-men often occupied key positions in the administrative and military systems of secular governments. But Gregory VII and his supporters insisted that the Church should assume its proper position at the head of society. Spirit, they argued, is greater than matter, and the spiritual authority of the Church ought to take precedence over the worldly authority of kings and magnates. Accordingly, clerics should judge the laity, not the reverse, and the Church should be supreme in the Christian commonwealth. Only then could Christian society achieve its rightful order.

The gulf between papal and secular opinion on this crucial matter resulted in a protracted and sometimes violent struggle. Pope Gregory VII, who had long fought simony and clerical marriage, raised the explosive issue of lay control in 1075 by issuing a formal ban against lay investiture. This ban, and the bitter Investiture Controversy that followed, focused on the ceremony by which a bishop was invested in his see. Traditionally, a lay lord formally bestowed on the initiate bishop a ring, symbolic of his marriage to the Church, and a staff, symbolic of his pastoral duties as shepherd of his Christian flock. Symbols and rituals had profound meaning in the Middle Ages, and in forbidding lay lords to invest new bishops with the ring and staff, Gregory VII was in fact striking at the vital principle of lay control of the clergy.

Because Gregory's chief opponent in the Investiture Controversy was Henry IV, king of Germany and prospective Holy Roman emperor, the fiery pope was not in a position to press the issue in England or Normandy. He could not fight all Europe at once. William the Conqueror, who had no intention of loosening his grip on the Anglo-Norman Church, received deferential treatment as a friend of the papacy and sincere opponent of ecclesiastical corruption. The issue of lay investiture did not explode in England until a generation later. During the Conqueror's reign it remained dormant.

Nevertheless, certain tensions did arise in Anglo-papal relations. William I and Gregory VII were both dedicated to church reform, but they had radically different ideas on the question of ecclesiastical supremacy. Gregory assumed that the preeminent spiritual position he claimed for the papacy carried with it broad secular powers. He persuaded a number of important Christian princes to acknowledge that they were papal vassals— that the pope was their "overlord." Indeed, he demanded the allegiance or "fealty" of the Conqueror himself, along with a request for the resumption of a papal tax known as Peter's Pence. William replied politely but firmly:

> Your legate, Hubert, Most Holy Father, coming to me on your behalf, has admonished me to profess allegiance to you and your successors, and to think better regarding the money which my predecessors were wont to send to the Church of Rome. I have consented to the one but not to the other. I have not consented to pay fealty, nor will I now, because I never promised it, nor do I find that my predecessors ever paid it to your predecessors.[4]

With this assertion, the issue was abruptly closed. The reform of the English Church proceeded, but always under strict royal supervision.

---

[4] From the translation in David C. Douglas and George W. Greenaway, eds., *English Historical Documents*, II, 2nd ed. (London, 1981), pp. 693–694.

The Problem of Feudalization

One of the most hotly contested scholarly problems relating to the Norman Conquest is the question of whether William the Conqueror introduced a "feudal revolution" into England—that is, whether the new Norman aristocracy established a network of feudal institutions in a previously nonfeudal land.[5] Scholars were once inclined toward the view that feudalism developed gradually in eleventh- and twelfth-century England, and that the Norman Conquest merely hastened a development that was basically inevitable. During much of the present century, however, the opposite view has prevailed: feudalism was introduced by the Normans quite suddenly, pre-Conquest England was fundamentally nonfeudal, and without Norman intervention it would probably have remained so. Today this feudal-revolution hypothesis is accepted by many scholars but questioned by others.

In order to understand the problem, one must explore carefully the nature of medieval feudalism. At heart, feudalism consisted of a network of personal and territorial relationships between members of a warrior aristocracy. It combined the old Germanic notion of the loyalty of a comitatus member to his lord with the early medieval concept of service in return for the holding of land. In its developed form, feudalism involved a relationship between two warriors—a lord and a vassal. The lord granted a parcel of land to his vassal and undertook to protect the vassal's interests. The vassal, in return, gave his allegiance (homage and fealty) to his lord and agreed to render him services of various sorts—most notably, knightly military service. The estate granted by the lord to his vassal was known as a fief or *feudum*—from which our word *feudal* is derived.

Feudalism was emerging in portions of France during the ninth and tenth centuries, at a time when Frankish military tactics were placing much emphasis on the heavily armed horseman. The cavalryman, or knight, required a fine horse, arms and armor, and a great deal of training in the art of mounted combat. In order to support such warriors, in an age when money was scarce, a lord might simply feed and maintain them in his own household. But gradually it became common for a king or a magnate to "pay" his knights by granting them land in return for their service.

---

[5] On this issue, see C. Warren Hollister, *The Military Organization of Norman England* (Oxford, 1965) and, by the same author, *Monarchy, Magnates, and Institutions in the Anglo-Norman World* (London, 1986), pp. 1–16. The classic account of the Norman Conquest as "feudal revolution" is Sir Frank Stenton, *The First Century of English Feudalism, 1066–1166* 2nd ed. (Oxford, 1961). Radically different views are expressed in H. G. Richardson and G. O. Sayles, *The Governance of Mediaeval England from the Conquest to Magna Carta* (Edinburgh, 1963), pp. 22–135. All the various points of view are represented in C. Warren Hollister, ed., *The Impact of the Norman Conquest* (New York, 1969). A good, fearlessly opinionated summary is R. Allen Brown, *Origins of English Feudalism* (London, 1973). See, finally, two contending articles with the same title, "The Introduction of Knight Service into England": John Gillingham, *Anglo-Norman Studies*, 4 (1982): 53–64; and Sir James Holt, *Anglo-Norman Studies*, 6 (1984): 89–106.

The practice of paying for service with land was by no means limited to the military sphere. The tenure-service relationship extended also to the fields of administration, justice, and even farming. A great landholder was expected, in return for his wealth in land, to assume the essential functions of public administration and to operate courts of law, as well as to provide knights for the army of his overlord. A villein, in return for his right to farm a particular plot, was required to contribute his labor on certain days of the week to the tilling of his lord's demesne land. Thus, in a money-poor society, wage service was secondary in importance to tenure service.

With the decline of central authority in Carolingian Francia during the Viking Age, the desperate need for local defense against the raids of the Norsemen resulted in an expansion and intensification of the lord-vassal relationship. Independent freeholders were forced to seek the protection of local lords, often becoming their vassals and giving them their lands. The lord would then return the land to his new vassal to be held as a dependent tenure in return for homage, fealty, and knightly service. Or, if the free-holder owned only a small farm, he might find himself sinking into the ranks of the villeins (or serfs). It should be understood that the fief-holding vassal did not ordinarily labor on his own lands. He drew his wealth from the obligations of his villeins to pay him a proportion of their crops and to work on his demesne fields. A considerable social chasm separated vassals from villeins: the villein was not directly involved in the network of feudal relationships, which principally concerned the aristocracy. On the other hand, the aristocracy depended ultimately on the toil of its villeins. Without them, farms and fiefs would be valueless.

During the eleventh century, France was beginning to regain a measure of political coherence. The power of the crown remained restricted to a modest territory in north central France embracing Paris and Orleans, and the French monarchs exerted little or no authority over the lands of their dukes and counts. But the regional principalities were themselves gradually developing stronger central governments. By the late eleventh or early twelfth century the counts and dukes of such principalities as Anjou, Champagne, Blois, Flanders, Poitou, and—above all—Normandy were succeeding in bringing their own magnates and lords of castles under control. If they could not eliminate private war in their dominions, they could at least reduce it considerably. By establishing networks of castles and exploiting various public and feudal revenues, they acquired the resources with which to dominate their principalities.

As a host of detailed regional studies have made clear, feudal arrangements varied enormously across eleventh-century France. In some principalities, feudal relationships were scarcely detectable; in others they coexisted with entirely different arrangements—lands held unconditionally, landless knights supported in noble households, political power based on public sovereign authority (rooted in the old Carolingian Empire) rather than on private lordship over vassals, and loyalties based on kinship or wages rather than homage and land tenure. These variations and qualifications have prompted some thoughtful historians to reject all use of the term *feudalism* on the grounds that it conveys a misleading sense of uniformity and universality. But one can raise the same objections to the use of many other general concepts: "democracy," for example, occurs in a great variety of forms and is sometimes said to exist where it does not. *Democracy* is a convenient term, nonetheless, and our world leaders today could not do without it. Similarly, as the distinguished medieval historian Marjorie Chibnall recently and wisely observed, the total expurgation of the term *feudalism* from our historical vocabulary is "too drastic."[6]

The student of English history can avoid much of the confusion over differing sorts of feudalism by concentrating on Normandy at the time of the Conquest. There, William the Conqueror's magnates rendered him homage for their estates and performed a number of other feudal services. By at least the early twelfth century, the obligations that a Norman vassal owed his lord had become quite explicit. Norman magnates were by then rendering a specific number of knights for service in the duke's army or in his castles, and they demanded similarly specific service from their own vassals. Often a magnate's vassals owed him, collectively, far more knights than he owed the duke. Whatever the case, the quantity of knight service eventually became fixed at all levels.

Besides supplying knights, a Norman vassal was obliged to join his lord's retinue on important ceremonial occasions and to serve in his court. Every important lord had a court, in which he exercised jurisdiction over his vassals and heard appeals from subvassals. The vassal also owed his lord certain monetary payments known as *aids* to be rendered on special occasions, such as the marriage of the lord's eldest daughter or the knighting of his eldest son. Vassals were also obliged to pay the lord's ransom should he be captured by an enemy.

The authority of a Norman lord over his vassals was further emphasized in four additional privileges: (1) the right to veto the marriage of a vassal's widow or heiress to his fief; (2) the right to occupy a fief during the minority of a deceased vassal's son and to serve as guardian of the young heir; (3) the right to collect a payment, known as *relief*, when the fief passed from a deceased vassal to his heir; and (4) the right to repossess the fief should the vassal die without heirs. All these rights and obligations became customary in post-Conquest England.

By the time of the Norman Conquest, feudal practices were spreading into parts of southern France, eastern Spain, and the lands in southern Italy that Norman military adventurers were bringing under their control. In the century after 1066 feudal customs made their way into Germany, the Crusader states of the Holy Land, and many other districts of Western Christendom, each region exhibiting its own peculiar characteristics. Most scholars would add that the post-Conquest century witnessed the advent of feudal-

---

6 Marjorie Chibnall, *Anglo-Norman England, 1066–1166* (Oxford, 1986), p. 2. On the other side of the battlefront, see Susan Reynolds, *Kingdoms and Communities in Western Europe, 900–1300* (Oxford, 1984), p. 9: ". . . 'feudalism' and 'feudal' are meaningless terms which are unhelpful in understanding medieval society."

A Knight, with Horse and Lance-flag, Does Homage to His Lord   From the Westminster Psalter, mid-thirteenth century. (Reproduced with permission of the British Library)

ism in England. It is beyond doubt that post-Conquest England was a feudal state; but scholars differ as to whether the genesis of English feudalism was sudden or gradual, and whether or not post-Conquest English feudalism was anticipated significantly in the development of Anglo-Saxon institutions.

At first glance, one is struck by the fundamental differences between Anglo-Saxon England and feudal Normandy. The shire and hundred courts, the danegeld, and the five-hide fyrd were all basically public institutions of a sovereign monarchy, whereas the feudal armies, feudal courts, and feudal aids were private in nature—products of a system in which privileges and responsibilities previously exercised by a royal government had become associated with private lordships. However, it is unsafe to stress this distinction too strongly. The public orientation of Anglo-Saxon institutions had been strongly modified by the spread of private lordship. A number of great lords—bishops, abbots, and lay magnates—received royal land charters granting not only extensive territories but also important jurisdictional rights. Many Anglo-Saxon lords operated hundred courts within their territories and led their own contingents of the fyrd. Even so, the courts continued to function as units of a kingdom-wide legal system that remained fundamentally public, and the fyrd was still, in both theory and practice, a royal army whose role was limited to the defense of the realm and service to the king. There were exceptions—such as the military confrontation between Earl Godwin and King Edward the Confessor in 1052—but Anglo-Saxon lords rarely led their fyrds against one another. In pre-Conquest England, unlike France, private war was uncommon. Even in Edward the Confessor's final years, when Harold Godwinson attended to the defense of the realm, the chroniclers often took the trouble to point out that Earl Harold led the fyrd "by the king's order."

The lord-vassal relationship of feudal Normandy undoubtedly existed in essence in pre-Conquest England. The practice of thegns and other men promising their loyalty—"commending themselves"—to lords was widespread, and the intensity of such relationships is clearly demonstrated in the devotion of Ealdorman Byrhtnoth's men at the battle of Maldon. No French lord could have asked for better vassals than these. In short, the personal relationship between lord and follower harked back to a Germanic tradition shared by both England and France. But although the Anglo-Saxons had their own equivalent of the vassal, it is doubtful that they possessed anything resembling the fief. The personal aspect of feudalism existed in Anglo-Saxon England; the territorial aspect probably did not.

Whether or not William the Conqueror can correctly be credited with having established "feudal" relationships in England, he clearly instituted a far more thoroughgoing feudal regime than England had known before. He and his great barons dotted England with castles and introduced private baronial courts alongside the older courts of hundred and shire. As a conqueror, he was able to initiate the significant concept, unknown in either Anglo-Saxon England or pre-Conquest Normandy, that all the land belonged either directly or indirectly to the ruler. Operating on this philosophy, and angered by the protracted English rebellions, he seized huge numbers of estates. Some of them he added to the royal demesne—the territory controlled directly by the crown. The remainder he granted as fiefs to trusted military followers. In the course of this vast process of redistribution, the lands of several thousand thegns were consolidated into large fiefs held by about 180 great Anglo-Norman barons—tenants-in-chief who held their land directly from King William. Most of these fiefs consisted of widely scattered estates rather than compact territorial blocks. And although the scattering of baronial estates had the effect in later years of diminishing local particularism, William apparently had no such object in mind. The scattering seems quite accidental, arising from the facts that (1) pre-Conquest estates themselves tended to be scattered (although to a lesser degree) and (2) William distributed lands in piecemeal fashion as the estates of one rebellious Anglo-Saxon lord after another fell successively into his hands.

By the 1070s William had assigned arbitrary quotas of knights' service to nearly all the lands outside the royal demesne, whether held by secular or ecclesiastical vassals. These quotas were sufficient to provide the king with a total force of about 5,000 knights. Aside from a handful of exempt monasteries (such as the Conqueror's own Battle Abbey), every English tenant-in-chief now owed a specific number of knights to the crown. In the years that followed, William's great vassals undertook to support the knights they owed the crown by creating smaller fiefs from portions of their larger ones. In the course of this process of "subinfeudation," English aristocratic society took the form of a complex chain of lord-vassal relationships.

Feudalism in Norman England, being the product of a single will, was far more orderly and thorough than its French counterparts. Above all, it was rigorously subordinated to the interests of the ruler, who was at once sovereign king and chief lord at the apex of the feudal pyramid. This lord-king—*dominus rex*—exerted a control over his vassals such as France had never known. In part, this authority was a product of the Conqueror's own forceful personality, but it also owed much to his skillful use of Anglo-Saxon traditions. He preserved the danegeld, as one might expect, and exploited it thoroughly as a unique and highly lucrative source of royal revenue, having discovered to his delight that all he had to do was to declare a danegeld and cartloads of money came rolling into the royal treasury. He also preserved the Old English fyrd and summoned it to his service on occasion. He tempered the centrifugal forces of feudalism by calling on the Old English custom of universal allegiance to the crown. In England, the subvassal owed primary loyalty not to his immediate lord but to the supreme overlord—the lord-king. In 1086, William summoned the more important landholders of England, tenants-in-chief and subtenants alike, to a great assembly at Salisbury to receive their oaths of allegiance. In doing so, he was following a venerable English tradition which had been exemplified long before in the oath King Edmund demanded of his subjects. Further, William permitted his great vassals to build castles, as they had been accustomed to do in Normandy. But, recognizing that these fortresses were potential centers of insurrection as well as strong points in England's defensive system, he allowed them to be built only by royal license. Finally, still following Anglo-Saxon tradition, he took much of the fun out of feudalism by prohibiting private war. The knights of Norman England, like the soldiers of the Anglo-Saxon fyrd, were to serve the king alone.

Thus, although deeply influenced by the royal centralization achieved by the Anglo-Saxons, England acquired greater cohesion under William the Conqueror than ever before. In a very real sense, the Anglo-Norman monarchy was greater than the sum of its parts, for the English and Norman traditions on which it was built were strengthened and enlarged by the Conqueror himself. William's claim to ultimate ownership of all English land, which went far beyond the claims of any prince in France, was equally unprecedented in England.

Feudal relationships had emerged long before to meet the needs of a money-poor, politically fragmented society. Such relationships were now adapted to a kingdom ruled by a strong monarchy—a land that enjoyed a vigorous commercial life and an expanding money economy. Thus, the feudalism of Norman England gave way increasingly, as time went on, before the steady growth of royal government and the progressive substitution of wage service for tenure service. The Conqueror himself had made good use of mercenary soldiers in his great invasion, and as the decades passed, mercenaries—serving the king as a regularly paid standing army of royal household knights—became steadily more important to the English military system. Furthermore, before the end of the eleventh century it was becoming customary for some tenants to pay money to the crown in lieu of military service. This tax—known as *scutage* or "shield money"—was usually employed by the post-Conquest kings to pay the wages of mercenaries. With the development of scutage, the fundamental feudal obligation of knightly service was converted into a new source of royal revenue. Feudal relationships persisted—and the aristocracy remained powerful throughout the Middle Ages and long beyond—but the basic principle of tenure service was gradually dissolving.

The Administrative Contributions of William the Conqueror

With a royal demesne twice the size of Edward the Confessor's, with danegeld revenues flowing in regularly, and with the backing of a loyal aristocracy, William ruled England with unprecedented authority. And, like his Anglo-Saxon predecessors, he ruled with the advice of a royal council. The council of the Norman kings—the *curia regis*—represents a blending of two parallel institutions: the ducal court of Normandy and the Anglo-Saxon Witenagemot. The *Anglo-Saxon Chronicle* describes William's counselors as his "Witan"; like the Old English Witenagemot, the Anglo-Norman curia regis could be either the small and more-or-less permanent council of household officials and intimate friends, or the larger and more formal council augmented by the presence of the great magnates and prelates. But it would be profitless to argue that the curia regis was more English than Norman. The councils of England and Normandy were similar, and William's large, formal councils, attended by the greater tenants-in-chief, were predominantly Norman in personnel.

While on their numerous visits to Normandy, the Norman kings left the administration of England in the hands of some trusted subordinate who was empowered to act in the king's name. William the Conqueror delegated his authority to different people at different times—to kinsmen, to loyal magnates, to a trustworthy household official, or to a powerful churchman such as Archbishop Lanfranc. In subsequent reigns, this viceregal authority came to be assigned permanently to a particular individual who, in the later twelfth century, bore the title of "chief justiciar." But the Conqueror, with his boundless energy, preferred to rule for himself or to delegate authority on an ad hoc basis. No one person shared William's authority for any significant time.

The vigor of English royal government under William the Conqueror, unmatched in Western Christendom, is illustrated vividly in his greatest administrative achievement: the Domesday survey. As the *Anglo-Saxon Chronicle* describes it:

> The king had important deliberations and deep discussions with his council about this country, how it was peopled and with what sorts of men. Then he sent his men all over England into every shire and had them determine how many hundreds of hides there were in each shire, and how much land and cattle the king himself had in the country, and what annual dues he ought to have from each shire. He also had recorded how much land belonged to his archbishops, his bishops, his abbots, and his earls, and— though I relate it at too great length—what and how much everybody had who was a landholder in England, in land or in cattle, and how much money it was worth. So very thoroughly did he have it investigated that there was not a single hide or virgate [a quarter of a hide] of land, or even—it is shameful to record but it did not seem shameful to him to do—one ox or one cow or one pig which was omitted from his record; and all these records were afterwards brought to him.

The Domesday survey, later consolidated into two large volumes known as Domesday Book, would have challenged any modern government. For its time, it was altogether unique. Although by no means free of errors and omissions (London and several other towns are left out), it is nevertheless an essentially trustworthy and immensely valuable historical source. It is organized by shires and, within each shire, by the estates of the royal demesne and the estates of royal vassals. Although cows and pigs were omitted from the final record, Domesday Book undertakes to list the name of every manor, its assessment in hides, its value both in 1066 and at the time of the survey (1086), and the number and social status of its tenants. Any social, economic, or institutional history of Saxon or Norman England must begin with this astonishing survey.

The Conqueror died in 1087. Injured while in the midst of a continental campaign, he was brought to Rouen, the chief city of Normandy. There he settled his affairs, made his last confession, and died. He had planned originally to leave England and Normandy to his eldest son, Robert Curthose ("short-boots"). But Curthose had rebelled against his father and was, indeed, in rebellion at the time of the Conqueror's death. William would probably have left both England and Normandy to his second son, William Rufus ("red-faced"), but he had earlier formally commended the duchy to Robert Curthose in order to stabilize the succession, and the Norman barons had affirmed this commendation by rendering homage and fealty to Curthose. These rituals could not easily be undone, and therefore the Conqueror was obliged to divide his dominions, leaving Normandy to Robert Curthose and England to William Rufus—King William II. To his youngest son, Henry—the future King Henry I—the Conqueror granted a treasure of £5,000 (the equivalent of several million dollars today). The struggles of these three sons over the next two decades resulted finally, as we shall see, in the reunification of England and Normandy.

Of William the Conqueror's ability there can be no question; but judgments of his character have varied widely. He enforced justice and kept the peace, and he was evidently faithful to his wife, but he was also avaricious and could be savagely cruel. A modern biographer describes him as "admirable; unlovable; dominant; distinct."[7] A similar ambivalence is to be found in the judgment of a well-placed contemporary observer—an anonymous Anglo-Saxon monk who had once lived at William's court:

> This King William of whom we speak was a very wise man, and very powerful and more worshipful and stronger than any king before him. He was gentle to those good men who loved God, but stern beyond all measure to those who resisted his will. . . . And he was such a stern and violent man that no one dared go against his will. Earls who resisted him he placed in chains, bishops he deprived of their sees, abbots of their abbacies, and thegns he imprisoned. . . . Among other things we must not forget the good order he kept in the land, so that an honest man could traverse his kingdom unharmed with his bosom full of gold. No one dared kill another, however much he had wronged him, and if any man raped a woman he was immediately castrated. He ruled over England and by his cunning it was so investigated that there was not one hide of land in England that he did not know who owned it, and what it was worth, and then set it down in his record. . . . Certainly in his time people had much oppression and very many injuries:
>
> > He had castles built
> > And poor men hard oppressed.
> > The king was very stark
> > And took from his subjects many a mark
> > Of gold and more hundreds of pounds of silver,
> > That he took by weight and with great injustice
> > From his people—with little need for such a deed.
> > Into avarice did he fall,
> > And loved greediness above all . . .
> > Alas! Woe, that any man should go so proud,
> > And exalt himself and reckon himself above all men!
> > May almighty God show mercy on his soul,
> > And grant unto him forgiveness for his sins.

These things we have written about him, both good and bad, that good men may imitate his good points and entirely avoid the bad, and travel along the road that leads us to the kingdom of heaven.[8]

---

[7] Douglas, *William the Conqueror*, p. 376.

[8] From the *Anglo-Saxon Chronicle*, A.D. 1087.

5

Norman England: William II, Henry I, and Stephen

As the Conqueror lay dying at Rouen, William Rufus left for England with his father's blessing. Through the good offices of Archbishop Lanfranc he received the customary approval of a council of magnates, and the aged archbishop crowned him in Westminster Abbey on September 26, 1087.[1]

The Reign of William Rufus (1087–1100)

William Rufus was an even greater puzzle than his father. The monk William of Malmesbury describes him as

> ...squarely built, with a reddish complexion and yellow hair, an open countenance and multi-colored eyes, varied with glittering specks—of astonishing strength, though not very tall, and his stomach bulged out.

Elsewhere, Malmesbury remarks,

> When he was in public and in large assemblies, he wore a haughty look and darted his threatening eyes on those around him, and with pretended severity and fierce voice he would assail those who conversed with him. From fear of poverty and of the treachery of others, presumably, he was excessively devoted to money and to cruelty. In private, when he was dining with his intimate companions, he gave himself over to joking and mirth.

To illustrate Rufus's extravagance, Malmesbury tells of how he exploded in anger at a chamberlain for buying him a pair of boots worth only three shillings:

---

[1] For the period from William Rufus through John, see Austin Lane Poole, *From Domesday Book to Magna Carta* (2nd ed., Oxford, 1955). A comprehensive selection of sources in English translation can to be found in David C. Douglas and George W. Greenaway, eds., *English Historical Documents* II (2nd ed., London, 1981). The best of several fine medieval historians is William of Malmesbury, *Deeds of the Kings of England*, A. Giles, tr. (London, 1847); cf. Rodney Thomson, *William of Malmesbury* (Woodbridge, Suffolk, 1986). On William Rufus, see Frank Barlow, *William Rufus* (Berkeley, 1983) and C. Warren Hollister, *Monarchy, Magnates, and Institutions*, pp. 97–115, and "William Rufus, Henry I, and the Anglo-Norman Church," *Peritia: The Journal of the Medieval Academy of Ireland*, 6–7 (1987–1988), pp. 119–140.

"You son of a whore! Since when has the king worn such cheap boots? Go and bring me a pair worth a silver mark." The chamberlain went, and bringing the king a much cheaper pair than before, told him falsely that they cost as much as he had commanded. "Yes, indeed," said the king, "these suit the royal majesty!"

Rufus was said to have "feared God but little, man not at all." He scorned religion (except at such times as he feared imminent death), and he exploited the Church ruthlessly, demanding that prelates render him large gifts of money in order to retain the royal favor. Not surprisingly, Rufus earned a bad press among the monastic chroniclers. His itinerant court was described as a traveling den of iniquity: the courtiers looted food, drink, and property from the people of the countryside through which they journeyed, molested local wives and daughters, pillaged the goods of villagers (later selling them), got drunk on stolen liquor and, when they could drink no more, washed their horses with what was left or poured it onto the ground.

Rufus's courtiers dressed in the height of fashion, with

> . . . flowing hair and extravagant clothes; and a new kind of shoes was
> introduced, with points that curled upwards. Then the model for young
> men was to rival women in delicacy of person, to walk with mincing steps
> and loose gesture, half naked. . . . Troops of effeminate men and gangs of
> harlots followed the court.

On the other hand, even Rufus's enemies conceded that he was an excellent soldier and was as loyal to his trustworthy vassals and his knightly followers as he had earlier been to his father. Although remorseless in his financial exploitation of the English Church and people, he was generous to his military companions and prodigal in the wages and bounties he gave to his numerous mercenary knights.

Rufus ruled with a rod of iron. By inspiring fear in his subjects and maintaining the devotion of his lesser knights, he managed generally to keep peace in his land. The *Anglo-Saxon Chronicle* may perhaps have been exaggerating when it branded Rufus as "hated by almost all his people and odious to God," but other writers of the period were scarcely more sympathetic. William of Malmesbury described him as a man much pitied by churchmen for losing a soul they could not save, beloved by the mercenary soldiers for his innumerable gifts, but unlamented by the people because he caused the plundering of their property.

Rufus's reign had scarcely begun when, in 1088, many of his barons rebelled in favor of Duke Robert Curthose of Normandy—a much more passive and amiable man than his royal brother. The rebels sought, through armed force against the king, to reunite the Anglo-Norman state under Robert's relaxed, dull-witted rule. But Rufus kept the loyalty of the Church, some of the barons, and most of the English freeholders. In view of the above appraisals of his character, it may well be wondered why the Church and the English stood by him. They did so for two reasons. First, the reign was young, and Rufus had yet to make his abhorrent impression. He won the English with lavish promises of just taxes and good government, which he did not keep. Second, the Church and the English consistently favored strong government, however harsh, over the prospect of baronial anarchy (usually accompanied by a good deal of aristocratic bullying and land-grabbing). Consequently, the English fyrd, the military tenants of the bishoprics and monasteries, and the remaining loyal barons rallied to Rufus and enabled him to put down the rebellion. Another baronial insurrection in 1095 was suppressed in similar fashion (although Rufus barely escaped a baronial ambush), and for the final five years of his reign he ruled in peace.

As the Anglo-Saxon chronicler observed, Rufus, even more than his father, claimed ultimate control of all the English lands—"he claimed to be the heir of every man, cleric or lay." Accordingly, he denied the security of a normal succession to laymen and churchmen alike. A baronial heir could succeed to his father's estates only after paying, as a relief, whatever sum struck the king's fancy—and Rufus's reliefs were notoriously high. He exploited the feudal privilege of vetoing the marriage of a vassal's widow or female heir by literally selling her in marriage to the highest bidder. He abused the right of wardship by taking possession of the estates of minor heirs and milking them dry before the heirs came of age. He treated church lands the same way, keeping abbacies and bishoprics unfilled for scandalously long periods after the deaths of their former incumbents, in the meantime diverting their revenues into the royal treasury and selling off their capital resources (plows, timber, cattle, etc.).

Indeed, Rufus did not hesitate to deal in this manner even with the archbishopric of Canterbury. At Lanfranc's death in 1089, Rufus seized the vast Canterbury lands, plundered them pitilessly, and left the archbishopric empty for four years. It might well have remained vacant still longer, but in 1093 Rufus suffered a near-fatal illness. Fearing death, he heeded to the pressures of his lay and ecclesiastical subjects—pressures that had been building ever since Lanfranc's death—and appointed to the archbishopric of Canterbury the saintly and scholarly Anselm, a distinguished Italian churchman who had spent many years in Normandy as prior and then abbot of the great monastery of Bec.[2]

It is ironic that such an irreligious king should appoint such a holy and remarkable archbishop. St. Anselm was not only a man of profound piety; he was the foremost theologian of his age and perhaps the greatest philosopher in Western Christendom since St. Augustine of Hippo, whom he admired. St. Anselm's philosophical and theological works constitute the initial achievement in the intellectual awakening of the High Middle Ages.

---

[2] Sir Richard Southern, *Saint Anselm and His Biographer: A Study of Monastic Life and Thought* (2nd ed., Cambridge, 1987) is a thoughtful, perceptive study. For a more sympathetic and persuasive appraisal of Anselm's political acumen, see Sally N. Vaughn, *Anselm of Bec and Robert of Meulan: The Innocence of the Dove and the Wisdom of the Serpent* (Berkeley, 1987). The Anselm debate continues with Sir Richard Southern, *St. Anselm: A Portrait in a Landscape* (Cambridge, 1991).

He stood at the beginning of a philosophical flowering that culminated in the thirteenth century with the works of men such as St. Bonaventure and St. Thomas Aquinas.

A man of deep integrity, Anselm was prepared to cooperate, at least in part, with the revolutionary drive toward papal supremacy and ecclesiastical independence that Pope Gregory VII had pioneered. Anselm was in his early sixties at the time of his appointment, and he claimed to have accepted the archbishopric reluctantly, remarking that he was like a weak old sheep being yoked to an untamed bull (i.e., William Rufus). But as archbishop, Anselm was far from sheepish in his defense of the prerogatives of Canterbury, and he soon found himself at odds with Rufus on a multitude of issues. Anselm wished to go to Rome to receive the *pallium*—the symbol of his spiritual authority—from the reform pope, Urban II (Gregory VII's second successor). Rufus refused to let Anselm out of the kingdom and for a time refused to recognize the claims of Pope Urban over those of an anti-pope supported by the Holy Roman emperor. Most trying of all to Anselm, Rufus forbade him to hold kingdom-wide ecclesiastical councils, meetings that had previously provided the chief means by which the archbishops of Canterbury ruled and passed legislation for the English Church. Late in 1097, these and other difficulties forced Anselm to abandon England for exile in Italy and France, and Rufus resumed control of the Canterbury revenues. Anselm eventually returned to England, at the beginning of the next reign, but for the time being the Norman monarchy was rid of its troublesome saint.

Rufus's financial exactions were carried out by a loyal subordinate and thoroughly roguish churchman, Ranulf Flambard, whom the king had made first a royal chaplain and later bishop of Durham. Flambard was Rufus's man Friday, responsible for a variety of executive and legal tasks. He served briefly as the king's regent in England when Rufus was overseas. His primary function, however, was the raising of revenues for the king, and he performed that mission with such malicious ingenuity that he was soon roundly hated. On one occasion he summoned the English fyrd to Hastings supposedly for service overseas, collected ten shillings from every soldier, then sent them directly home.

Rufus, a man of limitless ambition, needed every penny that Flambard could collect. Once secure in his kingdom, Rufus undertook to conquer Normandy, but his plots and campaigns against Duke Robert Curthose met with only partial success. He brought portions of Normandy under his control through warfare and bribes, but he could not win it all. In 1096, however, Duke Robert was seized with crusading fervor in response to Pope Urban II's appeal to Western Christendom's nobility to drive the Muslims from the Holy Land. Having determined to participate in this First Crusade, Duke Robert was hindered by a lack of money to support a worthy knightly retinue on the long journey. Accordingly, in 1096 the two brothers struck a bargain: Robert Curthose pawned Normandy to Rufus for three years in return for 10,000 silver marks, which the king obtained by levying a double danegeld on his kingdom. Robert could go crusading well financed, and

William Rufus had Normandy at last. By all indications, he never intended to return it.

Rufus quickly transformed Robert's casually governed duchy into a centralized, tax-ridden state on the English pattern. He defended Normandy's frontiers and endeavored to expand them, and shortly before his death he seems to have been bargaining to receive Aquitaine in pawn from its crusade-bound duke. One contemporary writer suggested that Rufus even aspired to the throne of France.

But these schemes went unfulfilled. On August 2, 1100, Rufus was killed by an arrow while hunting in the New Forest—a vast royal hunting preserve in southern England that William the Conqueror had established by evicting a number of peasants and imposing severe restrictions on those who remained. The New Forest had become a symbol of the Conqueror's "tyranny," and contemporaries thought it fitting that his son should die there.

The Reign of Henry I (1100–1135)

Rufus was in his early forties when he was killed, and his abrupt death provoked a crisis in the royal succession. Since he had never married and left no children, the kingdom might well have passed to his elder brother, Robert Curthose. But the luckless Robert was only now returning from the Crusade, whereas the Conqueror's youngest son, Henry, was on the scene. Henry had been a member of Rufus's final hunting party, and some historians have suggested that Henry may have deliberately instigated Rufus's murder. But this is a wild guess, unsupported by evidence or by the slightest hint of fratricide in the contemporary sources.[3]

After Rufus's death, Henry moved swiftly and surely. He galloped to nearby Winchester, seized the royal treasure, won the approval of a hastily assembled royal council, and then dashed to London where he was crowned at Westminster Abbey on August 5, a mere three days after the shooting.[4] In preparation for Robert's return, Henry did everything in his power to win the support of his subjects. He sought to appease the barons and the Church by issuing an elaborate coronation charter, known in later years as the

---

[3] See the entertaining but wrongheaded reconstruction of the event by Duncan Grinnell-Milne, *The Killing of William Rufus* (Newton Abbott, 1968), which interprets the killing as a political murder plotted by Henry I. Even more unlikely is Margaret Murray's theory that it was a ritual slaying in accordance with the rites of witchcraft and done at Rufus's request (*God of the Witches*, London, 1951). The question is reexamined in C. Warren Hollister, "The Strange Death of William Rufus," *Speculum* 48 (1973): 637–653, reprinted in *Monarchy, Magnates, and Institutions*, pp. 59–75.

[4] Henry's seizure of the throne is often described as an act of usurpation. But the custom of the eldest son succeeding was by no means a fixed rule at this time. It had occurred only rarely in England over the previous 250 years and was directly violated in the successions of such kings as Alfred the Great and William Rufus. Since Rufus and Robert Curthose were both born before 1066, Henry claimed to be the only one of the three brothers born of a reigning king.

Charter of Liberties, in which he agreed to discontinue the predatory practices of William Rufus. Among other things, Henry promised to

> . . . neither sell nor put at farm nor, on the death of an archbishop, bishop, or abbot, take anything from a church's demesne or from its vassals during the interval before a successor is installed. . . . If any of my barons or earls or other tenants shall die, his heir shall not redeem his land as he did in my brother's time, but shall henceforth redeem it by a just and lawful relief. . . . And if the wife of one of my tenants survives her husband . . . I will not give her in marriage unless she herself consents.

Henry did not keep all of these campaign promises. It has been estimated that they would have cost him four or five thousand pounds a year—perhaps a quarter of the total royal revenue under Rufus—and Henry was no less parsimonious than his predecessors. The coronation charter was neither a prelude to constitutional monarchy nor an open act of royal generosity, but one of several gambits that Henry employed to gain needed support in the oncoming confrontation with his brother.

To win Anglo-Saxon and Scottish backing, the new king married a Scottish princess named Matilda, who was a direct descendant of the Old English royal family—a great-granddaughter of Ethelred the Unready's son, Edmund Ironside. Henry I courted popular opinion still further by imprison-

Queen Matilda, Wife of Henry I From the Golden Book of St. Albans. (Reproduced with permission of the British Library)

ing the detested Ranulf Flambard in the Tower of London. But early in 1101, Flambard managed a daring escape from the Tower, climbing down a rope that had been smuggled into his cell inside a wine keg. Slipping out of London with very sore hands, he hastened across the channel to Normandy and joined Robert Curthose, who had by now returned from the First Crusade and was eager to wrest England from his younger brother. Henry I, alarmed by the growing threat, sent letters into every shire confirming his coronation oath and requesting that all his free subjects swear to defend England against all men—and especially against Robert of Normandy.

In late July 1101, Robert Curthose led a large force across the Channel to Portsmouth, where he was joined by many Anglo-Norman barons who longed for the reunion of the two lands and the more carefree rule of the Norman duke.[5] Meanwhile Henry had assembled a sizeable army of his own, consisting chiefly of episcopal contingents, common knights, and a large force of native Englishmen (rather like Rufus's army of 1088; see pages 123–124). Although some barons had joined King Henry's army, the loyalty of many of them was uncertain. Henry seems to have placed great confidence in the English, and we are told that he took pains to instruct them personally in the techniques of fighting against mounted knights. One contemporary writer asserts that Henry's army would have quickly driven Robert's forces out of the country, but as it happened the issue was settled by negotiation. "The more discreet on each side"—evidently the barons—arranged a truce, realizing perhaps that a decisive royal victory would weaken their own position. Henry was happy to avoid the uncertainty of a pitched battle, and Curthose was left no choice but to settle for what he could get. The duke recognized Henry's royal title in return for an annuity of two thousand pounds (which Henry discontinued two years later).

With the settlement of 1101, the great crisis of the reign passed and Henry's throne was secure. In 1102 he put down one further rebellion, centering on the earldom of Shrewsbury on the Welsh frontier, and thereafter he ruled England unchallenged until his death in 1135. Indeed, the lands he confiscated in the wake of the uprisings of 1101 and 1102 served as an invaluable new source of royal revenue and patronage in the years ahead.

Having secured England, Henry turned to the conquest of Normandy. Paving his way with bribes to Norman barons and neighboring princes, he campaigned in Normandy in 1104 and 1105. At length, on September 28, 1106, his army met Duke Robert's in open battle near the Norman castle of Tinchebray and won an overwhelming victory. Robert Curthose himself was captured and languished in comfortable imprisonment for the next twenty-eight years until his death in 1134.

Contemporaries noted that the battle of Tinchebray occurred forty years to the day after William the Conqueror's landing at Pevensey Beach. By this "English conquest of Normandy," Henry became master of the

---

[5] On Robert Curthose, see C. W. David, *Robert Curthose, Duke of Normandy* (Cambridge, Mass., 1920), a skillful work of technical scholarship.

duchy, reuniting the Anglo-Norman state which the Conqueror had forged. Thenceforth Henry spent a good part of his time in Normandy. Occasionally he was obliged to defend the duchy against invasions by the king of France and the counts of Anjou and Flanders, usually accompanied by Norman baronial rebellions. For the most part, however, Normandy remained at peace under his firm rule. William of Malmesbury credits Henry with establishing peace in Normandy such as had never been known before, even under the rule of his imperious father, William the Conqueror.

By the time of Henry's victory at Tinchebray, another, related crisis of his early years as king was nearing resolution. At the beginning of his reign Henry, in keeping with his conciliatory policy, had invited the exiled Archbishop Anselm to return to England, but Henry and Anselm were at odds from the first. The king was willing to concede all the issues that had divided Anselm and Rufus, but Anselm raised new issues. Henry expected Anselm to render him the customary homage for the Canterbury estates (which owed him sixty knights), but the archbishop, who had earlier done homage to Rufus, now felt conscience-bound to obey a recent papal decree—promulgated at a Roman ecclesiastical council in 1099 which Anselm had personally attended—forbidding churchmen to render homage to laymen. Anselm also regarded himself as morally bound to uphold another decree of the Roman Council of 1099 prohibiting the ritual of lay investiture—the granting of the symbols of ecclesiastical office, ring and staff, by a lay lord. Pope Gregory VII, as we have seen, had previously condemned this practice. But Anselm—who had tolerated investiture by William Rufus—could no longer condone a custom that had been formally forbidden by a great papal council in which he himself had participated.

Henry I, for his part, was just as determined to retain an important royal ritual that his predecessors had traditionally performed—a symbolic expression of the king's status and prestige. The positions of both men were reasonable, and neither would relent. At length, in 1103, Anselm returned to exile and Henry confiscated the Canterbury revenues, but the two men continued to negotiate throughout the archbishop's period of exile. Their negotiations reached a crisis in 1105 when Anselm, with skillful timing, threatened Henry with excommunication just in the midst of the king's Norman campaign against Curthose. The threat forced Henry to compromise, and after lengthy discussion the king, the archbishop, and the pope ratified an agreement in 1106 (on the eve of Tinchebray). Henry agreed to relinquish lay investiture, but the pope permitted him, reluctantly, to continue receiving homage from his ecclesiastical tenants-in-chief. (Anselm himself, however, never rendered homage to Henry I.) Although the English Church was never again quite so completely under the royal thumb, the king's authority remained substantial and Henry usually succeeded in controlling ecclesiastical appointments. He had agreed to allow his clergy the privilege of free canonical elections, but free elections and strict royal management were by no means incompatible, as is demonstrated by a royal writ from King Henry II to the monks at Winchester in the later twelfth century: "I order you to hold a free election, but nevertheless I forbid you to elect anyone except Richard, my clerk, the archdeacon of Poitiers."

Henry I was a very different sort of king from William Rufus. Quieter and more calculating, Henry was less given to explosions of anger—or of mirth. He was less reckless, less emotional, and considerably more intelligent. William of Malmesbury describes Henry in these words:

> He was taller than short men but shorter than tall ones. His hair was black and receding from his forehead; his eyes were sweetly serene, his chest muscular, his body fleshy. He was witty at appropriate times, nor did the press of business cause him to be any less genial when he mixed in company. Disinclined toward personal combat, he verified the saying of [the ancient Roman general] Scipio Africanus, "My mother bore me to be a general, not a common soldier." Thus he was second to no modern king in wisdom, and it might almost be said that he easily surpassed all his predecessors on the throne of England. . . . He was plain in diet . . . drank but to quench his thirst . . . slept soundly and snored lustily; his speech was informal, not oratorical—easy-paced, not rapid.

Henry was, in short, altogether less flamboyant than Rufus. In one respect, however, he stands out among all kings of English history. To the best of our knowledge, he holds the record for illegitimate royal offspring, having sired at least 22 bastards by a throng of mistresses. For this exploit, Henry has been severely reprimanded by a number of nineteenth- and twentieth-century historians, but the monastic writers of Henry's own time, thankful for his peace and strong government, did not hold his bastards against him. Indeed, William of Malmesbury sprang to Henry's support with this ingenious defense:

> He was free, during his whole life, of all lewd desires, for—as we have learned from those who know—he had sexual intercourse with women not for the gratification of lust, but for the sake of issue; nor did he yield to amorous delights except when he could effectively send forth the royal seed. Thus he was the master of his passions, not the passive slave of lust.

Another contemporary monk, Orderic Vitalis, describes Henry simply as "the glorious father of his country."

Despite Henry's reconciliation with Anselm, his reign was not, on the whole, a great age of Christian reform. In view of his personal life, he could hardly have been a dedicated proponent of clerical celibacy. He did agree to the official prohibition of clerical marriage but was lax in enforcing it. On more than one occasion, he simply assessed fines against married clergy as a trick to increase royal revenues. Henry's most powerful and trusted administrator, Roger bishop of Salisbury, made no secret of his mistress, and Roger's nephew Nigel, bishop of Ely, had a wife. Among Henry I's other bishops known to have had either wives, concubines, or children (or all of the above) are the bishops of Worcester, Lincoln, Chester, London, and two successive bishops of Durham (the second of whom served for a decade as Henry's chancellor). Moreover, Henry often kept bishoprics and abbacies unfilled for periods of time in order to enjoy their revenues—although in this regard he was far less culpable than Rufus. When Archbishop Anselm died in 1109, Henry kept Canterbury vacant for five years.

If the reign of Henry I is not noted for ecclesiastical reform, it is exceedingly significant from the standpoint of royal administration. Henry was known as the Lion of Justice, and it is quite true that he ruled firmly and, on the whole, justly. To defend the Anglo-Norman state, he required a flow of revenue for building castles along the borders of his dominions, bribing barons and neighboring feudal princes, and hiring mercenaries to curb rebellion and defend the frontiers. Henry and his ministers exploited the wealth of England to the fullest, although with more discretion and less gusto than had been customary in Rufus's reign. Henry's severity is a recurring theme in the *Anglo-Saxon Chronicle*:

> 1104: . . . It is not easy to describe the miseries this land was suffering at the time because of various and different injustices and taxes that never ceased or diminished. . . .

> 1110: . . . This was a very severe year in this land because of the taxes that the king collected for the marriage of his daughter.

> 1116: . . . This land and people were also this year often severely oppressed by the taxes which the king collected both in and out of the boroughs.

> 1118: . . . England paid dearly . . . because of the various taxes that never ceased during the course of all this year.

> 1124: . . . It was a very troublous year; the man who had any property was deprived of it by harsh taxes and harsh judgments at court; the man who had none died of hunger.[6]

The customary laws of Henry's time were harsh by modern democratic standards, and on occasion he could enforce them without pity. In 1125, discovering that his minters were producing adulterated coinage, the king ordered Roger of Salisbury to have many of them castrated and deprived of their right hands—thereby effectively ending their careers. Yet according to the *Anglo-Saxon Chronicle*, "it was done very justly, because they had ruined all the country with their great false dealing." And on Henry's death, the *Chronicle* remarked: "He was a good man, and people were in great awe of him. No one dared injure another in his time." In short, despite his severity—or because of it—he enforced justice and kept the peace.

Justice could be lucrative to an English monarch. Judicial fines added to the royal revenue, and by extending the scope of the king's justice, Henry increased the flow of money into his treasury. More importantly, effective royal enforcement increased the king's authority over his realm and contributed to the general peace by discouraging crime and encouraging people to settle private disputes amicably.

---

[6] Apart from 1110, these years of exceptional taxation are also, by no coincidence, years of major military campaigning in Normandy. Henry's three major Norman wars occurred in 1104–1106, 1116–1119, and 1123–1124.

Henry's reign witnessed significant growth in the royal judicial system and the royal administration. Although local justices were appointed in each shire to assist the sheriffs in judicial business, the king and his great men at the royal court judged the most important legal cases. Since it was often difficult for litigants to reach the court (which was always on the move), the practice developed of sending royal justices to various parts of England to hear pleas. These itinerant justices, or "justices in eyre," acted in the king's name. By hearing important cases in the shires, they greatly enlarged the scope of the king's justice, often diverting cases from the baronial courts or dealing with pleas that otherwise might not have been heard at all. When one of Henry's itinerant justices was present the shire

Henry I's Bad Dreams Henry I was reported, on good authority, to have had three nightmares in a single night in A.D. 1130—anticipating Scrooge by more than seven centuries. In the first panel (from a mid-twelfth-century manuscript), angry peasants threaten the king with their tools; in the second panel, knights approach him with drawn swords; in the third, churchmen attack him with the points of their staves. Such dreams were the psychological penalty for the building of a powerful centralized monarchy with an advanced system of taxation. (President and Fellows of Corpus Christi College, Oxford)

court was transformed temporarily into a royal court, and ordinary country people were brought face to face with the judicial authority of the royal curia. During the reign of Henry I, the judicial tours became increasingly systematic. They were a significant beginning of what would later become a comprehensive, regularized practice.

Henry's chief instrument of command over the considerable areas he ruled was the royal writ. We have already traced the origin of the writ to Anglo-Saxon times in Chapter 3 (see pages 75–76). Under the Norman kings it was employed much more commonly than before. In its Anglo-Norman form, it was a brief royal command or statement, written in Latin on a strip of parchment, witnessed, and authenticated by the attachment of the royal seal. Ordinarily a writ would be addressed to the local sheriff or justiciar, or to the baronial or ecclesiastical lord of an area, or to all the king's officials and faithful men of a particular shire or group of shires:

> Henry king of the English to Hugh of Bocland and Robert of Ferrers and William sheriff of Oxford and Nicholas of Stafford, greeting. I order that you

justly and immediately cause all fugitives of the abbey of Abingdon to return there with all their goods, wherever they are, so that I may hear no further complaint on the matter for lack of right; and in particular, restore to Abingdon the man who is on the land of Robert of Ferrers, and with all his goods. Witness: Robert fitz Richard. [Issued] At Wallingford.

Some 1,500 royal acts, including many writs, have come down to us from Henry I's reign (as compared with less than 300 surviving acts from William the Conqueror's), and we can be certain that those that have survived constitute only a small fraction of the original total pouring out of Henry's chancery. They deal with an immense variety of judicial and administrative matters: grants or confirmations of lands and privileges, orders of restitution, commands to act in some way or to cease acting in some way, exemptions from certain taxes, or freedom from tolls. Taken together, they convey a powerful impression of the scope and authority of royal government under Henry I. England had never before been so thoroughly administered. There were some who complained about the abuses of royal officials and wished to get "big government" off their backs. But for most, Henry's administration was a welcome contrast to the conditions of civil tumult and local thuggery that characterized most of Europe in the early twelfth century.

When Henry traveled to Normandy he left a regent in England to hear important legal cases, issue writs, and head the administration. During the first half of the reign, his English regent was usually his wife, Queen Matilda, assisted by such seasoned administrators as Roger bishop of Salisbury. After Matilda's death in 1118, Roger of Salisbury himself acted as regent in Henry's absence—as a kind of English viceroy.[7] One of medieval England's most gifted administrators, Roger supervised the royal administration even when Henry was in England. Although Roger had no official administrative title, similar viceroy-administrators of later reigns were called "Chief Justiciars." Bishop Roger's main responsibilities lay in the area of royal finances, and it was probably he, more than anyone else, who forged the powerful instrument of fiscal accounting known as the "exchequer."

In later generations the exchequer became an important department of state. But in its beginning stages under Henry I, it was not a department at all but a twice-yearly audit of the royal income from the shires. All the sheriffs of England were required to come to the treasury at Winchester to report their revenues to a panel of auditors. Some of the auditors were officials from the Winchester treasury, others were trusted barons and churchmen from the king's court. The audit was usually presided over by Queen Matilda or, after her death in 1118, by Roger of Salisbury. The term

---

[7] Conversely, when Henry was in England, his Norman administration was governed by one or more Norman regents—usually a royal steward and an administrator-bishop. See Edward J. Kealey, *Roger of Salisbury, Viceroy of England* (Berkeley, Calif., 1972), and C. Warren Hollister, "The Rise of Administrative Kingship: Henry I," *American Historical Review* 83 (1978): 867–891, reprinted in *Monarchy, Magnates, and Institutions*, pp. 223–245. See also Judith Green, *The Government of England Under Henry I* (Cambridge, 1986).

exchequer is derived from the table around which the auditors worked. On the table was a checkered cloth (British: "chequered cloth") resembling a checkerboard, divided into columns representing various denominations of money. The auditors placed markers on these columns to represent the accounts of sheriffs who reported in. The accounting method was based on the principle of the abacus and the decimal system of arithmetic, which had recently been introduced from the Islamic world. The exchequer accounts were recorded on long rolls of parchment known as "pipe rolls," now precious historical sources. Unfortunately, only one of Henry I's pipe rolls has survived, but we have a continuous set of these annual records from 1156 on. The single surviving pipe roll of Henry I, for A.D. 1129–1130, represents the earliest comprehensive fiscal account in the history of Europe.

The exchequer served as an important control over the activities of the king's sheriffs. In the early Norman period, these royal agents were by no means faceless professionals. Only a person of wealth and stature could protect the royal interests in the turbulent countryside of post–Conquest England. Indeed, many sheriffs seem to have grown too powerful for the king's liking. They often abused their authority to enrich themselves and their families and sought to make their positions hereditary. The exchequer audits restrained them to a degree, but Henry I was obliged to take further measures to ensure his control over his local officials. He deposed old sheriffs and appointed new ones from among his own trusted subordinates. The new sheriffs were often men from families of the lesser landholding class, men who had risen in the royal service and hoped to rise still further, who attached their hopes—and their unswerving loyalty—to the crown. Not uncommonly, such a man might become sheriff of several counties at once, thus extending his own power while simplifying royal governance.

Henry I's reign marks the coming of age of the royal administration. Indeed, some historians have seen it as the seedbed of the modern state. The functions of the royal household officials were growing in importance and specialization. The exchequer provided Henry with the first modern accounting office known to the medieval West. And the tightly controlled sheriffs and itinerant justices were forging the essential links between the royal administration and the countryside. Northern Europe had known no such coherent administrative machinery since Roman times, and no other northern monarch was as wealthy as Henry I. For Henry had discovered that efficient administration brought larger revenues, that strong government was good business, and, conversely, that a penniless king could not keep the peace.

Henry's regime contained many low-born administrators, and in enforcing public order he deprived his aristocrats of the freedom to fight one another. Still, Henry cannot be described as anti-aristocratic. The disasters of the reigns of later kings such as John, Henry III, and Edward II make it clear that a medieval English monarch could not succeed without support from a majority of his barons. And Henry proved himself adroit in winning the allegiance of many of his subjects—nobles and upstarts alike—through a well-oiled system of royal patronage. For those who demonstrated their loyalty and won his favor, he provided tantalizing opportunities to advance their careers and fortunes in the royal service. Such men were given an inside advantage in acquiring forfeited lands, wealthy wives, lucrative wardships, danegeld exemptions, administrative offices, and the various other spoils at the crown's disposal. Great baronial families flourished if they were loyal to the king, while a number of lesser aristocrats rose to high position, and men of still lower station ascended into the prosperous middle levels of the aristocracy. To be sure, these royal favorites had to pay the king for every privilege he gave them—in Henry's government nothing was cheap—and they seldom rose to high position overnight. Nevertheless, they were fully aware that they owed their success to the king's favor and that similar service in the future would continue to be rewarded. Through his astute use of patronage, Henry created a royalist core in the aristocracy. Royal patronage was to be a central and enduring element in English politics and society for many centuries thereafter. Under Henry I it made its first appearance as a fully articulated system.

Henry's government was complex, sophisticated, and to a degree impersonal, yet it depended ultimately on the existence of a strong, fear-inspiring king. Accordingly, Henry devoted much attention to the problem of the royal succession. Although he had a gaggle of illegitimate offspring, he produced only two legitimate heirs: a daughter named Matilda (or Maud) and a younger son named William, who was carefully groomed for the throne. It is the supreme tragedy of Henry's reign that William was killed on the eve of his manhood, in 1120, when a vessel carrying the prince and a distinguished but intoxicated party of aristocratic funlovers from Normandy to England sank. This catastrophe, known to history as the wreck of the White Ship, threw the royal succession into chaos. Henry, whose first wife had died two and a half years before, promptly remarried, but the second marriage proved childless. Finally, in 1127, Henry secured oaths from his barons to accept his daughter Matilda as the royal heir.

Matilda had earlier been married, at the age of eleven, to the Holy Roman emperor Henry V, but by 1127 she was a childless widow. Having secured his barons' pledges, Henry arranged a fateful marriage between Matilda and Count Geoffrey of Anjou. This was a bold stroke of policy, for it promised to end the long struggle between Normandy and Anjou for hegemony in northern France, but it also gave rise to myriad problems. For one thing, some Anglo-Norman barons were uneasy at the prospect of being ruled by a woman, particularly a woman of Matilda's explosive temperament. For another, Matilda and Geoffrey were poor mates. Matilda was a widow of twenty-five, Geoffrey a boy of fifteen, and their personalities clashed. After a year of marriage they separated, and Matilda returned to her father in England. At length, however, Geoffrey and Matilda reconciled, and in 1133 Matilda gave birth to a son, the future King Henry II. For a brief time Henry I relaxed, enjoying the pleasures of being a grandfather and the security of having obtained a male heir at last. But Matilda, now reconciled with her husband, prompted Geoffrey into a quarrel with her father.

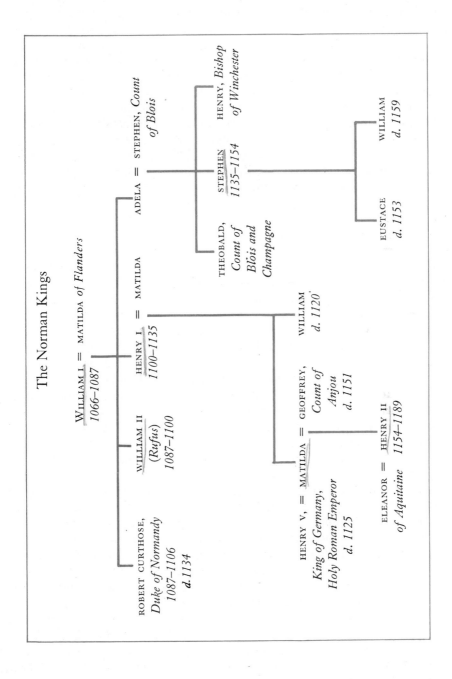

The Norman Kings

Matilda claimed a number of castles as her promised dowry; Henry refused to yield them, and in mid-1135 a small-scale frontier war broke out. Henry's armies triumphed once again, but in December the old king—now in his late sixties—died of indigestion. Because he was surrounded by his most loyal followers at the time of his death and was at odds with Matilda, Henry's death threw the succession into confusion. Henry's era of peace died with him, and Matilda's untimely quarrel with her father cost her the English crown.

The reign of Henry I was long and significant. He had reunited the Anglo-Norman state, kept the peace in England, successfully defended his far-flung frontiers, and instituted notable administrative advances. A perceptive modern scholar says of Henry's reign: "Looking to the future, it is here, we feel, that the history of England begins—a history which is neither that of the Norman conquerors, nor that of the Anglo-Saxons, but a new creation."[8]

The Reign of King Stephen (1135–1154)

When Henry I died, his grandson was a child of two whose ambitions did not yet extend to duchies and kingdoms. The English barons had sworn to accept Matilda and any son she might bear, but their enthusiasm was dimmed by the fact that they had been fighting on Henry's side against her in 1135—and that her eldest son was as yet an infant. Hence, the great English landholder Stephen of Blois, a son of the Conqueror's daughter and a nephew of Henry I, acting with much the same dispatch that Henry himself had demonstrated in 1100, seized the throne. Matilda had perhaps the better hereditary claim, but hereditary right was not everything in the making of an English monarch. Indeed, nearly a century had passed since an English king had been succeeded by his eldest offspring, and controversy had clouded the claims of all the Norman kings thus far.[9]

Stephen had long been a loyal follower of Henry I, and Henry had showered him with lands and privileges. At Henry's death, only one other Anglo-Norman landholder could compete in wealth with Stephen of Blois. That person was Robert earl of Gloucester, King Henry's favorite bastard.

Stephen was the most genial of the Norman kings and the least competent. Erratic and lacking in firmness, he was in many respects Henry's opposite. In the words of the *Anglo-Saxon Chronicle*, "he was a mild man, and gentle and good, and did no justice." During the first two years of his reign, he squandered Henry's treasure on bribes and wages for mercenaries,

---

[8] Sir Richard Southern, "The Place of Henry I in English History," *Proceedings of the British Academy* 48 (1962): 128–129.

[9] R. H. C. Davis, *King Stephen* (3rd ed., Berkeley, Calif., 1990), and H. A. Cronne, *The Reign of Stephen, 1135–1154: Anarchy in England* (London, 1970), are both excellent studies. See, further, Jim Bradbury, "The Early Years of the Reign of Stephen, 1135–1139," *England in the Twelfth Century: Proceedings of the 1988 Harlaxton Symposium*, ed. Daniel Williams (Woodbridge, Suffolk, 1990), pp. 17–30.

and managed, more or less, to keep the peace. In 1138, however, Count Geoffrey of Anjou attacked Normandy, Earl Robert of Gloucester rebelled in favor of his half-sister Matilda, and David king of Scots (Matilda's uncle) took up her cause by invading England. Stephen succeeded in defending himself against these threats, only to be faced with an invasion by Matilda herself. The next decade witnessed a seesaw battle between Stephen and Matilda, accompanied by warfare between baron and baron, and by a constant shifting of baronial allegiances from one side to the other. The barons by no means advocated weak kingship and the freedom to commit acts of mayhem against their neighbors. They had prospered during the previous reign under the firm rule of a monarch who was friendly to their interests. But now, with Stephen and Matilda battling on equal terms—a weak man against an impetuous woman—barons who sought strong royal lordship could find it nowhere.

The turbulence of these years was by no means universal—it was limited to particular areas and particular times (the same thing could be said of modern Lebanon)—but it was terrifying nonetheless and left a deep impression on contemporaries. The twelfth-century historian Henry of Huntingdon, commenting on the horrors of Stephen's reign, remarked that "whatever King Henry had done, whether in the manner of a tyrant or that of a true king, appeared most excellent in comparison." As an astute British historian recently described it, the reign of Stephen was "a true and terrible Anarchy."[10]

The most vivid descriptions of the civil war are to be found in the *Anglo-Saxon Chronicle*. While the chronicler's picture of general and total chaos is doubtless exaggerated, his specific impressions ring true:

> Every powerful man built his castles and held them against the king, and they filled the country full of castles. They oppressed the wretched people of the country severely with their castle building. When the castles were built they filled them with devils and wicked men. Then both by night and day they took those people that they thought had any goods, men and women alike, and put them in prison and tortured them with indescribable tortures to extort gold and silver from them—for no martyrs were ever so tortured as they were. They were hung by the thumbs or by the head, and armor was hung on their feet. Knotted ropes were placed around their heads and twisted until they penetrated to the brains. They put them in prisons where there were adders and snakes and toads, and killed them in that way. . . . Many thousands they killed by starvation.

> I have neither the ability nor the power to tell all the horrors and all the torments that they inflicted on the wretched people of this land. And all this lasted the whole nineteen years while Stephen was king, and it was always going from bad to worse. They levied taxes on the villages at intervals, and called it "protection money." When the wretched people had

---

10 David Crouch, *The Beaumont Twins: The Roots and Branches of Power in the Twelfth Century* (Cambridge, 1986), p. 138.

no more to give, they robbed and burned the villages, so that you could easily go a whole day's journey and find nobody occupying any village, nor any land tilled. . . . Some lived by begging, who had once been rich, and others fled the country. . . .

Wherever cultivation was done, the ground produced no grain, because the land was all ruined by such doings. And they said openly that Christ and his saints slept.

At length, the dynastic struggle settled into an uneasy truce. Robert of Gloucester's death in 1147 deprived Matilda of her ablest champion, and in 1148 she retired to the Continent. But in the meantime her husband, Count Geoffrey, had conquered Normandy. With the two contending parties separated by the English Channel, the conflict diminished—but only for a time.

By now Henry I's grandson, Henry of Anjou (or Henry Plantagenet), was approaching manhood and preparing to undertake an energetic struggle to make good his inherited claims. His father Count Geoffrey died in 1151, and two years later the young Henry—count of Anjou and duke of Normandy—invaded England.

This ambitious young man of nineteen was already the greatest prince in France. In addition to Normandy and Anjou and their satellite provinces (Maine, Touraine, etc.—see map on page 159), Henry Plantagenet had won the extensive duchy of Aquitaine in southern France by marrying its talented heiress, Eleanor.[11] He came to England as a man of great substance

Castle Acre, Norfolk, a Great Private Fortified Residence of the Warenne Earls of Surrey   Reconstructions, based on recent archaeological excavations, showing four successive phases of construction from the late eleventh century to about the mid-twelfth: (1) A two-story stone country house, lightly fortified by an encircling ditch and a palisaded mound. (2) The wooden palisade was replaced by a stone wall, with a fortified gate, but the central building remained essentially a house rather than a castle. (3) The country house was then remodeled internally for conversion to a strongly fortified castle tower, while the surrounding embankment was heightened and surmounted by a high stone wall. (4) Half of the former house was converted into a well-defended castle tower, the other half was demolished, and the encircling fortifications were greatly strengthened. Phases 3 and 4 appear to date from King Stephen's reign and bear witness to the growth of civil unrest and the increasing militarization of the countryside. (After R. Warmington; Courtesy of The British Museum)

---

[11] Eleanor of Aquitaine had recently divorced King Louis VII of France. Amy Kelly, *Eleanor of Aquitaine and the Four Kings* (Cambridge, Mass., 1950; paperback ed., 1959), is a highly readable account of her career and her relationships with her two husbands, Louis VII and Henry II, and her two royal sons, Richard the Lion-Hearted and John. The studies published in W. W. Kibler, ed., *Eleanor of Aquitaine: Patron and Politician* (Austin, Texas, 1976) provide greater scholarly accuracy and less entertainment.

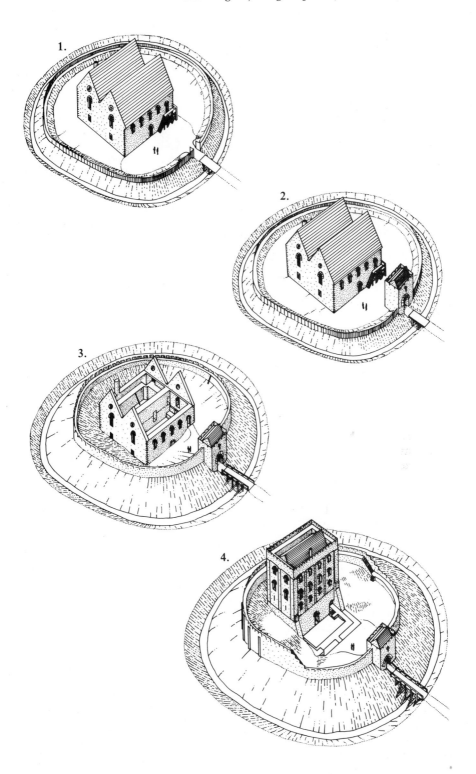

Great Seal of Stephen
One side shows the king enthroned as king of the English and, verso, mounted on horseback as duke of the Normans. (The Mansell Collection)

and significant resources, and as duke of Normandy he was in a position to terrify English barons by threatening to confiscate their Norman lands. He refrained from doing so, and they were grateful.

Henry's campaign in England was largely bloodless. With the reappearance of able and determined leadership, Stephen's baronial supporters declined to fight in his behalf and instead negotiated a series of truces favorable to Henry. Many now shifted to what was clearly the winning side. With declining support, advancing years, and sinking spirits, Stephen submitted to a compromise which deprived his own sons of the right to succeed him and assured Henry the throne. The agreement, known as the Treaty of Winchester (1153), stipulated that Stephen would rule England unmolested until his death, but that Henry Plantagenet would be his heir. Baronial partisans on both sides were guaranteed their lands and were promised immunity from punishment. England was to return at last to a state of peace. Nine months after the Treaty of Winchester, King Stephen died, and Henry Plantagenet acceded unopposed to the English throne as King Henry II. With his coronation, the Norman Age of English history came to an end, and the Angevin Age began.[12]

The troubled reign of Stephen was formerly regarded as an epoch of feudal anarchy, a reaction against the strong government of Henry I, and an age when a good but pliable king was exploited unmercifully by greedy barons. As a result of recent research, this interpretation requires drastic modification. For one thing, Stephen was not so open-hearted or simpleminded as he has sometimes been pictured. He was a cheerful man, by and large, but he could also be sly and treacherous. In particular, he had an irritating habit of arresting his barons and administrators by surprise and without good cause. His arrest of Henry I's great administrator Roger of Salisbury in 1139 damaged the royal administrative machinery. His peremp-

---

[12] The Angevin dynasty (1154–1399) is so called because Henry II and his successors were descendants in the male line of Count Geoffrey of Anjou. From about the fifteenth century onward the Angevin kings were often termed the "Plantagenets" after the broom flower native to Anjou—the *plante genêt*—which Count Geoffrey used as his emblem. On Henry's bloodless victory over Stephen, see Joe W. Leedom, "The English Settlement of 1153," *History* 65 (1980): 347–364.

tory arrests of two of England's most powerful magnates—Geoffrey de Mandeville earl of Essex, and Ranulf earl of Chester—prompted both of them, once released, to revolt against their king.

Moreover, most magnates preferred the rule of a strong, supportive king to a baronial free-for-all.[13] As the twelfth century progressed, the holdings of magnates great and small became increasingly subject to dispute, with disinherited families reviving old claims and rival heirs contending for the same estates. During the two closing decades of Henry I's reign, royal confiscation of baronial lands became exceedingly rare, and the royal court adjudicated most conflicting claims. In Stephen's reign, however, civil strife deprived the aristocracy of a single authoritative tribunal and a firm royal protector. Barons tended to assert every possible claim to every scrap of disputable land and to grab what they could. Disputes multiplied as Stephen and Matilda granted different persons the same estates and offices. Often, two contending claimants to a particular fief would be fighting on opposite sides in the civil war, and a shift of loyalty by one baron could prompt a countershift by a rival baron.

The Treaty of Winchester and the subsequent accession of Henry II marked a return to peaceful adjudication of disputes and secure inheritances. Indeed, the victory of the hereditary principle is nowhere more evident than in Henry's own succession to the throne. He succeeded in part by the approval of the council, in part by the designation of his predecessor—but above all, and unlike the Norman kings, he succeeded by hereditary right as the eldest grandson of Henry I. It was not, of course, a model instance of hereditary succession: Henry II succeeded Stephen, not Henry I. The difficulty was resolved first by having Stephen "adopt" Henry II, and later by declaring Stephen a usurper and his reign a "nonevent." But for all that, hereditary right based on primogeniture has governed the succession of English monarchs, with few exceptions, from that day to this.

---

[13] On royal patronage and royal-baronial relations, see Sir Richard Southern, "King Henry I," *Medieval Humanism and Other Studies* (Oxford, 1970), pp. 206–233; C. Warren Hollister, "Henry I and the Anglo-Norman Magnates," *Proceedings of the Battle Conference on Anglo-Norman Studies*, II, 1979 (Woodbridge, Suffolk, 1980), pp. 93–107, reprinted in *Monarchy, Magnates, and Institutions*, pp. 171–189; and RaGena DeAragon, "The Growth of Secure Inheritance in Anglo-Norman England," *Journal of Medieval History* 8 (1982), 381–391.

6

Henry II and Sons

Henry II reigned for thirty-five years (1154–1189), almost exactly as long as his grandfather, Henry I. The two reigns are similar in other respects as well, for Henry II undertook quite deliberately to revive Henry I's policies and strove to rule in his imperious tradition. Yet the new king was a vibrant personality in his own right. He has been aptly described as "a man of intense, mercurial temperament who could shift in a moment from sunshine to thunder."[1] His contemporaries regarded him as a fear-inspiring, peace-keeping monarch—impulsive, lecherous, always on the move, and overwhelming in personality. One writer of the time described him as

> . . . a man of reddish, freckled complexion, with a large, round head, grey eyes that glowed fiercely and grew bloodshot in anger, a fiery countenance and a harsh, cracked voice. His neck was poked forward slightly from his shoulders, his chest was broad and square, his arms strong and powerful. His body was stocky, with a pronounced tendency toward fatness, due to nature rather than self-indulgence—which he tempered with exercise.

Henry was almost perversely energetic. At the end of a hard day, he would refuse to sit down, before or after dinner, so that his courtiers, to avoid the risk of offending him, had to stand as well. As one of them complained, the king would "wear out the whole court by continually standing."

The scholar Peter of Blois, who spent some time at Henry's court, described it as a scene of chaotic confusion. Henry I had planned his itineraries carefully; by contrast, Henry II's movements through the countryside seemed to depend on no prearranged schedule but on the royal whim. "If the king promises to spend the whole day somewhere," Peter of Blois grumbled, "you can be sure that he will leave the place bright and early, and upset everyone's plans in his haste." Then everybody will be "rushing madly about, urging on the packhorses, hitching the teams to their wagons, everyone in total confusion—a perfect portrait of hell. . . . And I believe our plight added to the king's pleasure." The harassed scholar eventually elec-

---

[1] Christopher Brooke, in *The World of John of Salisbury*, Michael Wilks ed. (Oxford, 1984), p. 17. The best general biography is W. L. Warren, *Henry II* (Berkeley, Calif., 1973); see also Thomas K. Keefe, *Feudal Assessments and the Political Community Under Henry II and His Sons* (Berkeley, Calif., 1983).

Tomb Effigy of Henry II at Fontevrault Abbey in Anjou   The carving shows an idealized likeness of the king in his youth. (Copyright ARS NY/SPADEM 1987)

ted to resign from the royal entourage. "I shall dedicate the remainder of my days," he concluded, "to study and peace."

But Peter of Blois's portrayal of a vast yet directionless royal effort is surely exaggerated. Henry knew where he was going, even if his followers did not. And it is significant that a scholar of Peter of Blois's talents should be in the royal household at all. Henry II was the best-educated English king since the Norman Conquest. He delighted in associating with scholars and patronizing their works. As Peter of Blois himself said of Henry:

> Whenever he can get breathing space in the midst of his business cares, he occupies himself with private readings or endeavors to work out some difficult intellectual problem with his learned clerics. . . . With the king of England it is school every day, constant conversation among the best of scholars, and discussion of problems.

Military, Administrative, and Legal Reforms Under Henry II

Henry II began his reign by endeavoring to revive in all its fullness the royal authority his grandfather had exercised. He set about immediately to reverse the process of political disintegration that England had experienced under Stephen. He ordered the destruction of the unlicensed castles that barons had built during the height of the anarchy, and he was stingy in granting permission to build new castles. He worked energetically, first to reconstruct the powerful government of Henry I and later to expand it. Three areas of the royal government received Henry II's particular attention: military organization, administration, and above all, legal procedures.

Henry II's military reforms are well illustrated by two important documents from his reign: the *Cartae Baronum* (Barons' Charters) of 1166 and the Assize of Arms of 1181. The first is a series of written statements from all the tenants-in-chief of the realm, lay and ecclesiastical, in response to a royal inquest relating to knights' service. The inquest required the tenants-in-chief to tell the king (1) how many knights they had enfeoffed (bestowed a fief upon) before Henry I's death in 1135, (2) how many they had enfeoffed between 1135 and 1166, and (3) to what degree—if any—the enfeoffments fell short of the knightly military quotas the monarchy had imposed on them. The knights that the tenants-in-chief had enfeoffed were to be identified by name. The *Cartae Baronum* of 1166 constituted the first general survey of knights' service since William the Conqueror's establishment of the quotas. Henry II may well have wanted to discover the extent of his feudal military resources, but he also seems to have had two specific reasons for the inquest. First, he wished to identify all the knightly subvassals of England who had not yet rendered him their formal allegiance, so that he might secure their oaths in the near future. Second, on the basis of the data supplied by the *Cartae Baronum*, he attempted to obtain additional scutage payments from those vassals whose enfeoffments exceeded their royal quotas.

The Assize of Arms of 1181 was more radical in its implications than the *Cartae Baronum*. Coming at a time when the Anglo-Saxon fyrd had ceased to function and the feudal military obligation was tending to become a mere excuse for the levying of scutage, the Assize of Arms marked the first of a series of royal attempts—running through the thirteenth century—to reorganize the English military obligation on the basis of wealth.

Henry II divided the English military force into four categories. The first corresponded to the feudal army: the holder of each knight's fee was to have a shirt of mail, a helmet, a shield, and a lance. The second and third categories roughly paralleled the old five-hide fyrd, but the basis of the obligation shifted from the number of hides in a tenant's possession to the annual income from his land and the total value of his movable possessions. Every free layman with movables and rents of sixteen marks or more (the second category) was to have a shirt of mail, a helmet, a shield, and a lance—the equipment of a knight. Every free layman with movables and rents of ten marks or more (the third category) was to have a coat of light mail, an iron headpiece, and a lance. The fourth category embraced all freemen with chattels and rents of less than ten marks: they were to have quilted coats, iron headpieces, and lances. Finally, all four of these groups were to swear fidelity to Henry II and bear their arms in his service according to his command.

The Assize of Arms established a graded hierarchy of military obligations based on a single recruitment system extending from knightly service down to the general military duty of all freemen. It preserved the knight's fee of earlier times but equated it with an estate of sixteen marks or more. This equation between a knight's fee and an estate of some specified monetary value constitutes the beginning of a long process that incorporated the older system of arbitrary private feudal tenures into a larger and radically different structure—a standardized national system of military assessment.

Henry II's Assize of Arms of 1181 was merely the first of a series of such ordinances. Similar ones were issued by Henry III in 1230 and 1242 and by Edward I in his Statute of Winchester in 1285. These later ordinances increased the number of categories of nonknightly military service from three to five, incorporated the nonfree peasantry into the military system, and provided for new military classes, such as archers and light horsemen. And beginning in the thirteenth century, the monarchy sought to bring knights' service still more closely into line with the new system by requiring all men with estates of a certain annual value (usually twenty pounds) to become knights.

The shift from hides to annual income as the basis of land assessment is just as evident in the tax system. By Henry II's reign the ancient hide assessment was becoming anachronistic: it no longer served as a reliable indication of changing land values, and it failed to reflect adequately the growing wealth of townspeople. Responding to popular complaints, Henry II abolished the danegeld—the annual land tax based on hides. In its place there emerged a new tax, levied only occasionally to meet emergencies and assessed at some percentage of a subject's annual rents and chattels. Taxes levied on this new basis continued through the subsequent reigns of Richard I, John, Henry III, and long thereafter, paralleling the changes in the military recruitment system initiated by the Assize of Arms. From the standpoint of both taxation and military service, Henry II's reign marks the beginning of an epoch. In an era of commercial vitalization, the ancient assessment quotas based on land gave way to new, flexible criteria based on wealth and income.

In other aspects of royal administrative development, the reign of Henry II constitutes a revival and elaboration of Henry I's policies rather than a new beginning. As the functions of the household staff became more specialized, separate administrative departments began to emerge. The increasing professionalization of the exchequer (which moved from Winchester to Westminster, just outside London) is reflected not only in an unbroken series of annual pipe rolls but also in a treatise—*The Dialogue of the Exchequer*—which explains in detail the duties and procedures of exchequer officials. The chancery's work increased in both amount and sophistication and would continue to do so during subsequent reigns. In brief, the royal coterie of servants, advisers, scribes, and cronies was gradually evolving into a bureaucracy of professional administrators.

It was in the field of law, above all else, that Henry II made his unique contribution.[2] Under his rule the royal court widened the range of its judicial activities and the complexity of its organization until, by the reign's end, a number of separate bodies were hearing cases in the king's name. The great council—the assembly of magnates and prelates that met with the king on extraordinary occasions—served as the royal tribunal in cases of the highest importance, such as the trial of Archbishop Thomas Becket at Northampton in 1164 (see pages 155–156). Pleas of lesser significance usually fell to the ill-defined group of administrative officers and royal intimates who accompanied the king on his endless travels—a group that later historians have called the "small council."

The small council, in its judicial capacity, was presided over by the king or one of his chief judges. It evolved in later years into the separate tribunal known as the Court of the King's Bench. Because the small council labored under a great burden of royal business—judicial and nonjudicial—and was constantly on the move, it had its drawbacks as a body to which subjects might conveniently turn for royal justice. Litigants might have their cases postponed repeatedly as the small council shifted its attention to urgent political matters, or they might have to chase the king and his court hundreds of miles across England and France before finally catching up with them. To mitigate these difficulties, the twelfth-century kings—Henry II in particular—began to subdivide the royal court.

From the Norman Conquest onward, kings had routinely appointed regents to rule England during royal absences on the Continent. By Henry I's time, a well-defined viceregal court of seasoned administrators was functioning in England when the king was in Normandy, and a similar court operated in Normandy when the king was in England. On the king's return (in either direction), the viceregal officials merged into his entourage. Both viceregal courts, English and Norman, supervised the semiannual exchequer audits, where they served as a tribunal for cases concerning royal taxes and fines. In time the judicial scope of the exchequer court widened to include certain cases unconnected with the royal revenues. But because the king or his regent was usually present for the semiannual audits, and the "barons of the exchequer" (the members of the exchequer court) tended to be the same persons who normally heard cases in the viceregal court or the king's perambulating court, the gain in efficiency was slight.

Around 1178 Henry II took the further step of establishing a permanent body of royal justices at Westminster, which he empowered to hear all but

---

[2] The standard general work is Sir Frederick Pollock and Frederic W. Maitland, *The History of English Law Before the Time of Edward I* (rev. reissue of 2nd ed., 2 vols., Cambridge, 1968). A good summary is R. C. Van Caenegem, *The Birth of the English Common Law* (2nd ed., Cambridge, 1988). S. F. C. Milsom, *The Legal Framework of English Feudalism* (Cambridge, 1976), presents a fundamental reinterpretation of Henry II's possessory assizes; it is erudite, profoundly original, and—as one specialist has remarked—"almost impossible to understand." For an explanation and modification of Milsom's thesis, see Robert C. Palmer, "The Feudal Framework of English Law," *Michigan Law Review* 79 (1981): 1130–1164.

the most important royal pleas. This court, consisting sometimes of five men, sometimes of more, often included the treasurer and the chief justiciar (as the English regent now came to be called). It was distinguished by having its own separate seal and, in later years, a special name—the Court of Common Pleas. But under Henry II the court was still experimental: it occasionally met elsewhere than at Westminster; it was at times almost indistinguishable from the small body of exchequer officials that worked at Westminster year-round; and when the king visited Westminster, as he often did, it blended into the main royal court.

Henry II augmented the system of royal tribunals—the great council, the small council, the exchequer court, and the special court at Westminster—by reviving Henry I's policy of sending out itinerant justices to hear royal pleas in the shires. By the closing years of Henry I's reign, itinerant royal justices ranged across all of England. The system disintegrated under Stephen, but Henry II eventually rebuilt it into a series of kingdom-wide judicial circuits. He never completely regularized the schedule and scope of these circuits, however, for Henry II was inclined to experiment endlessly—increasing or decreasing the number of justices, the number and range of their circuits, and the scope of their duties. Besides their judicial activities, they served as royal agents in the countryside—helping to keep the sheriffs honest, holding inquests related to royal revenues, and safeguarding the king's rights over his demesne lands. Their jurisdiction was limited at first to certain kinds of royal pleas, but with the passing of time they acquired the power to hear every kind of case. Their judicial tours, known as "general eyres," or "assizes," succeeded as never before in extending royal justice across the kingdom.

Notwithstanding the activities of the itinerant justices, much of the king's power in the counties depended on the loyalty and effectiveness of the sheriffs, who were in theory his chief local deputies but were often ineffective instruments of royal authority in the shires. During Stephen's reign, the office of sheriff had tended either to pass directly into the hands of great hereditary earls (whose numbers had tripled under Stephen) or to fall indirectly under an earl's control through a sheriff whom he had handpicked. Henry II was determined to reassert his authority over the sheriffs and, above all, to prevent the supposedly royal office of sheriff from passing from father to son as a hereditary right.[3] In 1170 he ordered a thoroughgoing inquest of his sheriffs' activities, afterward replacing most of them with more dependable and loyal nominees. The king's authority depended heavily on his ability to control his sheriffs, for it was their responsibility to collect royal demesne revenues and account for them at the exchequer. The sheriffs were likewise obliged to carry out a variety of royal orders transmitted to them by sealed writs from the royal chancery. As the regional representatives of an increasingly literate administration, efficient sheriffs

---

[3] On this important point, see M. T. Clanchy, *England and Its Rulers, 1066–1272: Foreign Lordship and National Identity* (Oxford, 1983), pp. 120–123.

needed to be literate themselves. Indeed, Henry II's considerable authority in the countryside owed much to a significant rise in lay literacy. Government by the written word demanded local officials who could read.

Yet even with active itinerant justices and effective, trustworthy sheriffs, Henry II still faced the formidable problem of maintaining local law and order without a police force. In his Assize of Clarendon of 1166, augmented by the Assize of Northampton of 1176, he ordered that inquest juries of 12 men from each hundred and 4 men from each town be required to meet periodically. These juries were to report the names of notorious local criminals to the king's sheriff or itinerant justice. The accused criminals were then forced to submit to trial by ordeal and were suitably punished if they failed to pass it. The ordeal was an ancient procedure of Germanic law[4] that was passing out of favor with the twelfth-century Church. Although Henry II used it as a traditional method of determining guilt or innocence, he did so with some hesitation, taking the precaution of banishing people of unsavory reputation from the kingdom even if they passed the ordeal.

The juries established by the Assize of Clarendon were fundamentally different from the modern trial jury. The task of the modern jury—to decide whether the accused is guilty or innocent—was performed in Henry II's system by the ordeal. His juries were closer in spirit to our grand juries: they were indictment juries, whose function was to supply information. Similar juries had existed in the Anglo-Norman period, not only to identify criminals but also to funnel local data of various kinds to the royal administration. They were used during the Domesday inquest to supply the facts on which the survey was based, and their obscure genesis has been traced by contending scholars to both Anglo-Saxon England and the Carolingian Empire. In reality, the practice of conducting legal inquests by bodies of sworn jurors had been customary for centuries throughout Western Christendom, but no monarch had made as systematic use of them as had Henry II in the aftermath of the Assizes of Clarendon and Northampton. Thereafter, they became an integral part of royal criminal procedures. As such, they mark a significant advance of royal jurisdiction into areas traditionally reserved for the courts of hundred and shire.

Henry II also extended royal jurisdiction into the vast, bewildering area of land disputes. We have already traced the growth of rival claims to land in Norman England, and their explosive consequences during Stephen's reign. Stephen's treaty with Henry Plantagenet in 1153, restoring all lands to the families that held them in 1135, launched a new wave of conflicting claims. Although the Norman kings—particularly Henry I—had adjudicated disputes among their tenants-in-chief and had sometimes intervened in lesser conflicts over land, such issues were customarily handled in the private

---

[4] See Chapter 1, pages 24–25. It is difficult to determine what percentage of those who submitted to the ordeal passed and what percentage failed. A record of Hungarian legal cases in the early thirteenth century provides us with an important clue: of 208 people whose guilt or innocence was established by the ordeal of the hot iron between 1208 and 1235, 130 passed and 78 failed.

baronial courts. It was Henry II who first applied the authority of royal jurisdiction systematically to the crucial area of property law.

Historians used to interpret Henry's move as an encroachment on baronial prerogatives. In actuality, many magnates welcomed his intervention. Some were glad to have royal assistance in handling cases that defied solution and that were apt to turn the loser into a lifelong enemy. Other magnates were themselves involved in land disputes and benefited from the emergence of a clear and coherent royal policy. Further, baronial courts tended to favor sworn vassals in actual occupation of disputed lands—not only because of the close personal association of baron and vassal but also because of the baron's customary obligation to provide an evicted vassal with another estate of equal value. Thus, Henry II's purpose was not to take business from baronial tribunals but to help them function more effectively. Nevertheless, the ultimate effect of his intervention was to enlarge enormously the scope of royal jurisdiction.

The most important of Henry II's possessory assizes, the Assize of Novel Disseisin, was designed to protect property rights by providing legal recourse for anyone who was wrongfully dispossessed of an estate. Regardless of whether the plaintiff had the best claim to the estate in question, if he had been dispossessed without legal judgment, he was entitled to purchase a royal writ commanding the sheriff to assemble a jury to determine the facts of the case. If the jury concluded that the plaintiff had indeed been dispossessed wrongfully, the sheriff, acting with full royal authority, would see that the estate was restored.

Novel Disseisin was only one of several possessory writs established by Henry II. Another of them, of particular importance was the writ of Mort d'Ancestor. This writ required the sheriff to ask the jury whether the plaintiff's father had held the land in question when it last passed to an heir. If so, and if the plaintiff was the eldest surviving son, he was given the land. The writ of Mort d'Ancestor, when understood in the context of the less-crystallized inheritance arrangements of Anglo-Norman times, illustrates a growing insistence on hereditary succession through the principle of primogeniture.

The great merit of Henry II's possessory assizes is that they asked simple questions and provided rapid remedies. They did not inquire into the problem of right to land, which could often be heartbreakingly complex, but only into the issue of wrongful dispossession within a fixed and recent period of time—an issue that local juries could usually resolve without a lengthy investigation and without ambiguity.

Toward the end of his reign, Henry II instituted a legal action known as the Grand Assize, which addressed itself not to the question of wrongful dispossession but to the more fundamental question of who had the best title to the land. As in the case of the possessory assizes, the question was answered by a local jury consisting of men who were likely to know the situation well. Previously, questions of rights to land were commonly resolved in baronial courts by the custom of trial by battle; the two disputants or their representatives simply fought it out, and God presumably gave the victory to the person with the best claim. The new procedure commended itself to an age in which reason and logic were coming into high regard, and in which there was increasing reluctance to be constantly bothering God.

The ultimate effect of the royal land assizes was to make the royal courts the chief adjudicators of land quarrels of all kinds. The English were learning to turn to the king for quick, rational justice, and the baronial courts were outclassed in the competition.

Henry I and Henry II between them achieved an enormously significant extension of royal jurisdiction at the expense of feudal and local justice. The various regional peculiarities in legal custom—Kentish law, Northumbrian law, Danelaw—were giving way to a uniform royal law, a common law shared by all the English. Thus, the political unification of the West Saxon kings had its counterpart and consummation in the legal unification achieved by the two Henrys and their successors.

The emergence of a common law under Henry II and its dependence on literate lay officials are well illustrated by the appearance of England's first systematic legal treatise, attributed traditionally (and wrongly) to Henry II's chief justiciar, Ranulf Glanville.[5] "Glanville's" treatise is practical and utilitarian rather than philosophical—by and large, it is a manual explaining the nature and uses of the standardized judicial writs that plaintiffs could buy from the royal chancery. The English were not yet ready to speculate on the fundamental nature of their jurisprudence. But the treatise is nevertheless an intellectual landmark in the rise of a coherent body of royal law.

As the common law evolved under Henry II, a profoundly different legal tradition was developing on the Continent. Henry's law, although precocious in many respects, had its roots in Germanic custom. Continental law, on the other hand, was gradually passing under the influence of the Roman legal tradition, which was undergoing a revival in the newly emerging twelfth-century universities. In one sense, Roman law was republican law, resting as it did on the concept that ultimate political authority inhered in the Roman people. But it passed into the twelfth-century West in the autocratic form it had acquired from its late-imperial codifier, the sixth-century Byzantine emperor Justinian. For it was above all Justinian's *Corpus Juris Civilis* that continental specialists in Roman law studied and expanded. The legal concepts of the Roman Republic and early Empire had been colored deeply by sixth-century Byzantine absolutism. When these concepts began to influence Western Europe once again in the High Middle Ages, they tended to make continental governments not only more rational but also more autocratic.

---

[5] The actual author is unknown, but he was clearly someone associated with Henry II's court and intimately familiar with its methods. Historians commonly call the work, for convenience, Glanville's treatise. The best edition—with Latin text and English translation on facing pages—is *The Treatise on the Laws and Customs of England Commonly called Glanvill*, G. D. G. Hall ed. (London, 1965).

Roman law found greater acceptance on the Continent than in England. One reason for this was England's remoteness from Italy, where the study of Roman law centered. But a more important reason was the early development of a strong English monarchy. When the revived Roman law first made its impact on European politics in the mid-twelfth century, France and other continental states were still relatively disunited and amorphous, whereas the English monarchy already had a powerful administrative and legal tradition behind it. To continental monarchs, Roman law seemed an ideal tool with which to build centralized political regimes. But the Angevin kings of England relied more heavily on the Germanic traditions of the Saxon and Norman kings, which had already served the monarchy so well. Hence, although Roman law made a distinct mark on England's legal development, its influence was not decisive. The common law remained distinctively English. It would evolve in later centuries into one of the dominating legal traditions of the world.

Henry II and the Church

For all its achievements in the realms of commerce and political administration, the twelfth century remained an age of faith. A great deal of the creative originality of the period was devoted, in one way or another, to the service of Christianity. The best historians of the age regarded historical development as the progressive unfolding of a divine plan. Scholars such as St. Anselm and John of Salisbury reflected primarily on God and his relationship to humanity. Kings, barons, and knights embarked on crusades to the Holy Land. Architects devoted their talents to the building of abbeys and cathedrals.

High-medieval Europe experienced a series of ecclesiastical reform movements and an intensification of piety at all levels of society. The struggles over lay investiture left the twelfth-century papacy and episcopacy more powerful than ever before, and appointments to high Church offices, no longer subject to total lay control, often produced churchmen of high character as well as practical wisdom. Of course, kings and nobles retained a strong voice in ecclesiastical appointments, and the universal Church still suffered unworthy, self-serving bishops and abbots, and priests who were incompetent or licentious (or both). Even so, the moral caliber of the clergy was undoubtedly rising, as the papacy tightened its control over the Church through its wide-ranging legates and its increasingly effective administrative organization.

In England, as elsewhere, the Church devoted more and more attention to such areas as law, administration, and education. Monasteries and cathedrals grew increasingly active in the education of the young, and under ecclesiastical auspices, centers of higher education such as Oxford and Canterbury emerged. Canon law was developing into a vast, coherent body of knowledge, administered by an increasingly elaborate network of ecclesiastical courts separate from those of king and barons. In the area of secular administration, too, clerics played a decisive role. Well-equipped by the excellence of their education, they ran the exchequers and chanceries, served as trusted royal counselors, wrote the histories of their times, and carried on the work of scholarship. Archbishops and kings might clash on occasion, but there could be no separation of church and state.

Henry II's effort to extend the scope of the royal courts ran directly counter to the growth of ecclesiastical jurisdiction. But the papacy at the time was again deeply involved in a struggle with the Holy Roman emperor, and had Henry enjoyed the full cooperation of the English episcopacy, he might well have succeeded in carrying out his policies unhindered. As it was, however, his attempt to limit the jurisdiction of the ecclesiastical courts aroused the violent opposition of the new archbishop of Canterbury, Thomas Becket, resulting in a savage struggle between the king and his primate.[6]

The public career of Thomas Becket went through two phases of about equal length. For eight years, from 1154 to 1162, he served as Henry II's chancellor and boon companion. In 1162, Henry appointed him archbishop of Canterbury, and for the following eight years, until his murder in 1170, Becket was Henry's implacable foe. Much has been written of the transformation in Becket's character from the roistering, worldly chancellor to the stern archbishop, but the complexities of Becket's personality will always remain obscure. It is clear that he was an exceedingly talented man, the offspring of a London merchant family who ascended, by virtue of his intelligence and charm, up through the ecclesiastical hierarchy into the royal chancellorship, and finally into the supreme ecclesiastical office in Britain. His career was dazzling, and as he rose, he devoted himself to fulfilling each of his successive responsibilities. As chancellor, Becket served his king faithfully and skillfully; as archbishop, he fought with equal ardor for the interests of the Church. The perfect chancellor, and one of England's most celebrated churchmen, he has been described as a mere actor who played each of his roles to the hilt. This judgment is superficial. Becket in fact hoped to maintain a cooperative relationship with Henry II, but he also took his archiepiscopal responsibility very seriously. As archbishop, he felt duty bound to uphold the rights of God's Church—all the more so because some churchmen had criticized him for being the first archbishop since the Norman Conquest who had not previously served as a monk or regular canon. Deeply aware of this alleged shortcoming, Becket went to considerable lengths to demonstrate his piety—to his contemporaries and doubtless to God as well. He adopted the ascetic custom of wearing a miserably scratchy hairshirt concealed under his religious habit. Although he desired Henry's continued friendship, he would not be Henry's tool. If the archbishop sometimes lacked generosity of spirit, one must nevertheless recognize that he made his later years immensely more difficult for himself by his uncompromising dedication to what he took to be his religious duties. We must grant him the honesty of his convictions.

---

[6] The best biographical study is Frank Barlow, *Thomas Becket* (London, 1986).

Henry II, on the other hand, could not have anticipated Becket's change of heart. In appointing Becket to the archbishopric, the king must have supposed that he was installing a chum at the apex of the British Church. But Becket soon asserted his independence in a variety of ways. He declined Henry's request, for example, that he continue to serve as royal chancellor, and he began to treat Henry not as his master but as his political colleague and spiritual son. Henry was surprised and resentful, and hostility soon developed between the two.

Early in 1164, Henry brought the issue to a head by forcing Becket and the other English bishops to consent to a list of customs dealing with church-state relations—a document known as the Constitutions of Clarendon. These customs were, of course, strongly pro-royal. Henry II maintained that they represented common practice in the days of Henry I, and with one or two possible exceptions they did. Yet for several reasons they were difficult for reform clergy to accept. For one thing, although Henry I had often acted contrary to the spirit of ecclesiastical reform, he had never been so bold—or so foolish—as to commit his practices to writing. He may have ignored many of the privileges that ecclesiastical reformers claimed, but he never asked his clerics to give their written approval to his policies. Moreover, the English Church had achieved a considerable measure of independence during Stephen's reign, rising to a position much more in harmony with contemporary reform ideology. Some of the provisions in the Constitutions of Clarendon would therefore have appeared to reformers as distasteful backward steps. This was particularly true of the ban on appeals to Rome without royal permission (a policy that dated back to William the Conqueror) and the provision establishing a degree of royal jurisdiction over "criminous clerics," who had previously been subject to church courts alone.

The proper treatment of criminous clerics was the most bitterly disputed issue in the Henry/Becket controversy. Henry complained that such offenders often received absurdly light sentences from ecclesiastical tribunals. In the royal courts the penalty for murder was death or mutilation, but a cleric who murdered someone might simply be banished from the priesthood (defrocked) and released. The Constitutions of Clarendon provided that once a cleric was tried, convicted, and defrocked by an ecclesiastical court, the Church should no longer prevent his being brought to a royal court for further punishment: "If a cleric has confessed or been convicted, the Church shall protect him no further." Becket replied that no one ought to be put in double jeopardy.

The Becket dispute discloses two worlds in collision: the secular world of the royal bureaucracy and the spiritual world of the English and international Church. Two different governments—royal and ecclesiastical—met head-on. Similar disputes occurred off and on throughout high-medieval Europe and, indeed, pointed to a deeper conflict—a power struggle between the universal Church and the rising secular states. The battle between Henry II and Becket was one of its most dramatic episodes, and it might well have been avoided if both men had possessed cooler heads.

Shortly after subscribing to the Constitutions of Clarendon, Becket reversed himself and appealed to Pope Alexander III for support. Alexander equivocated: he could hardly repudiate Becket, yet his own conflict with the Holy Roman emperor, Frederick Barbarossa, left him reluctant to make further enemies among Europe's monarchs. Moreover, as a trained legal scholar, Alexander would have realized that Becket's position on clerical immunity was more radical than that of most canon lawyers.

Henry II had by now lost all patience with Becket and resolved to break his spirit. Toward the end of 1164, Henry ordered him to stand trial before the king's great council in Northampton, which accused Becket of various offenses allegedly committed during his service as chancellor. Claiming clerical immunity from royal jurisdiction, Becket fled the country to appeal his case to the pope. In so doing, he challenged one of the basic articles of Henry's Constitutions of Clarendon—the prohibition of unlicensed appeals to Rome.

There followed a protracted struggle between the fiery king and the exiled archbishop. For nearly six years, the papacy managed to placate Becket while restraining him sufficiently to avoid a complete break between England and Rome. The crisis reached its climax in June 1170. Henry II, anxious to forestall another succession crisis after his death, took steps to have his eldest surviving son crowned. Since the archbishop of Canterbury was unavailable, Henry turned to Canterbury's ancient rival, the archbishop of York. When Becket heard that the archbishop of York had presided over a royal coronation, he was furious at the affront to the dignity of Canterbury. With papal backing, he threatened to lay England under the ban of interdict. Alarmed at this threat, which would have resulted in the closing of all of England's churches, Henry II worked out a temporary reconciliation with Becket that left all major issues unresolved but allowed the archbishop to return to England.

A truce that failed to resolve anything was perhaps worse than no truce at all. Just before returning to England, in the late autumn of 1170, Becket shocked Henry by excommunicating all the bishops who had participated in the coronation of the Young Henry. Henry II, livid with rage, is reported to have cried out to his court, "Will no one rid me of this turbulent priest?" And four of his barons, responding to their king's fury, journeyed to Canterbury with vengeance in their hearts. On the evening of December 29, 1170, they hacked Becket to pieces in Canterbury Cathedral before a group of terrified onlookers. Becket murmured, "I accept death for the name of Jesus and his Church." And he fell to the stone floor with his arms outstretched in prayer.

The deed had a powerful impact on public opinion in England and the Continent. Becket was hailed as a martyr, and his tomb at Canterbury became an immensely popular pilgrimage center. He was quickly canonized, and his bones were reputed to be a source of miraculous cures. His stance on criminous clerics now won the assent of Europe's canon lawyers, and the papacy itself issued legislation protecting clerics from secular punishment.

Becket's Murder in Canterbury Cathedral, 1170 In the upper panel of this nearly contemporary manuscript illumination, the archbishop, while dining, is warned of the arrival of four hostile barons. In the lower panel he is murdered while his monks hide in terror. (Reproduced by courtesy of the Trustees of the British Museum)

To Henry, Becket's murder was a source of profound political embarrassment. The king denied that the four barons had acted under his orders, and one can well believe that Henry would not have been so foolish as to undertake deliberately such a violent and self-defeating policy. Nevertheless, Henry by no means escaped responsibility completely. He had been Becket's archenemy, and if the four killers were not acting on his command, they were at least responding to his anger. The Church and a strong public outcry obliged the king to do penance by walking barefoot through the Canterbury streets and undergoing a ceremonial whipping by the Canterbury monks. He was also compelled to repudiate the Constitutions of Clarendon, to permit appeals to Rome without specific royal license, and to refrain from subjecting criminous clerics to capital punishment. On the surface of things, the martyred archbishop would seem to have won.

In reality, the expansion of royal justice at ecclesiastical expense suffered only a partial eclipse. Although Henry withdrew the Constitutions of Clarendon, most of their provisions remained effective in fact if not in law. Henry continued to place trustworthy royal servants in high ecclesiastical offices, and in the later years of his reign he kept tight control over the Church without any dramatic violations of canon law or harsh conflicts with the papacy. His earlier policy of flamboyant aggression, symbolized by the Constitutions of Clarendon, gave way to a more effective policy of subtle backstairs maneuvering. Learning from the Becket affair, Henry II succeeded, in ecclesiastical affairs as elsewhere, in advancing his realm toward administrative and legal centralization.

The Angevin Empire

In discussing the development of England under Henry II, one must never overlook the fact that Henry's authority extended far beyond the island kingdom. He was the first of England's kings to possess greater wealth and power outside England than within it. He applied many of his English legal and administrative policies to his continental dominions as well—Normandy in particular. The Norman ducal court and exchequer continued to parallel those of England. Henry issued a military ordinance for his French lands similar to the English Assize of Arms, and he undertook a feudal survey of Normandy in 1172 that echoed the *Cartae Baronum* of 1166. Nevertheless, one can separate England from the remainder of the Angevin Empire without doing excessive violence to historical reality, for Henry's constellation of territories was really no empire at all. Each principality he controlled had its own separate government and distinct customs; only their allegiance to a single individual linked these heterogeneous lands. There was no central imperial government, no unified body of imperial law, but rather myriad separate administrations of varying efficiency, held together by Henry's intelligence and energy. Still, from the military and diplomatic standpoint—if not from the standpoint of law and administration—the Angevin Empire must be regarded as a single entity. England was its most tightly administered district and a major source of wealth, whereas the continental territories required the bulk of Henry's military efforts.

Having inherited a huge conglomeration of territories, Henry aspired to still more. He campaigned—with only partial success—to extend his authority into the province of Toulouse in southern France (see map, opposite). And he won a degree of control over eastern and central Ireland when a few of his ambitious vassals invaded and settled there and, later, when he intervened directly. In 1185, he went so far as to install his son John as lord of Ireland, recalling him later when John suffered a military disaster at Irish hands. But for Henry II, the Irish campaigns, so significant to later English history, were of mere secondary importance—little more than an afterthought. From the beginning of his reign to the end, he focused his military and political interests primarily on France.

During the years of Henry II, the French monarchy was coming of age. Since 987, the crown had rested in the hands of the Capetian family. This dynasty had managed to secure its hold on the French throne by producing male heirs at the proper time. But until the twelfth century, its direct authority extended only to the district around Paris and Orléans, known as the Ile de France, and even here the Capetians were plagued by a host of unruly minor barons. In theory, the great dukes and counts of France—even the duke of Normandy himself—were vassals of the French kings, but they tended to ignore their obligations toward their feeble monarch unless it was in their interest to ally with him.

In the twelfth century, however, Capetian power was growing. King Louis VI (1108–1137) succeeded in taming the barons of the Ile de France, thereby providing the monarchy with a secure, if limited, territorial base.

THE ANGEVIN EMPIRE

DOMINIONS OF HENRY II

Held from Henry II by vassals.

Ruled by Henry II directly as king.

Royal Domain of the King of France.

Held by Henry II as vassal of the King of France.

Held by vassals of the King of France

His successor, Louis VII (1137–1180), was a genial, pious man who extended the monarchy's prestige by serving as a rallying point for the French nobility against the Angevin Empire's immense power. More and more, the French nobles outside Henry II's dominions looked to Louis VII for leadership and submitted their disagreements to the court of this self-effacing, honest king.

To Louis VII, the growth of the Angevin Empire presented an ominous threat. From his modest possessions in the Ile de France, he faced a vast configuration of territories controlled by his nominal vassal, Henry II. England, Normandy, Maine, Anjou, Brittany, Touraine, and Aquitaine were now joined together in an empire that dwarfed the French royal domain. On the other hand, the Capetian monarchy enjoyed the advantage of a formal overlordship over Henry II's French dominions, and the further advantage that these territories were heterogeneous—too extensive to defend easily and in some cases quite loosely governed. Aquitaine, in particular, had a long tradition of baronial independence, and outside the northern Aquitainian province of Poitou, the ducal authority tended to be nominal.

Thus, the Angevin Empire had serious weaknesses that the French monarchy might exploit. But Louis VII took only half-hearted advantage of the overextended Empire, primarily by fomenting revolt among Henry II's sons and Henry's much-abused wife, Eleanor of Aquitaine (Louis's own former wife). Henry left himself open to such tactics. He alienated his wife by his infidelities (Eleanor of Aquitaine absolutely loathed Henry's mistress, "the Fair Rosamund" Clifford), and he annoyed his sons by giving them titular authority over various districts of his empire while reserving actual political authority for himself. Urged on by the French king, and resentful of their father's authoritarian ways, Henry II's three eldest sons, Henry, Richard, and Geoffrey, rebelled against him in 1173–1174. Their mother supported them; indeed, because the three rebellious sons were, at the time, fourteen, fifteen, and barely eighteen years old, Eleanor must have been the primary architect of the revolt. A number of nobles in Henry II's continental possessions joined the rebels, but they were able to win the backing of only a few English barons. In the end, the rebellion collapsed and, to prevent future uprisings, Henry II consigned his wife to comfortable imprisonment in a castle in France and placated his sons with greater responsibility and authority. All this did little good. Young Henry and Geoffrey both died in the midst of their plots or insurrections—Henry in 1183 and Geoffrey three years later. At Louis VII's death in 1180, the French crown passed to his shrewd and ruthless son, Philip II "Augustus" (1180–1223), who adopted a far more aggressive anti-Angevin policy than his father had pursued.

Consequently, trouble marred Henry II's final years. The great king could keep the peace everywhere except within his own family, and Philip Augustus was able to exploit to the fullest the rebelliousness of Henry's offspring. In the late 1180s, both of Henry's surviving sons, Richard and John, conspired with Philip Augustus and rebelled against their aging father. On the eve of Henry's death in 1189, their hostile coalition forced him to submit to them, and tradition has it that Henry's dying sentence was one of bitter self-reproach: "Shame, shame on a conquered king."

But Henry II's defeat in 1189, although a personal tragedy, had little effect on French or English history. For despite Philip Augustus's involvement, the rebellion was fundamentally a family affair, and on Henry II's death, the Angevin Empire passed intact to his eldest surviving son, Richard the Lion-Hearted. Philip Augustus's machinations had done him little good. But Philip was both patient and persevering, intent on destroying the Angevin Empire and prepared to devote his whole life to the task if necessary. Henry II had clung grimly to his continental lands. It remained to be seen whether his sons could do as well.

Richard the Lion-Hearted (1189–1199)

Richard the Lion-Hearted was above all else a warrior. The military nobility greatly admired him for his skill at arms, his mastery of siegecraft, and his passion for battle. While crusading in the Holy Land, Richard conducted the siege of Acre with such enthusiasm that, even when he was ill, he had his men carry him to the city walls on a litter so that he might fire his crossbow at the enemy.

Richard was also in tune with the new aristocratic style of courtly manners, witty talk, and chivalrous display that was becoming fashionable among the Anglo-French nobility. A troubadour at the court of Henry II had complained about its lack of style: "There was no banter, no laughter, no giving of presents." At Richard's court the mood was different, for the new king had spent his youth in Aquitaine—the homeland of the troubadours—and he wrote troubadour songs himself. There were those who criticized him for his outbursts of temper and his acts of cruelty; the contemporary writer Gerald of Wales described him as a person who "cared for no success unless it was reached by a path cut by his own sword and stained with his enemies' blood." But many of Richard's contemporaries nonetheless respected him as a warrior and crusader, and in subsequent generations his reputation rose to heroic heights.

Richard has fared less well at the hands of modern historians. He made no personal contribution to English constitutional and legal development and, indeed, spent less than six months of his ten-year reign in England. (This statistic is enshrined in every textbook, and we have no intention of neglecting it here!)[7] The nineteenth-century historian Sismondi dismissed him as "a bad son, a bad brother, a bad husband, and a bad king." But historians who condemn Richard in such uncompromising terms are judging him by anachronistic standards: Because we now know that the Angevin Empire was ephemeral and the crusading movement ultimately a

---

[7] John T. Appleby entitled his history of the reign *England Without Richard 1189–1199* (Ithaca, N.Y., 1965). An excellent, sympathetic biography is John Gillingham, *Richard the Lion-Heart* (London, 1978).

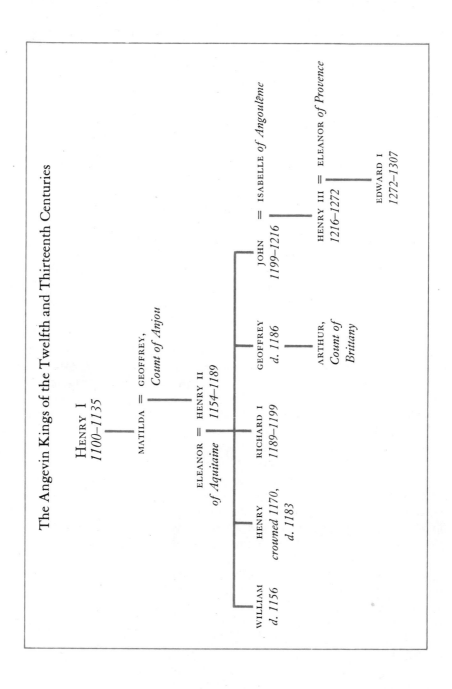

The Angevin Kings of the Twelfth and Thirteenth Centuries

HENRY I
1100–1135

MATILDA = GEOFFREY,
Count of Anjou

ELEANOR = HENRY II
of Aquitaine 1154–1189

WILLIAM
d. 1156

HENRY
crowned 1170,
d. 1183

RICHARD I
1189–1199

GEOFFREY
d. 1186

ARTHUR,
Count of
Brittany

JOHN = ISABELLE of Angoulême
1199–1216

HENRY III = ELEANOR of Provence
1216–1272

EDWARD I
1272–1307

failure, we are prone to discount Richard's defense of his French territories and his glory on the Third Crusade. Yet these are the very activities that earned him respect among his contemporaries and ensured the success of his reign. His military prowess and chivalric reputation retained for him the loyalty of his vassals and subjects, even when he himself was far away. Hence he preserved the Angevin Empire's integrity and was never seriously threatened by internal rebellion.

The Reign of Richard I

Immediately after his coronation in 1189, Richard began preparing for a crusade. Jerusalem, which had fallen to the Christian warriors of the First Crusade in 1099, had been retaken by the talented Muslim leader Saladin in 1187. Beginning in 1190, a multitude of European warriors set off on the Third Crusade with the goal of recapturing the Holy City. They were led by three monarchs: Emperor Frederick Barbarossa of Germany, King Philip Augustus of France, and King Richard I of England. Considering the magnitude of the effort and the distinction of its leaders, the Third Crusade must be regarded as a failure—but it was a romantic failure that added much to Richard the Lion-Hearted's fame. Richard became the real leader of the movement. Frederick Barbarossa drowned while crossing a river on his way to the Holy Land, and Philip Augustus—whose dour temperament was unsuited for crusading—abandoned the venture after joining with Richard in the capture of the important port of Acre. The longstanding French-Angevin conflict made the two monarchs natural rivals, and having quarreled with Richard, Philip returned to France to plot against him. Richard was left in command of the campaign against Saladin.

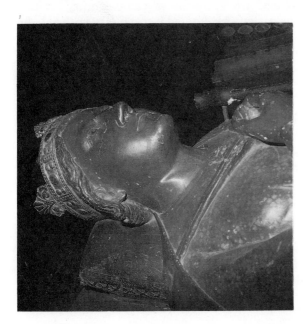

King Richard I from Rouen Cathedral, 1157–1199
(Ronald Sheridan/
The Ancient Art &
Architecture Collection)

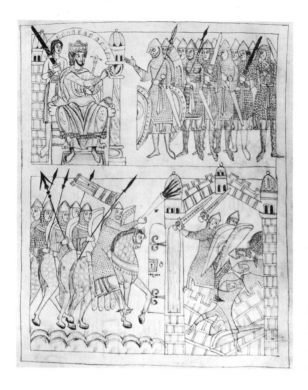

**Knights in Chain Mail
Attacking a Castle**
From a twelfth-century
manuscript. (Walters Art
Gallery, Baltimore)

In this great Muslim chieftain, Richard found an adversary as valiant as himself. While fighting one another, the two warriors developed a strong mutual admiration. And when, after months of campaigning, Richard found it impossible to take Jerusalem, he entered into a treaty with Saladin that guaranteed the rights of Christian pilgrims in the Holy City. He then set out for home to take his revenge on Philip Augustus. On his return journey, he had the extreme bad luck to be captured by the duke of Austria and handed over to his enemy, Emperor Henry VI of Germany, Frederick Barbarossa's son and heir.

Europe was outraged that a crusading hero should receive such treatment, but Henry VI refused to give up his valuable hostage until England met his terms. In the end, the English submitted to ruthless taxation to raise the immense sum of one hundred thousand pounds—literally a king's ransom—and Richard was obliged to grant Henry VI the overlordship of England, to hold his kingdom as a fief of the Holy Roman Empire as long as Richard lived. Only then was Richard set free.

On his return in 1194, Richard had several scores to settle. Philip Augustus had been working to subvert the Angevin Empire, which was held together by the loyalty of its barons to their chivalric, ill-treated lord, and by the heroic efforts of Richard I's mother, Eleanor of Aquitaine, who, at the news of his captivity, assumed a position of direct authority in England. King Philip had even sought to persuade Emperor Henry VI to keep Richard in perpetual custody. Accordingly, Richard spent the last half of his reign waging war against France. And it soon became clear that on the battlefield Philip Augustus was no match for Richard. By 1198, Richard had recovered all the lands and castles lost during his captivity, and at his untimely death from a battle wound in 1199, he was threatening the French throne itself.

In England, during Richard's absence, the Anglo-Norman and Angevin tradition of family discord had asserted itself in the person of his younger brother, John. When Richard departed from England for the Crusade, he left the kingdom in the control of his chancellor, William Longchamp, bishop of Ely. Longchamp was an able but heavy-handed administrator whose low birth and pompous behavior made him widely unpopular. John attempted to place himself at the head of the movement against Longchamp, with the ultimate goal of wresting England from Richard's control. He succeeded in removing Longchamp from office but failed to win the Angevin Empire for himself. Thereupon he began to plot against his absent brother with the ever-willing Philip Augustus, but again without success. On Richard's return, John begged for his mercy and forgiveness. Richard is recorded as replying in a generous but patronizing tone: "Think no more of it, John; you are only a child who has had evil counselors."

In the years after Longchamp's fall, England's administration passed into the hands of a skillful royal official, Hubert Walter, who rose in 1193 to the archbishopric of Canterbury. More an administrator than a pastor, Hubert Walter did not distinguish himself as a spiritual leader. But he provided Richard with something that Henry II had sought in vain: a trusted supporter at the head of the English Church. More than that, Hubert Walter, who dominated the English administration during the last half of Richard's reign and the first third of John's, presided over an immensely significant era in English administrative history. In addition to his exalted position as archbishop of Canterbury, he served as Richard's justiciar and as John's chancellor. In his time, the royal administration functioned with unprecedented efficiency (the hundred-thousand-pound ransom is merely one illustration of this), and royal records were maintained far more systematically than ever before.

Hubert Walter and his able administrative colleagues provided a degree of continuity between the reigns of Richard and John. The two brothers were so contrary in personality, however, that their reigns form two distinct epochs. Royal administration had made great progress in the twelfth century, but the quality of individual royal leadership remained fundamentally important. And even more than the chivalrous Richard, John was to make his own impression on the development of the English state.

King John (1199–1216): An Evaluation

John's reign witnessed three great conflicts: with the French monarchy, with the papacy, and with the English barons. Each of these struggles ended in failure for John, and his failures were of momentous consequence for the making of England. They resulted in the disintegration of the Angevin

Empire, the establishment of papal lordship over the English realm, and the issuing of Magna Carta.[8]

John himself is an elusive figure. In many respects, he was Richard's opposite—unchivalrous, moody, suspicious, a mediocre general, but highly intelligent and deeply interested in the royal administration. He is at once repulsive and fascinating. Historians of the nineteenth century tended to regard him as a brilliant, unscrupulous villain. J. R. Green described him in these words, beginning with a quote from the thirteenth-century chronicler Matthew Paris:

> "Foul as it is, hell itself is defiled by the fouler presence of John." This terrible view of his contemporaries has passed into the sober judgment of history. . . . In his inner soul John was the worst outcome of the Angevins. He united into one mass of wickedness their insolence, their selfishness, their unbridled lust, their cruelty and tyranny, their shamelessness, their superstition, their cynical indifference to honor or truth.[9]

Since the time these words were written, historians have modified their appraisal of John. A French historian, writing in the 1930s when Freud's theories were popular, ascribed John's difficulties to mental illness: "It is our opinion that John Lackland was subject to a mental disease well known today and described by modern psychiatrists as the periodical psychosis. . . . Among his Angevin ancestors were fools and madmen."[10] Modern psychology shares with medieval penance the happy quality of forgiving all sins; by portraying John as a psychotic, it allows us to absolve him.

Subsequent historians have also attempted to rehabilitate John—in a variety of ways. Modern scholars tend to be skeptical of such concepts as the foulness of hell, corrupt inner souls, masses of wickedness, and even of Freud. Some have argued that John was considerably maligned by his contemporaries. Many of the most infamous atrocity stories relating to his reign, for example, come from the writings of two thirteenth-century historians from St. Albans Abbey—Roger Wendover and Matthew Paris—both of whom were strongly biased against him. Roger Wendover despised John, and Matthew Paris copied from Wendover and elaborated his tales. From the works of these men comes the story that John ordered his soldiers to seize Archdeacon Geoffrey of Norwich, bind him with chains, cast him into prison, and torture him to death by crushing him beneath a covering of lead.

---

[8] King John has received much attention. Two scholarly accounts are highly recommended: Sidney Painter, *The Reign of King John* (Baltimore, 1949), and W. L. Warren, *King John* (London, 1961; Berkeley, Calif., 1978). The latter is somewhat more popular in approach and more readable. More popular still, and thoroughly entertaining, is W. L. Warren, "Painter's *King John*—Forty Years On," *The Haskins Society Journal: Studies in Medieval History* I (1989): 1–9, which suggests parallels between King John and Richard Nixon.

[9] J. R. Green, *History of the English People*, I (special ed., Nations of the World Series, n.d.), p. 237. Green's *History* was first published in London in the years 1877–1880.

[10] Charles Petit-Dutaillis, *The Feudal Monarchy in France and England* (London, 1936), p. 215.

Tomb Effigy of King John in Worcester Cathedral, Carved Shortly After His Death Beside him are depictions of two Anglo-Saxon bishops of Worcester, Oswald and Wulfstan, whom John regarded as patron saints. (A. F. Kersting)

This grisly event is said to have occurred in 1209. Yet sixteen years later, in 1225, this same Archdeacon Geoffrey became bishop of Ely. It is known that there were several Geoffreys connected with Norwich and that Roger Wendover may have gotten them confused; but if so, we can accept the remainder of the anecdote only with grave reservations. Again, Matthew Paris reports that at the death of Archbishop Hubert Walter in 1205, John made the disrespectful statement: "Now for the first time I am king of England." The same historian relates that when John's talented justiciar, Geoffrey Fitz Peter, died in 1213, the monarch exclaimed: "By the feet of God now for the first time am I king and lord of England." Unless we wish to add redundancy to John's numerous sins, we must view both tales with skepticism.

Still, even though such stories may be exaggerated or even false, John was the sort of person about whom they could be believed. He was a repellent, unlovable man who probably murdered his nephew (Arthur of Brittany) in a drunken rage, and who killed hostages, starved prisoners, and broke his word with exuberant abandon. Such conduct fell far short of the standards that twelfth- and thirteenth-century England demanded of its kings. John's behavior cost him the respect of his subjects and diminished his effectiveness as a political and military leader. The story is told of how St. Hugh, bishop of Lincoln, once tried to frighten John into changing his ways by showing him a carving of tormented souls in hell at the Angevin abbey of Fontevrault. But John turned aside to gaze at some carvings of proud kings, telling Bishop Hugh that he intended to pattern himself after them.

Richard had successfully preserved his patrimony because his barons and lesser subjects trusted and respected him. John failed because he lost his barons' confidence. They did not demand a living saint as their monarch— many of John's predecessors had been ruthless and cruel—but they did expect consistency of policy and military prowess. And John was, above all, inconstant. He was capable of almost senseless lethargy, excessive caution, even panic. The barons, who could forgive much in an able warrior-king, gave John the humiliating nickname "Softsword," and right or wrong the image had a fatal effect on John's leadership. His barons, regarding him as suspicious and untrustworthy, often refused to join his military expeditions or fight his battles. The more they did so, the more suspicious and untrustworthy John became. In the generations since the Norman Conquest, monarchy and nobility had often been at odds, but never before was the rift so deep. As one historian observed: "John was the most incompetent and overrated of the Plantagenet kings."[11]

Nonetheless, John's reign was not without its triumphs. His military and diplomatic policies toward Wales and Scotland succeeded as seldom before. His vassals extended their authority over two-thirds of Ireland, and the native Irish kings of the remaining third recognized him as their overlord. He undertook to build a strong, well-organized navy: by 1205 it numbered fifty-one oared galleys and could be expanded to several times that figure by commandeering merchant ships. He devoted much intelligent attention to the royal administration. He enforced the law strongly and—unless it was against his interest—justly. Indeed, his accession marks the beginning of a great new epoch in the administrative history of the realm. Three of medieval England's foremost administrators worked under him and evidently received his full support: the chancellor-archbishop, Hubert Walter; the justiciar, Geoffrey Fitz Peter; and the treasurer, William of Ely. Royal records became more abundant and exact. Now for the first time, royal charters and other correspondence issuing from the chancery were systematically copied and preserved.

Like his predecessors, John was keenly acquisitive, and his tightening of royal law and administration brought a significant increase in taxation. But John carried the revenue-raising practices of his royal predecessors to extremes—demanding arbitrarily high reliefs, abusing royal authority over wardships and marriages, and adding to these abuses new fiscal expedients such as higher and more frequent scutage levies and a greater incidence of taxes on rents and chattels. England was prosperous enough to afford such exploitation, and John needed money desperately. He had inherited an empty treasury from Richard, and his reign was marked by a surge of

---

[11] John Gillingham, "The Unromantic Death of Richard I," *Speculum* 54 (1979): 18.

inflation. Nevertheless, John's financial policies served to increase his unpopularity and to heighten his reputation as an arbitrary tyrant.

The Collapse of the Angevin Empire

When John acceded to the throne of England and assumed the leadership of the Angevin Empire, he faced a multitude of difficulties.[12] His reputation was already damaged, not so much by his earlier machinations against his crusading brother (filial and fraternal disloyalty were by no means unprecedented) as by their utter futility. He inherited from Richard an effective but expensive and demanding military policy in France. Moreover, he was confronted from the first with a rival to the throne in his nephew, Arthur of Brittany—son of his late brother Geoffrey and grandson of Henry II. Because John managed to win England and most of the continental territories, Arthur predictably received the full support of the persistently troublesome Philip Augustus of France.

Philip and Richard the Lion-Hearted had been at war when Richard died, and the hostilities continued into the early months of John's reign. In 1200 the two kings arranged a truce, but Philip continued to await his opportunity to shatter the Angevin inheritance. The opportunity came a mere three months later when John, on a tour of Aquitaine, suddenly and unexpectedly entered into marriage. The bride was a girl in her early teens, Isabel, heiress of the important Aquitainian county of Angoulême.

John's motives in selecting his young wife seem to have been a blend of passion and politics. Isabel was a beautiful girl, and Angoulême was one of the more disorderly principalities in turbulent Aquitaine. By establishing firm control over Angoulême, John could extend his authority in southern France considerably. But Isabel's hand was already promised to the neighboring lord of another important Aquitainian principality—Hugh the Brown of Lusignan. In making Isabel his wife, John forestalled a dangerous alliance between Lusignan and Angoulême; he also gravely offended the Lusignan family. According to the custom of the day, he might have smoothed things over by granting Hugh the Brown certain territorial compensations, but the headstrong king chose to scorn the Lusignans and thereby earned their hatred. In the months that followed, John alienated other Aquitainian barons by seizing their lands and accusing them of treason. He was creating a dangerously hostile faction within his continental dominions.

In the spring of 1202, King Philip Augustus made his move. Taking advantage of an appeal by the Lusignans to his court, Philip summoned John to Paris to answer their complaints. As king of England, John was subject to no one; but as duke of Aquitaine and Normandy, count of Anjou, and lord of

---

[12] The collapse of the Angevin Empire under John is treated masterfully and in great detail by Sir Maurice Powicke, *The Loss of Normandy, 1189–1204* (2nd ed., Manchester, 1961). See further Sir James Holt, "The End of the Anglo–Norman Realm," in his *Magna Carta and Medieval Government* (London, 1985), pp. 23–65.

The Ruins of Chateau-Gaillard   Built by Richard I in 1197–1198 to guard the Seine approach to Normandy, the castle was lost by King John after a long siege. (Ronald Sheridan/ The Ancient Art & Architecture Collection)

numerous other continental principalities, he was the vassal of the king of France. As such he was bound by feudal custom to answer the summons to his lord's court. And when he refused to do so (very sensibly) Philip formally deprived him of his French fiefs. Philip had cunningly maneuvered himself into the position of the good lord whose vassal had wronged and defied him. He sent his armies against Normandy, backed by the full force of feudal law.

The campaign went well for John at first. In a bold military stroke, he captured Hugh the Brown, several of Hugh's Lusignan kinsmen, and Arthur of Brittany. But John nullified his victory with subsequent blunders. He released the Lusignans in return for a ransom and promises of loyalty that they did not keep, and he apparently murdered his nephew Arthur. Conclusive proof of the murder has never materialized, but rumors of it spread quickly and John's reputation disintegrated still further. Meanwhile, the king continued to abuse his barons, friend and foe alike, and his unpopularity increased among his continental vassals.

Ultimately, John had to depend on the loyalty of these vassals for the defense of his continental inheritance, and his mistreatment of many of them proved a fatal error. In the course of the year 1203, one Norman castle after another fell to Philip Augustus, while John roamed aimlessly around the duchy watching his patrimony crumble. In December 1203, with much of Normandy still under his control, John departed for England, apparently in panic, leaving his Norman loyalists in the lurch. By the middle of 1204, all Normandy lay in King Philip's hands. Meanwhile, Maine, Anjou, and all of John's former continental territories north of Aquitaine also fell to the French monarchy. All that remained were portions of distant Aquitaine, whose barons preferred a remote and ineffective lord like John to a powerful monarch near at hand. The Angevin Empire was defunct. John had sustained a monstrous military and political disaster.

England's French territories were not severed completely and would not be until the mid-sixteenth century. But from 1204 onward, England was far more autonomous than before, and its kings tended to devote most of their attention to the island kingdom itself. Modern English historians, looking at events in retrospect, are inclined to regard this development as fortunate. To John, however, it was a profound humiliation that had to be avenged. For the next decade, he devoted his considerable political and diplomatic talents to creating an alliance system designed to crush Philip Augustus and permit the reconquest of Normandy and Anjou.

The Struggle with the Papacy

In the meantime, John had become involved in a struggle with the papacy over the selection of a new archbishop of Canterbury to replace Hubert Walter, who died in 1205. The archbishopric of Canterbury had been a storm center in the reigns of William Rufus, Henry I, and Henry II. Under John as well, the basic issue remained ecclesiastical independence versus royal sovereignty over the English Church, a trial of strength between the claims of the universal Church and the kingdom of England. But far more than ever, the church-state struggle in John's reign became a direct confrontation between monarchy and papacy.

The Investiture Controversy had been settled long before with compromise, but the question of lay control over the appointments of bishops and abbots remained unresolved. The kings of England subscribed overtly to the policy of free canonical elections but in fact controlled appointments to important offices in the English Church through subtle—or sometimes not so subtle—maneuvering. As long as they applied royal influence quietly and without serious opposition, all was well. But if a king acted clumsily and created a messy issue, the papacy could be expected to intervene in behalf of proper canonical practices. This was particularly true in the opening years of the thirteenth century, when Innocent III—a man of keen intelligence and resolution—occupied the papal throne. Innocent III was history's most powerful pope; it was John's misfortune to lock horns with him.

Hubert Walter had been a masterful royal administrator but a less than inspiring prelate. The monks of Canterbury, who enjoyed the traditional canonical privilege of electing the archbishop, were anxious not to have another royal agent on the Canterbury throne. John was just as anxious to install one of his own loyal subordinates. Working quickly to forestall the king, the Canterbury monks elected one of their own number and sent a delegation to Rome to have him confirmed. Infuriated at their insubordination, John forced the monks to retract their choice, elect his own man, and send another delegation to Rome to obtain confirmation of the new candidate. Thus the issue had been raised, and Innocent III was in a position to judge the dispute. The pope made wise use of his opportunity by repudiating both Canterbury nominees and persuading the Canterbury monks in Rome—by now a goodly number—to elect a churchman of his own choice. The new archbishop was a noted English scholar, Stephen Langton, who had been out of the country for some years teaching on the Continent.

Stephen Langton, as Depicted on His Personal Seal (The Mansell Collection)

John refused to accept an "outsider" and rejected Innocent's interference. Every archbishop of Canterbury in memory—even troublesome ones like Anselm and Becket—had been royal nominees, and John refused to abandon control of the Canterbury succession. Accordingly, he barred Stephen Langton from entering England. Innocent III, for his part, regarded Langton's election as strictly canonical and gave him full support. As a result of the impasse, Innocent laid England under interdict, suspending all church services and sacraments except baptism and confession for the dying.

The interdict lasted seven years. John survived this ecclesiastical penalty remarkably well and even turned it to his financial advantage by confiscating ecclesiastical revenues, but in the end he was obliged to submit. Innocent III was threatening to depose John, and Philip Augustus was contemplating an invasion of England. And John himself—whose grand design for the reconquest of Normandy and Anjou was reaching its climax—needed all the support he could obtain. Hence, he made peace with the papacy in 1213, and in the following year Innocent lifted the interdict. Stephen Langton returned to England and received his archbishopric, and John agreed to restore at least a portion of the confiscated revenues.

Having surrendered, John determined to salvage as much as possible from the situation by winning the full support of the pope. Of his own accord, he gave to Innocent III what William the Conqueror had long ago refused to Gregory VII: he made England a papal fief, undertook to become Innocent's vassal, and promised an annual tribute payment to the papacy (above and beyond the traditional Peter's Pence).[13] He took the further step of vowing to lead a crusade to the Holy Land. The crusade never materialized, for John always claimed more urgent business at home. But by his submission and his crusading vow, he succeeded in capturing the friendship of Rome. Consequently, historians have credited John with snatching victory from defeat. This interpretation seems doubtful, for Innocent's future support was of no great use to John, and Archbishop Stephen Langton turned out to be a man of independent spirit. Nevertheless, in 1214 John still nurtured hopes of recouping his previous territorial losses. With the papal struggle over, he was ready to move decisively against Philip Augustus.

During the years of the interdict, John had been building a coalition of French and German princes against the French monarchy. In 1214, the chief parties in the coalition were (1) Otto of Brunswick, John's nephew and a serious contestant for the disputed throne of the Holy Roman Empire; (2) the counts of Flanders and certain neighboring principalities; and (3) John himself. After several false starts, John set out for the county of Poitou in northern Aquitaine with as many English knights as he could persuade to accompany him. He intended his campaign to be part of a grand design: he was to attack Philip Augustus through Poitou while his German and Flemish allies invaded France from the northeast. The strategy was well conceived, but it ended disastrously. John subdued Poitou and incorporated a large number of Poitevan knights into his army. But when these knights encountered an army led by Philip Augustus's son, the future King Louis VIII, they refused to fight, claiming that they could not engage in armed conflict against their overlord. In rage and frustration, John withdrew from the campaign.

Philip Augustus himself led an army against John's German and Flemish allies and won an overwhelming victory over them near the Flemish village of Bouvines. Philip's victory extinguished John's last hope of recovering the lost continental lands. It also marked a significant advance in the authority of the French monarchy, which surged ahead of Germany as the great power on the Continent. Thus, the decisive French triumph at Bouvines in 1214 confirmed the disintegration of the Angevin Empire in 1204. France was jubilant. Philip's subjects strewed flowers in the path of his triumphant army as it returned home, and the students of the University of Paris partied for two straight weeks.

Magna Carta (1215)

There were no flowers for John. Ten years of savage taxation had come to nothing, and he returned to England to face a sullen baronage. In the wake of Bouvines, the calamitous failure of John's foreign policy became clear to all.

---

[13] The English monarchy continued to pay papal tribute off and on until the fourteenth century, repudiating it officially only in 1366. At the time of John's submission, a number of other kingdoms—Poland, Sicily, Denmark, Sweden, and Aragon—were also papal vassal states.

His prestige had never been lower, and many of his taxridden English barons were on the verge of rebellion. Early in 1215, the insurrection began, and by early summer it was obvious that the king could not contain it. His enemies demanded a written guarantee of good law and just governance based on the coronation charter of Henry I, which Henry II had confirmed in 1154. In June 1215, after protracted negotiations, John capitulated on the meadow of Runnymede and affixed his seal to Magna Carta.[14]

The Great Charter was a much broader statement of rights and privileges than the charter of Henry I. It was the product of long bargaining between John, Stephen Langton, barons who remained loyal to John, and barons of various degrees of hostility toward him. Its sixty-three clauses embraced the full spectrum of baronial grievances, mapping the limits of royal authority much more precisely than ever before. Despite the specific and practical nature of many of the provisions, collectively they reflected— at least by implication—the rudiments of a coherent political philosophy.

Historians have not always agreed on the implications of Magna Carta. Many used to regard it as the fountainhead of English liberty and the bulwark of constitutional monarchy. Some historians, reacting against this naive view, have described Magna Carta as a reactionary document—an assertion of feudal privileges at the expense of the enlightened Angevin monarchy. In reality, the Great Charter was both feudal and constitutional. It looked backward but also pointed forward. It was a step in the transition from the ancient Germanic notion of sacred custom, and the feudal idea of mutual contractual rights and obligations, to the modern concept of limited monarchy and government under the law. In 1215, however, the dissident barons were looking neither backward nor forward; they were grappling with problems of the moment.

Their demand for a written confirmation of privileges had precedents not only in earlier English coronation charters but also in documents drafted elsewhere in Europe—by Emperor Frederick Barbarossa to the towns of Lombardy in 1183, by King Alphonso VIII of Leon to his barons in 1188. And European subjects were winning similar charters from their rulers throughout the thirteenth century—in Germany, Hungary, southern Italy, Sicily, and elsewhere. These documents were products of many of the same forces that underlay Magna Carta: military misfortune; the rising expenses of government; more effective administration, which usually meant more inventive and ruthless means of collecting taxes; and a growing conception on the part of powerful subjects of their specific legal rights. But whereas other charters aimed at achieving autonomy for provinces or other local districts, Magna Carta was kingdom-wide in scope and viewpoint. King John's barons, perhaps because their ancestral holdings had been scattered here and there across the land ever since the Conquest, sought not to cripple the royal government but to influence it—to make it act in their interests and respect their customary rights.

---

[14] On the Great Charter, see Sir James Holt, *Magna Carta* (Cambridge, 1965).

Baronial rights and privileges were the chief items of business in Magna Carta, yet the barons were capable of a wider social vision. They incorporated into the charter the concept that tradition and custom limited the king in his relations with free Englishmen of every class—burghers and peasants as well as knights and barons. And when the document referred to "Englishmen," it sometimes included women as well. For example, "No widow shall be compelled to remarry so long as she wishes to live without a husband." "To no one," John promised, "will we sell, deny, or delay rights of justice." "No free man may be arrested or imprisoned or deprived of his land or outlawed or exiled or in any way brought to ruin, nor shall we go against him or send others in pursuit of him, except by the legal judgment of his peers or by the law of the land." The exact nature of "the law of the land" remained vague, but the barons felt it important to assert that there was such a law, to be discovered in custom and traditional usages, and that the king was bound by it. The concept was expressed more precisely a generation later in the great legal treatise traditionally (and wrongly) ascribed to Henry de Bracton: "The king should be under God and the law." Political philosophers of the twelfth and thirteenth centuries were drawing sharp distinctions between the king who abided by the law and the "tyrant" who abused and ignored it. In Magna Carta, these notions received practical expression.

John had said, "The law is in my mouth." Such a doctrine clearly threatened baronial rights and interests. The king whose will was law could, at least in theory, charge reliefs, levy scutages, and confiscate property as he pleased. Magna Carta specifically forbade such practices: "Scutage and aid shall be levied in our kingdom only by the common counsel of our kingdom"; "No one shall be required to render greater service from a knight's fee or from any other free holding than is in fact owed from it." It was with practical building blocks such as these that the structure of the English limited monarchy was constructed. For implied in the numerous, specific, and pragmatic provisions of Magna Carta was the concept of an overarching body of customary law that circumscribed the power of the king.

There remained, however, the problem of creating some kind of machinery to force the king to honor his concessions. Henry I had offered many promises to his subjects in his coronation oath, but he forgot a number of them once the crisis of his accession had passed. A series of royal promises was obviously insufficient to control an ambitious king backed by the full power of the royal administration. The search for some institutional means to incorporate the nobility into royal government was to occupy England for centuries to come. The later Middle Ages found a tentative solution in Parliament. The barons of 1215 relied on the simpler sanction of a watchdog committee of twenty-five barons who were to summon the English people "to distrain and distress him in every way possible" if the king violated the charter. The committee was not long idle.

"In 1215," writes Sir James Holt, "Magna Carta was a failure. It was intended as a peace and it provoked war. It pretended to state customary law and it promoted disagreement and contention. It was legally valid for only three months, and even within that period its terms were never properly executed." Nevertheless, the charter survived the turbulence of John's final months, was reissued several times in the thirteenth century, and became a part of the common law. Although largely ignored in the days of the Tudors, it was revived, reinterpreted, and passionately supported by the opponents of the seventeenth-century Stuart kings. It has never been entirely forgotten. In later centuries, it was regarded as a document fundamental to the protection of individual liberty. This was far from the intention of its original drafters, but it is a tribute to the quality of their work. "It was adaptable. This was its greatest and most important characteristic."[15]

But for John, Magna Carta was merely an expedient to escape a temporary difficulty. He had no intention of honoring his promises; he quickly secured from his sympathetic papal overlord absolution from his oath to the barons, which was, he argued, obtained under duress and therefore invalid. Consequently, John's reign ended in the midst of a full-scale insurrection. The rebelling barons appealed to King Philip Augustus for aid, and the French king sent an army to England led by his son, Prince Louis. John died in 1216 with the French in London and the country wracked by war.

The dissident barons were fighting not against the traditions of Angevin kingship but against a single man—a monarch who had earned their hostility with his duplicity and ruthlessness. This fact is dramatically demonstrated by the speed with which the baronial insurrection dissolved in the wake of John's death. In the words of an earlier historian, the French invasion "was doomed to fail when the kingdom ceased to be divided against itself; and the one insuperable obstacle to the healing of its divisions was removed in the person of John."[16]

---

[15] Holt, *Magna Carta*, pp. 1, 2.

[16] Kate Norgate, *John Lackland* (London, 1902), p. 286.

PART THREE

The Community of the Realm

1216 to 1307

A GIFT OF A RING   *(The Granger Collection)*

7

Civilization and Its Discontents in High-Medieval England

Back in Chapter 4, when exploring the effects of the Norman Conquest, I said that with or without the Normans England would surely have experienced its share of the economic and cultural developments that were then transforming Europe. In discussing this transformation, it is not always easy to separate England from the Continent; all of Western Europe shared in the economic boom and cultural flowering of the High Middle Ages (c. 1050–1300). Nor is it easy or particularly helpful to cram a discussion of high-medieval civilization into the chronological framework of Part III of this book—1216 to 1307, the reigns of Henry III and Edward I. Instead, this chapter will examine the civilization of high-medieval England in its larger European context and in its full chronological dimensions, ranging across the years from the Norman Conquest to the death of Edward I.

The Civilization of the High Middle Ages

High-medieval civilization rested on the material framework of a productive agriculture and accelerating commerce. By the time of the Norman Conquest the European commercial revival was well under way. Indeed, some historians would prefer to begin the High Middle Ages somewhat earlier than 1050—perhaps in 1000 or 950. The process was gradual, commencing in the tenth century in some districts of Europe, gathering momentum in the eleventh, and achieving full speed in the twelfth. Across these years, devices such as the tandem harness and redesigned horse collar allowed people not only to substitute animal for human labor but also to increase substantially the energy available for cultivation. The heavy plow, drawn by a team of oxen, was the machine most basic to medieval agriculture, but horses were important as well. They were enormously more significant in the High Middle Ages than in Roman times because the new horse collar permitted them to pull loads with their shoulders instead of their necks. Additional energy was supplied by tens of thousands of water mills and, later, by windmills (Europe's first known windmills appeared in eastern England during Henry II's reign). Food was becoming available in greater abundance and variety than before: protein-rich peas and beans

A Reconstruction of a Fourteenth-Century Windmill excavated in Buckinghamshire   The upper structure in this reconstruction is based on contemporary manuscript illuminations. (Courtesy of The British Museum)

became an important element in the European diet, and people consumed cheese, eggs, fish, and meat in much greater quantities.

Consequently, England's population was not only much larger in 1300 than at the time of the Norman Conquest, but healthier and more energetic as well. The best scholarly guesses put England's population at about two million at the time of the Domesday survey of 1086, and at two to three times that figure by the early fourteenth century. To feed the millions of new mouths, the process of land clearing accelerated. Existing agrarian communities expanded into nearby wilderness regions, and by the thirteenth century, cultivators began to make major inroads into the previously protected royal forests.

With the rise in population and food production came a decisive shift toward urbanization. Although society remained primarily agricultural throughout the Middle Ages and long thereafter, by 1300 cities had become a crucial factor in the economy, culture, and social structure of England and continental Europe. Although small by present standards (the population of London in 1300 probably did not far exceed 50,000), high-medieval cities transformed Europe for all time to come. They were themselves the products of a tremendous intensification of commerce, which the historian Robert S. Lopez described as a commercial revolution: "For the first time in history an underdeveloped society succeeded in developing itself, mostly by its own efforts."[1] The awesome cathedrals of Europe's high-medieval cities have been viewed traditionally as symbols of an Age of Faith, but they could have risen only in a period that was also an age of commerce.

The economic transformation of the High Middle Ages was accompanied by far-reaching changes in political and social organization and in mental attitudes. England evolved during these generations from a pre-literate to a literate society. Although it is true that the majority of the English people in 1300 could not read (or at least not very well), they nevertheless had come to depend on written records—deeds, letters, wills, government surveys—to define their rights, property, and status. Whereas England's inhabitants had previously left much to memory and oral tradition, by 1300, English freeholders and even some serfs were having their property transactions recorded in writing. The production and preservation of government documents increased spectacularly: about 15 royal acts per year have survived from the reign of William Rufus; the figure rises to about 41 per year from Henry I's reign and 115 per year from Henry II's. These figures reflect only documents that have survived. The actual production of Henry I's chancery has been estimated, very roughly, at 4,500 acts per year, and the figures for William Rufus and Henry II should doubtless be revised upward comparably. But by whatever measure, the volume of parchment-work issuing from the chancery rose constantly and swiftly across the High Middle Ages. By the thirteenth century, the English government was recording the amount of wax that the chancery was using to seal royal letters. The records disclose that in the years between Henry III's coming of age and his death (1226–1272) the use of sealing wax increased tenfold, suggesting a parallel increase in the number of letters themselves.

Financial records, too, were becoming more and more widespread and systematic. In the recording and accounting of royal financial transactions, England established a clear and early lead over the remainder of high-medieval Europe. Annual written accounts of royal revenues commenced in England around 1110, in France around 1190. Fiscal accounting systems also emerged in Flanders and Catalonia, but only toward the end of the twelfth century. The single exception to this continental lag was Normandy, where Henry I established an exchequer accounting system parallel to, and probably concurrent with, that of England.

Taken together, these new records bear witness to increasingly effective and complex royal administrative systems, first in the Anglo-Norman state and later throughout Western Christendom. As a result of these developments, skills such as reading, writing, and mathematical calculation became vital to the functioning of secular and ecclesiastical governments,

---

[1] Robert S. Lopez, *The Commercial Revolution of the Middle Ages, 950–1350* (Englewood Cliffs, N.J., 1971), p. vii.

urban businesses, and even agricultural enterprises. Possessors of these skills, the reasoners and reckoners, sifted into positions of control throughout society, changing its attitudes and its character. Schools sprang up everywhere, and the age of the university dawned.

The growing complexity of high-medieval society opened much greater possibilities than before for social mobility. Clever social nobodies could rise to power in royal and ecclesiastical administrations. Devout Christians could now choose from a rapidly increasing number of new religious orders. And to restless serfs and poor freeholders, the towns beckoned. Most sons and daughters continued to follow in their parents' footsteps, but the more daring and ambitious found opportunities to break from the family pattern. The result was greater social vitality and, for many, increased anxiety: one's career choice was no longer as narrowly predetermined as before, and it could be a traumatic experience to move from a small village community of one or two hundred familiar faces into a town bustling with thousands of strangers. Some historians have seen as a consequence of this fluidity an increased awareness of self and a growth of introspection. In high-medieval Europe more people were collecting and preserving their personal letters. Autobiographies began to appear for the first time since St. Augustine of Hippo wrote his *Confessions*.

One of the best-known autobiographers of twelfth-century France, Peter Abelard, also pioneered in the development of a new, rational attitude toward humanity and the universe. The seeds of such an attitude had existed in the Judeo-Christian doctrine that the world was created by God yet separate from God (and thus natural rather than supernatural). Nevertheless, early medieval people viewed the world as a theater of miracles: a storm or fire was a divine punishment for sin, a military victory was a mark of God's favor. But in the view of Abelard and many who followed him, God's creation was a natural order that could function by its own rules, without incessant divine tinkering. Miracles were possible, of course, but they were rare. Similar attitudes were circulating in England before and after Abelard's time. When the central tower of Winchester Cathedral collapsed in 1107, many attributed the event to the fact that the blaspheming King William Rufus lay entombed beneath it, but the historian William of Malmesbury (Abelard's contemporary) had his doubts: "The structure might well have fallen because of faulty construction even if the king had never been buried there."

The spread of such attitudes encouraged a growing skepticism toward the judicial ordeal—the appeal to God for a "miracle on demand" to determine guilt or innocence. We have seen how Henry II used the ordeal in his Assizes of Clarendon and Northampton but stipulated that persons of notorious reputation be banished even if they passed it. Earlier, in the 1140s, the English theologian Robert Pullen had expressed his firm belief that ordeals ought to be abolished from God's Church. Later in the twelfth century, the ordeal came under increasingly severe attack in university circles, and in 1215 a great church council known as Lateran IV, chaired by Pope Innocent III, prohibited clergy from participating in ordeals, thereby dooming the procedure to gradual extinction. The judgment of God gave way to the testimony of witnesses and the deliberation of juries. The twelfth century also saw the introduction in church courts of a novel procedure that in time evolved into a major characteristic of European jurisprudence: the cross-examination of witnesses.

These deeply significant shifts in attitude toward self and the world, and the fundamental economic and social changes that accompanied them, have been described as Europe's coming of age. Such metaphors are obviously inadequate; historians might argue endlessly (if they chose to) over the date of Europe's "puberty" or "adulthood." But whether they see the High Middle Ages as childhood's end, or the opening phase of Europe's "modernization," or the time of economic "take-off" (or, for that matter, the climax of the Age of Faith), the changes were essential preconditions for modern Western Civilization. Behind the seventeenth-century scientific revolution lay the high-medieval idea of a universe functioning by natural rules and open to rational inspection. Behind the fifteenth-century invention of printing lay the high-medieval shift from a pre-literate to a literate society. Behind the nineteenth-century Industrial Revolution lay the commercial revolution of the twelfth and thirteenth centuries. Our word *civilization* comes from the Latin *civitas*—"city." In this strict sense, Europe became civilized in the High Middle Ages.

Towns and Commerce in High-Medieval England

Towns had dotted Western Europe ever since classical antiquity. In fifth- and sixth-century Britain, with the withdrawal of the Romans, urban life virtually disappeared, but on the Continent the administrative-military towns of the Roman Empire evolved into the smaller cathedral towns of the early Middle Ages, with their episcopal courts and churches, and the legends and sacred relics of their saints. The revival of town life in England dates back at least to the time of King Alfred and his West Saxon successors. As commerce revived in the tenth and eleventh centuries, it invigorated old towns and stimulated new ones to emerge as centers of trade and production. By William the Conqueror's time, it became necessary to move a number of old rural bishoprics to the new centers of urban population. Lichfield was moved to Chester, Sherborne to Salisbury, Elmham to Thetford and then to Norwich, and Dorchester (Oxfordshire) to Lincoln.

The high-medieval city remained faithful to its saints and religious establishments while at the same time expanding its commercial districts and developing its political and legal institutions. Church, commerce, and urban government coexisted in a balanced relationship within the city's walls. But where trade was lively, merchants spilled outside the walls into new suburbs.

Town life, centering on the town market, remained rustic by modern standards, but it grew steadily more vigorous, and money became more and more abundant. England's ports became increasingly active in international trade: cloth from Flanders, wine from Bordeaux, silks and spices from the

Mediterranean Basin, iron and olive oil from Spain. The English exported a variety of products in return—wool, tin, beer, and, later, woolen cloth. As commercial networks developed all across Europe, various regions could now specialize increasingly in the agrarian and manufactured products for which they were best suited. Trading in various grains, meats, and fruits brought a marked improvement in diet. The English people were now consuming more iron-rich and protein-rich foods and were living longer as a result. The increase in iron in the diet contributed particularly to a longer life expectancy for women, who now, for the first time, began to outnumber men.

The century between 1150 and 1250 saw the emergence of new towns in unprecedented numbers. But this surge was merely the peak of a much longer period of urban growth running from late Anglo-Saxon times to about 1300. Staffordshire, for example, had only three towns at the time of the Domesday survey of 1086, but by 1300 it had twenty-two. The boroughs of Devonshire increased from five in 1086 to eighteen in 1238. And as archaeological investigations disclose, existing towns were growing in size during the twelfth and thirteenth centuries—expanding their limits, raising new houses and buildings on previously undeveloped land, and, in some instances, relocating from a cramped site to a more commodious one nearby. Salisbury, for example, moved from its restricted hilltop location within an ancient ring-fort down to the neighboring plain.

With town growth and commercial vitality came a general improvement in urban architecture. By the late twelfth century, wealthy merchants

A Shop in Medieval London   (Lauros-Giraudon)

were often living in impressive stone houses with roofs of slate or tile. Such houses have been excavated in towns as widely separated as Southampton and Norwich, Lincoln and Canterbury. The shift from wood to stone occurred not only in urban domestic architecture but also in the construction of town and village churches, castles, and manor houses. For rich merchants, large stone homes with tiled roofs provided not only comfort and protection against fire but, as well, a way of showing off.

Increasingly, town government was dominated by merchant guilds or craft guilds, consisting of those within and outside the town who were privileged to sell goods in its market. Towns such as Bristol, Newcastle, Northampton, and, above all, London were becoming major commercial centers. The monarchy, recognizing their importance, granted them charters containing valuable privileges, such as the right to operate a borough court, freedom from taxes and tolls, and various commercial monopolies. Henry I granted his Londoners the privilege of appointing their own sheriffs and justices, and by the early thirteenth century, they were electing their own mayor—which they have been doing ever since. Of course, the kings did not grant such privileges out of sheer goodheartedness. Townspeople had to buy their charters of liberties, usually at a stiff price, and they continued to pay the crown a yearly lump-sum tax—an annual "farm." But town dwellers regarded their charters as well worth the price. The new urban privileges freed the burghers of the obligations and tenurial complexities of manorialism and feudalism: "A burgher can give or sell his land as he pleases and go where he wishes, freely and undisturbed."[2]

Most urban manufacturers worked for themselves in their own shops, producing their own goods and selling them directly to the public. Each craft tended to have its own guild—a voluntary organization that functioned primarily as a social and religious association and a drinking club. The guild also served as an official craft association that, working through the town government, was often able to protect its members from competition by establishing a regional monopoly on its product. Typically, these craft associations imposed strict admission procedures and stringent rules on prices, wages, standards of quality, and operating procedures. Young artisans learned their trade as apprentices in the shops of master craftsmen. After a specified period, sometimes as long as seven years, the apprenticeship ended, at which time—with good luck and rich parents—the apprentice might become a master. But most young artisans had to work for some years beyond their apprenticeships as day laborers—"journeymen" (French: *journée* = "day")—sharpening their skills and saving their money until they could establish shops of their own and become guild masters. Toward the end of the High Middle Ages, as prosperity waned and urban society crystallized, it became increasingly common for artisans to spend their whole lives as wage earners, never becoming masters.

Throughout the High Middle Ages and beyond, women took an active

---

[2] From the customs of Newcastle-upon-Tyne at the time of Henry I.

part in town life. Because the master craftsman's shop was also his home, the modern distinction between home and workplace, between public and private spheres of activity, did not exist (nor did it in aristocrats' castles or peasants' cottages). This blurring of domestic and business life worked to women's advantage: a master's wife and daughters could learn his skills just as his apprentices could—by observing and practicing. Indeed, master craftsmen and their wives normally shared authority over apprentices, on the assumption that the wife was well acquainted with her husband's craft. Widows commonly carried on the businesses of their deceased husbands, and the tendency for urban women in their teens to marry established businessmen in their late twenties or early thirties, resulted in an abundance of lively, prosperous widows. Even while still married, women sometimes owned and operated their own businesses, distinct from those of their husbands. Town records show women collecting taxes, exchanging money, and engaging on their own in a wide variety of craft and merchant enterprises.

There were many who made their fortunes in commerce and manufacturing. England was astir with new life, and for one who was clever and enterprising the possibilities were virtually limitless. In the twelfth and thirteenth centuries, English and foreign merchants traveled continuously along the roads and rivers of England and in and out of its ports. At some point in the course of the medieval commercial revolution, perhaps toward the end of the twelfth century, commerce outdistanced agriculture to become the chief vitalizing force in the English and European economy, and it has remained so ever since. What occurred was more than a great boom. It was a permanent change, and of such historic magnitude that several scholars have described it as Europe's economic "take-off." In centuries thereafter, England would endure depressions, plagues, and wars, but it would never revert to the primarily agrarian economy of the early Middle Ages.

Twelfth-Century London

One can sense the texture of medieval urban life by looking at London as it existed toward the close of the twelfth century. With a population of about 35,000 and growing, London was by far the largest city of its time in the British Isles and one of the leading commercial centers of northwestern Europe. Many of England's bishops, abbots, and barons maintained townhouses there, and the king himself conducted much of his business at a palace, built by William Rufus and standing to this day, in London's western suburb of Westminster. Londoners were served by 139 churches, whose bells pealed over the city and its suburbs to mark the hours of the day.

London's narrow streets were lined with houses and shops, some built of stone in the new fashion, but most of them still built of wood. Fire was an ever-present danger. The streets were mostly unpaved and during the day teemed with people, dogs, horses, and pigs. (The French monarchy was launching a major project just then to pave the streets of Paris where, half a century earlier, a crown prince had been killed when his horse tripped over a pig.) By today's standards, London was a small, filthy, evil-smelling fire-trap. But by twelfth-century standards, it was a great, progressive metropolis. The old wooden bridge across the Thames River was being replaced by a new London Bridge made entirely of stone. The city employed sanitation workers to clear the streets of garbage. There was a sewer system—the only one in England—consisting of open drains down the centers of streets. There was even a public lavatory—the first of a nationwide network of "Public Conveniences" that now grace England.

Twelfth-century Londoners were proud of their city. One of them, William fitz Stephen, writing around 1175, described it in these glowing words:

> Among the noble and celebrated cities of the world, London, the capital of the kingdom of the English, extends its glory farther than all others and sends its wealth and merchandise more widely into far distant lands. It lifts its head higher than all the rest. It is fortunate in the healthiness of its air,[3] in its observance of Christian practice, in the strength of its fortifications, in its natural situation, in the honor of its citizens, and in the modesty of its wives. It is cheerful in its sports and the fruitful mother of noble men. . . . [4]

> It has on the east the Palatine castle [the Tower of London], very great and strong. The tower and walls rise from very deep foundations and are fixed with a mortar tempered by the blood of animals. On the west there are two castles very strongly fortified, and from these there runs a high and massive wall with seven double gates and with towers along the north at regular intervals. London was once also walled and turreted on the south, but the mighty River Thames, so full of fish, has with the sea's ebb and flow washed against, loosened, and thrown down those walls in the course of time. Upstream to the west there is the royal palace [Westminster Palace] which is conspicuous above the river, a building incomparable in its ramparts and bulwarks. It is about two miles from the city and joined to it by a populous suburb. . . .

> Those engaged in business of various kinds, sellers of merchandise, hirers of labor, disperse every morning into their several localities according to their trade. Besides, there is in London on the river bank, among the wines for sale in ships and in the cellars of the vintners, a public cook shop. There daily you may find food according to the season, dishes of meat, roast, fried and boiled, large and small fish, coarser meats for the poor and more delicate for the rich, such as venison and big and small birds. . . .

The delicacies offered by this medieval Colonel Sanders could be enjoyed not only by Londoners but also by visitors from afar:

> To this city from every nation under heaven merchants delight to bring their trade by sea. The Arabian sends gold; the Sabaean spice and incense. The Scythian brings arms, and from the rich, fat lands of Babylon comes oil

---

[3] Actually, London had a smog problem even in the twelfth century.

[4] Among the noble "men" born in twelfth-century London, William fitz Stephen proudly includes the empress Matilda.

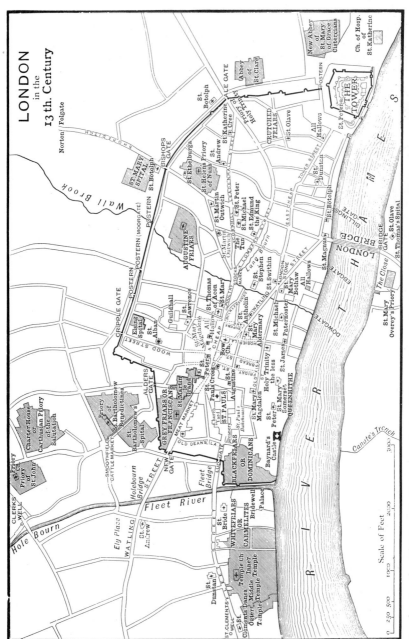

London in the Thirteenth Century It would have changed relatively little since William fitz Stephen's time, except for the coming of the two great thirteenth-century religious orders, the Grey Friars or Franciscans, and the Black Friars or Dominicans. Westminster Abbey and Westminster Palace are just off the map to the left. (The Mansell Collection)

of palms. The Nile sends precious stones; the men of Norway and Russia, furs and sables; nor is China absent with purple silk. The French come with their wines.

William fitz Stephen goes on to describe the entertainments and sports of the metropolis: religious plays showing the miracles of saints and martyrs; the festivities of the annual Carnival Day; cock fights; and ballplaying in the fields outside the city, with teams representing various London schools and guilds competing with one another. "On feast days throughout the summer the young men indulge in the sports of archery, running, jumping, wrestling, slinging the stone, hurling the javelin beyond a mark, and fighting with sword and buckler." And in winter,

> . . . swarms of youths rush out to play games on the ice. Some, gaining speed in their run, with feet set well apart, slide sideways over a vast expanse of ice. Others make seats out of a large lump of ice, and while one sits on it, others with linked hands run before it and drag him along behind them. So swift is their sliding motion that sometimes their feet slip, and they all fall on their faces. Others, more skilled at winter sports, put on their feet the shinbones of animals, binding them firmly around their ankles, and, holding poles shod with iron in their hands, which they strike from time to time against the ice, they are propelled as swiftly as a bird in flight.[5]

Not everyone found London so delightful. The twelfth-century chronicler Richard of Devizes quoted a Jewish merchant from France as giving this advice to a friend who was about to visit England:

> If you come to London, pass through it quickly. . . . Whatever evil or malicious thing that can be found anywhere on earth you will find in that one city. Do not associate with the crowds of pimps; do not mingle with the throngs in eating houses; avoid dice and gambling, the theater and the tavern. You will meet with more braggarts there than in all France. The number of parasites is infinite. Actors, jesters, smooth-skinned lads, Moors, flatterers, pretty boys, effeminates, pederasts, singing and dancing girls, quacks, belly dancers, sorceresses, extortioners, night wanderers, magicians, mimes, beggars, buffoons: all this tribe fill all the houses. Therefore, if you do not want to dwell with evildoers, do not live in London.

The same merchant is equally gloomy about other English towns. At Bristol, "there is nobody who is not or has not been a soap maker." York "is full of Scotsmen, filthy and treacherous creatures—scarcely human." Exeter "refreshes both men and beasts with the same fodder." Bath, lying amidst "exceedingly heavy air and sulphurous fumes, is at the gates of hell. . . . Ely stinks perpetually from the surrounding fens."[6]

---

[5] The description is translated in full in *English Historical Documents*, 2 (2nd ed., London, 1981), pp. 1024–1030.

[6] *The Chronicle of Richard of Devizes*, John T. Appleby, ed. (London, 1963), pp. 65–66. Richard of Devizes may well have invented the whole business.

A recent calculation of thirteenth-century London's annual murder rate reinforces the French merchant's warning. The rate was some 12 homicides per 100,000 people, many times the per-capita murder rate of modern Britain—although far below the rate of New York and Los Angeles in the 1980s and much lower than the rate of Miami or Washington D.C.[7] The violence of medieval London can perhaps be explained in part by the existence (in 1309) of 354 taverns and more than 1,300 ale shops, a fact that gives added dimension to such terms as "High Middle Ages" and "tight little island." Ale consumption seems to have been equally heroic in the medieval English countryside, where the per-capita murder rate was even higher than in the towns.

The Jews of Medieval England

Well might a twelfth-century Jewish merchant criticize urban life in England or, for that matter, throughout much of Western Christendom. In an almost unanimously Christian civilization, members of a minority faith were apt to suffer. In most regions of Europe, Jews had long been subjected to legal disabilities and popular bias. In England there were no significant Jewish communities until after the Norman Conquest, when Jews from Normandy and elsewhere migrated to London under royal protection and later established colonies in other English cities. While engaging in a variety of commercial activities, they prospered particularly through the lending of money at interest—a practice forbidden to Christians. Despite this prohibition, Christians are known to have engaged in moneylending for profit—including royal clerks in minor orders and even an occasional bishop. Some Christian moneylenders devised cunning schemes to evade the Church's ban, such as taking productive property as a pledge and enjoying its revenues until the debt was repaid. But until the late thirteenth century, Jews predominated in the essential business of banking and lending. Christian burghers and landholders rejoiced in the opportunity to borrow from Jewish lenders but resented the obligation to repay.

In the course of the High Middle Ages, popular attitudes toward Jews became increasingly hostile, with the growth of Christian self-awareness, crusading militancy, and popular devotion to the suffering Christ. Good Christian theology insisted that Christ died for the sins of all humanity, but popular sentiment often held that he was murdered by the Jews (conveniently overlooking the fact that Jesus, the Virgin Mary, and all the Apostles were Jewish themselves). There were even those who arrived at the grotesque conclusion that Christ's "murder" should be avenged. Thus, beginning in the reign of Henry II a series of bloody anti-Jewish riots occurred in various English cities whose Christian inhabitants were infuriated by popular rumors that Jews desecrated the transfigured bread of the

---

[7] James B. Given, *Society and Homicide in Thirteenth-Century Britain* (Stanford, 1977), pp. 36, 38.

Holy Eucharist, or that they murdered Christian infants (as they had allegedly murdered Christ). A pope decreed in 1272 "that Jews arrested on
such an absurd pretext be freed from captivity."

On this occasion, as on others, the papacy took responsibility for protecting Jews from mindless grassroots savagery, and Christian kings and
princes shared the responsibility. But these enthroned guardians demanded
much of the Jews in return for protection. The kings of England, like
Christian monarchs elsewhere, borrowed heavily from Jewish lenders;
milked them through arbitrary taxes; seized the property and loan accounts
of Jews who had died without heirs; and charged Jews enormous sums for
the rights to travel freely, to enjoy a fair trial, and to pass property on to their
heirs. With these sources of revenue and credit fattening the royal treasury,
it is no wonder that the kings protected the Jewish communities.

Nevertheless, toward the end of the High Middle Ages the monarchs of
Christendom turned savagely against the Jews. Edward I of England, Philip
IV of France, and other monarchs expelled Jews from their kingdoms en
masse, cancelling royal debts to Jewish lenders and stripping the Jews of
their wealth. By then their moneylending services were no longer essential;
Christian banking houses from southern France and Italy were providing an
alternative source of credit. Many Jews later filtered back or were invited to
return when royal policy shifted. But by the time of the Renaissance Jews
were being segregated into ghettos. And persecution continued unabated
throughout England and most of Europe for generations thereafter, reaching
its savage climax in the Nazi Holocaust of the twentieth century.

The Jews of high-medieval England contributed much to its commercial revitalization by providing a source of credit at a time when the
Church's doctrine on usury had not yet adjusted to commercial reality. But
their contributions were not limited to moneylending alone. They enlivened commerce and helped to modernize commercial practices through
their contacts with other Jewish urban communities throughout Western
Christendom, Byzantium, and Islam. They achieved a much higher literacy
rate than their Christian contemporaries—every substantial Jewish community had its own school—and their contributions to medicine, biblical
scholarship, and philosophy were all out of proportion to their numbers. In
commerce and learning alike, they helped break the barriers that had isolated Europe during the early Middle Ages.

The Landholding Aristocracy

The commercial revival substantially changed the life of the English aristocracy. For one thing, the large increase in the circulation of money eroded
the tenure/service relationship central to early feudalism. The monarchy
came to depend less and less on the military and administrative services
that its tenants-in-chief performed in return for their fiefs, resorting
increasingly to the use of mercenary soldiers and paid officials.

Moreover, money and commerce made new luxuries available to the
landed aristocracy: pepper, ginger, and cinnamon for baronial kitchens;

finer and more colorful clothing; jewelry; fur coats for cold winters; grandiose stone manor houses; and—inside the houses—carpets, wall hangings, and elaborate furniture. These amenities in turn drove many nobles into debt, thereby increasing the business—and the unpopularity—of Jewish lenders. Many aristocrats, women and men alike, regarded overspending as a virtue—the mark of a generous spirit. An Anglo-Norman monk provides this disapproving portrait of the late eleventh-century magnate, Hugh earl of Chester, whose life-style was perhaps more flamboyant than most:

> He was a great lover of the world and its pomp, which he regarded as the greatest blessing of the human lot. He was always in the vanguard in battle, lavish to the point of prodigality, a lover of games and luxuries, entertainers, horses, dogs, and similar vanities. He was always surrounded by a huge following, noisy with swarms of boys, both low-born and high-born. Many honorable men, clerics and knights, were also in his entourage, and he cheerfully shared his wealth and labors with them. . . . He kept no check on what he gave or received. His hunting was a daily devastation of his lands, for he thought more highly of hawkers and hunters than of peasants or monks. A slave to gluttony, he staggered under a mountain of fat, scarcely able to move. He was given over to carnal lusts and sired a multitude of bastards by his concubines.[8]

The medieval aristocracy was above all a military class, trained from early youth to fight on horseback. Mounted on a charger and clad in helmet and chain mail, the knight was a kind of military machine—the medieval equivalent of the modern tank. The analogy comes still closer when, in the fourteenth century, chain mail gave way to plate mail in response to the coming of the longbow.

War could ravage the land, destroying farms and churches, as England learned to its sorrow during Stephen's reign. But medieval warfare was less dangerous to the aristocracy than might be supposed. Pitched battles were rare, and even when they occurred the knight was well protected by armor. According to a contemporary report of the one major battle between Henry I and King Louis VI of France:

> I have been told that in the battle between the two kings, in which about nine hundred knights were engaged, only three were killed. All the knights were clad in mail and spared each other on both sides because of their fear of God and their fellowship in arms. They were more concerned to capture fugitives than to kill them.[9]

In peacetime, tournaments took the place of battles, and it was often difficult to distinguish between the two. Tournaments typically involved daylong mock battles among groups of as many as a hundred knights, in the course of which a participant might be killed, maimed, or taken for ransom.

---

[8] *The Ecclesiastical History of Orderic Vitalis*, Marjorie Chibnall, ed. and tr., 2 (Oxford, 1969), pp. 262–263; 3 (Oxford, 1972), pp. 216–217.

[9] Orderic Vitalis, 6 (Oxford, 1978), pp. 240–241.

The Church legislated against tournaments but to little avail. The aristocracy relished these melees as opportunities to train for war or to collect ransoms—or simply for the sheer joy of fighting.

Magnates had more sober tasks as well: presiding at their baronial courts, giving council to their lords—including the lord-king—and managing their revenues and estates. As the commercial revolution stimulated the circulation of money and encouraged a profit mentality, the Hugh-of-Chester types became rarer. In the thirteenth century, when the profits of agriculture were at their height, the aristocracy undertook to buy out peasant holdings and increase the demesne lands under their direct control. Late in the century, when profits dipped, the landholders once again began letting out demesne lands to peasants for a fixed rent. These trends reflect a degree of aristocratic calculation and avarice quite uncharacteristic of Earl Hugh.

For recreation, aristocrats continued throughout the Middle Ages to enjoy hawking and hunting in their private forests. Besides the sheer fun of it, hunting rid the forests of dangerous beasts—wolves and wild boars—and provided tasty venison for the baronial table. Lords and ladies alike engaged in falconry, a sport that consisted of releasing a trained falcon to soar upward, kill a wild bird in flight, and return it to earth uneaten. Both hunting and falconry developed into complex arts during the High Middle Ages.

The process of gradual refinement characterized high-medieval aristocratic life as a whole, and it was much needed. Most baronial castles of the eleventh and early twelfth centuries were nothing more than square towers, often of wood, rising two or three stories from the ground (see illustration, page 99). They were usually set atop hills or artificial mounds and surrounded by barracks, storehouses, stables, workshops, kitchen gardens, manure heaps, and perhaps a chapel—all enclosed, along with assorted livestock, within a stockade. The tower, or "keep," was apt to be stuffy, gloomy, and badly heated. Built for defense, not for comfort, its windows were narrow slits for outgoing arrows, and its few rooms accommodated not only the lord and lady and their family but also servants, retainers, and guests. In that world of enforced togetherness, only the wealthier aristocratic couples enjoyed the luxury of a private bedchamber.

By the late thirteenth century, however, rich aristocrats lived in much more commodious dwellings—castles or manor houses built of stone and

Ladies Hunting Deer
(The Mansell Collection)

mortar. Privacy remained rare, for great lords now commanded larger retinues than before. But the sweaty, swashbuckling life of the eleventh-century nobility had evolved by 1300 into a new, courtly life-style of good manners, troubadour songs, and gentlemanly and ladylike behavior. Warfare had diminished in the English countryside, and the barracks atmosphere was softening. Handbooks of etiquette became popular in the thirteenth century and remained so long thereafter. They encouraged aristocratic refinement with advice such as this:

> Wash your hands in the morning and, if there is time, your face; use your napkin or handkerchief [not your hands]; eat with three fingers only, and don't gorge; don't pick your teeth with your knife or wipe them on the tablecloth; don't butter your bread with your finger; don't spit on the table, or over it.[10]

As the old military elite learned good manners and courtly ways, it evolved into a "high society," increasingly conscious of itself as a separate class, more exclusive and more rigidly defined than in its earlier, less stylish days.

Aristocratic Women

Women were subordinate to men in almost all premodern civilizations, but less so in Western Christendom than, for example, in Islamic lands, where the veil and harem flourished. We saw in Chapter 3 how late Roman and Christian influences softened the antifeminine attitudes embodied in early Anglo-Saxon law codes. But Christianity itself was highly inconsistent in its view of women. St. Paul—at once a Jew, a Roman citizen, and a Christian evangelist—injected a typically early Roman antifeminine bias into the Christian mainstream. He conceded that, in God's eyes, there was no distinction between men and women or between slave and free—"All are one in Christ." But this cosmic equality did not extend to daily life. "Let your women keep silent in churches," Paul wrote, "for it is not permitted to them to speak. . . . And if they wish to learn anything, let them ask their husbands at home."

Medieval Christianity echoed some of Paul's antifemale views. Women could not be priests. They could hold no church office except as an abbess or lesser official in a nunnery. Holy men were apt to regard women as threats to male purity, and thus as objects—instruments of diabolical temptation. The canons of a thirteenth-century priory agreed to avoid all women "as we would avoid poisonous beasts."

But there is an enormous body of evidence to show that medieval women frequently rejected the submissive role that church and society expected of them. Shortly after the Norman Conquest, so we are told:

> . . . certain Norman women, consumed by raging lust, sent message after message to their husbands in England urging them to return home at once,

---

10 From Charles H. Haskins, *Studies in Medieval Culture* (Oxford, 1929), p. 80.

and adding that, unless they did so with all possible speed, they would find other husbands for themselves. . . . Many men left England heavy-hearted and reluctant, because they were abandoning their king while he struggled in a foreign land. They returned to Normandy to oblige their wanton wives.[11]

The monk who relates this story objects to the women's initiative, but their all-conquering husbands rushed home nonetheless.

Some 300 years thereafter, Geoffrey Chaucer related the story of an oft-married Wife of Bath whose fifth husband persisted in reading aloud to her from a "book of wicked wives" that recounted the evil deeds of innumerable wives from biblical, classical, and later times. As the Wife of Bath explained it:

> When I saw that he would never stop
> Reading this cursed book, all night no doubt,
> I suddenly grabbed and tore three pages out
> Where he was reading, at the very place,
> And fisted such a buffet in his face
> That backwards down into our fire he fell.

Along with notions of wanton women and wicked wives, high-medieval Christianity developed a concept of idealized womanhood from its emphasis on Mary, the virgin mother of Jesus. The cult of Mary was especially strong in late Saxon England, and it reemerged after the Norman Conquest as a characteristically English devotion—a vital religious link between Saxon and Norman England. (The renowned Norman abbey of Bec, which produced the first two post-Conquest archbishops of Canterbury—Lanfranc and Anselm—was dedicated to the Virgin Mary.) As the symbol of maternal compassion, Mary became the subject of countless miracle stories in England and throughout Christendom. Sinners who trembled at the prospect of God's judgment turned their prayers to Mary, confident that she could persuade Christ to forgive them, for what son could refuse his mother?

The high-medieval troubadour songs and the rise of stylized courtesy in aristocratic households resulted in another kind of idealization. Romanticizing them as "ladies fair," men placed women on pedestals from which they are only now managing to descend. This idealization of women was itself a kind of dehumanization, for high atop their pedestals women remained objects still. But at least pedestals elevated women from their former lowly status as threats to male purity, or objects of casual knightly seduction and rape, or victims of boorish, wife-beating husbands. The courtly lady remained an object, but a more revered and idealized object than before.

Such at least was the condition of women in most of the courtly songs and romances. But social and literary conventions seldom reflected real life.

---

[11] Orderic Vitalis, 2, pp. 218–221.

Tomb Effigy of Eleanor of Aquitaine   Her tomb lies beside that of her husband, Henry II (p. 145) and her son, Richard I (p. 163) at Fonteurault Abbey in Anjou. (The Granger Collection)

Medieval lords and ladies did not ordinarily behave like characters from courtly fiction. Wife beating persisted and, on a much lesser scale, husband beating as well (recall the Wife of Bath). Wives of all classes were immobilized for long periods by the bearing and breast-feeding of numerous children, necessary for the preservation of family lines in an era of high infant mortality. Eleanor of Aquitaine, the most celebrated woman of her generation and a patroness of troubadours, bore no less than eleven children—but was survived by only two. Her blatantly unfaithful husband Henry II imprisoned her for urging their sons to rebel, and she spent many years in comfortable but strict confinement in one of his French castles. Only on Henry II's death was she released to live out her final years as a valued adviser to her royal sons, Richard and John, and as a wealthy and independent grande dame of the realm.

Aristocratic women occupied passive roles as noncombatants living in a warrior's world. But if the medieval English aristocracy was a warrior class, it was also a class of hereditary landholders, and women could play a crucial role in the inheritance of land. In the absence of sons, a daughter might become a wealthy, coveted heiress. Even if she had brothers, a well-born daughter might bring a large estate to her husband as a dowry and retain some control over it. Women, whether married or single, could sometimes hold and grant fiefs. They could own goods; make contracts and wills; and, under certain conditions, engage in litigation. A widow normally received a third of her husband's lands (their eldest son received the rest), and since aristocratic wives, like urban wives, were usually much younger than their husbands, landholding widows were common.

A strong king might compel a wealthy maiden or widow to marry some royal favorite. Indeed, the granting of an heiress in marriage to a loyal courtier was an important element in the royal patronage system of medieval England—and a source of royal revenue as well. In the financial accounts of Henry I, one encounters items such as these: "Robert de Venuiz renders account to the king for sixteen shillings eightpence for the daughter of Herbert the Chamberlain with her dowry"; and "The sheriff of Hampshire renders account to the king for a thousand silver marks for the office, lands, and daughter of the late Robert Mauduit."[12] One great English heiress, the thrice-widowed Lucy countess of Chester, paid the king a handsome sum for the privilege of not having to marry again for five years.

Many a family fortune was built on strategic marriages of heirs to heiresses. In a landed society such as medieval England's, marriages were crucial to a family's well-being, and marriages for love alone were luxuries that no family could afford. It has been said that medieval warfare was a game but medieval marriage a deadly serious business. Parents arranged sons' as well as daughters' marriages, and it was not uncommon for the mother to do the arranging. Although it is true that medieval canon law demanded that both partners "consent" to the marriage, most brides and bridegrooms would have been programmed from early childhood to view marriage in the context of family economic and social advancement. Shortly after the Norman Conquest, William I ordered a young heiress to marry one of his favored barons, who happened to be an elderly hunchback. She refused and the Conqueror was furious, but the problem was resolved and the desired family alliance achieved when she agreed to marry the hunchback's son.

Marriages based on family strategies sometimes did develop into loving relationships. As current divorce statistics suggest, youthful infatuation may serve no better than family arrangement as the basis for a lifetime union. But arranged marriages, which often paired teenaged girls with much older men, do seem to have encouraged the extramarital romances that occurred in courtly literature—and sometimes in the real world as well. We have already read about the numerous bastards of Earl Hugh of Chester. Eleanor of Aquitaine, during her stormy first marriage with King Louis VII of France, was suspected of an extramarital affair with her uncle. The Church condemned adultery as a mortal sin, but aristocratic society was tolerant of the escapades of well-born husbands. Their wives, however, were judged by a double standard that demanded wifely fidelity to ensure the legitimacy of family lines. Earl Hugh could sire bastards across the Cheshire countryside and beyond, but he expected his wife's children to be his own. This juxtaposition of male "wild oat-sowing" and female virtue has persisted into the present century.

Despite their dowry rights, wives were very much under their husbands' control according to both law and custom. But in the day-to-day functioning of aristocratic life, a wife might exercise a great deal of power.

---

12 *The Pipe Roll of 31 Henry I, Michaelmas, 1130,* Joseph Hunter, ed. (London, 1833; reprinted 1929), p. 37, translated from the original Latin.

In the castle and manor house, as in the urban shop-dwelling, home and workplace were one. The wife usually governed the castle and barony when her husband was absent—as husbands often were, on wars or crusades. If the castle was attacked while the lord was away, his wife frequently commanded its defense. When the earl of Northumberland rebelled against King William Rufus in 1095, he charged his young wife (who bore the unoriginal name, Matilda) with defending his chief castle while he scouted the countryside. Matilda defended it courageously against the full force of Rufus's army, surrendering only when Rufus captured her husband, brought him before the castle wall, and threatened to gouge out his eyes.

Even when the lord was at home, the wife might enjoy considerable authority. In medieval marriages, as in modern ones, husband and wife might relate in a variety of ways. Some husbands were cruel and domineering. Others might be obliging, absentminded, or senile, in which case—despite social and legal conventions—the wife ruled the barony. One such person was the Anglo-Norman countess, Avicia of Evreux:

> The count of Evreux's intellect was by nature rather dim as well as being blunted by age. And putting perhaps undue trust in his wife's ability, he left the government of his county entirely in her hands. The countess was distinguished for her wit and beauty. She was the tallest woman in all Evreux and of very high birth. . . . Disregarding the counsels of her husband's barons, she chose instead to follow her own opinion and ambition. Often inspiring bold measures in political affairs, she readily engaged in rash enterprises.[13]

The Anglo-Norman monk who wrote these words, Orderic Vitalis, clearly disapproved—in part because he disagreed with Avicia's policy of rebelling against King Henry I. But his account discloses an aspect of aristocratic womanhood absent from the arid records of legal custom and the romances of the troubadours.

The High-Medieval Peasantry

Peasant life in the High Middle Ages was grim by modern American suburban standards. A year or two of drought, cattle plague, or excessively heavy rains could bring on widespread starvation. In 1125, for example, the *Anglo-Saxon Chronicle* reported that "many villages were flooded and many people drowned, and bridges collapsed, and grain and meadows were utterly ruined, and famine and disease spread among people and cattle. And there was more bad weather for all crops than there had been for many a year."

Nevertheless, the standard of living was improving. For several centuries, the climate of northwestern Europe had been growing warmer and drier, reaching a climatic optimum between about 1000 and 1200. Summers were longer, frosts were fewer, and crops were more abundant. During this

---

[13] Orderic Vitalis, 6, p. 148.

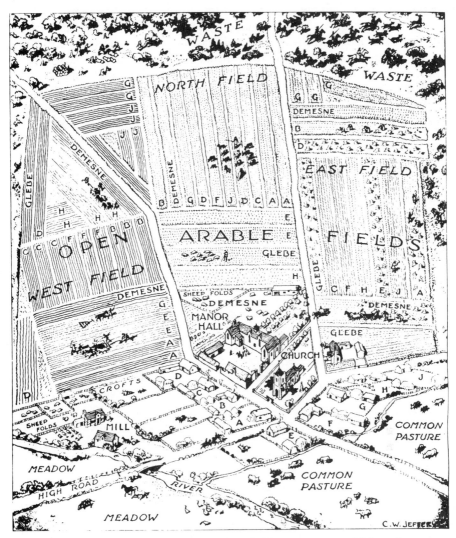

A Modern Reconstruction of a Medieval English Manor It would be safest to regard this not as a "typical" manor but as a "possible" manor. The *glebe* is the property set aside for the manorial priest, and the capital letters indicate particular fields allotted to families occupying particular cottages. The crofts are small enclosed fields adjoining cottages and used for pasture and small-scale tillage. (The Granger Collection)

lengthy period of fair weather, slavery disappeared from the English countryside. Domesday Book records a small but distinct minority of enslaved farm workers in 1086—about 10 percent of the total population—but one finds no trace of slaves in the records of the twelfth and thirteenth centuries. By then they had risen into the semi-free class of landholding villeins, bound to their land and subject to their manorial lord, but possessing their own strips in the village fields. According to the customs of the time, "no lord can eject his cultivators from their land as long as they can perform their due service." On the other hand, those villeins "who leave the estate on which they were born" are to be arrested and sent back.[14] Most villeins cherished their lands, and the ban against leaving them was not as intolerable as it might seem to footloose Americans today. Still, considerable numbers of peasants in pre-Conquest England who had been free to go where they pleased lost this liberty under the Norman and Angevin kings. These previously free workers descended into the villein class at the very time the slaves were ascending into it.

The twelfth- and thirteenth-century peasantry, in short, became a more uniform group than the peasantry of former times. Peasants were now characteristically of villein status, subject to their manorial lords, living in agrarian villages, tilling their strip fields with heavy plow and ox teams, and devoting certain days to cultivating their lords' demesne fields. Their lives were tied to the agricultural calendar of plowing, sowing, and harvesting. They ground their grain in the manorial flour mill and had it baked into loaves in the lord's bakery. When they were not working in the fields, they tended their oxen, pigs, and chickens; raised vegetables in kitchen gardens next to their cottages; and occasionally broke the routine of work with church festivals and country dances, religious celebrations and "church-ales" (where everyone got drunk in the village church).

But the uniformity of the high-medieval peasantry must not be exaggerated, for there remained immense diversity in agrarian life and organization. In certain areas, the single-family farm persisted. Regions of less fertile soil were devoted to cattle or sheep raising. Some manors had no demesne strips at all, and their lords lived off the rents and taxes of their peasants. Other manors consisted entirely of demesne strips, worked by hired laborers. In general, manors varied widely in the relative proportions of peasants' strips and demesne strips. There was wide variation, too, in the authority that lords might exercise over the peasants on their manors. And in some of the more remote portions of England, there was no manorial organization at all: the villagers pursued their routine under only the loose authority of a distant lord.

Whatever the local customs and conditions might be, life for the average peasant would have seemed almost changeless from year to year. But the economy of high-medieval England was in fact becoming steadily more active and prosperous. The work of forest clearing and swamp draining undertaken by the Anglo-Saxons was now reaching its climax. And with the growth of commerce and the increased circulation of money, peasants could produce for profit rather than for mere subsistence. The Cistercians, an austere monastic order that rose to great prominence in twelfth-century

---

[14] *Leis Willelme*, 29.1, 30.1 (a twelfth-century compilation).

Europe, established many abbeys in England—often in remote wilderness areas—and began to raise sheep on a large scale.[15] Wool production had long been important to England, but farmers now pursued it with unprecedented efficiency. Neighboring Flanders had developed a vigorous textile industry, and in the course of the twelfth century, England became Flanders' chief source of wool. A large-scale trade developed between the two lands, and Kings Henry I and Henry II were able to turn the situation to their own diplomatic advantage by threatening the counts of Flanders with suspension of the trade if they did not cooperate with English royal policies. As thirteenth-century commerce progressed, England increasingly was able to manufacture its own cloth from its own wool.

Grain production also became more efficient. The traditional system of dividing manors into two fields, farmed in alternate years, had been giving way over the previous several centuries to a more complex and more productive three-field system of crop rotation. Field 1 would be planted in the fall (with wheat or rye), field 2 would be planted the following spring (with oats and barley), and field 3 would lie fallow all year, to be planted the following fall—and so on around. The effect was that two-thirds of a village's arable lands could be planted and harvested each year rather than half as under the two-field system. Three-field agriculture was possible only in the more fertile regions, however, and the two-field system continued to be used in parts of England throughout the Middle Ages. Indeed, a single manor might rotate part of its land on a three-field basis and part on a two-field basis. Nevertheless, three-field rotation contributed much to the increased productivity of medieval agriculture.

The English agrarian economy also benefited from the increased use of mechanical power. Water mills abounded in Anglo-Saxon times—over 5,000 are recorded in Domesday Book—and before the end of Henry II's reign, the windmill had made its debut in the flat, windblown East Anglian countryside. These innovations are difficult to trace—the historians of the age gave them scant attention—but their importance is incalculable. For despite the surge of commercial activity, grain production remained the economic foundation of medieval England, and significant improvements in agrarian organization and technology were bound to have a buoyant effect on the realm's prosperity. Such innovations were by no means the exclusive products of English inventive genius; they were appearing at the same time on the Continent. Hence, the economic surge of twelfth- and thirteenth-century England was paralleled in France, Germany, Italy, Spain, Scandinavia, and elsewhere in Western Christendom. But the economic prosperity of the High Middle Ages would give way eventually to the depression and economic uncertainties of the plague-ridden fourteenth and fifteenth centuries. There was trouble ahead.

---

[15] See pp. 208–210.

Life in an English Peasant Village

By today's standards, peasant life in the High Middle Ages is almost beyond our imagining. Village life was tied to the cycle of the seasons and vulnerable to the whims of nature—drought, flooding, epidemics among humans and animals, crop diseases, the summer's heat and the winter's chill. Today, most inhabitants of the industrialized world are insulated from nature by a screen of modern technological wonders: central heating, air conditioning, a secure food supply, plumbing, deodorants to spare us the smell of human sweat, modern medicine, and much more. We enjoy the protection of police and fire departments; we defy distance and terrain with our freeways and jets. All these we take for granted, but they are all products of the recent past. They were undreamed of in the Middle Ages and remained unknown for many centuries thereafter.

From the viewpoint of modern middle-class America, the medieval English peasantry lived in unspeakable poverty and filth. A typical peasant's house consisted of a thatched roof resting on a timber framework, with the spaces between the frame filled by webbed branches covered with mud and straw. Wealthier peasants' houses might have had two or more rooms, furnished with benches, a table, and perhaps a chest. Recent excavations have made clear that some prosperous peasants of the thirteenth century could afford to build stone houses, and archaeological research has also shown, from the wear revealed on the cobblestone or flagstone floors of peasant cottages, that they were brushed spotlessly clean. But poorer peasants continued to dwell in one-room, half-timbered cottages virtually bare of furniture.

Manuscript Illumination Showing a Well-Dressed Peasant Woman Milking (Bodleian Library, Oxford, MS. Bodley 764, f. 41v)

The straw on which the family slept was apt to be crawling with vermin. The smells of sweat and manure were ever-present, and therefore went largely unnoticed. Flies buzzed everywhere. A single cottage might shelter not only a large family but its domestic livestock as well: chickens, dogs, geese, occasionally even cattle. Windows, if any, were small and few (and of course had no glass). Arthritis and rheumatism were common, along with countless other diseases whose cures lay far in the future. A simple fire served for cooking and heating, but in the absence of chimneys, smoke filled the room before escaping through holes or cracks in the ceiling. Candles were luxury items, and peasants had to make do with smoky, evil-smelling torches made of rushes soaked in fat. There was always the danger that a stray spark might set the thatched roof on fire.

The daily routine of a family of village-dwelling villeins might run more or less as follows: there would be a predawn breakfast—perhaps of coarse black bread (don't try it!) and diluted ale—after which the husband, wife, and post-toddling offspring would work from daybreak to nightfall. Peasants' work required close partnerships among husband, wife, and children. Indeed, young peasant men were expected to marry before inheriting land, so that their wives and children could fulfill their essential roles in the peasant work force. The father and his sons did most of the heavy plowing. The wife and daughters took primary responsibility for the "inside" work—not only performing domestic chores such as cooking and cleaning but also manufacturing the family's food and clothing (making cheese and butter, spinning and weaving cloth). They milked the cows, fed the livestock, tended the vegetable garden outside the cottage, and joined with the men in activities such as haymaking, thatching, sheep shearing, sowing and reaping of grain, weeding, and sometimes even plowing. In the winter, when the fields were often frozen, the whole family might stay indoors making and repairing tools. The evening meal might consist of a pot of vegetable broth, more coarse black bread, more ale, and possibly an egg. Then it was early to bed, to rest for the toils of the following day.

Even this somber picture is a bit idealized. Often, one or more members of the peasant family would be immobilized by illness (for which there were

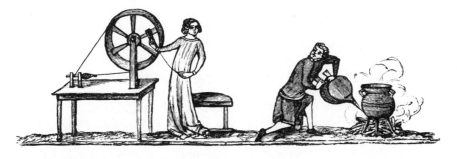

Spinning and Heating a Fire with a Billows Early fourteenth century. (North Wind Picture Archives)

no available doctors and no effective medicines) or tormented by injuries, wounds, aches, and pains (no aspirin, just ale). Wives endured one pregnancy after another; childbirth presented a mortal danger to mother and baby alike, and infant mortality ran high. (In medieval and early modern Europe, approximately two-thirds of all children died before the age of ten, and over one-third died during their first year.)

In a typical peasant village, the most substantial buildings were the residence of the lord or his bailiff and the parish church. The lord's residence, the manor headquarters, was usually surrounded by a walled enclosure that also contained a bakehouse, kitchen, barns, and other structures. The kitchen was normally (but not always) located in a building separate from the main house to ensure that if the oven fire should spread out of control, it would not threaten the lord's residence. To the manor house, the peasants brought portions of their crops, which they owed as customary dues. There, too, they brought their disputes to be settled at the manorial court.

The parish church often stood in the center of the village. Its priest was seldom well educated, although he might have learned the rudiments of reading and writing. He played a central role in the villagers' lives, baptizing infants, presiding at marriages and burials, and regularly celebrating the Mass. The church was likely to be painted inside with scenes from the Bible or the lives of local patron saints. Such paintings provided an elementary form of religious instruction to an illiterate congregation.

The church usually doubled as a village meeting hall. And despite canonical prohibitions, it might be used on festival days for dancing, drinking, and revelry. The feast days of the Christian calendar—Christmas, Easter, and many lesser holy days (holidays)—provided joyous relief from an otherwise grinding routine. In some parts of England, people celebrated the feast of Candlemas (February 2) with a candlelight procession followed by a pancake dinner. On the eve of May Day, the young men of some villages would cut branches in the forest and lay them at the doors of houses inhabited by young unmarried women. St. John's Day (midsummer) brought bonfires and dancing. Throughout the year, villagers found time for the informal sports of wrestling, archery, cock fights, drinking contests, and a rough, early form of soccer. But for most of their days, the peasantry labored to raise the food on which their families and social superiors depended for survival.

In examining the lives of the townspeople, aristocrats, and peasant villagers of high-medieval England, I have tried to show not only what their lives were like but also how their lives were changing. Across the generations between 1066 and about 1300, the changes were most evident among the town dwellers and aristocrats. The former participated in a commercial and urban revolution of decisive significance to Western Civilization; the latter experienced a drastic transformation in taste and style as they moved from grim square towers into elaborate, well-furnished dwellings that echoed with the songs of troubadours. Changes in the lives of the peasant villagers were less visible to the naked eye, but perhaps no less

important. Villagers, too, were drawn increasingly into the web of a bur-
geoning money economy that provided markets and profits for surplus food.
And the gradual improvement of the diet of both peasants and aristocrats,
too gradual to have been perceived at the time, may well have fostered the
vitality and longevity of the English people.

High-Medieval Christianity

The ever-increasing scope of the Church, along with the rising self-
awareness of the new age, resulted in a deepening of popular piety throughout high-medieval England and all of Western Christendom. The High
Middle Ages witnessed a shift in religious attitude from one of awe and
emphasis on ritual (characteristic of earlier Christianity) to a new emo-
tionalism and dynamism. The shift appears in changing devotional practices, as the divine Christ sitting in judgment gave way to the tragic figure
of the human Christ suffering on the cross. As a result of this change, and of
the growing devotion to the Virgin Mary, Christianity became increasingly
a doctrine of love, hope, and compassion. The God of justice became the
merciful, suffering God of love.

Papal power reached its apogee in the High Middle Ages. The papacy
controlled the universal Church as never before—through its legates, its
authority over bishops and abbots, and its superbly developed central
administrative machinery. But success and affluence are always apt to
present dangers to a spiritual institution (as to others), and there can be no
question that the high-medieval Church had lost its lean and hungry look.
Its prelates had become increasingly absorbed in the problems of political
power at the expense of their spiritual and pastoral responsibilities. And
despite the Church's theoretically centralized command structure (popes to
archbishops to bishops to priests), lines of communication had a way of
getting clogged. Ecclesiastical courts were deluged with jurisdictional disputes in which abbots sought exemption from the control of bishops, and
bishops from archbishops. The archbishops of York struggled and maneuvered throughout the High Middle Ages to establish their freedom from the
jurisdiction of the archbishops of Canterbury. A bishop who deliberately
ignored or "misunderstood" papal commands was difficult to dislodge. And
travel and communications were agonizingly slow. It might take half a year
for an archbishop of Canterbury to journey to Rome, consult with the pope,
and return to England.

Furthermore, an immense gulf separated the religious beliefs of popes
and theologians from those of common townspeople and peasants. The
supernatural ideas of ordinary people in any society, including our own,
include a variety of odd notions (a relative of mine transcribes messages
from the dead; a "nonfiction" bestseller insisted that the pyramids were
built by extraterrestrial visitors). It should come as no surprise, then, that
popular attitudes in prescientific societies tended to be at least as implausi-
ble as our own. The God of the high-medieval theologians was a god of love
and reason. But in the popular mind he became a kind of divine magician

who could shield his favorites from the hunger, pain, disease, and sudden death that afflicted all humanity until quite recent times (and that indeed afflicts much of humanity still).

To such people, religion offered three desperately needed ideals: the hope of eternal salvation from a harsh, threatening world; an explanation for human suffering (as a spiritual discipline necessary for paradise); and the promise of a better life here and now. Of course, religion continues to offer these things, but in the Middle Ages, when human need was more intense and more immediate, the popular practice of Christianity was quite unlike what it is today. People placed far greater emphasis on seeking divine favor through mechanical means such as charms, pilgrimages, holy images, and the relics of saints.

The most cherished relics of all were those associated with Christ and the Virgin Mary. Because both were believed to have ascended bodily into heaven, relics of the usual sort (body parts) were ruled out. But there remained pieces of their clothing, fragments of the true cross, vials of Christ's blood and the Virgin's milk, Christ's baby teeth, his umbilical cord, and the foreskin removed at his circumcision. Reading Abbey, founded in southern England in the 1120s, had acquired hundreds of relics by the end of the twelfth century, including twenty-nine relics of Christ, six of the Virgin Mary, nineteen of the Old Testament patriarchs and prophets, and fourteen of the Apostles. As a result of its avid collecting, Reading became a prosperous pilgrimage center—yet it was merely one of many. Chartres had the Virgin Mary's gown; Canterbury housed the body of St. Thomas Becket; Santiago de Compostela in northwestern Spain claimed the bones of St. James the Apostle (except for his arm, which was at Reading); La Sainte Chapelle in Paris acquired Christ's crown of thorns after participants in the Fourth Crusade had taken it from Constantinople. Indeed, there was scarcely a town or rural district in all Christendom that did not possess some relic or protective image.

Each medieval trade honored its own particular saint. Potters offered special devotions to St. Gore; painters to St. Luke; horse doctors to St. Loy; dentists to St. Apolline. There was an appropriate saint for almost every known disease. Plague sufferers prayed to St. Roch; St. Romane specialized in mental illnesses; St. Clare in afflictions of the eye; St. Agatha in sore breasts. The miraculous healing powers associated with such saints satisfied a widespread longing for supernatural protection against dangers and afflictions that seemed beyond human control. The doubts of the theologians were drowned out by the clamor of popular demand.

Such attitudes received encouragement from ill-educated parish priests, and from bishops and abbots anxious to attract floods of pilgrims to their churches. The Catholic doctrine of the Communion of Saints (the caring fellowship of all Christians, whether in this world or the next) justified the relic cult up to a point. But in its obsession with the supernatural powers of material objects, popular belief carried an ideological residue from long-ago days of pagan magic.

A Monk and His Mistress Are Accused and Punished, yet Continue to Profess Their Innocence From Queen Mary's Psalter, fourteenth century. (Reproduced with permission of the British Library)

The high-medieval Church suffered not only from popular credulity but from occasional corruption as well. Corrupt churchmen were in evidence throughout the era—a result of the unfortunate necessity of staffing the Church with human beings. Historians have always found it tempting to describe instances of larcenous bishops, gluttonous priests, and licentious nuns. I have no intention of resisting that temptation. An archiepiscopal visitation to a small thirteenth-century Norman nunnery yielded these dark secrets:

> Johanna de Alto Villari kept going out alone with a man named Gayllard, and within a year she had a child by him. The subprioress is suspected with Thomas the carter, her sister Idonia with Crispinatus, and the prior of Gisorcium is always coming to the convent for Idonia. Philippa of Rouen is suspected with a priest of Suentre, of the diocese of Chartres; Margurita, the treasuress, with Richard de Genville, a cleric; Agnes de Fonteney, with a priest of Guerreville, of the diocese of Chartres. . . . All wear their hair improperly and perfume their veils. Jacqueline came back pregnant from visiting a certain chaplain who was expelled from his house as a result of this. Agnes de Monsec was suspected with the same chaplain. Ermengard and Johanna de Alto Villari beat each other. The prioress is drunk almost every night.

Such instances are far from typical, however. Widespread ecclesiastical corruption was more common in subsequent centuries. If there were licentious nuns in Normandy, there was also a stern archbishop to investigate and discipline them. The Church retained a powerful impulse toward piety and reform that manifested itself in the spiritual dedication of countless lay and clerical believers, in the exemplary lives of many great prelates, and in the emergence of new religious orders.

The New Orders

The kings and magnates of Norman England had been generous in founding and patronizing Benedictine monasteries, granting them numerous productive estates. With the revenues from their manors, Benedictine communities erected enormous abbey churches, dormitories, meeting halls, dining halls, kitchens, and cloisters joined in a single architectural group usually built entirely of stone. Within their abbeys, Benedictine monks and nuns lived lives of communal prayer, meditation, and relative luxury. The "better" houses admitted only the sons and daughters of aristocratic families, who normally committed one or more of their younger offspring, while they were still children, to a particular monastery or nunnery. Thus, future monks and nuns, like future brides and grooms, found their lives shaped by parental decisions based on family strategy. They themselves had little choice in the matter. Many developed into devoted servants of God; others simply served out their time.

But new, rival orders emerged in the Anglo-Norman period and continued to proliferate throughout the High Middle Ages. All were founded by reformers dissatisfied with traditional Benedictine monasticism and were peopled by men and women who had chosen their religious vocations for themselves, as adults. In religious life, as in economic life, the increasing range of career choices encouraged greater self-awareness. This knowledge reflected not so much a rise of individualism, in the modern and rather lonely sense, as it did a new freedom to choose among many different kinds of communal life—to discover oneself through community.

Perhaps the most popular new order in Norman England was that of the Augustinian Canons (or "Austin Canons"). Breaking sharply from Benedictine tradition, the Augustinian Canons modeled their lives on a rule derived from disciplinary and spiritual directions prepared by St. Augustine of Hippo for his own cathedral clergy back in the fifth century. Although they submitted to the rigor of a strict rule of conduct and devotion, the Augustinian Canons carried on normal ecclesiastical duties in the world, serving in parish churches and cathedrals or doing charitable work in the towns where most of their priories were situated. The founding of Augustinian priories became a favorite form of religious benefaction among the Anglo-Norman aristocracy, in part because a priory was far less costly to establish than a great Benedictine house with its elaborate buildings and vast estates. The fusion of monastic discipline and secular activity culminated in the twelfth-century crusading orders—the Knights Templars, Knights Hospitalers, and similar groups—whose ideals synthesized the monastic and the military life to expand the political frontiers of Western Christendom.

The greatest new monastic force of the twelfth century was the Cistercian order, which followed a more austere, more strictly regulated version of the cloistered Benedictine life. The order began in 1098, when a little group of Benedictine dissenters migrated to Citeaux, in the wilderness of eastern France. For a time, the Cistercians expanded only gradually. But in its early years, Citeaux had the good fortune to be governed by an abbot of

Ruins of Fountains Abbey This aerial view of the great Cistercian abbey, built in a Yorkshire wilderness around the mid-twelfth century, shows the bell tower (left), church, and domestic buildings (right). (Aerofilms Ltd.)

extraordinary gifts, the Englishman St. Stephen Harding, who framed the original version of the rule that shaped Cistercian monasticism. Known as the Charter of Divine Love, the Cistercian "constitution" was revised on various occasions to meet current needs. From the beginning, however, it emphasized a simple life of work, love, prayer, and self-denial. Although Cistercians regarded themselves as Benedictines—indeed, as the perfect Benedictines—they distinguished themselves from the monks of other Benedictine houses by wearing white habits rather than black. Some Benedictine monks of the older tradition regarded this change as showy and affected, and they resented the Cistercians' tendency (as they saw it) to put on puritanical airs. The Cistercians departed from traditional Benedictine monasticism in other ways as well. Their abbeys admitted no children, only adults able to choose their religious vocation for themselves. (Many older Benedictine houses now began to follow the Cistercians in ceasing to accept children.) Like the Benedictines, the Cistercian order came to include nunneries, but they were established (or incorporated) with great caution. The Cistercians accepted only grants of undeveloped land, or, in some cases, they accepted developed land and then relocated its serfs elsewhere. They then developed their estates by their own labor or, increasingly, by the labor of illiterate peasant lay brothers known as *conversi*. Although bound by vows of chastity and obedience to the abbot, the *conversi* were permitted to follow a less-demanding form of the Cistercian life. The incorporation of *conversi* into the order represents a compassionate outreach to the illiterate peasantry and, at the same time, a solution to the labor shortage on the unmanorialized Cistercian lands.

The Cistercian order began a notable epoch of international expansion when the Frenchman St. Bernard of Clairvaux joined the community c. 1113. A supremely eloquent, strong-willed mystic, St. Bernard was also gifted and effective in the realm of practical affairs. He was to become the most admired churchman of his age, and as his fame grew, the Cistercian movement grew with it. By 1115, Cîteaux had founded four daughter houses, one of which—Clairvaux—had St. Bernard as its first abbot. By 1200, some 500 Cistercian monasteries were scattered across Europe.

Inevitably the movement spread to England—in the later years of Henry I—and by Stephen's death in 1154 the kingdom had some fifty Cistercian abbeys. They were stark, undecorated buildings, contrasting dramatically with the elaborate churches and conventual buildings of some of the wealthier centers of traditional Benedictinism. Yet even now the simple beauty of Cistercian ruins such as Fountains and Rievaulx, set in wilderness areas of Yorkshire, is deeply moving. In such remote abbeys, encircled by their fields and pastures, white-clad Cistercian monks lived out their stark and prayerful lives.

Early in the thirteenth century, St. Francis of Assisi and the Spaniard St. Dominic established new religious orders that reinvigorated the spiritual life of Western Christendom.[16] Franciscan and Dominican friars lived by a rule, but like their Augustinian predecessors they shunned the walls of the monastery. Instead, they traveled far and wide to preach among the people—especially those of the rising towns who exhibited a spiritual thirst that the traditional ecclesiastical organization could not quench. The Franciscans directed their energies primarily toward the poor, while the Dominicans preached to the wealthy and powerful, and to heretics. Both orders dedicated themselves to chastity, obedience to their superiors, and individual and collective poverty. At first, the Franciscan and Dominican orders had no property at all. And even though their immense success and popularity soon forced them, in the interest of organizational coherence, to accept jurisdiction over houses, churches, and small parcels of land, they never remotely approached the vast, landed wealth of the Benedictines or Cistercians.

The Dominicans came to England in 1221, the Franciscans in 1224. Before long, their activities spread to every major town. In England, as on the Continent, these orders brought vigorous new life to the Church by

---

[16] On English monasticism in general, see the works of David Knowles, *The Monastic Order in England, 940–1216* (2nd ed., Cambridge, 1963), and *The Religious Orders in England*, I, *1216–c. 1340* (Cambridge, 1948). See, more generally, C. H. Lawrence, *Medieval Monasticism* (2nd ed., London, 1989).

their fervent, compassionate preaching, their unpretentious holiness, and their boundless enthusiasm. To these virtues, the Franciscans added yet another: the joyous, artless simplicity inherited from their remarkable founder, St. Francis of Assisi.

Intellectual Life

Despite their original simplicity, however, the Franciscans quickly joined the Dominicans in enriching the intellectual life of the European universities, which were now rising to great prominence. Several important universities—including Paris and Bologna—had emerged in the vibrant intellectual environment of the twelfth century, but they matured into organized and established educational institutions only in the thirteenth. Bologna became Europe's greatest center for the study of civil and canon law. Paris excelled in philosophy and theology, which Europeans regarded as the supreme intellectual disciplines of the day, and which thirteenth-century scholars developed and elaborated in brilliant fashion. Franciscan and Dominican theologians of remarkable ability graced the Paris faculty, which included, at one time or another, the three finest philosophical minds of the age: the Franciscan minister-general St. Bonaventure (1221–1274), and the Dominicans St. Albertus Magnus (1206–1280) and St. Thomas Aquinas (1225–1274). In his rigorously organized multi-volumed *Summa Theologica* and *Summa Contra Gentiles*, Aquinas created a comprehensive fusion of reason and Christian revelation—a synthesis harmonizing logic with faith. His work stimulated vigorous controversy in its own time and has done so ever since, but it has also proven remarkably durable. It is an impressive illustration of the profundity of thirteenth-century intellectual life at its best and stands as a major achievement in the history of thought.

England shared in this intellectual revival in many ways. In the tradition of the great Northumbrian historian Bede, England produced some of the ablest historians in high-medieval Europe. William of Malmesbury, working in the first half of the twelfth century, wrote histories of the English kings and of important English churchmen with an elegance and insight worthy of Bede himself, and the historical works of William of Newburgh in the late twelfth century and of Matthew Paris in the thirteenth are similarly impressive. Many other English historians scarcely less talented were writing at the same time.

High-medieval England also witnessed a proliferation of schools—some of them church-related, some private—that trained children and adolescents to read, write, and perform the rudiments of mathematics and other liberal arts. There were several hundred such schools in thirteenth-century England. In developing centers of higher education, England lagged behind France, and it was common during the twelfth century for bright English students to obtain their university training at French intellectual centers—often at the University of Paris. But by the end of the twelfth century, Oxford University had begun to grow, and in the course of the next century it developed into one of Europe's foremost scholarly institutions. Cambridge soon followed as a center of higher learning, and its schools received a major infusion of talent early in the thirteenth century on the arrival of a colony of intellectual dissidents on strike from Oxford. Archbishop Theobald of Canterbury (1139–1161) had earlier gathered around him an impressive scholarly circle that included figures such as the future archbishop, Thomas Becket, and the great twelfth-century humanist and philosopher, John of Salisbury (c. 1120–1180).

John of Salisbury was an Englishman, as his name implies, but his career was international in scope. Having obtained his early schooling in England, he journeyed to France to study under Peter Abelard and other masters at the University of Paris, and possibly at Chartres as well. Around 1154, following his service as a papal official, he became Archbishop Theobald of Canterbury's personal secretary, one of his close advisers, and his diplomatic agent at the courts of King Henry II and other princes. After Archbishop Theobald's death in 1161, John remained at Canterbury to serve Theobald's successor and his own good friend, Thomas Becket. John supported Becket against Henry II and absented himself from England during Becket's years of exile, returning to Canterbury in 1170 in time to be an eyewitness to Becket's murder. John spent his final years in high ecclesiastical office in France, as bishop of Chartres (1176–1180).

The writings of John of Salisbury, executed in highly polished Latin, are no less varied than his career. They include histories; a biography of Becket; an important philosophical work (the *Metalogicon*) defending the correct use of Aristotelian logic; and a significant work of political philosophy, the *Policraticus* (1159). Drawing on the political thought of classical antiquity and the early Middle Ages, the *Policraticus* stresses the divine nature of kingship but emphasizes equally its responsibilities and limitations. The king receives his authority from God, not from the people, yet God commissions him to rule for the good of his subjects rather than for his own good. The king is responsible for giving his subjects peace and justice and for protecting the Church. If he abuses his divine commission and neglects his responsibilities, he loses his God-given authority, ceases to be a king, and becomes a tyrant. He thus forfeits his subjects' allegiance and is no longer their lawful ruler. Under extreme circumstances, and if all else failed, John of Salisbury suggested the possibility of tyrannicide: a good Christian subject, although obliged to obey his king, might assassinate a tyrant. John qualifies his novel doctrine of tyrannicide to such a degree that he may simply be making a rhetorical point—that Christian kings must not tyrannize their subjects. In other respects, the views expressed in the *Policraticus* are in tune with the general political attitudes of the twelfth century: responsible limited monarchy and government on behalf of the governed. These theories, in turn, were idealized reflections of the monarchies of the day whose power was held in check—as King John's career so aptly demonstrates—by the nobility, the Church, and ancient custom.

From the Anglo-Norman era to the time of Isaac Newton and on to the present, the English have excelled at science. Adelard of Bath, a younger contemporary of Henry I, pioneered in bringing the Greco-Arabic scientific tradition to Western Europe. A great traveler, Adelard made contact with and admired Greek and Islamic science. He introduced several ancient Greek works of major importance to Western Christendom by translating them into Latin—Euclid's *Elements*, for example—and also produced important scientific treatises of his own. He wrote a treatise on the abacus and may have been associated with the early administration of Henry I's exchequer. Adelard was by no means the only Western European of his age with keen scientific interests, nor was he the only English scholar working in the fields of mathematics and science. He and others like him represent the genesis of the rich scientific tradition of medieval and modern England.

It has been argued that the greatest scholar and churchman of thirteenth-century England, and the foremost progenitor of modern European science, was Robert Grosseteste (c. 1170–1253). Against all previous scholarly opinion, Robert Grosseteste's most recent and astute biographer, Sir Richard Southern, has argued persuasively (although not conclusively) that unlike many of his gifted contemporaries, Grosseteste obtained his entire education in England.[17] Born of impoverished parents, he could not afford the University of Paris (which did not yet have a scholarship program). Consequently, so Southern argues, Grosseteste was unacquainted with the best and latest scholastic philosophy of his day, and this deprivation liberated him to blaze a new intellectual trail. Whatever the case, Grosseteste was both an ecclesiastical statesman active in the politics of his day—a chancellor of Oxford University and subsequently bishop of Lincoln—and also a deeply original theologian and scientist, and a keen student of the two contending philosophical traditions of his time—Platonic and Aristotelian. Hungry for more and better translations of Greek philosophical texts, he undertook in his sixties to learn the Greek language and then translated important Greek works into Latin. Grosseteste pioneered in the area of scientific methodology. His scientific works convey, as Southern puts it, "the outline of a scientific method extending from the first fragmentary observations of the senses to the generalities of scientific laws." Grosseteste's attempts to explain phenomena such as comets, tides, rainbows, color, and light (which he regarded as the basic element in the universe) seem primitive by modern standards, as one might well expect. Grosseteste himself was keenly aware of the inadequacies of his scientific conclusions: "I can only hope," he wisely and modestly wrote, "that others may be stimulated to inquire more deeply, and to do better, and to discover more than I have been able to find out." But his belief in mathematics as the key to the secrets of the physical universe, his emphasis

---

[17] R. W. Southern, *Robert Grosseteste: The Growth of an English Mind in Medieval Europe* (Oxford, 1986). See also James McEvoy, *The Philosophy of Robert Grosseteste* (Oxford, 1982), which points out that Grosseteste rejected Aristotle's generally accepted distinction between the corrupt sublunar region (the earth and its environs) and the uncorruptible heavens. The entire universe, Grosseteste taught, functioned in accordance with the same mathematically precise natural laws.

on the investigation of nature through innumerable exact observations illuminated by human insight, and his articulation of an experimental method paved the way for the scientific advances of subsequent centuries. Grosseteste outlined a procedure that anticipated modern scientific approaches: observe phenomena carefully, frame a hypothesis, and check the hypothesis against the behavior of natural phenomena—a process akin to what we would now term experimental verification. Sound methodology is basic to science, and in Grosseteste's work it was set forth in detailed, rational form, although in a terminology strange to modern scientists. Grosseteste cannot be regarded as the father of science, for he drew heavily from his Greek and Islamic predecessors. But from the Western European standpoint, we may well regard him as its foster father.

Robert Grosseteste exerted a deep influence on his successors, particularly among English scholars of the Franciscan order. Although not a Franciscan himself, Grosseteste became the master teacher of the Franciscans at Oxford. The scientific orientation of English Franciscanism derived from Grosseteste's inspiration, and perhaps also from the deep love of nature exhibited by St. Francis himself.

The most celebrated and controversial scientist of late-thirteenth-century England was the Franciscan friar Roger Bacon. His extensive writings contain, along with a good deal of superstitious fancy, a passion for experimentation and for the application of mathematics to scientific investigation reminiscent of Grosseteste: "Reasoning does not disclose these matters," Bacon wrote. "On the contrary, experiments are required, performed on a large scale with instruments and by other necessary means." At times, Roger Bacon assumed the role of scientific prophet: "Experimental science controls the conclusions of all other sciences. It discloses truths which reasoning from general principles [the favored method of the Paris theologians] would never have discovered. Finally, it sets us on the way to marvelous inventions which will change the face of the world." Bacon then goes on to describe telescopes, submarines, automobiles, and airplanes.

Art and Literature

In the course of the High Middle Ages, the Norman Romanesque style of architecture and sculpture gave way to an incredibly beautiful new style described by its later, dull-witted critics as "Gothic" ("barbaric"; it was described by contemporaries as "modern architecture"). The reign of Henry III, and that of his illustrious French contemporary, Louis IX (St. Louis), marked the zenith of the Gothic style. Originating in the twelfth-century Ile de France, Gothic architecture—with its radically new principles of design and standards of beauty—reached its culmination in such French cathedrals of the thirteenth century as Chartres, Reims, and Amiens. It was less massive than the Romanesque style it superseded and more graceful. The thick walls necessary to the structural stability of Romanesque churches were made superfluous by such Gothic innovations as the flying buttress, pointed arch, and ribbed vault. The new churches were skeletal

Westminster Abbey
Henry III rebuilt the abbey
in the French High Gothic
style, which emphasizes
vertical lines and window
walls. (The Mansell
Collection)

frameworks of stone in which walls served only as screens and were
replaced more and more by huge, lustrous windows of colored glass.

These structural ideas quickly spread to England where, in one
instance, they inspired a nearly perfect imitation. In the thirteenth century,
century, King Henry III, a devotee of French culture, personally directed the
rebuilding of Westminster Abbey in the French High Gothic style, much as
Edward the Confessor had supervised the building of its Norman Romanesque predecessor. Henry III's Westminster Abbey has survived gloriously to
this day, although its beauty is tarnished by the outrageously bad taste of
the eighteenth- and nineteenth-century tomb sculptures that creep up its
venerable walls like dry rot.

Elsewhere, however, English builders modified the new French style in
accordance with their own tastes into a distinctive variation known as
Early English Gothic. The vaulting of Early English churches did not rise to
such heights as their French counterparts, nor were their windows quite so
large. Architects often painted the churches' interiors, and sometimes
enlivened them with dark marble columns (of "Purbeck" marble—i.e.,
from the island of Purbeck) that contrasted with wall surfaces and arches
made of light-colored stone. The east ends of these churches, behind their
high altars, were squared rather than rounded as in France. Strong horizontal lines held the upward thrust of the columns and pointed arches firmly in
check, creating a sense of harmonious balance. Early English Gothic was
less audacious, less tautly dramatic than French High Gothic, but, to some
tastes, just as impressive and a good deal more restful. It inspired the

Salisbury Cathedral
Approximately
contemporary with
Westminster Abbey,
Salisbury exemplifies the
very different style of Early
English Gothic, with its
smaller windows and
strong horizontal lines.
(Courtesy of the Royal
Commission on the
Historical Monuments of
England)

building of great cathedrals such as Salisbury, Wells, and Lincoln, as well as countless village and abbey churches, many of which, like the cathedrals, still stand essentially unchanged.[18]

Cathedrals were not, as is sometimes thought, mere monuments to ecclesiastical vainglory, built through the toil and impoverishment of unwilling masses. Evidence suggests that they were products of a common faith—of a powerful religious culture embodying a Christian world view shared by all orders of society. These buildings were the highest artistic achievements of an age of belief in which architects, sculptors, glass-makers, and ordinary builders worked together to adorn their towns and manifest their faith. Artisans achieved the fullest exercise of their creative powers not in spite of the prevailing ecclesiastical culture but through it. Their finest works, the high-medieval abbey churches and cathedrals, illus-

---

[18] Two excellent works that relate Gothic architecture to the cultural background of the High Middle Ages are Erwin Panofsky, *Gothic Architecture and Scholasticism* (reprint, Cleveland, 1957), and Jean Bony, *French Gothic Architecture of the 12th and 13th Centuries* (Berkeley, Calif., 1983). For the English styles, see the richly illustrated *English Cathedrals* by Geoffrey Grigson, Martin Hurlimann, and Peter Meyer (new ed., London, 1961). On cathedral building, see Henry Kraus, *Gold Was the Mortar: The Economics of Cathedral Building* (New York, 1979).

trate even today that romantic individualism is not the only path to artistic excellence—that in certain periods of cultural vitality, great works of art can emerge from a self-effacing commitment to the ideals of the wider community. In the High Middle Ages, these ideals included civic pride, devotion to the Church and its saints, and love of God. High-medieval cathedral builders, although no less human than modern artists, seem to have been less alienated. They did not believe in art for art's sake. Self-expression, rather than being a goal in itself, was a means to a wider goal that the artist shared with society.

The literature of the High Middle Ages, although perhaps less dazzling than its architecture, is nevertheless impressive. Lay literacy expanded to the point where written records were maintained at many baronial courts and manors. Secular music and vernacular literature flourished in a variety of forms: the political song; the round (England's first known round, "Sumer is icumen in," dates from the thirteenth century); and, most strikingly, the romance. The French-speaking Normans' conquest and settlement of England had made Old French the language of polite society. English remained the common language of the peasantry. And aristocratic children, often reared by English-speaking nannies, were usually bilingual. But French remained the dominant language among the aristocracy until the fourteenth century, and in the romance it found a congenial form of expression.

The romance synthesized two earlier literary forms: the *chanson de geste* (song of great deeds) and the lyric poem. The *chanson de geste* was popular in northern France and England during the Anglo-Norman era. A bellicose narrative poem, it stressed the heroic virtues of loyalty and warlike prowess typical of the earlier feudal aristocracy. Its characteristics are splendidly exemplified in the "Song of Roland," an exciting, bloodthirsty tale of a battle between a powerful Muslim army and a small knightly band led by Charlemagne's nephew. The "Song of Roland" is said to have been a favorite of William the Conqueror himself.[19]

The lyric poem, a product of the very different cultural milieu of southern France, was short, sometimes witty, and often romantic. In the course of the later twelfth century, the southern lyric, with its emphasis on idealized love and refined behavior, was transmitted into the courts of northern Europe by aristocratic southerners such as Eleanor of Aquitaine and her daughter Marie, countess of Champagne. There it helped romanticize the knightly ideal and significantly transform poetic expression from the epic style of the *chanson de geste* to the shorter, gentler thirteenth-century

---

[19] William of Malmesbury alleges that at the onset of the Battle of Hastings, the Normans advanced against the English singing the "Song of Roland." If so, it was probably in an earlier form than the earliest version known to us today (transcribed by an anonymous author sometime between c. 1100 and 1130). If the poem had been as long in 1066 as in its earliest manuscript version, the Battle of Hastings would have been much delayed.

romance. As Bernard de Ventadour, Eleanor of Aquitaine's own troubadour, expressed it:

> Singing isn't worth a thing,
> If the heart sings not the song.
> And the heart can never sing
> If it brings not love along.

In a longer poem for which the music has survived, Bernard de Ventadour poured out his heart, expressing the new sentiments that he and Eleanor of Aquitaine shared:

> When I see the lark beat its wings
> Facing the sun's rays,
> Forgetting itself, letting itself sing
> Of the sweetness that enters its heart—
> Ah! Such a great longing enters me,
> From the happiness I see,
> That only a miracle prevents my heart
> From consuming itself with desire.
> Alas! I thought I knew so much of love
> And I know so little.
> For I can't help loving a lady
> Whom I cannot attain.
> She has all my heart,
> She has me entirely. . . .
> She has left me nothing but desire,
> And a foolish heart.

The romance was narrative in form like the *chanson de geste*, but romantic in mood like the lyric poem. Thirteenth-century romances drew heavily for their subject matter from a series of tales relating to the court of the half-legendary British monarch King Arthur—tales that originated in Wales and were given international publicity by Geoffrey of Monmouth. Geoffrey was a churchman active in England and Wales at the time of Henry I and Stephen, and his fanciful *History of the Kings of Britain* was read widely on both sides of the Channel. In the later twelfth and thirteenth centuries, the Arthurian legends, along with other ancient Welsh tales such as the adventures of Parsifal and Tristan, were beautifully and imaginatively developed by poets in France and Germany. The sensitivity of the twelfth- and thirteenth-century romance, contrasting sharply with the power of the *chanson de geste*, further exemplifies the growing sophistication and international scope of high-medieval civilization.

8

Henry III: Monarchy, Community, and Parliament

When King John died in 1216, he left as heir his nine-year-old son Henry III, who governed and misgoverned England for the next fifty-six years.[1] During the first decade of Henry's long reign, a group of regents directed the royal government. Fortunately for the realm, they included men of ability and good sense. One was the legate Cardinal Guala, who exercised the right of guardianship on behalf of England's papal overlord. Another was William Marshal, England's most respected magnate, a valiant and aged warrior who had risen from a threadbare life of tournament jousting to become earl of Pembroke, and who had remained faithful to King John through all his various moods and fortunes. A third was the talented justiciar Hubert de Burgh, who had ascended from a minor landed family to the highest post in the royal administration and had won for himself the earldom of Kent. These three men, together with several others, comprised a select group of leading barons and high ecclesiastics who ruled England in the name of the child-king. Together they worked to heal England's old wounds and to restore unity. They forced Louis of France to abandon his campaign against England, they reissued Magna Carta (in slightly revised form), and they freed England of strife.

From Regency to Personal Rule

As the years passed, the personnel of the governing group changed. Cardinal Guala left the country in 1218, to be replaced by another papal legate. And William Marshal died the following year. In the meantime, Archbishop

---

[1] The two most detailed works on the period are both by Sir Maurice Powicke: *The Thirteenth Century, 1216–1307*, Oxford History of England, 4 (2nd ed., Oxford, 1962), and *King Henry III and the Lord Edward* (2 vols., Oxford, 1947). The most important recent works are Robert C. Stacey, *Politics, Policy, and Finance Under Henry III, 1216–1245* (Oxford, 1987); David A. Carpenter, *The Minority of Henry III* (Berkeley, 1990); M. T. Clanchy, *England and Its Rulers, 1066–1272* (London, 1983), pp. 199–283; and David A. Carpenter, "Kings, Magnates, and Society: The Personal Rule of King Henry III, 1234–1258," *Speculum*, 60 (1985), 39–70. These interpretations differ quite sharply: Carpenter views Henry III as much friendlier and more lenient toward native English barons, and more tolerant of the extension of baronial power in the shires, than Clanchy or Powicke would have it.

Tomb Effigy of William Marshal From the Temple Church, London (c. 1230). (A. F. Kersting)

Stephen Langton, having returned from a visit to Rome, assumed an important position in the regency. In the early 1220s, Langton and Hubert de Burgh were the chief architects of royal policy. Although Hubert, being of low birth, was the object of a certain amount of baronial jealousy, the regency government continued, by and large, to govern effectively.

At length, in 1227, the young king declared himself of age. At nineteen, he felt ready to assume the responsibilities of government. In retrospect, it's fair to say that he was as ready at nineteen as he would ever be. Stephen Langton died the following year, but Henry III remained more or less under the influence of Hubert de Burgh until Hubert's fall from power in 1232. Indeed, the period of Henry's personal rule did not truly commence until 1236, when the king married Eleanor of Provence and at the same time chose new councilors (including the new queen's uncle) to replace men who had been providing counsel since King John's time.

Henry possessed many talents, but they were not of the sort that led to effective governance. He was well educated; he was usually amiable (though he had a hair-trigger temper); and he was pious. According to the contemporary historian Matthew Paris, who was not one of Henry's admirers, "In proportion as the king was thought deficient in prudence in worldly affairs, so was he the more distinguished for his devotion to the

Lord—for it was his custom each day to hear three Masses . . . and when the priest elevated the body of our Lord, Henry usually held the priest's hand and kissed it." Henry was a person of discrimination, but only in judging art, not counselors. Generous with his friends, loyal to his papal overlord, and faithful to his wife, he lost the respect of many of his barons and prelates because of his mercurial temperament and acid tongue. At times he could seem firm, but too often his firmness was mere obstinacy. His reign was long but inglorious.

Matthew Paris describes Henry as "of medium stature and compact in body. One of his eyelids drooped, hiding some of the dark part of the eyeball. He had robust strength but was careless in his acts." A court jester is reported to have remarked that Henry III was like Jesus Christ. When asked why, the jester replied that, like Jesus, Henry was as wise at his birth as he would ever be.

Law and Administration Under Henry III (1216–1272)

In spite of Henry III's shortcomings, or perhaps because of them, his reign brought impressive progress in law and administration. The rising affluence of the lesser knights, freeholders, and burghers gave them a growing sense of political responsibility and an increasing participation in local administration. Members of the knightly gentry staffed the shire courts, which were beginning to play an ever-greater role in the royal judicial system. Town governments and courts fell more and more under the control of the burghers themselves—in particular, the wealthy merchants and master craftsmen. Although the great majority of the population remained politically inarticulate, participation in the business of government was broadening nonetheless.[2] Even the semi-free villeins became slightly more involved in the affairs of the kingdom. Before the thirteenth century, only freemen enjoyed the privilege of bearing arms (the possession of arms traditionally being a mark of free status). In the thirteenth century, however, arms were permitted to villeins, who thereby assumed some small share of the responsibility for defending the land and maintaining internal order.

Out of this diffusion of responsibility there emerged a concept vital to the politics of the age and to the future development of English government: the notion of a "community of the realm." The "community" was by no means all-inclusive. At first restricted to the king and his great landholders, lay and ecclesiastical, it gradually came to include prosperous members of the lesser knightly class and the burghers. These groups contributed much to local administration and to the realm's prosperity. They therefore insisted, reasonably enough, on having some voice in governance. There was much disagreement as to precisely what their political role ought to be, but as the century progressed the notion became firmly rooted

---

[2] See J. R. Maddicott, "Magna Carta and the Local Community, 1215–1259," *Past and Present*, 102 (1984), 25–65; and R. G. Davies and I. H. Denton, eds., *The English Parliament in the Middle Ages* (Philadelphia, 1981).

that a ruler who ignored the interests of the "community of the realm" was no king but a tyrant.

This notion did not hinder the continued growth of a centralized government. Even more than at the time of Magna Carta, the issue was not whether a strong royal administration should exist, but who should control it. In the course of the thirteenth century, the struggle for control grew violent at times, but the royal administrative machinery itself became steadily more elaborate.

The chief agency of government under the king was the small council with its varied responsibilities—administrative, fiscal, and judicial. It advised the king, handled financial matters too great or too complex for the exchequer, served as the nucleus of all meetings of the great council, and functioned as the high tribunal of the realm. It was a court of common law—the King's Bench—with jurisdiction over major civil and criminal cases. It could also act as a feudal court, adjudicating disputes between royal vassals. It had also become a court of equity, handling cases that the baronial, shire, or common-law courts could not settle properly or fairly. The council eventually delegated more and more of its judicial business to a body of specialized royal justices. Not infrequently, these justices sat with the king and his small council, and occasionally they merged into a still larger tribunal of king, small council, and great council. But much of the time, they functioned as a separate court with something of the same independence as the Exchequer court and the court of Common Pleas. Ultimately, the King's Bench evolved into an independent body, commissioned to try major criminal cases in the king's name.

The small council maintained close relations not only with the common-law courts but also with the major administrative offices of exchequer and chancery, whose chief officers, the treasurer and chancellor, were themselves major participants in the council. The exchequer, now permanently at Westminster, shared financial responsibility with the wardrobe—the financial office that accompanied the king on his travels and handled day-to-day expenses. Exchequer recordkeeping became ever more rigorous, and exchequer procedures achieved an unparalleled level of efficiency.

The chancery, an increasingly active branch of the royal household, maintained custody of the Great Seal. Chancery officials were responsible for drawing up a growing variety and number of royal documents—charters, royal letters, administrative and judicial writs—and authenticating them with the Great Seal. Since the time of King John, the chancery had been regularly preserving copies of these documents—"enrolling" them—in records such as the charter rolls, patent rolls, and close rolls. Under Henry III, a new type of seal, the Privy Seal, accompanied the royal court on its travels, enabling the chancery with its Great Seal to function as a separate department at a fixed location. But this process of differentiation remained incomplete until the fourteenth century.

Royal administration and royal law grew side by side. The court of Henry III produced an impressive, systematic legal treatise—*On the Laws and Customs of England*—traditionally but incorrectly credited to the mid-thirteenth century jurist Henry de Bracton.[3] The work is a thoughtful, rigorous description and interpretation of the law of the thirteenth-century royal courts, dwarfing the work of "Glanville" in the previous century and illustrating clearly that English law had come of age. "Bracton" demonstrated a keen knowledge of Roman law, as well as a mastery of the vast accumulation of precedents forming the foundation of English common law. The work searched beyond the precedents themselves to discover the fundamental principles that shaped them. One such principle was the idea that the king, although himself subject to the law, was the ultimate source of justice in the realm. This notion underlay the age-long trend toward a single, uniform body of law common to all English people.

The thirteenth century saw the establishment of a coherent and comprehensive legal system. The royal courts of King's Bench, Common Pleas, Exchequer, and justices in eyre were staffed for the first time by what can be described as professional judges[4] and were provided a sturdy juridical and philosophical foundation by the treatise ascribed to Bracton. With the evolution of a strong royal bureaucracy, a well-structured and professional judiciary, and the vital concept of community, feudal monarchy was being left far behind. Yet it was the contractual assumption of feudalism itself—the notion of vassals' rights before their lord-king—that gave the thirteenth-century English monarchy its tone and direction.

The Limitation of the Royal Prerogative

The age of Henry III was a crucial epoch in the history of English constitutional development. The historian G. O. Sayles has aptly described the reign as "a commentary upon the Great Charter." More than that, it was a commentary on one of the central problems inherent in Magna Carta and in medieval political theory as a whole: given that the king's authority is bound by customary limitations—that "the king should be under God and the law," as the author of "Bracton" put it—how could such a principle be translated into workable political institutions? The answer lay in the concept that the king should govern in the interests and with the active cooperation of the "community of the realm."

English government had always been, at least to a degree, the product of a dialogue between monarchy and community. The Anglo-Saxon kings acted on important occasions in consultation with their Witan. The Norman and Angevin kings usually summoned their great councils to advise

---

[3] In fact, Bracton merely revised earlier versions of a work written originally in the 1220s and 1230s by someone associated with the royal tribunals. See Henry de Bracton, *De Legibus et Consuetudinibus Angliae*, G. E. Woodbine, ed. (4 vols., New Haven, 1915–1942; reissued Cambridge, Mass., 1968–1977). The later edition includes commentary and a translation by Samuel E. Thorne, who demonstrated that Bracton was not the author.

[4] See pp. 132–133 and 148–149 of this text and Ralph V. Turner, *The English Judiciary in the Age of Glanville and Bracton, c. 1176–1239* (Cambridge, 1985).

Gilt-Bronze Effigy of King Henry III   In Westminster Abbey (c. 1294). (A. F. Kersting)

them on weighty decisions and drew continually on the advice and administrative support of their small councils. Well into the thirteenth century, however, the great and small councils had neither a power of veto nor a fixed membership. If the king chose to abuse his rights over the baronage, ignore their counsel, and overtax his subjects, his people had little recourse short of rebellion. The search for a more effective means for the king and his great landholders to share in governance became the major concern of English politics under Henry III. And throughout most of his reign, dissident barons worked toward that end by striving to gain control of the king's small council. In this way they hoped to protect the rights set forth in Magna Carta.

As his reign progressed, Henry III chose more and more to forgo the advice of his English magnates and to exclude some of them from participating in the central government. Particularly after about 1236, the king surrounded himself with his own professional administrators and with favorites, whom his baronial critics described contemptuously as "foreigners." These outsiders constituted two unrelated, and usually antagonistic, kin groups. First, a cohort of Queen Eleanor's uncles from her homeland of Savoy and Provence followed her to England, joined the court of her husband King Henry, and catapulted into high office. One of Eleanor's uncles became the king's chief counselor, another became earl of Richmond, and a third became archbishop of Canterbury. The other group of "foreigners" were Henry III's own half-brothers—the products of a rather unlikely second marriage between his mother, Isabel of Angoulême, and the same Hugh of Lusignan to whom she had been betrothed before King John galloped off with her. Henry III made one of his Lusignan-Poitevin half-brothers the heir by marriage to William Marshal's vast earldom of Pembroke, another ascended to the wealthy bishopric of Winchester, and two more received large royal pensions.

All these royal kinsmen, jockeying for position around the king, were eager to win fame and fortune through Henry III's favor in this rich island realm. The chronicler Matthew Paris remarked that the king was losing day by day the affection of his natural subjects:

> He enticed to his side all the foreigners he could, enriched them, and, despising and despoiling his English subjects, intruded aliens into their place. . . . Men from Poitou busied themselves in oppressing the nobles of the country, and especially religious men, in a thousand ways.

The king's dislike and distrust of various English nobles aggravated the problem. Matthew Paris tells how Henry flew into a rage against the important Earl Robert de Ros and called him a traitor. "You lie," the earl replied. "I have never been a traitor and never will be. If you are just, how can you harm me?" "I can seize your grain and thresh and sell it," the king responded. "Do so," answered the earl, "and I will send back your threshers minus their heads." Friends interceded to quiet the quarrel, but Matthew Paris observes that the windy words bred anger and hatred. On another occasion, Henry infringed on the traditional liberties of the lords of the Welsh March (the Welsh frontier, "where the king's writ does not run") by sending a royal writ to the marcher lord Walter Clifford. Infuriated at this royal presumption, Walter forced the king's luckless messenger to eat the writ, seal and all.

Henry III was by no means the first king to govern without serious regard for the advice of his magnates. The English political tradition was still sufficiently fluid to allow a king to rule arbitrarily, as long as his policies were reasonably successful and palatable to the barons, and as long as he maintained fairly good personal relations with most of them and did not squeeze them too hard. King John had squeezed and failed, and the result was Magna Carta. Similarly, Henry III's governance aroused widespread opposition, and for two reasons. First, his policies—which included lavishly expensive and dismally unsuccessful efforts to reconquer the old Angevin Empire—seemed subversive to baronial interests. He was obliged to appeal frequently for baronial aids, and many barons granted them with increasing reluctance. Second, the barons were mindful of the recent example, during the regency, of a successful government based on baronial advice and counsel. This memory sharpened the traditional notion that the king's "natural counselors" were his great hereditary landholders.

The Struggle with Dissident Barons

From the beginning of his personal rule, Henry III found himself at odds with a strong aristocratic faction. In 1236, a group of barons demonstrated against foreign participation in royal governance, forcing Henry to take refuge for a time in the Tower of London, but the incident effected no change in the council's makeup. At a great council meeting in 1237, the barons refused his request for aid unless he purged the small council and brought in "natural counselors." Henry again submitted, again momentarily: he appointed twelve men acceptable to the barons, including several of their own number. Once the great council disbanded, however, the king brought back his favorites. Although English magnates exercised relatively little influence in the royal council despite their efforts during these years, they were steadily tightening their power over the governments of their shires, thereby increasing the threat of conflict between court and countryside.

The pattern of temporary royal accommodation to aristocratic pressures recurred with variations in the great council of 1244, and baronial dissatisfaction steadily intensified. But the king managed to muddle through from crisis to crisis until 1258. At that time a crisis occurred that proved too much for Henry. As a consequence, the royal government was forced to undergo a drastic reorientation.

Henry's successive clashes with his barons arose because of his incessant need to appeal to them for money beyond the customary royal revenues. Basically, the financial position of the mid-thirteenth century monarchy was sound. The difficulty lay in the fact that medieval monarchies had nothing to correspond to the national debts of modern governments. There were no normal means of raising funds to meet extraordinary expenses, except to borrow at short-term and high interest from individuals or groups (merchants, churchmen, Jewish bankers), or to beg the barons' permission to levy a special tax. Matthew Paris mentions various undignified money-raising methods Henry was forced to employ. He pawned his jewels and even sold them. He trumped up charges against Jewish bankers and threatened them with imprisonment unless they paid thousands of pounds into the royal treasury. To the abbot of Ramsey he wrote: "My friend, I earnestly beg you to assist me by giving, or at least lending me one hundred pounds, for I am in need and must have that sum without delay." On one occasion he approached each of his barons in turn, saying: "I am a poor man and entirely destitute of money . . . and whoever will do me this favor, to him I will return it when an opportunity occurs; but whoever denies me the favor, to him will I also deny any."

Henry's financial difficulties were largely of his own making, for the virtue of thrift was unknown to him. In Maurice Powicke's disapproving words:

> He maintained a great household, swollen by foreign kinsmen and their protégés, by a company of knights and by a crowd of officials. He was hospitable and liked big ceremonial feasts. He was a lavish patron of the arts and had a passion for building, for the decoration of his castles and houses, for jewels and precious stones and fine clothes. Tenacious of his rights, he was involved in frequent lawsuits at Rome, where he had to maintain expensive guardians of his interests not only as his proctors but as pensioners among the cardinals and officials of the Curia. The sums he

spent annually on gifts of wood, venison, robes, pensions would have been the despair of a modern committee of ways and means.[5]

Added to all these expenses were the high costs of Henry's ambitions in foreign affairs. He tried repeatedly but fruitlessly to recover Normandy and Anjou—paying soldiers, bribing allies, and financing rebellions against the king of France. When these efforts failed, he turned his attention to more distant parts. The crisis of 1258 between Henry and his barons resulted directly from Henry's attempt to place a son on the throne of the kingdom of Sicily.

For a century, the papacy had been engaged in a power struggle with the Hohenstaufen dynasty of Holy Roman emperors. Following the death of the brilliant and dangerous Emperor Frederick II in 1250, the pope sought Henry III's cooperation in dividing the vast territories in Germany and Italy that the Hohenstaufens had ruled. In the 1190s, this dynasty had added the rich Norman kingdom of Sicily and southern Italy to its dominions through a marriage between Emperor Henry VI and the heiress of the Norman kingdom of Sicily. Now the papacy was determined to sever these southern districts from the remainder of the Holy Roman Empire and place them under a new dynasty. In 1254, after much diplomatic bargaining, the pope offered the Sicilian crown to Edmund, Henry III's second son.

The offer was less generous than it might seem. The pope had been trying for several years to dispose of the Sicilian crown, and two princes had already rejected it. They were probably wise to do so. In accepting the crown for his son, Henry III had to assume the enormous debt the papacy had incurred by campaigning against the Hohenstaufens in Sicily. The debt exceeded ninety thousand pounds—a sum almost as great as King Richard the Lion-Hearted's ransom. To make matters worse, the papacy did not actually control the kingdom of Sicily: whoever purchased the Sicilian crown would then have to conquer the kingdom. In the years following 1254, the actual control of the Sicilian kingdom fell into the hands of an able bastard Hohenstaufen named Manfred. Edmund's hopes of winning a kingdom to go with his new crown seemed dim.

But once committed to paying the papal debt, Henry III could not renege without great difficulty and embarrassment. He found himself tied to a ruinously expensive and fruitless venture. When he fell behind in his payments, the Vicar of Christ threatened to excommunicate him. Henry was obliged to turn to his barons for financial aid, and they agreed to help him only in return for radical political concessions. In 1258, he submitted to their demands and allowed them a significant degree of control over the royal administration.

Henry's Sicilian dream emptied his treasury and jeopardized his royal independence. Moreover, it forced him to come to terms at last with the

---

5 Powicke, *Henry III and the Lord Edward*, I, p. 303.

French monarchy. In the Treaty of Paris (1259), he formally recognized the Capetian dominion over the former territories of the Angevin Empire in northern France and did homage to Louis IX for Gascony and other southern French lands that had remained under English control since the catastrophes of John's reign. In the end Henry lost Sicily, too. Eventually, the papacy found a more stalwart champion against Manfred in the person of Charles of Anjou, Louis IX's younger brother, and it was Charles rather than Edmund who finally wrested Sicily from the Hohenstaufens.

In 1258, however, the fate of Sicily was still uncertain, and Henry III had to come to terms with his magnates. Gritting his teeth, he conceded

> ... that by twelve faithful men of our council already elected, and by twelve other faithful men elected by the nobles, who are to convene at Oxford one month after the coming feast of Pentecost, the condition of our kingdom shall be ordered, rectified, and reformed in keeping with what they shall think it best to enact for the honor of God, for our faith, and for the good of our kingdom. . . . And whatever is ordained in this manner by the twenty-four elected by both sides and sworn to the undertaking—or by the majority of them—we will observe inviolably. . . . Moreover, the aforesaid earls and barons have promised that on the completion of the business stated above they will in good faith endeavor to arrange that a common aid is rendered us by the community of our realm.

The deliberations of the twenty-four men produced an agreement known as the Provisions of Oxford (1258), which sought at one blow to make the community of the realm a political reality. First of all, the great council was to meet formally at least three times each year. It was to include in its membership not only counselors chosen by the king but also twelve men "elected" by the "community"—i.e., selected by the magnates. The agreement further stipulated that "the community shall regard as binding whatever these twelve shall do." Moreover, the small council came under the control of a baronial executive committee—the Council of Fifteen—with the power of "advising the king in good faith regarding the government of the kingdom and all matters pertaining to the king or the kingdom, and of amending and reforming everything that they shall consider in need of amendment or reform." The Council of Fifteen dominated the royal administration through its power to appoint three of the great officers of state—the chancellor, the treasurer, and the justiciar—to yearly terms. It exercised authority over the exchequer and worked with the king to supervise the activities of sheriffs and other local officials.

The Provisions of Oxford also included a number of administrative reforms, designed particularly to correct abuses in property laws. Other similar reforms were established in a corollary document, the Provisions of Westminster (1259). In general, the magnates accepted the growth of the central administration that had occurred over the past several generations. But now, because of what they regarded as royal incompetence, they sought to seize control of the government. Their methods of limiting royal authority—through the Council of Fifteen and through frequent meetings of the great council—constitute a much more sophisticated approach to shared governance than that of John's barons in 1215.

Still, their solution was too extreme to last. Under the Provisions of Oxford, the central administrative machinery remained as powerful as ever, but the king himself was reduced to near parity with the greater magnates. Many barons were troubled over the emasculation of kingship that the Provisions of Oxford implied and gradually became disenchanted with their more radical leaders. In time, the experiment in limited monarchy became wracked by baronial dissension, and by 1262 Henry III found himself in a position to abolish the Provisions altogether. Absolved of his oaths by the pope, he undertook once again to rule by his own authority.

Some of Henry's barons had evidently hoped that the king might learn from his misfortunes. They were bitterly disappointed, for Henry's renewed personal rule was as willful as ever. Consequently, in 1263 baronial opposition asserted itself once again. The leader of the insurgents was Simon de Montfort, earl of Leicester and brother-in-law of the king. Earl Simon was a remarkable character—passionate, adventurous, fearlessly self-confident, and avidly pious—a friend and admirer of theologians such as Robert Grosseteste. Simon inspired some with intense loyalty and high hopes, others with terror and hatred. A younger son of a great baronial family of central France, Simon had come to England to seek his fortune and had become earl of Leicester by right of his grandfather's marriage to a Leicester heiress. Simon himself married one of Henry III's sisters and basked for a time in the royal favor. Eventually, like other magnates, he had a falling-out with the king. Simon was one of the powers behind the Provisions of Oxford and had served on the Council of Fifteen. When Henry rescinded the Provi-

An Equestrian Simon de Montfort, as Depicted on His Personal Seal, c. 1258 (The Granger Collection)

sions in 1262, Simon went into exile, but he returned in 1263 to lead a powerful faction of disaffected magnates.

Toward the close of 1263, king and magnates agreed to submit their dispute to the arbitration of the universally respected King Louis IX of France. St. Louis's impartiality was famous, but he had an uncompromising respect for the prerogatives of royalty. The barons' notions of cooperative government and community of the realm were beyond his experience. His verdict, known as the Mise of Amiens (1264), constituted a ringing denunciation of the baronial cause:

> We suppress and annul all the aforesaid provisions, ordinances, statutes, and obligations, by whatever name, and all that has followed from them. . . . We also decree and ordain that the said king, of his own will, may freely appoint, dismiss, and remove the justiciar, chancellor, treasurer, counselors, lesser justices, sheriffs, and any other officers and ministers of his kingdom and household, as he was used and able to do prior to the time of the aforesaid provisions.

Left without a scrap of their hard-fought program, Henry's baronial opponents took up arms.

The rebellion of 1264–1265 was not simply a struggle between king and baronage. As has been suggested, the barons were by no means of one mind. Few of them approved wholeheartedly of Henry III, but many had a keen respect for the royal office and distrusted the opposition leaders' radical goals. Nobody, of course, wished to abolish the monarchy—the day of Oliver Cromwell lay almost four centuries in the future—but insurgents such as Simon de Montfort would not hesitate to govern the realm in the name of a captive king.

Thus there were barons on both sides, and not a few of them switched teams in the midst of the struggle. The opposition was led by Simon de Montfort, and the royalist force by Henry III's eldest son, the Lord Edward, now near manhood. Many looked hopefully toward this chivalrous young warrior, wishing that he, not his bumbling father, were their king.

The first phase of the rebellion culminated in a pitched battle at Lewes, near the Channel coast, in May 1264. The Lord Edward fought well, but the insurgents won the field. Henry III had to submit to the rebellious magnates, and the barons held Edward hostage to ensure the king's cooperation. For the next fifteen months, Simon de Montfort was the de facto ruler of England, governing in Henry's name.

Simon attempted to govern in the spirit of the Provisions of Oxford. He summoned the great council frequently and strove to broaden its representative structure. He shared his authority with two colleagues, the earl of Gloucester and the bishop of Chichester, and the three received assistance from a permanent executive council akin to the former Council of Fifteen but with only nine members. Nobody could justly accuse Simon of harboring dictatorial ambitions, but many remained suspicious of his casual attitude toward the royal dignity. His government represented too sharp a break from the traditions of his age. As the months went by, he saw his party eroded by disaffection, and his widespread support dissolved. His colleague, the earl of Gloucester, jumped over to the royal cause, and in May 1265 the Lord Edward escaped from imprisonment and hurried to raise an army. At the battle of Evesham, in August 1265, Edward routed Simon de Montfort's army. Simon himself was slain and then hideously chopped to pieces. The experiment in baronial governance collapsed, and Henry III resumed his authority.

Henry lived another seven years, but his power passed more and more into the hands of his able son and heir. The issues of the long crisis of 1258–1265 were settled finally in the royal favor in the Dictum of Kenilworth (1266) and the Statute of Marlborough (1267). But the Lord Edward had the good sense to be a gracious victor and to respect the interests and opinions of the "community." The Dictum of Kenilworth, for example, not only asserted royal rights but also provided for the restoration of confiscated rebel lands—upon the payment of stiff fines. Edward rejected the severe limitations on royal power that the Provisions of Oxford imposed but accepted the enlightened legal reforms that the barons at Oxford had urged. Hence, England was at peace with itself once again, and by the time Edward succeeded to the throne on his aged father's death in 1272, he had already won the confidence of his subjects.

The Emergence of Parliament

From our modern perspective, the rise of Parliament is the most significant political development in thirteenth-century England. Parliament emerged amidst the internal disputes of Henry III's reign, and the military expenses of Edward I stimulated its early growth. Most historians would agree on these two propositions but on little else. The origin and nature of the medieval English Parliament are subjects of continuing, sometimes acrimonious, historical debate. For the writer of a general textbook, presenting a coherent account of the rise of Parliament is rather like walking through a mine field.[6] With this warning in mind, let me proceed—very cautiously.

Throughout the High Middle Ages, the word *parliament* was used in a variety of contexts. It is derived from the French verb *parler*, "to speak," and originally applied to a meeting of any kind at which views were exchanged—a parley. It was used in the early twelfth-century "Song of Roland" to describe a mere dialogue. But by the later twelfth century, it was acquiring the more specialized meaning of a large deliberative meeting. It was used, for example, to describe Henry II's great dispute with Becket at the Council of Northampton in 1164 and John's confrontation with his barons on the occasion of Magna Carta. During the thirteenth century, its meaning narrowed gradually to meetings of the king with his great council

---

[6] For various approaches, see Bertie Wilkinson, *The Creation of Medieval Parliaments* (New York, 1972), an essay plus original sources; E. B. Fryde and Edward Miller, eds., *Historical Studies of the English Parliament*, 1, *Origins to 1399* (Cambridge, 1970), a collection of scholarly studies; G. L. Harriss, *King, Parliament and Public Finance in Medieval England to 1369* (Oxford, 1975); G. O. Sayles, *The King's Parliament of England* (New York, 1974).

or his small council—particularly when functioning as a high tribunal. Only during the thirteenth century did *parliament* come to apply specifically to an important meeting of the great council, and not until the later Middle Ages did the term describe a permanent body that met regularly. Until then there was no "Parliament"; there were only "parliaments."

Kings had been summoning their great councils since time immemorial, but only after the early 1230s were they called parliaments. Up until this time, the chief justiciar, chairing the exchequer and regency government, had provided unity to the royal administration. But with Hubert de Burgh's fall from power in 1232, Henry III abolished the office of chief justiciar. Moreover, by the mid-1230s the courts of Common Pleas and King's Bench had both separated from the king's itinerating court. To counteract this process of decentralization, Henry III began to summon larger and more frequent councils to discuss royal policy and to deal with difficult cases referred to the king from his several courts and administrative departments. These council meetings were the first to be described consistently as parliaments.

Scholars disagree as to precisely what constituted a thirteenth-century parliament. What were its functions? What groups participated in it? What classes were represented in it? The evidence is unclear. During the closing decades of the thirteenth century, contemporaries seem to have agreed on which great council meetings were parliaments and which were not, but the composition and functions of such assemblies remained ill defined.

Of some things we are certain. Parliaments emerged not as a counterweight to royal authority but as an extension of it. Parliaments were royal assemblies, summoned by the king to meet in his presence. They were not representative bodies in the modern sense, yet they were assumed to represent the interests of the entire community of the realm and to serve as its voice. The king's small council, with its increasingly professional expertise, functioned as the vital core of every parliament and exercised responsibility for initiating and transacting most of its business. Earls, magnates, and prelates also attended. The greater of them were summoned individually by royal writs, although there remained for a time some doubt as to precisely which landholders were entitled to a summons. Late thirteenth-century parliaments sometimes also included representatives of the towns, the shires, and the lower clergy (but often they did not). In retrospect, the tendency to add these representative elements to the great council was a constitutional development of enormous significance. We must not imagine, however, that members of the lower social orders—peasants or landless workers or urban journeymen—were included. Rather, it was the prosperous middle group of landholding shire knights and established merchants and artisans who sent their representatives.

The functions of these assemblies were as varied as their composition. They sat as the high court of England, hearing pleas of unusual significance. They settled thorny issues of law and administration. They advised the king on great matters of state, such as undertaking a war or concluding a peace, and they declared their support in moments of crisis. From Edward

I's reign onward, they entertained petitions from subjects and local groups for the redress of grievances—particularly those arising from the misconduct of royal officials. And from the beginning, they held the power to grant the king special aids.

Ultimately, Parliament's role in approving extraordinary taxes would become the key to its power, but in the thirteenth century that role was limited. "Scutage and aid shall be levied in our kingdom only by the common counsel of our kingdom." Such was John's promise in clause 12 of Magna Carta. As the thirteenth century progressed, the concept of consent became increasingly important. In 1297, Edward I made the concession more explicit: no extraordinary taxes would be levied without the assent of the whole community of the realm. Such permission did not require polling the entire population but winning the concurrence of the wealthy and powerful—who were taken to be the community's natural spokesmen. Thus, parliaments served as a particularly convenient way to obtain the community's assent. As the king's customary revenues became less and less adequate to meet the rising costs of administration and war, parliamentary grants became ever more essential and frequent.

It should not be concluded that nonfiscal parliamentary functions were of mere secondary importance. Throughout the thirteenth and fourteenth centuries, parliaments remained, in essence, supreme tribunals. But a politically insensitive monarch such as Henry III valued parliaments more for their financial support than for their judgment and counsel. When Henry summoned a parliament in 1237, for example, he placed no business whatever before his magnates and prelates but simply asked them to approve an aid. The resentment aroused by this sort of royal treatment of the great landholders—the "natural counselors" of the king—underlay the Provisions of Oxford and the crisis of 1258–1265.

Royal financial need seems to have been a primary motive for the inclusion of representatives from the towns and shires. John summoned shire knights to a meeting of the great council in 1213, and Henry III did the same in 1254. On both occasions, the knights' chief function was to speak for their shires in approving an aid to the king. In 1261, Henry III summoned them once again to give moral and financial support to his struggle with his baronial opponents. The shire knights joined the barons in a parliament summoned by Simon de Montfort in 1264; and in 1265 Simon summoned a parliament that included, in addition to the magnates and prelates, two knights from every shire and two burghers from every town or city. Simon's chief aim was to broaden the base of his rebellion by winning over not only great landholders but also the urban elite and the shire gentry.

Burghers and shire knights appear again in some of the parliaments of Edward I. King Edward experimented constantly and creatively in the composition of his parliaments. The two lesser orders were present at only four of the thirty parliaments held during the first quarter-century of his reign, but during Edward's final decade of rule they were called frequently to serve alongside the great lords. Edward summoned representatives from the towns and shire gentry to his first Parliament in 1275 "to discuss together

Parliament of Edward I Edward I presides over a parliament, flanked by the king of Scots, the prince of Wales, and, beyond them, the archbishops of York and Canterbury. Churchmen are seated to the left and barons to the right, with royal judges seated between them on sacks of wool. (Society of Antiquaries, London)

with the magnates the affairs of our kingdom." They granted him an aid, but the new king was probably as anxious for their moral support as for their financial help.

Edward I summoned his most famous parliament—the so-called Model Parliament of 1295—at a crucial moment in his reign: a Scottish war, a Welsh rebellion, and a French invasion of Gascony combined to threaten the security of the realm. The three groups represented in the Parliament of 1275 appeared once again in 1295, and to them Edward added representatives of the lower clergy. Despite its name, the Model Parliament did not serve as a model for the future. The knights and barons met together in one group, the clergy in a second group, and the townsmen in a third—on the pattern of the later French Estates-General. In the fourteenth century, the lesser clergy resolved to exclude themselves from parliaments altogether, preferring to meet separately and deal with the king in ecclesiastical convocations. And the burghers and shire knights began to meet in a separate group that became the nucleus of the House of Commons. The magnates and highest prelates, left to themselves, evolved into the House of Lords.

The increasing participation by burghers and shire knights in thirteenth-century parliaments signified that the power of the English monarchy was to be shared not only with the magnates and prelates but with lesser classes as well. The community of the realm was significantly broadened and was becoming a political reality. Still, one must be cautious when speaking of parliaments and limited monarchy in thirteenth-century England. These concepts are apt to convey to the modern mind a degree of constitutionalism undreamed of in the High Middle Ages. As the century closed, the power of parliaments was still vague. Their members continued to serve the monarchy as judges and counselors no less than as grantors of royal subsidies. They sometimes bargained modestly and discreetly for policies favoring the interests of the community in return for the granting of fiscal support. But if any bargaining was done, either explicitly or implicitly, it was the magnates who took the lead. Lesser orders might sometimes be represented in parliaments, but their voices were scarcely audible.

Why was it that these lesser orders came to achieve representation at this particular historical moment? The reason is not difficult to discover. In the thirteenth century, they were growing in affluence, and their political and social importance increased accordingly. Their allegiance and support became more and more important to the central government—whether controlled by Henry III, Edward I, or Simon de Montfort. Moreover, shire knights and burghers in thirteenth-century parliaments represented a considerable degree of wealth, and the monarchy needed their financial support to meet its soaring expenses. With the decline of baronial courts, the magnates gradually lost the authority and confidence to commit the resources of their knightly tenants. Sometimes the monarchy sought aids from its knights and burghers by sending its officials out into town and countryside to meet with them separately. But it could deal with them more conveniently in a parliament.

The political events of thirteenth-century England were not solely responsible for the evolution of Parliament. During the High Middle Ages, parallel institutions emerged throughout Western Christendom: the French Estates General; the Spanish Cortes; and representative bodies in Italy, Sicily, Germany, and the Low Countries. Townsmen were represented in the cortes of Aragon, for example, as early as 1164, and in 1232 two representatives from every town were summoned to a royal assembly of the kingdom of Sicily.[7] Underlying all these developments was the old and

---

[7] For a thorough discussion and thought-provoking reinterpretation of high-medieval assemblies, see Susan Reynolds, *Kingdoms and Communities in Western Europe* (Oxford, 1984), pp. 262–331.

widely shared tradition that kings—and lesser lords as well—should consult with their great men and were bound by custom and law. These views owed something perhaps to early Germanic procedures and something also to feudal custom. They are reflected in the opinions of contemporary philosophers such as John of Salisbury in the twelfth century and St. Thomas Aquinas in the thirteenth—both of whom asserted that a king must rule in accordance with good law and in the interests of his people; otherwise, he need not be obeyed. This was in no sense a democratic idea—St. Thomas was a dedicated monarchist—but it was, potentially, constitutional.

Medieval representative assemblies elsewhere in Europe succumbed to the rising royal absolutism of the early modern era, but the English Parliament lasted. It derived its strength from the unique character of the medieval English political experience. More than any other such assembly, it was a national body—not a fusion of regional groups. It was not a potential rival to the royal government, but an integral part of it. The English parliament rose on the solid foundation of vigorous local government. Representatives of shire and town came to parliaments with valuable political experience gained from their local administrative activities. Ever since Henry II's time, shire knights had handled judicial, financial, and administrative affairs in the counties. Through the procedure of the sworn inquest, they served on juries to provide information for royal justices—identifying suspected criminals, reporting on local conditions, and performing a variety of other duties on behalf of the king's government. Town representatives were equally rich in political experience, having served in their borough courts or as inquest jurors charged with indicting criminous townspeople before the king's itinerant justices at the shire courts. Parliament, therefore, evolved naturally out of a political system in which the middle ranks of the social order shared administrative responsibility with king and magnates and were accustomed to participating in royal governance.

There is obviously nothing democratic about thirteenth-century parliaments, nor can it be said that they limited royal power. Most of the parliaments of the age were summoned on royal initiative for the purpose of doing the king's judicial business, granting him an aid, or supporting his policies. Rather than limiting the monarchy, they served it. Simon de Montfort notwithstanding, the parliamentary idea emerged in thirteenth-century England because the monarchy—particularly under Edward I—regarded parliaments as useful instruments of royal policy. In retrospect, we now know that, many centuries later, Parliament did become a deeply significant democratic institution—that in the broadest sense it served as a bridge between medieval feudalism and modern democracy. But the kings and magnates of the thirteenth century, who would have despised democracy had they known about it, hadn't the slightest intention of engaging in institutional bridge building. They had problems enough of their own.

9

The Reign of Edward I

Edward I's reign (1272–1307), a crucial epoch in the development of parliamentary custom, was significant for other reasons as well.[1] The new king had demonstrated his ability long before his father's death by defeating Simon de Montfort at Evesham and by his intelligent exercise of power during Henry III's final years. Contemporaries regarded him as a skillful and highly competent leader, although extraordinarily ambitious and occasionally devious. Whatever his shortcomings, he was seen as a spectacular improvement over his father. When Henry III died in 1272, Edward was away on a crusade but had no worries about his succession. He returned in a leisurely fashion, settling affairs in Gascony on his way and reaching England only in 1274.

Edward was the first king since the Norman Conquest to bear an English name—the result of his father's devotion to the cult of Edward the Confessor who, in the words of a modern historian, displayed some of Henry III's own qualities of piety and incompetence. As a mature, self-confident man of thirty-five, Edward I began ruling in a style radically different from that of his father. For Edward was a king whom the nobles could trust and admire. He was a courageous warrior, a man of chivalrous instincts, an aristocrat among aristocrats. His presence was almost awesome: he was so tall that he stood head and shoulders above an ordinary crowd. His hair was dark but turned snowy white as he grew old. His handsome features were marred only by a drooping left eyelid, like his father's. And his long, powerful arms and legs enabled him to excel at swordsmanship, riding, and jousting. One contemporary called him "the best lance in the world." Despite a tendency to lisp, he spoke fluently and persuasively. At times he could terrify his adversaries with his explosive temper: when an ecclesiastical synod objected to his levying a tax against the Church, he flew into such a rage that the dean of St. Paul's, London, dropped dead on the spot.

---

[1] See the works cited in note 1 of Chapter 8. On the reign of Edward 1, see Michael C. Prestwich, *Edward I* (Berkeley, 1988). John Chancellor, *The Life and Times of Edward I* (Totowa, N.J., 1981), is a deft work of popularization. On Edward's legal achievements, see T. F. T. Plucknett, *The Legislation of Edward I* (Oxford, 1949); on his relations with the Church, see J. H. Denton, *Robert Winchelsey and the Crown, 1294–1313: A Study in the Defence of Ecclesiastical Liberty* (Cambridge, 1980).

Law and Administration

Although Edward's great passions were fighting and hunting, he could, when necessary, devote himself to the less robust pursuits of law and administration. He possessed a profound respect for law, characteristic of the best of an age that produced the treatise ascribed to Bracton and the works of Thomas Aquinas. Like these authors, Edward I had an intense desire for system and definition, which led him to bring to completion the legal achievements of Henry II, Hubert Walter, and the administrators of Henry III.

In the admiring words of a seventeenth-century chief justice, "The very scheme, mould and model of the common law was set in order by King Edward I, and so, in a very great measure, it has continued the same in all succeeding ages to this day." Edward I gave structure and system to the common law, but in doing so he rendered it less flexible than before. No longer could monarchs extend their jurisdiction merely by deciding to create new writs—new forms of action. No longer could the law develop freely from precedent to precedent. The extensive series of statutes under Edward I limited the latitude and individual interpretation previously exercised by royal judges. By and large, judge-made law gave way to enacted law; thereafter, only by issuing new statutes could the royal government effect significant changes in the legal structure.

It was under Edward I that *statute* became a meaningful concept. The ancient notion that law was traditional and unchanging had long proved inconsistent with the realities of legal development. As far back as Alfred the Great, the promulgation of law had depended on the judgment of the king. The imposition of the danegeld under Ethelred the Unready constituted new law, and the possessory assizes of Henry II unquestionably bore the mark of original legislation. Nevertheless, contemporaries tended to regard the Anglo-Saxon dooms as mere clarifications or interpretations of existing custom, the danegeld as a desperate expedient (later, as an old tradition), and the Angevin assizes simply as new administrative procedures. By Edward I's time it was coming to be understood more clearly that the king, with baronial consent, might indeed change old laws and create new ones. But original legislation was regarded as an act of unusual significance and solemnity that could be introduced only in the form of a statute.

The issuing of statutes per se long antedated Edward I's reign. Later medieval jurists came to regard Magna Carta as the first statute, and the term is used to describe several acts of Henry III. Even under Edward I, a great deal of the statutory law continued to do no more than summarize earlier practice. But in Edward I's reign, and not before, it becomes possible to distinguish statutes from more routine royal ordinances. In the fourteenth century, the distinction becomes progressively sharper: an ordinance might be issued by the king in his small council; a statute could be enacted only by the king in Parliament. This necessary association between parliaments and statutory law was enormously important, for it eventually

**A Manuscript Illumination
of King Edward I**
(Reproduced with
permission of the British
Library)

led to Parliament's power to legislate. In Edward's time, however, parliaments were relatively subservient, and the king took the initiative in issuing statutes.

"Bracton's" treatise declared that the king was the fountainhead of all justice—that magnates and prelates who operated courts of their own did so only by royal permission. Edward I undertook to translate this theory into reality. The royal administration insisted that it would recognize private franchises[2] only if they could be shown to have been granted by royal charter. As early as Henry III's reign, the monarchy had tried to enforce this principle through writs of *quo warranto* ("by what warrant?"), which initiated investigations of the legal foundations of private franchises. Between 1278 and 1294, Edward I initiated *quo warranto* proceedings on a large scale. His Statute of Gloucester (1278) stipulated that

> . . . all those who claim rights of jurisdiction by charters of the king's predecessors as kings of England, or by any other title, shall come before the

---

[2] Private franchises were districts where some great private landholder operated the legal machinery.

king or the itinerant justices on a certain day and at a certain place to show what sorts of franchises they claim to have, and by what warrant. . . . And if those who claim to have such franchises fail to come on the aforesaid day, those franchises shall be taken into the king's hand by the local sheriff.

Predictably, these royal efforts evoked a baronial furor. The *quo warranto* proceedings were largely ineffective because Edward's administration lacked the capacity to implement a new policy of such massive scope against stiff baronial resistance. Most magnates in fact had no charters to authenticate their jurisdictional claims. Baronial families had exercised their franchises for generations without royal challenge and, understandably, had no intention of surrendering them now. A fourteenth-century chronicler tells a story that, whether accurate or embroidered, catches the outraged spirit of Edward I's nobility. The elderly Earl Warenne, summoned to defend his jurisdictional rights, waved a rusty sword before the royal justices:

Here, my lords, here is my warrant. My forefathers came over with William the Bastard and conquered their lands with this sword. And I will defend them with the same sword against anyone who tries to take them from me. The king did not conquer and subdue this land alone. Our ancestors were his comrades and confederates.

The confrontation between royal initiative and baronial opposition resulted in a bevy of complex, case-by-case disputes. The monarchy continued to press its jurisdictional claim in principle, but with sufficient restraint to avoid widespread hostility. In the Statute of *Quo Warranto* of 1290, Edward modified his policy: his administration would recognize franchises backed not only by royal charter but by ancient privilege as well. By endorsing unchartered franchises that could be shown to date back to at least the time of Richard I, Edward in fact submitted to the argument of the rusty sword. The potency of immemorial custom in medieval legal thought left him no choice.

Thereafter, Edward's government continued to tread softly, often confirming franchises unsupported by either criterion. But while doing so, the king's officials held to their basic principle that a landholder might exercise private justice only by royal delegation. As a consequence, the primacy of royal jurisdiction gained ever wider acceptance.

Edward's statutes also made significant contributions to property law, clarifying and simplifying some of the bewildering issues arising from the labyrinth of feudal tenures. By the later thirteenth century, William the Conqueror's original land distributions had become hopelessly entangled by many generations of disputes over rights, inheritances, marriage settlements, "temporary" grants, forfeitures, and subinfeudations. Great chains of lord-vassal relationships, running down through many degrees of subordination, created considerable confusion regarding rights to land and often resulted in endless buck-passing when it came to performing feudal obligations. A certain Roger of St. German, for example, held an estate in Huntingdonshire in fief from Robert of Bedford, who held it of Richard of Ilchester, who held it of Alan of Chartres, who held it of William le Boteler, who held it of Gilbert Neville, who held it of Devorguil Balliol, who held it of the king of Scotland, who held it of King Edward I. Such a situation could have hardly commended itself to Edward's orderly administration, and it would have equally frustrated great magnates trying to exact services and aids from their tenants.

Consequently, Edward strove to bring some degree of order to the anachronistic feudalism of his day. The Statute of Westminster of 1285 undertook to (1) specify conditions under which a lord might confiscate the land of a tenant who failed to perform his required services and (2) establish clear rules governing conditional and temporary land grants. The Statute of Mortmain ("dead hand") of 1279 prohibited land grants to the Church without the license of the grantor's lord, for once an estate was granted to the Church—which never "died"—the land passed permanently out of lay control. Most significant of all was the Statute of *Quia Emptores* (1290), which established an absolute prohibition against further subinfeudation.[3] Thereafter, if a tenant sold a part of his land, he no longer retained any claim of lordship over the buyer. The buyer then held the land directly of the seller's lord, and the seller himself dropped out of the feudal chain altogether. *Quia Emptores* by no means abolished feudalism, but it did have the effect, as time went on, of diminishing the importance of lord-vassal relationships below the level of the king and his tenants-in-chief. It was an important partial step away from the feudal concept of dependent landholding toward the modern practice of outright ownership of land.

The same passion for system that infused Edward's statutes prompted him to institute major administrative reforms. The assertion of royal legislative supremacy in the statutes of Gloucester and *Quo Warranto* mirrored the growth and systemization of the king's own legal machinery. The highest tribunal in the land consisted of the king himself sitting in Parliament or passing judgment with the advice of his small council. But unless a legal case involved particularly important persons or raised some unusually difficult legal subtlety, it passed to one of the three royal common-law courts sitting at Westminster—Exchequer, Common Pleas, or King's Bench—or to itinerant judges working in the shires. At Westminster, all three courts were staffed with professionals—trained lawyers or, at the Exchequer, skilled accountants. The King's Bench handled cases of special royal concern, the Exchequer dealt with cases involving royal revenues, and Common Pleas heard all remaining cases.

The Exchequer was of course not only a court but also, and preeminently, the key institution in the royal fiscal system. Exchequer, chancery, council, and household were the four chief organs of royal administration under Edward I. The exchequer, usually supervised by the treasurer, contin-

---

[3] *Quia Emptores* means, literally, "Because Buyers." Like papal bulls, the statute took its name from its two opening words. (Had I adopted this custom, the present book would bear the interesting title, *History As*, the first two words in Chapter 1. I chose instead to name the book after its four concluding words.)

ued to serve as the central accounting office for royal revenues. By Edward's time, it held responsibility not only for the accounts of the sheriffs but also for those of numerous other local officials who collected money for the king.

By the end of Edward I's reign, the chancery had become increasingly independent of the royal household. As the fourteenth century progressed, the chancery evolved from a mere royal record-keeping office into a separate department of state that, like the exchequer, became permanently stationed at Westminster. There it carried on and expanded its traditional work of issuing royal documents and judicial writs under the Great Seal and preserving copies of them in ever increasing numbers and types of chancery records. The chancellor and his clerks were by now professional, salaried administrators.

Heretofore we have distinguished between great council and small council. But under Edward I, great councils were coming to be called parliaments, and the term *council* thereafter applied exclusively to the smaller group of royal advisers—judges, administrators, bishops, and baronial intimates. This group remained flexible and ill-defined in membership and continued to accompany the king as he traveled through his lands. In 1258, the magnates had attempted to assert control over the council, and they would make further attempts in the course of the fourteenth century. But in Edward I's reign, the small council was an obedient and increasingly professional instrument of the royal will.

The household, too, accompanied the royal person. It had grown considerably since late Saxon and Norman times, but it retained its essential character as a body of royal servants whose tasks ranged from menial duties to high administrative responsibilities. Since chancery and exchequer had become separate departments, it was necessary for the king to maintain smaller, parallel institutions in his own household so that he could transact business quickly no matter where he was. The Great Seal stayed in the chancery at Westminster, but the traveling household included its own staff of writing clerks and a keeper of the Privy Seal. In the late thirteenth and early fourteenth centuries, the king's household used the Privy ("private") Seal with increasing frequency to authorize the chancery to issue documents under the Great Seal. In this way, chancery authentication of household documents became more or less automatic.

Similarly, some of the financial duties formerly performed by the exchequer had by now passed to the clerks of the royal wardrobe. They supervised receipts and disbursements in the king's household, and they sometimes assumed responsibility for paying troops' wages and other military expenses when the king was engaged in foreign campaigns. Thus, considerable tax revenues went directly into the wardrobe without being received or recorded by the exchequer.

In the twelfth century, the sheriffs and itinerant justices had been the chief connecting links between crown and countryside. Both continued to function in Edward I's reign, but in the meantime many new shire officials had emerged. Local justice was sometimes handled by royal judges on special commission to hear a particular case or series of cases. At other times, royal judges joined important regional landholders to hear, in the king's name, all the cases in a particular shire. As always, the efficient execution of royal justice at the local level brought in higher royal revenues, and it was now increasingly apparent that the king's justices in eyre were, in effect, draining money from the countryside. The general county eyre developed an evil reputation, and as the fourteenth century progressed, popular opposition forced the monarchy to limit the activities of its traveling justices, and, eventually, to abolish them completely.

Royal administration in the counties involved a delicate balance between central authority and local initiative. This balance proved immensely important in the evolution of English government, for it meant that the royal administration could function effectively at the local level without suppressing the political vigor of the counties themselves. Rather than resisting the royal administration or being crushed by it, local notables could participate in it, protecting their own interests and gaining political experience in the bargain. Magnates and gentry thus became involved not only in their own regional affairs but also in the affairs of the realm. Their sense of community and local responsibility increased accordingly.

This phenomenon can best be appreciated by contrasting Edward I's governance of England with contemporary France. By and large, the French royal government ruled its provinces through officials sent from the royal household—men without local roots, whom the monarchy transferred regularly from one district to another. English kings, too, shuffled their local and regional officials in and out of offices, but less often than did French kings. Important local personages worked actively in the administration of the shires. They accompanied the royal judges on circuits of the counties, often served as the king's sheriffs, came in large numbers to sessions of the shire courts, and filled numerous offices charged with keeping peace and collecting royal revenues. The coroners, who investigated murders and other felonies, normally came from the local gentry. So too did the keepers of the peace, who maintained order and apprehended criminals. Local men also abounded among the host of assessors, customs officials, and tax collectors who served the king in shire and town.

Royal officials great and small might hope to rise, through the king's favor, to higher social and economic positions. Royal service was by no means an unobstructed road to riches, but the patronage policies systematized by Henry I continued and grew. More than a few spectacular careers were built on royal rewards for faithful service. By skillfully using the vast patronage at his disposal, an able king such as Edward I could usually count on the devoted service of his acquisitive subordinates. At a time when the once powerful feudal concepts of homage and fealty were dissolving, greed and ambition remained powerful incentives for loyalty between a lord and his men.

Even in the early days of Anglo-Norman feudalism, kings had used money to buy loyalty and hire troops. Now more than ever, money played a dominant role in society. Feudal personal ties persisted after a fashion, but

Edward I's prohibition of subinfeudation hastened their decay. The aristocracy retained and solidified its position atop the social order; the knightly ideology endured and intensified as nobles indulged increasingly in elaborate tournaments, heraldic devices, and other colorful expressions of the cult of chivalry. But the old feudal concept of service in return for land tenure was dead, and the armies of Edward I fought for wages.

Edward I's reign witnessed the development of the deadly longbow and a decline in the importance of cavalry. Mounted knights formed merely the small cores of armies that abounded in mounted archers and infantry. Edward's Statute of Winchester of 1285 defined the military responsibilities of the English population along the lines of Henry II's Assize of Arms (1181),[4] which Henry III had already amended and expanded more than once. The monarchy began to grant "commissions of array" to local notables, licensing them to raise forces in their shires from among the local inhabitants, whose military obligations were set forth in the Statute of Winchester. The king could still summon his tenants-in-chief to bring their knights to the royal host, but the knights now demanded wages for their services. More important was the use of mercenaries under contract. Edward I employed the policy—which his fourteenth-century successors developed much more fully—of entering into contracts for life with important lords, binding the lords to supply mercenary contingents for the army in return for regular retaining fees. This arrangement—known as the *indenture* system—was extended to contracts between the lord and his own military followers. Just as the lord undertook to supply troops to the king in return for regular payments, so the lord's own men undertook to follow him into battle in return for similar payments. Since the contracts were normally for life, the relationships created by the indenture system tended to be stable and permanent, and the subordination of man to lord that the system entailed gradually replaced the older lord-vassal relationships. The vastly expanded indenture system of the fourteenth century has been called "bastard feudalism." It created, in effect, a social hierarchy bound together by money.

Under Edward I, the indenture system was still in its infancy, but it was already becoming a burden on the royal treasury. Indeed, by medieval standards, the numerous wars of Edward I were immensely expensive. His military ambitions far outran the normal resources of the monarchy, and he was obliged to exploit every conceivable source of revenue. His desperate need for money drove him to summon numerous parliaments and to include in them, with increasing frequency, representatives from the shire gentry and the towns. Edward's parliaments often granted him authority to collect a substantial percentage of his subjects' chattels or annual rents—although sometimes only after considerable persuasion. He taxed the clergy with similar severity and thereby aroused vigorous opposition from the Church. He collected heavy customs dues, particularly from Italian mer-

---

[4] See pp. 145–147.

chant-banking companies to which he had granted a monopoly on English wool exports. He turned to these same Italian merchant-bankers for large loans when his tax revenues failed to meet his expenses, and in return he took the Italian financiers under his special protection. Previous kings had done most of their borrowing from the English Jewry, but in 1290 Edward expelled the Jews from England to get his hands on their wealth. Yet for all his skillful and sometimes cruel ingenuity, Edward failed to balance his books. When his favorite Italian merchant-banking house, the Riccardi Company of Lucca, went bankrupt in 1294, Edward found himself facing some of the most serious crises of his reign with inadequate financial backing. Later in the reign he was able to replace the Riccardi with another company of Italian merchant-bankers, the Frescobaldi, who continued to serve the English monarchy into the early years of Edward II's reign.[5]

The Wars of Edward I

The reign of Edward I splits into two distinct periods. Between his return from the crusade in 1274 and the beginning of his war with France in 1294—coinciding with the collapse of the Riccardi Company—his foreign policy was highly successful, and he pursued his domestic policies of administrative and legal centralization without significant opposition from his subjects. But from 1294 until his death in 1307, his wars were inconclusive, and his relations with his subjects were stormy.

Edward reigned in an age when older concepts of feudal monarchy were gradually giving way to a new concept of national sovereignty. We should not regard Edward I's England as a national state in anything like the modern sense. Yet in England, France, and other European kingdoms of the time, the royal political authority was growing. Edward had considerable respect for the traditional aristocratic ties between lord and vassal, but he often exploited his rights of lordship to the fullest in order to increase his own power and prestige. This was particularly true in his relations with Wales and Scotland—over which English kings had long claimed a vague suzerainty. Edward's troubles with France arose from the fact that his French contemporary, King Philip IV "the Fair" (1285–1314), shared his policy of exploiting rights of lordship over vassal states. Edward, as duke of Aquitaine, was Philip's vassal for his lands in Gascony, and he resented Philip's behaving toward Gascony as he himself behaved toward Wales and Scotland.

Edward's greatest military triumph was his conquest of Wales. The Anglo-Welsh controversy had been going on ever since the Anglo-Saxon

---

[5] See Richard W. Kaeuper, *Bankers to the Crown: The Riccardi of Lucca and Edward I* (Princeton, 1973), and "Royal Finance and the Crisis of 1297," in *Order and Innovation in the Middle Ages: Essays in Honor of Joseph R. Strayer*, William C. Jordan, Bruce McNab, and Teofilo F. Ruiz, eds. (Princeton, 1976), pp. 103–110. For a more general overview, see Kaeuper's *War, Justice, and Public Order in England and France in the Later Middle Ages* (Oxford, 1987).

invasions (and has been going on ever since). The aggressions of the Anglo-Norman frontier lords, although periodically subjected to Welsh counter-attacks, had resulted ultimately in a significant westward extension of English authority at Welsh expense. Still, despite innumerable royal expeditions into Wales, Welsh independence endured.

Edward's Welsh campaign began in 1277 as a result of Prince Llywelyn's refusal to do homage. Marching into Wales, Edward succeeded in winning Llywelyn's homage and restricting his authority. But in 1282, Llywelyn and other Welsh princes rose in rebellion once again. Edward raised a large army and invaded for a second time. In the course of the struggle, Llywelyn was killed (December 1282). By the spring of 1283, all Wales lay in Edward's hands, and its independence was permanently lost. Thereafter, it became a province of the kings of England. "Prince of Wales" no longer referred to an independent Welsh ruler but became the title for the king or queen of England's eldest son, and so it has remained.

Considering the antiquity of the Anglo-Welsh conflict, Edward's conquest was remarkably swift and easy. The Welsh rebelled in 1287 and again in 1294–1295. But although the latter rebellion succeeded in embarrassing Edward and delaying a projected expedition against France, neither uprising threatened seriously to undo the conquest of 1282–1283. Edward tightened his hold on Wales—at staggering expense—by building throughout the area a network of enormous castles of the most advanced design to awe the Welsh and discourage further resistance. Edward's Welsh castles were perhaps the greatest system of fortifications in medieval Europe. Their ruins haunt Wales to this day.

Ruins of Beaumaris Castle, North Wales   A superbly designed fortification built under Edward I. The standard pronunciation—"bo-*mare*-iss"—is enough to cause apoplexy among the French. (Aerofilms Ltd.)

Edward's struggle with Scotland promised for a time to bring him an even more notable victory, but in the end Scotland eluded his grasp. Again, the issue turned on Edward's claims to suzerainty. As overlord of Scotland, he was called upon by the Scottish nobility in 1290 to adjudicate a disputed royal succession. He began his task by demanding and receiving the allegiance of the Scottish magnates and thereupon took temporary possession of Scotland while pondering the relative merits of the two royal claimants— Robert Bruce and John Balliol. At length, late in 1292, he decided in Balliol's favor. For the next three years, he enraged the Scots by asserting his overlordship in a heavy-handed and altogether unprecedented fashion. He violated custom by hearing judicial claims of Balliol's Scottish subjects at Westminster, and even summoned Balliol himself to answer a complaint by one of his Scottish countrymen. Some Scottish magnates evidently preferred Edward to Balliol, but the English king's imperious behavior created a dangerous legacy of resentment. In 1295, with Edward deeply involved in French affairs, Balliol and the Scots rebelled.

Abandoning for the moment his plan to invade France, Edward turned his attention northward and in 1296 led a brilliantly successful expedition against the Scots. Forcing Balliol to abdicate, Edward assumed direct control of Scotland. He dramatized his achievement by bringing back to England as a souvenir of his campaign the Stone of Scone, on which by ancient custom the Scottish kings were crowned. Edward ordered that an elaborately carved "Coronation Chair" be built to enclose the Stone of Scone, and both the chair and the stone—on perpetual display in Westminster Abbey—continue to be used in English coronation ceremonies to this day.

But although they never recovered the Stone of Scone, the determined Scots quickly challenged Edward's conquest of 1296. In the following year, a new Scottish insurrection broke out, led by a member of the lesser nobility named William Wallace. The rebellion alternately flared and simmered as repeated English campaigns failed to reestablish Edward's power in its former fullness. At length, in 1304, most of the Scottish nobles submitted to Edward, and the uprising ended with the capture of Wallace in 1305.

In 1306, the Scots rebelled again, led this time by Robert Bruce, grandson of the former claimant to the Scottish throne. As it turned out, Bruce was the real hero of this Scottish war of independence. Crowned king of Scots by his followers in 1306, he lost a battle to Edward but retained his poise and carried on the struggle. Edward I died in 1307 on the road to Scotland, still seeking the tantalizing but elusive prize. His son, Edward II, proved no match for Robert Bruce, and consequently Scotland was able to consolidate its independence. Not until the seventeenth century were the two crowns joined—in the person of James I—and even then, it was a Scottish king who became king of England.

The tenacity of the Scots themselves won them their independence, but the fact that at crucial moments in the conflict Edward I was preoccupied with his struggle against King Philip the Fair of France immeasurably aided the Scottish cause. The Anglo-French controversy had begun long before, with the Norman Conquest, when the English monarchy first became involved in preserving and extending its French territories. The rivalry persisted off and on into the nineteenth century. Over this vast span of time, the two countries fought numerous wars separated by peaceful intermissions, sometimes of long duration. When Edward I ascended the throne, England and France had not engaged in serious hostilities for a generation. The outstanding issues between the two monarchies had been resolved by the Treaty of Paris of 1259, which provided that the English king should hold Gascony—as a vassal of the king of France.

In the course of the thirteenth century, England and Gascony had developed a considerable degree of economic interdependence. England exchanged cloth, grain, and other products for large quantities of Gascon wine, for which the English had acquired a special thirst. The trade between the two lands gradually assumed such importance that Gascony's prosperity came to depend heavily on its English connection. Edward himself valued Gascony highly. He spent many months establishing order there in 1273–1274, on his return journey to England from the crusade, and in the later 1280s, he spent the better part of three years strengthening his authority over the Gascons. Edward was touchy about his rights in Gascony and could not be expected to relinquish them without a stiff fight.

The Anglo-French conflict was rekindled primarily when Philip the Fair insisted on enforcing to the fullest his overlordship in Gascony. For the first two decades of Edward's reign, England and France were at peace, but in 1293, Philip the Fair, on the pretext of a dispute between English and Gascon pirates, summoned Edward to his court. Like John nearly a century before, Edward refused the summons. Philip responded in 1294 by undertaking to conquer Gascony.

It has been said that after 1294, Edward I's ambitions became too great for his resources. This is not altogether true. Long before 1294, Edward had pursued his three basic diplomatic goals: the conquest of Wales, the establishment of hegemony over Scotland, and the retention of Gascony. His troubles in the 1290s stemmed chiefly from Philip the Fair's aggressive new policy. With respect to Gascony, Edward was on the defensive.

Philip's hostile actions prompted Edward to take expensive countermeasures. He wove a network of alliances against France—much as John had done earlier—and prepared for a large-scale invasion. But in undertaking the daunting task of holding distant Gascony, Edward presented a tempting opportunity to his previous victims. The Welsh rebellion of 1294–1295 forced him to delay his expedition to France, and the Scottish uprising of 1295–1296 necessitated still another postponement. By 1297, when his French expedition was ready at last, Edward's alliance system had broken down, his prestige was damaged, and his finances were in disrepair. He had not yet found another banking company willing to provide him credit on the scale of the now defunct Riccardi Company, and the more he taxed his subjects, the more they grumbled.

Edward crossed to France in the summer of 1297 in an atmosphere of unrest and disaffection; he returned in the early fall after an inconclusive campaign. After several years of complex negotiations, France and England concluded a peace in 1303 on the basis of the *status quo ante bellum*. Edward gained nothing and, apart from a heavy outflow of money, lost nothing. The pact was sealed by marriages between Edward I and Philip the Fair's sister and between Edward's son (the future Edward II) and Philip's daughter Isabella. The latter marriage would provide future English kings with a claim to the French throne, thereby contributing to the outbreak of the Hundred Years' War in the fourteenth century.

Edward succeeded in retaining Gascony. But the struggle with France, together with concurrent campaigns in Scotland and Wales, clouded the king's relations with his English subjects. The great difficulty was money. The normal royal revenues were grossly inadequate to meet the costs of these widespread military enterprises. Between 1294 and 1298, Edward's military expenses alone ran to something like £730,000. Over these same years, the crown's ordinary income—from demesne lands, the profits of justice, the forests, customs revenues, and other sources—came to roughly £150,000. Consequently, Edward had to borrow from everyone in sight and to request special aids from his subjects. He collected a tenth of all his lay landholders' income in 1294, an eleventh in 1295, a twelfth in 1296, and a ninth in 1297. He won similar substantial grants from his burghers and clergy, as well as special taxes on exports over and above the normal customs dues. But each of these special taxes required that the groups being taxed acquiesce, and they did so with increasing reluctance. In short, the year 1294 marked the end of a long political honeymoon between Edward and his subjects.

The great domestic crisis of Edward I's reign occurred in 1297. By then his foreign policy was straining English resources dangerously. The Gascon threat, the bribes to allied princes on the Continent, and the nearly concurrent uprising of Robert Bruce in Scotland constituted a military and diplomatic crisis of major proportions. Moreover, Edward's heavily taxed subjects resisted additional exactions for a foreign policy of questionable outcome. The gentry opposed Edward's effort to make everyone with an annual landed income of twenty pounds or more take up the burdensome responsibilities of knighthood. Some of Edward's magnates refused to serve abroad. And the Church, led by the archbishop of Canterbury, Robert Winchelsey (1294–1313), declined to pay additional taxes without express papal approval. In taking this stand, English churchmen were following the policy of the pope himself. In 1296, Pope Boniface VIII issued the bull *Clericis Laicos*, which specified that every occasion of royal taxation of the clergy required specific papal permission. Although Pope Boniface's stance accorded with canon law, it conflicted with custom at the time and aroused violent royal opposition in both England and France. When the bull arrived in England, Archbishop Winchelsey undertook to promulgate it throughout the kingdom. Edward responded promptly with a writ of prohibition, thereby generating a royal-archiepiscopal showdown.

Threatened from many directions, Edward handled the crisis of 1297 with great skill and emerged without serious wounds. He managed to coax from the clergy and laity the taxes he needed to continue his campaigning, and although his relations with his subjects thereafter were more troubled than before, he remained in control. His conflict with the Church subsided toward the end of 1297 when Pope Boniface modified his bull *Clericis Laicos*. Earlier in the year, Edward had soothed the laity by confirming Magna Carta and granting further concessions. He promised, among other things, that extraordinary taxes would be levied only by consent of the community of the realm assembled in a parliament.

Historians have traditionally interpreted this last concession as a major setback for the crown, but Edward probably did not regard it as such. He controlled his parliaments, as we have seen, and used them to advance the royal interest. Because they were his most convenient means of obtaining consent for uncustomary taxes, his promise to employ them for that purpose cannot have troubled him deeply. From the constitutional standpoint, the concession was a milestone in the growth of Parliament; from Edward's standpoint, parliaments were his tools.

During the final decade of the reign, as before, Edward I continued to assert his royal prerogatives. On the election of a docile pope in 1305, Edward obtained papal permission to repudiate certain of his earlier concessions on royal forest rights and managed to suspend his old antagonist, Archbishop Winchelsey, and force him into exile. Edward was a determined monarch, and events seemed once again to be tilting in his favor. It is possible that he might have won Scotland, too, for at his death in 1307 he was on his way northward with a powerful military expedition. But in his closing years the obedience of his subjects was based more on force from above than on affection from below. His remorseless insistence on his self-styled rights at home and abroad had severely overstrained his realm's resources.

But despite Edward's severity, and despite the inconclusive outcomes of his Gascon and Scottish wars, his reign remains one of the most productive in the annals of England. It was a period of immense legal and administrative accomplishment and decisive constitutional development. Under Edward I, the royal administration became truly professional, the common law reached maturity, and Parliament became an indispensable component of English government.

PART FOUR

The Realm in Crisis

1307 to 1399

HUNDRED YEARS' WAR   English soldiers scaling a fortress in Gascony during the reign of Edward III. *(North Wind Picture Archives)*

10

The Bloom Fades: England in the Age of Edward II

The adjective *transitional* can be applied with some justice to any historical epoch, but it is particularly appropriate to the fourteenth century.[1] In this era, many of the characteristic institutions of the Middle Ages were decaying, yet their modern counterparts had not yet appeared in recognizable form. The fourteenth century was not an age of feudalism but of "bastard feudalism." Devotion to the medieval Church was giving way to rebellious anticlericalism, but patriotic devotion to the state still lay in the future. The medieval intellectual synthesis of faith and reason was breaking down, but nothing comparable had emerged to take its place. The century closed in a mood of deep dissatisfaction with the traditional political, social, economic, and religious structures, but there was little consensus about what new forms might replace them.

The Change in Mood

On the Continent no less than in England, the prosperity and relative social cohesion of the thirteenth century were giving way to a new mood of violence and unrest. In the eleventh, twelfth, and thirteenth centuries, the population had increased rapidly on the wings of a vigorous economy, and the frontiers of Christendom had expanded significantly. Within Europe, new farmland had been created out of forests and swamps, and Western civilization had advanced far beyond its earlier boundaries—into Spain, Sicily, Syria, and the Baltic lands. But as the fourteenth century opened, these external and internal frontiers had ceased to expand, and they began to shrink. The Christian reconquest of Spain had come to a halt in the 1260s; Granada—the remaining Muslim foothold on the Iberian Peninsula—continued under Islamic control until 1492. The Teutonic Knights,

---

[1] The classic work on fourteenth–century England is May McKisack, *The Fourteenth Century, 1307–1399* (Oxford, 1959). Another excellent survey, covering the period from 1290 to 1485, is M. H. Keen, *England in the Later Middle Ages* (London, 1973). Edmund King, *England, 1175–1425* (London, 1979), integrates economic, social, and political history succinctly and skillfully, and Michael Prestwich, *The Three Edwards*, continues to provide skillful and judicious guidance. An important comparative study is Richard Kaeuper, *War, Justice, and Public Order: England and France in the Later Middle Ages* (Oxford, 1988).

who had pushed German-Christian power far eastward and northward along the Baltic shore, were gradually driven back by Russian and Baltic peoples. In 1291 Acre, the last important bridgehead of the crusaders in the Holy Land, fell to the Muslims, and by the mid-fourteenth century an aggressive new Islamic people, the Ottoman Turks, were moving into the Balkans.

The fourteenth century also saw the onset of a widespread agrarian and commercial depression, although its impact varied from year to year and from place to place. The clearing of forests and draining of marshes continued on a minor scale in certain parts of England, but the process of opening new fields to cultivation was generally complete by the later thirteenth century. The medieval system of strip fields and heavy plow had by then expanded to its limits. What new lands were cleared tended to be only marginally productive. As the population continued to expand, it either spilled onto these marginal lands or made do with smaller holdings. In either case, the result was a decline in the peasants' standard of living and a precarious situation in which one or two bad crop years could cause widespread starvation.

The increasingly burdensome royal taxes necessitated by the wars of Edward I and, on a much larger scale, Edward III aggravated these conditions of agricultural saturation. Taxes and land shortages together brought a decline in prosperity and in the birthrate. By the late thirteenth century, England's population had ceased growing at its former pace; by the early fourteenth century, it had reached a plateau of something between four and six million persons. Thereafter, the population held constant or perhaps began to decline—slowly at first, but cataclysmically with the onset of the Black Death in the mid-fourteenth century. Land revenues fell in the wake of the plague, and the peasantry abandoned marginal fields and villages on a large scale. To aggravate the situation, the climate of the entire northern hemisphere began changing for the worse. The prosperous civilization of the High Middle Ages had enjoyed a cycle of unusually warm, dry weather—a blessing for a land like England, which today tends to be chilly and damp. But in the later thirteenth century, and more so in the fourteenth, the weather turned colder, rainier, and much less predictable. As a result, harvests were often skimpier than before, and people were hungrier.

Famine and plague caused unimaginable suffering among the English peasantry of the fourteenth century. But by decimating the peasant population, these crises created a labor shortage that worked ultimately to the advantage of the wealthier peasant families, who extended their holdings, built more commodious homes, and ascended into the class of yeoman farmers. The nobility, previously unchallenged in the social structure, now faced reduced land revenues. At the same time, their military importance as a knightly cavalry force declined. Common infantry, which had always played an important role in English warfare, became more significant than ever with the advent of the longbow under Edward I. In fourteenth-century battles, a body of trained archers often proved the key to victory. With the coming of gunpowder and the consequent development of artillery later in the century, the armored knight became more vulnerable still—although armor would remain in use for many generations to come, and mounted cavalry charges would retain their tactical importance until the present century. The decline in nobles' authority relative to that of lesser social classes is illustrated by the marked increase in the power of burghers and gentry in fourteenth-century parliaments. Still, the decline must not be exaggerated. At the end of the fourteenth century, and for countless generations thereafter, the landed nobility remained powerful. It shared its power more and more with other classes and underwent a severe economic squeeze, but despite all, it retained its position at the top of the social order.

As land income dropped, England's commercial structure changed dramatically. During the first half of the fourteenth century, Italian merchants continued by and large to serve as the chief royal bankers, and Italians, Flemings, and Germans from the cities of the Hanseatic League controlled about two-thirds of the wool trade. But English merchants struggled to obtain more of the trade for themselves. They sought to concentrate the sale of English wool in one foreign trading center under English control—in a single town that would have a royal monopoly on wool exportation. Such a center was called a "staple."

During the 1290s, Edward I had established the first staples at Dordrecht and Antwerp in the Low Countries. Anxious to build up his war chest, he found it advantageous to concentrate the wool trade so that it could be supervised easily and taxed efficiently. In 1314, Edward II set up the first compulsory staple at St. Omer in Flanders. And Edward III, responding to the financial squeeze of the Hundred Years' War, established staples at one time or another at Antwerp and Bruges. Foreign merchants still played an important role in the trade, but now, unless specially privileged, they were obliged to buy their wool at the staple from English traders.

The monarchy began to favor English merchants more wholeheartedly after the collapse in 1339 of the Bardi and the Peruzzi—the two Italian banking firms on which Edward III had particularly depended for loans and whose fall resulted in part from his failure to repay them. For a time, Edward turned for credit to merchants of the German Hansa towns. But beginning in the 1350s, he depended primarily on domestic loans and subsidies and granted favors in return. In 1363, the king established a staple at Calais—in northern France but under English occupation—and gave control of it to a group of English merchants known as the Company of the Staple. This company acquired a monopoly of the wool trade, the one exception being that wool could still be shipped by sea to Italy. The wool monopoly enabled the Company of the Staple to dominate the trade for many years thereafter.

During these years, however, the wool trade as a whole was declining as a result of the steady rise of the English cloth industry. From about 1200 onward, English textile workers consumed more and more wool to manufacture English cloth, and the amount remaining for export decreased steadily.[2] English weavers were exempt from the high royal duties on wool and, as relative newcomers on the economic scene, did not have to abide by cumbersome guild regulations. They were therefore able to undersell their continental rivals and, in time, to win large markets not only in England but all across Europe. As the fourteenth century closed, English merchants themselves were beginning to penetrate deep into the Continent, competing successfully in areas where the merchants of Flanders and the Hanseatic League had long dominated. No longer merely a source of raw materials, exploited by foreign traders, England had become a great textile producer. Its merchants were beginning to demonstrate the sort of initiative that would, in later centuries, make their kingdom the commercial nexus of the world.

English towns also underwent fundamental changes. The economic forces of the fourteenth century brought about the decline of many towns—Oxford and Lincoln, for example—that served as agricultural markets or centers of the faltering wool trade. But at the same time, the rise of cloth manufacturing transformed towns such as Norwich, York, and Coventry into thriving textile centers. The profits from cloth production enabled a number of East Anglian villages to build lavish churches in the late-medieval Gothic style. The intensifying cloth trade made London more prosperous than ever (although it was afflicted by serious gang warfare from the late thirteenth century onward). The port of Bristol, on England's western shore, was rising to become London's chief commercial rival. But the establishment of new towns fell off sharply in the general economic slump of the late Middle Ages: some 265 boroughs appeared for the first time in records of the thirteenth century but only 17 in records of the fifteenth.

The labor shortage resulting from the population decline presented tempting new opportunities to the lesser urban classes—the journeymen and minor artisans—whose services were now much in demand. But these opportunities, opened momentarily by social and economic change, were closed by political force. The wealthy and privileged merchant guilds and the important craft associations—such as those connected with cloth manufacturing—maintained their longstanding control of urban economic life and town government. They clung to their valuable monopolies, supressed the rising journeymen's organizations and lesser crafts' guilds, and did everything in their power to keep wages down. Consequently, urban workers during the later fourteenth century took to the streets in a series of severe riots, which terrified the ruling merchants but did not dislodge them. Even though the lesser classes had economic conditions on their side, they advanced only very slowly. And the towns themselves, although winning ever-wider privileges and increasingly generous charters from the monarchy, remained under royal control. Independent city-states of the sort abounding in Italy and northern Germany were unknown in England.

---

[2] A. R. Bridbury, *Medieval English Clothmaking: An Economic Survey* (London, 1982), argues persuasively for this early beginning of large–scale cloth manufacturing in England.

In the countryside, too, the post-plague labor shortage gave lower classes of employees the advantage of being in greater demand. The dominant groups in town and country alike reacted by bending every effort toward forcibly preserving the economic status quo; suppressing dangerous lower-class associations; and, through Parliament, procuring royal statutes that fixed wages at artificially low, pre-plague levels. The rebellious unrest that resulted from these policies culminated in the Great Revolt of 1381, known traditionally as the "Peasants' Revolt," which will be discussed in the final chapter. Similar popular uprisings sprang up on the Continent as well. A particularly bloodthirsty revolt known as the Jacquerie Rebellion broke out in France in 1358, and between 1378 and 1382, popular insurrections afflicted Germany, Italy, and the Netherlands. Fourteenth-century Europe suffered from a surge of violence, rebellion, and murder; a sharpening of class conflict; and increased factionalism among the nobility. Added to these misfortunes were the twin horrors of plague and war. France was devastated by contending armies and rampaging bands of ill-disciplined mercenary soldiers. England suffered little from military violence, but its inhabitants endured severe taxation to support English armies and allies on the Continent, and at times the English monarchy teetered on the edge of bankruptcy.

Changes in architecture accompanied the shifts in social and economic conditions. The Early English Gothic style of the thirteenth century—balanced, graceful, and restrained—gave way in the late thirteenth and early fourteenth centuries to a new English variation known as Decorated Gothic. Buildings in the new style—the stunning "Angel Choir" of Lincoln Cathedral, for example, and the marvelously sculpted chapter house at

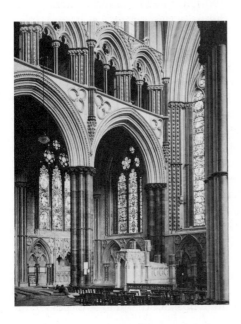

The Angel Choir, Lincoln Cathedral (1256–1320)
An example of English Decorated Gothic architecture. (Dr. Martin Hürlimann)

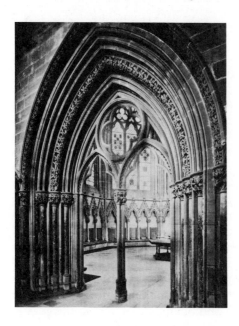

Chapter House, Southwell Minster   The portal displays a profusion of sculpted foliage in the Decorated Gothic style. (Courtesy of the Royal Commission on the Historical Monuments of England)

Southwell Minster—exhibited rich, naturalistic carving and elaborate vault ribbing. Stone tracery in windows and on walls became increasingly complex, as simple arcs and circles evolved around 1290 into twisting serpentine curves. Capitals and choir screens displayed wonderfully lifelike stone foliage, attesting to the artists' keen perception of the natural world and their skill with the chisel.

In the 1330s there emerged the last great style of English medieval architecture—Perpendicular Gothic—which spread gradually across the kingdom and remained in vogue for the next two centuries. It remains a distinctively English achievement. Indeed, the contemporary French "Flamboyant Gothic" was closer in spirit to the English Decorated style than to the Perpendicular, and probably developed through English inspiration. As exemplified by the cloister and remodeled choir of Gloucester Cathedral, Perpendicular Gothic architecture featured intricately patterned vaulting and sculpted walls, uninterrupted upward lines, and vertical bar tracery in its windows and choir screens. A progressive thinning of columns and arches resulted in a new feeling of plasticity—a flowing unity of overall design. Immense windows flooded spacious interiors with light; the Gothic dream of window walls set in a slender framework of stone had seldom been realized so completely. The stately harmony of earlier Gothic architecture, based on the principle of horizontal/vertical equilibrium, gave way to the aspiring upward thrust—the passionate verticality—of Perpendicular Gothic.

In the realm of intellect, the fourteenth century witnessed a series of powerful scholarly attacks against the fusion of reason and revelation that thirteenth-century philosophers, Thomas Aquinas in particular, had achieved. The English Franciscan John Duns Scotus (d. 1308) began the

Choir, Gloucester Cathedral The Norman Romanesque choir was remodeled during the mid-fourteenth century in the Perpendicular Gothic style, with elaborate ribbed vaulting and unobstructed vertical lines. (National Monuments Record)

criticism, and another English Franciscan, William of Ockham (d. 1349), carried it to its climax. Duns Scotus was far more than a mere critic; he constructed his own elaborate philosophical system—of such complexity as to captivate some later scholars, repel others, and bewilder the rest. His system of thought tended to place narrow limits on humanity's ability to approach God and religious truth through reason. In the tradition of the Franciscan scientists, he taught that the most appropriate object of human reason was the natural world rather than the supernatural, and he maintained that many Christian dogmas that Aquinas had regarded as rationally verifiable could be accepted only on faith.

William of Ockham went much further, insisting that empirical facts and Christian doctrine were completely separate. He believed in both but concluded that the dogmas of the Catholic religion transcended reason. The existence of God had to be taken on faith. It could not be proven, and all efforts to create a rational theology were futile. The scope of human reason was limited to the world of visible phenomena. Ockham's splitting of reason from faith severed the age-long bond between theology and natural science, freeing science to follow its own independent course.

The most striking intellectual achievement of the thirteenth century had been the welding of reason and faith into a single coherent system of thought, and the fourteenth-century philosophers subjected that system to intense logical criticism. In doing so, they helped accomplish on an intellectual level what Western civilization was achieving concurrently on the social, economic, and cultural levels: the erosion of an old ethos and a tentative, uncertain approach toward a new one.

The Reign of Edward II (1307–1327)

Three kings ruled England through most of the fourteenth century: Edward II (1307–1327), Edward III (1327–1377), and Richard II (1377–1399). Of these three, two had their reigns cut short by rebellion and deposition. Edward II was the most despised and least successful of them. His inadequacies stand out in sharp relief against both the iron strength of his father, Edward I, and the success and popularity of his son, Edward III. A perceptive scholar recently described him as one of the most incompetent men to sit on the throne of England, and the history of his reign "is one of successive political failures punctuated by acts of horrific violence."[3]

Edward II inherited from his father an ambitious foreign policy, an empty treasury, and a restive nobility. But Edward I failed to pass on to him the intelligence and resolution necessary to cope with these problems. Even as a youthful Prince of Wales, the future Edward II had demonstrated his willfulness and incapacity, and before accepting him as their king, the barons forced him to take a coronation oath of unusual scope. The oath took the form of a series of questions posed to the prospective king by Robert Winchelsey, archbishop of Canterbury (who had returned from exile on the death of Edward I). Significantly, the oath was neither in Latin nor in French but in English:

> "Sire, will you grant and keep and confirm to the people of England by your oath the laws and customs given them by the previous just and God-fearing kings, your ancestors, and particularly the laws, customs, and liberties granted the clergy and people by the glorious king, the sainted Edward,[4] your predecessor?"
>
> "I grant and promise them."
>
> "Sire, will you in all your judgments, to the best of your ability, preserve to God and the Holy Church and to the clergy and people full peace and concord before God?"
>
> "I will preserve them."
>
> "Sire, will you, to the best of your ability, have justice rendered rightly, fairly, and wisely, in compassion and truth?"
>
> "I will so do."
>
> "Sire, do you grant to be held and kept the laws and just customs which the community of your realm shall choose, and, to the best of your ability, defend and enforce them to the honor of God?"
>
> "I grant and promise them."

The last of these four promises was the most novel and doubtless the most important, embodying as it did the concept of community that had provoked such contention in the thirteenth century. By now it was under-

---

[3] Michael Prestwich, *The Three Edwards*, pp. 79, 295, and, more generally, 79–114. See also Natalie Fryde, *The Tyranny and Fall of Edward II, 1321–1326* (Cambridge, 1979), and J. R. Maddicott, *Thomas of Lancaster, 1307–1322* (London, 1970). A valuable contemporary history of Edward II's reign is N. Denholm–Young, tr., *Vita Edwardi Secundi* (London, 1957).

[4] Edward the Confessor, not Edward I.

stood that Parliament was the instrument through which the community expressed its will, and of necessity Edward II summoned parliaments frequently. The new king was as willing to make promises as his predecessors had been, and as ready to break them. The coronation oath is useful in disclosing to us in very general terms what the community expected of its king, but more than an oath would be required to bridle the obstinate Edward II.

At the time of his coronation, Edward was twenty-four years old. A contemporary described him as "fair of body and great of strength." But in character he was mercurial and unknightly. His many-faceted personality was described admirably by Bishop William Stubbs well over a century ago:

> He was a trifler, an amateur farmer, a breeder of horses, a patron of playwrights, a contriver of masques, a smatterer in mechanical arts; he was, it may be, an adept in rowing and a practiced whip; he could dig a pit or thatch a barn; somewhat varied and inconsistent accomplishments, but all testifying to the skillful hand rather than the thoughtful head.

In short, Edward was an eccentric. He was "a weakling and a fool," who was lacking "not only in military capacity, but also in imagination, energy, and common sense."[5] Because he lacked a knight's chivalric and military virtues, he could not win the respect of his barons, who preferred their kings to be warriors, not dilettantes. His coronation ushered in a generation of civil strife.

Throughout his career, Edward II demonstrated a dangerous and self-defeating tendency to engage in emotionally consuming love affairs with ambitious young men and to fall hopelessly under their influence. The first such man, and one of the most important, was Piers Gaveston—a Gascon knight of modest birth whose courage and ability were tainted by arrogance. Gaveston had been exiled prior to Edward I's death because of his influence on the Prince of Wales, but when the prince inherited the throne he brought Gaveston back to England and made him earl of Cornwall. The friendship with Gaveston caused Edward II endless difficulties. As one contemporary expressed it:

> [Baronial antagonism] mounted day by day, for Piers was very proud and haughty in bearing. All those whom the custom of the realm made equal to him, he regarded as lowly and abject, nor could anyone, he thought, equal him in valor. On the other hand the earls and barons of England looked down upon Piers because, as a foreigner and formerly a mere man-at-arms raised to such distinction and eminence, he was unmindful of his former rank. Thus he was an object of mockery to almost everyone in the kingdom. But the king had an unswerving affection for him.[6]

It must have seemed to the barons that the bad old days of Henry III had returned: Edward II ignored the will of the community, scorned the advice

---

[5] McKisack, *The Fourteenth Century*, p. 95.

[6] *Vita Edwardi Secundi*, p. 3.

of his nobles, and listened only to the vainglorious Gaveston. Predictably, disgruntled magnates conspired against the king. Their coalition soon fell under the leadership of Thomas earl of Lancaster, Edward II's first cousin and one of the wealthiest and most powerful magnates that England had ever known. A magnate of Thomas's resources would have been unthinkable under the Norman and early Angevin kings, whose wealth far exceeded that of their greatest vassals. But over the generations the disparity between king and magnates had been reduced by royal grants of demesne lands and the consolidation of baronial estates through intermarriage. The wealth of the crown was much less overshadowing in the fourteenth century than it had been in the twelfth: a handful of super-magnates could now present a far more formidable threat to the king than in earlier times. And no magnate was more formidable than Thomas of Lancaster. At the height of his power, Thomas held five earldoms—Lancaster, Leicester, Derby, Salisbury, and Lincoln—together with vast estates in northern and central England. He defended his lands and interests with a large private army. His impact on English history would have been greater still had not his policies been short-sighted, capricious, and limited by and large to the satisfaction of his personal ambition. Recent attempts to present his career in a more favorable light fail to dispel the impression that he was a grasping, stupid blunderer.

Nevertheless, Earl Thomas's royal opponent was at least as blundering as he. Edward II's fruitless attempts to carry on his father's aggressive Scottish policies put the monarchy in desperate need of money. He and Gaveston exploited every possible source of tax revenue and borrowed heavily from Italian bankers, particularly the Frescobaldi of Florence, who had served as the monarchy's principal creditors since Edward I's later years. Ultimately, however, the king was obliged to seek supplemental financial support from his barons in Parliament.

Edward's financial dependence enabled the magnates to establish limited control over the unwilling king. In 1310, they forced him to accept a committee of notables empowered to draw up a series of ordinances for the governing of the realm. The fruits of their work, the Ordinances of 1311, echoed the Provisions of Oxford of half a century earlier but were much more elaborate and thoroughgoing. They provided that both Gaveston and Edward's chief banker, Amerigo dei Frescobaldi, be exiled from England. Parliaments were to be summoned at least twice a year and were empowered to endorse or reject the appointment of high administrative officers such as the chancellor and treasurer. More than that, parliaments held veto power over the appointments of important officials in the king's household itself—the master of the wardrobe and the keeper of the Privy Seal. Finally, and perhaps most humiliating of all, the king could declare war only with parliamentary approval.

In 1311, as in 1215 and 1258, the magnates forced the monarchy to accept a comprehensive series of limitations on royal power. And as before, the king submitted only temporarily, sparking a period of civil turbulence. The irrepressible Gaveston returned to England from exile late in 1311, and by

Christmas he was again at Edward's side. The exasperated magnates responded by taking up arms, seizing the royal favorite, and hanging him. With Gaveston's execution, Edward II's reign entered a new phase, unhappier than the last.

Gaveston's murder cost the insurgents some support. Several magnates, restive under Thomas of Lancaster's inept leadership, felt that opposition to the king had become too extreme. The country was on the verge of civil war when, in 1313, the magnates and king arranged a reconciliation. For the moment, the Ordinances of 1311 dropped from sight. The war clouds evaporated, but the kingdom's condition remained far from peaceful. The many complex and bitter rivalries among the nobility, which had troubled Edward II's reign from the beginning, reached their climax. The second and third decades of the fourteenth century saw not only a continual struggle between monarchy and nobility but also feuds between magnate and magnate that sometimes erupted into private war: in 1317, the personal armies of the earls of Lancaster and Surrey clashed openly. And throughout this period, the English suffered a series of military disasters in their conflict with Scotland.

Edward II had great difficulty with the Scots from the start, and in 1314 an overwhelming Scottish victory over a large English army at Bannockburn shattered the entire northern policy of the first two Edwards. This spectacular Scottish triumph was so complete as to doom all further efforts to subdue the northern kingdom. In the years that followed, the Scots took the offensive against England—often with the support of dissident English earls—until Edward II arranged a peace with them in 1323. Scotland had won its independence, and Robert Bruce ruled his kingdom unchallenged. Edward II's prestige, none too high to begin with, was tarnished still further by this humiliating military failure.

Meanwhile, the king continued to quarrel with his magnates and his parliaments. Thomas of Lancaster, who had held aloof from the disastrous Scottish campaign of 1314, was now more powerful than ever. In a parliament held in the autumn of that year, he succeeded in reestablishing the Ordinances of 1311. In 1316 and 1317, he was the king's chief counselor and the foremost figure in the royal administration. He never succeeded, however, in winning Edward's confidence, nor indeed did he even try. Not only Edward II but many of his magnates were becoming alarmed at Lancaster's growing authority, and in 1318 a group of barons more accommodating to the king rose to power in the court. Lancaster remained a potent force in the English government, but he was no longer supreme. The new men were suspicious of Lancaster and less interested than he in forcing royal government into the rigid framework of the ordinances. This group included a youthful nobleman of intelligence and ruthless ambition—Hugh Despenser the Younger—who rose quickly to power by winning from Edward II the romantic affection the susceptible king had once lavished on Gaveston.

Despenser was the son and namesake of a royal official who had rendered faithful service to Edward I. Hugh Despenser the Elder continued to

Detail of the Tomb Effigy of Edward II, Gloucester Cathedral   (A. F. Kersting)

serve the monarchy under Edward II, and father and son both profited prodigiously from the royal favor. Being a well-born Englishman, the Younger Despenser could not be denounced as an upstart foreigner like Gaveston. He was a much abler man than Gaveston had been, and even more ambitious. With Edward II's ardent backing, he and his father acquired vast landed wealth. By 1321 he had ascended, through the king's affection, to a position of overwhelming authority in the royal court. It was the Younger Despenser, rather than Edward II or his other magnates, who now ran the government.

Once again, the magnates formed a coalition against the king and his favorite, led by notables such as Thomas of Lancaster and the Mortimers— a family of marcher (frontier) lords who resented Despenser's brazen policy of collecting lordships for himself in the Welsh Marches. Now at last, the struggle between king and insurgent nobles broke into open warfare, and at. the crucial battle of Boroughbridge in March 1322, Thomas of Lancaster was routed by a royal army. The earl surrendered and was summarily tried and condemned for treason. His captors mounted him on a skinny white nag, placed a ragged old hat on his head, led him through a jeering crowd that pelted him with snowballs, and had him beheaded. With Thomas of Lancaster's defeat and death, the king—or rather the Younger Despenser—won unchallenged dominion over the kingdom.

In the aftermath of Boroughbridge, Edward and Despenser, blatantly disregarding law and custom, executed their major opponents, confiscated their lands, and imprisoned their kinfolk—including children and elderly relations. Their tyranny spawned an era of violence, plundering, and a breakdown of law and order unparalleled since the Norman Conquest.

The years following the royal military triumph at Boroughbridge, 1322–1326, witnessed peace abroad but terror at home. Wales was won, Scotland lost, and Gascony at peace. The dramatic reduction in military and diplomatic expenses, combined with a heavy influx of taxes from frightened, browbeaten subjects, replenished the royal treasury and made Edward II the wealthiest English monarch in living memory. Edward I had left his son a debt of some £200,000, whereas Edward II, at the close of his reign in 1327, had a surplus of over £60,000—nearly a year's income in reserve. There had been nothing like it since Henry I, nearly two centuries earlier in 1135, had left nearly £100,000 to his luckless successor, Stephen. But Edward II, in the course of enriching himself and his few friends, had also earned the passionate hatred of his subjects.

In the years after Boroughbridge, the Younger Despenser ruled imperiously over king and kingdom, amassing estates and enemies. But his power and success made him overconfident—as so often happens—and he carelessly allowed a new coalition to develop that ultimately would prove fatal to his ambitions. The Welsh marcher lord Roger Mortimer, imprisoned during Edward's crackdown after Boroughbridge, escaped from the Tower of London in 1323 and took refuge in France. Two years later Queen Isabella, whose place in the royal affections Despenser had usurped, was sent across the Channel to negotiate with her brother, King Charles IV, on the long-standing Anglo-French dispute over Gascony. Once in France, the neglected

Queen Isabella Returning from France to Dethrone Her Husband, Edward II
From a fourteenth-century manuscript. (Bibliothèque Nationale, Paris)

Isabella broke with her husband and became the mistress of Roger Mortimer, and in 1326 Mortimer and Isabella returned to England with an army. With them was young Prince Edward, son of Edward II and Isabella and heir to the throne.

Mortimer and Isabella at once became the center of a general uprising of English magnates against the hated Despenser and his crowned puppet. Late in 1326, the rebels captured and imprisoned the king and executed Despenser after first chopping off his genitals and burning them before his eyes. In January 1327, a parliament formally deposed King Edward II in favor of his fourteen-year-old heir, Edward III. To avoid any possibility of a royal comeback, Edward II's enemies forced him to abdicate, imprisoned him in Berkeley Castle, and apparently had him murdered. About a decade later, a letter from a papal notary to Edward III related a beguiling but unlikely tale of Edward II escaping from the castle just ahead of his would-be killers. On his way out, he is said to have murdered a porter, whose body was alleged by the bungling assassins to be that of the king. Afterwards, Edward supposedly wandered in disguise through England, Ireland, and the Continent, paying a secret visit to the pope in Avignon and ending his years in an Italian hermitage.

The deposition of a king, unprecedented in English history, was an event of awe-inspiring magnitude. Although a parliament was the formal instrument of the deposition, the real agents of Edward II's downfall were Mortimer and Isabella, aided by English magnates hostile to the king. Edward II was defeated and imprisoned by means of armed rebellion. The parliament of 1327 was controlled by the insurgents and merely ratified their wishes. Nevertheless, the fact that the formalities of the royal deposition were carried out in a parliament is itself significant. It was through

The Execution of Hugh Despenser the Younger at Hereford in 1326 (Bibliothèque Nationale, Paris)

The Fourteenth-Century Kings

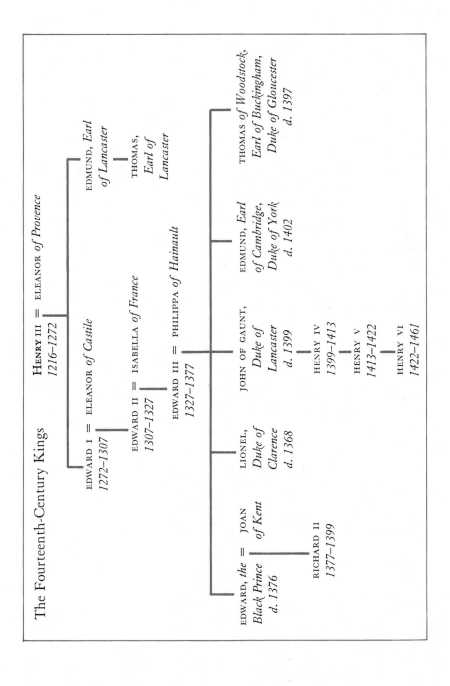

HENRY III = ELEANOR *of Provence*
1216–1272

EDWARD I = ELEANOR *of Castile*
1272–1307

EDMUND, *Earl of Lancaster*

THOMAS, *Earl of Lancaster*

EDWARD II = ISABELLA *of France*
1307–1327

EDWARD III = PHILIPPA *of Hainault*
1327–1377

EDWARD, *the Black Prince* = JOAN *of Kent*
d. 1376

LIONEL, *Duke of Clarence d.* 1368

JOHN OF GAUNT, *Duke of Lancaster d.* 1399

EDMUND, *Earl of Cambridge, Duke of York d.* 1402

THOMAS *of Woodstock, Earl of Buckingham, Duke of Gloucester d.* 1397

RICHARD II
1377–1399

HENRY IV
1399–1413

HENRY V
1413–1422

HENRY VI
1422–1461

parliaments that the community of the realm spoke, and in 1327 the community gave its legal sanction to what otherwise would have been an act of high treason. Never before had it been asserted so straightforwardly that royal authority required the assent of the community. A constitutional means had at last come about for justifying the removal of a king who refused to abide by customary laws and the community's will: the representatives of the English community, acting in parliament, could cast him from the throne. No subsequent medieval king could safely ignore that lesson.

In Edward II's time, as before, the monarchy remained the central force in English politics. And for that very reason, the reign of a savage nincompoop such as Edward II robbed the kingdom of its political balance and brought on civil turmoil. Despite the ever-growing importance of English political and administrative institutions, the strength and wisdom of the monarch remained essential to the community's well-being. Edward III proved a far abler king than his father, and his rise to power transformed the political orientation of England.

The immediate effect of the revolution of 1327, however, was to renew the bitterness and disaffection from which England had so long suffered. Although Edward III inherited the kingdom, he was still too young to rule. Actual power passed to Mortimer and Isabella, who dominated the regency government. Mortimer proceeded to enrich himself handsomely from the lands of Edward II's defeated associates, and the baronial faction that had supported the revolution soon turned to internal bickering. Moreover, the sexual relationship between Mortimer and Queen Isabella was becoming a national scandal. The two were well on their way to making as many enemies as Despenser when, in 1330, they were unexpectedly brought to ruin. Seemingly secure in their control of England, they fell victim to a court conspiracy led by the young king himself. Mortimer was seized in his room in Nottingham Castle by Edward III's followers, tried by a parliament, and hanged. Isabella was permitted a generous allowance but was deprived of power. And King Edward, having proclaimed his coming of age in this emphatic fashion, proceeded to the essential work of healing England's divisions by restoring vigorous royal leadership to his troubled kingdom.

11

Edward III and the Hundred Years' War

Like Richard the Lion-Hearted, Edward III was a warrior-king.[1] Chivalrous and magnanimous, he enjoyed immense popularity—except during a brief standoff with some dissident barons in 1341 and in his final, senile years. Some historians have accused him of being a grandiose fool, addicted to extravagance, dissipation, ostentatious display, and spectacular but ultimately fruitless military campaigning. Yet he succeeded to a remarkable degree in maintaining the loyalty of his magnates and his six sons. Earlier kings of England—William I and Henry II, in particular—had been tormented by the revolts of ambitious offspring. But the sons of Edward III respected and supported him, and at no time in his entire fifty-year reign did his barons raise the standard of rebellion.

One key to Edward's success lay in his cheerful, amiable disposition. He was, as one contemporary observed, "not accustomed to be sad," and he never pushed his royal prerogatives to the point of openly challenging the laws and customs of the realm. More important was his taste for chivalry and his triumphant military campaigns—which historians have often, too quickly, dismissed. The magnates esteemed pageantry and military victories above all else, and Edward III's theatrical behavior and soldierly exploits won him the admiring loyalty of his barons and the obedience of his subjects. To contemporaries, he was "our comely king," "the famous

---

[1] There is, at the time of this writing, no satisfactory modern scholarly study of Edward III's reign in print, but an excellent one by Scott Waugh, which I have had the pleasure of reading in typescript form, will be published in 1992 by the Cambridge University Press: *England in the Reign of Edward III*. See also Michael Packe's popular biography, *King Edward III*, L. C. B. Seaman, ed. (London, 1983). On political institutions in the early part of Edward III's reign see J. F. Willard et al., eds., *The English Government at Work, 1327–1336*, 3 vols. (Cambridge, Mass., 1940–1950). An excellent older survey of the Hundred Years' War is Edouard Perroy, *The Hundred Years War*, W. B. Wells, tr. (London, 1951). A more recent survey is Christopher Allmand, *The Hundred Years War: England and France at War, c. 1300–c. 1450* (Cambridge, 1988). See also Richard Barber, *Edward, Prince of Wales and Aquitaine: A Biography of the Black Prince* (New York, 1978), and Juliet Vale, *Edward III and Chivalry: Chivalric Society and Its Context, 1270–1350* (Woodbridge, Suffolk, 1982). On Edward's parliaments, see Sir Goronwy Edwards, *The Second Century of the English Parliament* (Oxford, 1979); G. L. Harriss, *King, Parliament and Public Finance in Medieval England to 1369* (Oxford, 1975); and George Holmes, *The Good Parliament* (Oxford, 1975).

and fortunate warrior," under whom "the realm of England has been nobly improved, honored, and enriched to a degree never seen in the time of any other king." His victories abroad kindled a glow of national pride by creating an international reputation for English military prowess: "When the noble Edward first gained England in his youth," a French writer observed, "nobody thought much of the English, nobody spoke of their prowess or courage. . . . Now, in the time of the noble Edward, who has often put them to the test, they are the finest and most daring warriors known to man."[2]

The Reign of Edward III (1327–1377)

Reversing the political equation of Edward II's final years, Edward III's reign witnessed peace at home and war abroad. Between 1333 and 1336, he led a series of successful though brutal and inconclusive expeditions into Scotland. Later, in 1346, the English won a decisive victory over the Scots at the battle of Neville's Cross, capturing King David II of Scotland and devastating the Scottish countryside. But Edward III directed his chief military efforts against France, and it was there that he won his greatest renown.

Edward's French campaigns mark the opening phase of a protracted military struggle known as the Hundred Years' War. The name is inappropriate for several reasons. For one thing, the "war" lasted not 100 years but 115—from 1338 to 1453. For another, the campaigns of this period were separated by prolonged truces, often lasting many years. In fact, one might reasonably regard the Hundred Years' War as a series of much shorter wars. And it should be obvious by now that the conflict between England and France began not in 1338 but shortly after 1066. Almost every king since the Norman Conquest had campaigned against the French at one time or another, and the Hundred Years' War was in many respects a continuation of these earlier struggles. Nevertheless, the term has been hallowed by custom and will be used here for the sake of convenience and out of respect to past scholars—no matter how misguided.

One theme that links the various campaigns of the Hundred Years' War and distinguishes them from previous Anglo-French conflicts is the English monarchy's claim to the French throne. When Charles IV, the last of the Capetian kings, died childless in 1328, Edward III became a serious contender for the French royal succession through his mother Isabella, Charles's sister. But the French, alleging an ancient custom that the royal succession could not pass down the female line, gave the crown to Philip VI (1328–1350)—a first cousin of Charles IV and the founder of the long-lived Valois dynasty. At first, Edward did not dispute this decision, but later, when other matters prompted him to take up arms against the French, he revived his claim and used it to justify his invasions. Subsequent kings of England would also claim the throne of France, and the Valois succession was not finally recognized in England until after the war ended in 1453.

---

[2] Jean le Beau, *Chroniques*, I, 155–156, quoted in May McKisack, *The Fourteenth Century*, p. 150.

Edward III's Tomb Monument in St. Stephen's Chapel, Westminster (The Mansell Collection)

In the middle and later 1330s, Anglo-French relations were severely strained by a number of other disputes. The two kingdoms were at odds over Flanders, which France had long endeavored to control but which was extremely important to England as a market for its wool. Moreover, the French had supported the Scots in their warfare with England. The old dispute over the remaining English fiefs in southern France remained alive and reached a crisis in 1337 when Philip VI, after cancelling his plans for a large-scale crusade to the Holy Land, ordered the confiscation of Gascony. Underlying these issues was the fact that the young King Edward and the chivalrous nobles he had gathered around him were hungry for adventure and for the pursuit of military glory. In short, a warrior-king and his warrior nobility needed a war.

So it was that in 1338, after elaborate preparations, Edward III led a glittering and hopeful army southward across the English Channel. His plan was to invade France through the Low Countries—to attack on a huge scale not only with his own soldiers but with those of his continental allies as well. For Edward III, like John and Edward I before him, had created a system of alliances with important princes in the Netherlands and Germany. Such a system required staggeringly heavy expenditures for subsidies and bribes ("foreign aid," as we would call it now) and imposed a considerable strain on English resources. Edward attempted to finance his soldiers and diplomats by means of heavy taxes on wool and by various complex but ineffective schemes to create artificial wool shortages, thereby raising prices and customs revenues. But Edward found that his allies' thirst for money was unquenchable and that, when the time came for action, they demanded more than he was able to give. Accordingly, the fighting between 1338 and 1340 accomplished little except to drive the English monarchy back into debt. Edward salvaged one military triumph from the early phase of the war when, in 1340, his fleet annihilated a French armada at the battle of Sluys off the Flemish coast. The victory at Sluys enabled the English to control the Channel for the next several years. But Edward's initial land campaigns were both frustrating and expensive.

During the 1340s and afterward, Edward altered his military strategy. Finding that an alliance system was costly and inefficient, he undertook to invade France with English armies that were lightly supplied but prepared to forage off the land. The new policy proved its worth in 1342, when a series of English raids against Brittany established English control over that strategic province. Again, in 1345, Edward sent armies into France—one to Brittany, another to Gascony. In 1346, the king himself crossed the Channel with an army of 10,000 men—immense by the standards of the age. Campaigning in Normandy, he plundered the important town of Caen and from there led his force first southeastward toward Paris, then northward into Ponthieu. At Crécy, a few miles from the Channel, he encountered the French royal army, and the two forces clashed in the first great land battle of the Hundred Years' War.

The battle of Crécy, fought on August 26, 1346, brought overwhelming victory for Edward III. It was the most stunning military triumph of his career. Edward's longbowmen decimated the mounted French nobles, crippling their military capability for years to come. The triumph enabled Edward, a year later, to take the key channel port of Calais, which remained in English hands for the next two centuries. The campaign of 1346–1347 gave Edward the success and prestige to which he had aspired only in his wildest dreams and brought the hegemony of high medieval France to a decisive close.

A decade after Crécy, the English, again depending heavily on their longbowmen, won another major victory over the French at Poitiers. Edward III was not present at the battle; the English army was led by his eldest son, Edward the "Black Prince." Although badly outnumbered, the English put the French to rout; captured their incompetent king, John the

The Battle of Crécy, August 26, 1346 Detail of an illustration from a fourteenth-century manuscript of Froissart's Chronicles. (The Granger Collection)

Good (a very bad king indeed); and returned to England with the royal prisoner. The English had triumphed dramatically once again, and the Black Prince won acclaim as "the most valiant prince that ever lived in this world, throughout its length and breadth, since the days of Julius Caesar or Arthur."

The battles of Crécy and of Poitiers were separated by the cataclysmic arrival of the Black Death in Europe. Shattered by two military disasters, the plague, the loss of its king, and the harrying of mercenary companies, France lay prostrate in the later 1350s. In 1358, the monarchy suppressed a large-scale rebellion of French peasants only after a savage struggle, and in 1359 the Black Prince led his army across France from the Channel to Burgundy virtually unopposed. In 1360, the two kingdoms concluded a truce on terms exceedingly favorable to Edward III. King Edward temporarily dropped his claim to the French throne but was given vast territories in France, approaching those of the twelfth-century Angevin Empire. And the French ransomed King John for the staggering sum of half a million pounds—five times the ransom of Richard the Lion-Hearted in the late twelfth century.

All that the English had won in these French campaigns they lost in the course of the next two decades. This reversal in military fortunes resulted from a revival of French royal authority and the dogged, unrelenting pressure of French armies against the overextended English positions. England

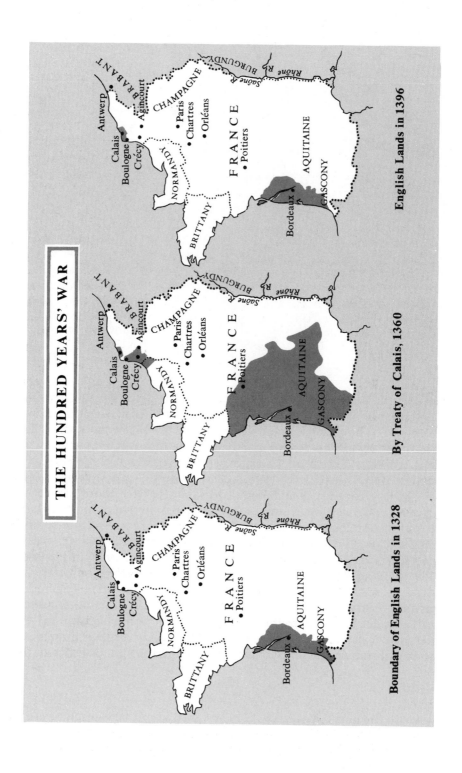

THE HUNDRED YEARS' WAR

English Lands in 1396

By Treaty of Calais, 1360

Boundary of English Lands in 1328

prospered during the greater part of the 1360s, Edward III basked in the prestige of his earlier victories, and the royal treasury drew rich nourishment from French ransom payments. But as the 1360s drew to a close, the balance of quality in French and English leadership tipped in France's favor. Edward III's high living—primarily drinking and chasing women—had driven him into an early dotage; he became senile in his late fifties and passed his later years as a tool of unscrupulous courtiers and of his mistress at the time, Alice Perrers. His eldest son, the Black Prince, fell victim to a lingering illness. On the French side, the inept King John died in 1364, leaving the kingdom to his intelligent and energetic son, Charles V (1364–1380). King Charles had the good fortune to be served by an astute military commander, Bertrand du Guesclin, reputed to be the ugliest man in France and the best general in Europe. Charles and du Guesclin adopted a military policy of remorseless harassment. They avoided major battles but won many skirmishes. From 1369 on, England's French possessions dissolved steadily until, at Edward III's death in 1377, the English held only Calais, Cherbourg, a little territory around Bordeaux, and a few Breton harbors. A generation would pass before England, under the bold leadership of Henry V, made any serious attempt to recover its losses and resume its quest for the throne of France.

Parliament in the Fourteenth Century

Against the background of foreign military campaigning that characterized much of the fourteenth century, Parliament developed significantly.[3] Huge military expenditures forced the monarchy to depend increasingly on extraordinary taxation, and kings could obtain the revenues they so desperately needed only by parliamentary consent. Hence, the parliaments of the fourteenth century were in an ideal bargaining position. The magnates generally approved of Edward III's French wars and were not inclined to be parsimonious in giving him their financial support. His policies and chivalric tastes placed him in close rapport with his nobles. But fourteenth-century parliaments included classes other than the nobility, and Edward III's overseas adventures proved less captivating to the townspeople and gentry, who had little to gain from his campaigns and objected most heatedly to the repeated subsidies necessary to finance them. Consequently, it was they who gained the most politically from his dependence on parliamentary grants.

As the fourteenth century dawned, Parliament's membership and function was ill-defined. But by the close of the century, parliament had assumed something of its modern form. It had split into Lords and Com-

---

[3] On Parliament, see the references cited in Chapter 8, note 7, and Chapter 11, note 1, and also H. G. Richardson and G. O. Sayles, *Parliaments and Great Councils in Medieval England* (London, 1961) and *The English Parliament in the Middle Ages* (London, 1981): a collection of the authors' earlier articles. See further the valuable essays assembled in *The English Parliament in the Middle Ages*, R. G. Davies and J. H. Denton, eds. (Philadelphia, 1981).

mons, and the Commons had acquired a crucial role in taxation and legislation. By 1399, the parliamentary tradition had become etched indelibly into the English political system.

The fourteenth century was a crucial epoch, therefore, in the development of Parliament and, more specifically, in the rise of the Commons. By the time of Edward I's death, the summoning of representatives of townspeople and gentry was becoming customary practice, and although they attended only three of the first seven parliaments of Edward II, they participated in all but two of the parliaments between 1310 and 1327. They became a customary component of Edward III's parliaments and were invariably present from the mid-fourteenth century onward.

Just when representatives of town and shire were forming an integral part of Parliament, the two groups were also coalescing into a single political body. Gradually, they came to realize that they had strong common interests. The shire knights remained more assertive than the burghers in fourteenth-century parliaments. But the economic resources of the urban elites, relative to those of other classes, expanded throughout this period, and both gentry and townspeople discovered that they could accomplish more by cooperating than by defending their interests alone. Frequent intermarriages between members of the two classes cemented their community of interest. Before the fourteenth century was half over, they had fused politically into a single parliamentary group—the Commons.

This process of fusion began under Edward II and reached its completion under Edward III. Representatives of town and shire may have met together in 1332, and they unquestionably did so in 1339—to deliberate jointly over a royal grant. They were described in the rolls of Parliament at that time as "men of the Commons." Thereafter, joint meetings became customary, and the Commons took its place as a vital element in the government of England.

The development of Commons as a separate parliamentary group meant that the members of Parliament who did not participate in the Commons became, in effect, a separate group themselves. These men—the great magnates and prelates of the realm—became a distinct body known as the House of Lords. The term *house of lords* does not appear in documents until the sixteenth century, but the institution itself existed by the mid-fourteenth.

In the thirteenth century, many notables had regarded attendance in parliaments as a burden, but as the fourteenth century progressed, they began to consider it a privilege. Eligibility for attendance in parliaments was now much more rigorously defined than before. Under Edward II, there evolved a fixed list of barons who alone and invariably received parliamentary summonses. This select group came to be known as the peerage. And although the term *peer* literally means "social equal," the peers were in fact, to paraphrase George Orwell, more equal than anyone else in the realm. Fourteenth-century barons who were eligible for a parliamentary summons fell into two groups: (1) the greatest magnates and prelates, who received individual summonses to Parliament; and (2) lesser lords, whose tenures were regarded by custom as "baronial" rather than merely "knightly" and who were called by a general parliamentary summons (but often failed to attend). The right of a lord to attend Parliament became hereditary, passed down like a great baronial estate from father to eldest son. Thus, the peerage became a permanent and clearly defined group at the apex of the social order.

The process of selecting particular individuals to represent their shires or towns in Commons was more fluid and complex, and many of the details of the selection process are lost to us. Normally, the shire representative was chosen at a meeting of the shire court, which only the more substantial men of the district usually attended. The sheriff was the chief figure at these meetings and often manipulated the elections in his own favor or on behalf of the monarchy. Indeed, the electoral procedures were frequently so ill defined that the sheriff could simply name his own slate of representatives. Similarly, a powerful local magnate might overawe the court with his private army of retainers and secure the election of his own henchmen. In the later fourteenth century, John of Gaunt exerted nearly absolute control over the selection of shire knights from his vast palatinate of Lancaster, and the great magnates of Yorkshire appear to have dominated the elections of Commons representatives from their county. Such manipulation increased sharply in the fifteenth century, when the military power and local autonomy of the great lords were at their height. Before 1399, manipulation of county elections by sheriffs or magnates, although widespread, was by no means universal. Left to themselves, the county courts tended to elect knights or squires of wealth and substance. The same was true of the towns, where electoral arrangements were so varied as to defy generalization. Whatever the details, the Commons generally chose as its representatives pillars of their community (unless they were paid royal or baronial agents), and one will look in vain in the fourteenth-century Commons for lower-class protest or revolutionary ferment.

Nevertheless, the emergence of Commons and the progressive extension of its power is a matter of immense significance in the development of the unwritten English "constitution." In the crisis of 1297 the royal government of Edward I had conceded that all uncustomary taxes must be approved by the community of the realm. It was assumed by then that the community was embodied in parliaments. Under Edward III, this power to approve taxes passed gradually into the hands of Commons. It was to be the key to all of that body's future power, and the members of Commons seem to have understood this. When they approved a particular grant, they would often demand and receive greater control over grants in general. Commons was now in a strong position, for the increasingly affluent classes it represented were supplying the monarchy with much of its tax revenues. Accordingly, by the end of the fourteenth century, the Commons was coming to exercise the exclusive right to originate parliamentary taxation. In 1395 a parliamentary grant was made "by the Commons with the advice and assent of the Lords." This was the first time these exact words were used, but they became the norm in years thereafter.

Thus, by 1399 the approval of Parliament, more specifically the Commons, was required for all extraordinary taxes, direct or indirect—even tolls and customs from merchants. Parliament even supervised and audited tax revenues and began to specify the uses for particular taxes. Profiting from the military dangers and general unrest of Richard II's reign (1377–1399), Parliament used its fiscal power to establish ever-greater control over government policies. In 1377, it insisted on overseeing the use of its grant and succeeded in securing the appointment of two London merchants as treasurers of war. And in 1382, parliamentary representatives imposed their own foreign policy on the royal government by insisting on a military campaign in Flanders. The right to grant or refuse taxes, they were discovering, was an effective avenue to political power.

The relationship between taxation and power is nowhere better illustrated than in the gradual growth of Commons' role in eliciting legislation. This function, undreamed of at the close of the thirteenth century, was well established 100 years later. Edward III's first Parliament, meeting in 1327, introduced for the first time a Commons petition—a list of grievances that Parliament expected the monarchy to consider seriously in return for the granting of taxes. Parliaments had long been accustomed to receiving and passing on to the king petitions from individuals or groups. The Commons petition differed from these earlier requests in that it dealt with matters of general interest to the community of the realm. The Commons petition of 1327 concerned issues such as the maintenance of Magna Carta, the soundness of English currency, and the size of cloths sold in English markets. Coming at a time of grave political crisis, it received the sympathetic attention of the royal government and gave rise to two statutes and several ordinances and decrees. More important, it set a precedent. Similar petitions were introduced in the parliaments of 1333 and 1337, and they appeared regularly from 1343 onward. Fourteenth-century parliaments used the Commons petition repeatedly as a device to put pressure on the king to grant their wishes, and as time went on it became increasingly customary for a Commons petition to give rise to royal statutes. Thus the Commons petition was a significant step in the direction of parliamentary legislation. In later years, the Commons petition evolved into the Commons bill, and the will of the House of Commons became the law of England. Indeed, after the mid-fourteenth century, most statutes resulted directly from Commons petitions or bills rather than from royal initiative, as in the days of Edward I. The mechanism for Commons legislation was thereby established. It remained only to refine it.

The original procedure consisted of Commons presenting a petition and voting a grant. The king would then approve the petition, and it would be translated into statute. But if some item in the petition was offensive to the king, he might ignore it or alter its meaning. To prevent this sort of royal tampering and to ensure that the statute perfectly matched the petition, the Commons developed the principle of "redress before supply." Only when the king satisfied their petition, both in matter and spirit, would Commons make the requested grant. Redress before supply, which had become a normal procedure by the early fifteenth century, was a key factor in transforming Parliament's privilege to petition into its power to make law.

Law and Administration

The evolution of other branches of the fourteenth-century English government was less spectacular than that of Parliament. The functions of the council—now a fixed body of sworn royal counselors—became steadily more elaborate and varied. It remained the organizational core of every parliament. It supervised the entire system of royal justice and functioned, although on a declining scale, as a court of equity to settle cases unadaptable to the common-law courts. It counseled the king (as before), kept watch over the great departments of chancery and exchequer, handled affairs of diplomacy, and enacted royal ordinances—many of which gave rise to royal statutes in Parliament. As the fourteenth century progressed, the council became increasingly an executive body, authorizing under the Privy Seal, without direct royal mandate, most of the ordinary business of state. These activities and responsibilities by now had become much too complex for direct royal supervision; and as time passed, the council operated more and more on its own initiative. By the century's close it had achieved sufficient independence to keep separate records of its meetings.

Baronial attempts to control council and household had begun, as we have seen, under Henry III and were revived under Edward II—never with lasting success. Edward III, a friend of the barons, normally made it a point to fill his council with nobles or men acceptable to them. This was not invariably the case: in 1341, he submitted briefly to a degree of parliamentary control over his officers of state. And again, in his old age, the "Good Parliament" of 1376 crippled Edward's regime for a time by refusing to grant subsidies. It challenged his authority by forcing the appointment of a new royal council and dismissing from court—through the novel process of impeachment—the king's chamberlain and the king's mistress. But within months the impeachments were quashed. The crises of 1341 and 1376 proved to be isolated, momentary disturbances in a long and otherwise untroubled period of royal/baronial harmony.

The two departments of chancery and exchequer continued to drift further away from direct royal control. Each had acquired its own seal; both were now removed from the court and were carrying on their functions at Westminster. During the fourteenth century, the chancery's administrative independence declined as it began to share more and more of its authority with the household departments of wardrobe and chamber. By the end of the century, the chancery's initiative was limited largely to the automatic issuing of judicial writs and the drafting and authenticating of royal documents already authorized elsewhere. The chancellors themselves—most of whom were clerics, as in earlier times—devoted less and less attention to supervising the chancery and its clerks and more to great matters of state. Throughout much of the fourteenth century the chancellor was the dominant figure in the council, and he eventually assumed the additional task of presiding over a special tribunal responsible for hearing cases in equity.

As we have seen, such cases had been heard traditionally by the full council. But now the council's administrative burdens were growing to such a point that it could no longer serve effectively as a tribunal. The chancellor, as chief officer in the council, was particularly well equipped to take equity cases under his own jurisdiction. He was likely to be an expert jurist, and his responsibilities included channeling pleas into the appropriate common-law courts—King's Bench, Common Pleas, or Exchequer. He was therefore in a strategic position to identify cases that were appropriate to none of these courts—cases requiring special, equitable treatment in a court unhampered by the hardening rules and procedures of the common law. Such a court developed in the course of the fourteenth century—a group of learned justices and lawyers selected by the chancellor to aid him in judging cases. Only later did this tribunal disentangle itself completely from the council to become the official Court of Chancery. But by the end of Edward III's reign, the tribunal was already, for all practical purposes, functioning on its own and draining off most of the pleas formerly heard by the council. Its development illustrates once again the growing professionalization and departmentalization of the royal government and the steady drift of its components farther and farther away from direct royal supervision.

American presidents have complained of the difficulty of imposing their will on a vast, inert federal bureaucracy. Fourteenth-century English kings faced the same problem on a smaller scale. It had been convenient enough for William the Conqueror to issue his documents under the Great Seal. But by Edward I's time—with the Great Seal in the chancery's custody at Westminster—the Privy Seal became necessary for the day-to-day exercise of the royal will. In the course of Edward III's reign, the keeper of the Privy Seal himself drifted out of court and settled in Westminster with his large clerical staff, so that the king was obliged to depend on various new household seals. Richard II sealed many of his documents with his own signet ring—so many, in fact, that the ring acquired its own office and its own staff of clerks.

Meanwhile the judicial structure evolved slowly along the general lines established by Edward I. There were no great legal systematizers among the kings of fourteenth-century England, and the common law remained more or less as it had been at Edward I's death. The lords in Parliament continued to function as the highest tribunal. The common-law courts grew increasingly specialized—and increasingly jealous of one another. The court of King's Bench now primarily heard criminal cases; Common Pleas, civil cases; and the Exchequer, royal revenue cases. The role of the itinerant justices declined through the early decades of Edward III's reign, as the volume of local judicial business became greater than the eyres could handle, and as the traveling justices became increasingly unpopular. Edward abolished the eyres altogether in 1361—at Commons' insistence—and thereafter the king's justice in the countryside was handled by a new group of officials—usually drawn from the local gentry—known as justices of the peace. The rise of these new officers meant that the gentry had, in effect, won control of the local courts.

The fourteenth-century justice of the peace remained a dominant figure in the administrative and judicial organization of the counties for centuries to come. The office evolved out of Edward I's keepers of the peace, who exercised police functions under the authority of the sheriff. A statute of 1330 gave them the responsibility to indict criminals as well as apprehend them, and this new judicial function was broadened greatly when a statute of 1360 empowered the keepers to try felons and trespassers. In effect, the statute of 1360 transformed the keepers of the peace into justices of the peace. Their judicial functions were elaborated further in 1362, when they were directed to hold courts four times a year. These "quarter sessions" gave the justices of the peace preeminence in legal affairs over all other county officials, including sheriffs. By the century's close, their jurisdictional supremacy had ripened into a general supervision of the county administration, and the quarter sessions had superseded the older shire courts. The justices had also assumed by then the obligation of supervising the recruitment of shire levies. In short, justices of the peace had replaced sheriffs as the chief royal officers in the counties and the primary links between crown and shire.

Edward III and the Decline of Royal Authority

The Hundred Years' War and concurrent warfare against the Scots placed a tremendous burden on the royal administration. The staggering expenses of foreign campaigns left Edward III even more dependent on parliamentary grants than his predecessors had been, and he won the financial backing of the community only by acceding to most of its demands. He soothed Parliament by consulting with it on important matters of policy and appointing no high-handed royal ministers who might offend it. His pliancy contributed much, as we have seen, to the growth of the power of Commons. And in agreeing to abolish his itinerant justices, he speeded the decline of royal authority in the countryside. In the absence of justices from the royal court, magnates often could dominate law and administration in their regions—bribing the local justices of the peace or intimidating them with private armies.

Overall, Edward III achieved splendid success in restoring the prestige of the crown after the disasters of Edward II's reign and in working harmoniously with his subjects—but at a cost. All was well as long as England remained under the spell of a victorious, venerated king. But Edward's less pliant and less triumphant successors would suffer for his concessions. The Commons, through their control of taxation, could hamstring any royal policies with which they disagreed. And the magnates' unprecedented power in the shires would drive England toward political chaos in the next century. Not until the coming of the Tudors would the crown regain the supremacy over the nobility that it had enjoyed in the twelfth and thirteenth centuries. And never again could it safely ignore the Commons.

12

The Strange Death of
Medieval England

During the second half of the fourteenth century, England's foreign struggles and constitutional transformation occurred against a background of
plague, cultural change, and growing social upheaval. The Black Death
served as the somber backdrop to a deepening economic crisis, a bitter
popular insurrection (known as the Peasants' Revolt) in 1381, and growing
social tensions and religious restlessness. These problems cannot be brack-
eted within an arbitrary date range such as historians too often impose on
them. They continued to torment English society well after 1399, the
terminal point of this book, and many of them will be discussed more fully
in the next volume of this series. Together, they constitute a turbulent
epilogue to England's medieval experience.

The Black Death

As the fourteenth century opened, the general prosperity of the High
Middle Ages was fading. The ever increasing pressure of population on
resources, and the shift to a colder, rainier climate, caused widespread hunger and malnutrition. The towns suffered, too, for they depended on food
from the countryside. Poor harvests and crop failures brought famine to
townspeople and peasants alike. The population already seems to have been
leveling off when a series of terrible floods and famines struck England
between 1315 and 1317, followed by an equally devastating cattle disease in
1319–1321 and a disastrous crop failure in 1321. Together, these catastrophes provoked the greatest kingdom-wide agrarian crisis since the aftermath of the Norman Conquest. English agriculture made a partial
comeback in the years after 1321, but for the next generation, famine
remained near at hand. Then, in 1348–1349, the Black Death struck, carrying off at least a third of the population of England and Western Europe.

There is much dispute among scholars over the demographic effects of
these various factors—weather, soil exhaustion, sheep and cattle disease,
the extension of cultivation into marginal districts, and the overpopulation
of fertile lands. Kingdom-wide population figures for the first half of the
fourteenth century are few and unreliable. Studies of particular agrarian
communities provide more exact information, but we are left to wonder

how far such case studies reflect general trends. A particularly rigorous analysis of the West Midlands parish of Halesowen shows the population growing through the late thirteenth and early fourteenth centuries, until the calamities of 1317–1321 reduced it by some 15 percent. Growth resumed during the 1320s, reaching a peak in the late 1340s, but then the Black Death reduced the inhabitants of Halesowen by nearly half.[1] The crisis of 1317–1321 and the Black Death would have affected vast areas of England in much the same way it affected Halesowen. Yet it remains uncertain whether England's entire population grew slowly, declined slowly, or held even during the half-century before 1348. On the enormous demographic impact of the Black Death, however, all would agree.

The Black Death appears to have been a combination of two diseases: bubonic plague, carried by black rats and spread by the fleas that they carried and infected, and pneumonic plague, spread by direct human contagion. Bubonic plague came first, arriving from the East aboard rat-infested merchant ships and spreading swiftly among a population whose resistance may perhaps have been weakened by malnutrition. It was quickly followed by pneumonic plague—which results when a person with a respiratory infection contracts bubonic plague. In these two forms, the Black Death was spread by contacts both between human and flea and between human and human. The lively European trade in (rat-infested) grain may explain why the plague spread so swiftly.

Arriving at the Mediterranean ports of southern Europe during the winter of 1347–1348, the plague moved northward into France. The French monk Guillaume de Nangis described it as

> . . . so great a mortality of people of both sexes . . . that it was scarcely possible to bury them. They were only ill for two or three days and died suddenly, their bodies almost sound. And he who was in good health one day was dead and buried the next. They had swellings in the armpits and groin, and the appearance of these swellings was an unmistakable sign of death. . . . In many towns, great and small, the priests were terrified and fled, but some monks and friars, being braver, administered the sacraments. Soon, in many places, of every twenty inhabitants only two remained alive. The mortality was so great at the hospital in Paris that for a long time more than 500 bodies were carried off on wagons each day, to be buried at the cemetery of the Holy Innocents. And the holy sisters of the hospital, fearless of death, carried out their task to the end with the most perfect gentleness and humility. These sisters were all wiped out by death. . . .

In the summer of 1348 the Black Death reached England. It first broke out at the port of Melcombe Regis in Dorset, then spread through the southwestern shires. By winter it was in London, and by the following

---

[1] Zvi Razi, *Life, Marriage and Death in a Medieval Parish: Economy, Society and Demography in Halesowen, 1270–1400* (New York, 1980).

A Physician and His Assistants Provide Care for a Plague Victim (The Granger Collection)

summer it was at its peak, ravaging the heavily populated counties of eastern England. "So great a pestilence," wrote a Lincolnshire monk, "had never been seen, heard, or written of before this time. . . . Even the flood of Noah's days had not, it was thought, swept away so great a multitude." The fourteenth-century historian Henry Knighton described it in these words:

> In Leicester, in the little parish of St. Leonard, more than 380 people died; in the parish of the Holy Cross more than 400; and in the parish of St. Margaret in Leicester more than 700. And so in each parish they died in great numbers. . . . And the sheep and cattle wandered about through the fields and among the crops, and there was nobody to go after them or to collect them. They perished in countless numbers everywhere, in secluded ditches and hedges, for lack of watching, since there was such a lack of serfs and servants that nobody knew what he should do. . . . Meanwhile there was such a lack of priests everywhere that many widowed churches had no divine services—no masses, matins, vespers, sacraments, or sacramentals. . . . Likewise many small villages and hamlets were completely deserted; not a single house remained in which any inhabitants were still alive. Many such hamlets will probably never again be inhabited.

Contemporary writers, shocked and terrified, may have exaggerated, but modern studies make it clear that the plague's toll was heavy. Some 35 percent of the population of Bristol succumbed. About 44 percent of the clergy perished in the dioceses of York and Lincoln, and nearly 50 percent in the dioceses of Exeter, Winchester, Norwich, and Ely. It has been estimated that half the English clergy may have died of plague. And yet the surviving population somehow endured the calamity without general panic or widespread flight. Life went on, agriculture and commerce continued, and the war with France persisted.

By the end of 1349 the Black Death had run its course. There is evidence of unusually numerous marriages and births in the years just following, as the English endeavored to preserve family lines and repopulate the land. But in 1361–1362 the plague returned, striking especially hard at the young people born since 1349. This "children's plague" was only the first of a long series of epidemics. The plague returned in 1369, 1374–1375, 1379, 1390, 1407, and periodically throughout the fifteenth century. For generations it remained a recurring hazard, keeping the people in a state of perpetual anxiety for their lives and the lives of their families. The population of England and the Continent dropped drastically in the wake of the plague and appears to have continued to decline for the next century and a half. It began to rise again only in the late fifteenth century. England's population in 1500 was probably only about half of what it had numbered two centuries earlier.

It is impossible to measure the grief brought by the plague, but one can comprehend its effects in more tangible ways—in the deserted villages, the temporary decline of the European wool market, and the severe shortage of labor. The Black Death vastly accelerated the already evident breakdown of high-medieval civilization. Among other things, it hastened the demise of the old manorial regime. Because the labor shortage brought about rising wages, and the population drop crippled the grain market, land profits and land values plummeted. Demesne farming became increasingly profitless and gradually disappeared almost entirely. Landlords tended to abandon direct farming, preferring to divide their old demesne lands into individual peasant plots and to live entirely off the rents, or, in some instances, to convert their lands to sheep raising. The effects of plunging population on the English peasantry were mixed, but many of the plague's peasant survivors profited from a more open, fluid society than they had known before and from a dramatic reversal of the previous land shortage. As one historian put it, the economic effects of the Black Death may well have been more purgative than toxic.

Political and Social Conflict

Social turmoil had been intensifying early in the fourteenth century during Edward II's reign, and in the later years of Edward III it increased still more. The Black Death played a large part in this, as did Edward III's failing leadership in his old age. But most important was the unhealthy trend toward so-called bastard feudalism, which had been gaining momentum ever since Edward I's reign. By the later fourteenth century, the custom of assembling permanent private armies of retainers—supported by their lords' wages and clad in their lords' liveries (uniforms)—was reaching its height. This practice of "livery and maintenance" was, in effect, the old feudal household system run amok. The contract, or indenture, between king and lord and between lord and military retainer had achieved full development during Edward III's French campaigns, and in the following decades, it contributed substantially to the general social chaos. Private military retinues sometimes terrorized the countryside, bringing about a breakdown in local government and an epidemic of local warfare. The English countryside had enjoyed relative peace in the High Middle Ages; in the fourteenth and fifteenth centuries, it was afflicted by widespread violence.

The social crisis reached its peak in Edward III's final years and in the reign of his successor. When Edward passed from his long dotage in 1377, he was succeeded by his ten-year-old grandson Richard II (1377–1399), son of the Black Prince. For the next decade, a regency government dominated by contending baronial factions ruled England. Plague, social disorder, and faltering royal leadership all contributed to the general gloom, as did the series of military humiliations England was suffering in France. Fear that the French would invade England darkened the years between 1377 and 1380, ending only with the death of the able French monarch, Charles V. But France had been suffering too, and the succession of a child to the French throne in 1380—the fitfully insane Charles VI—brought on a long era of strife centering on the rivalry of two royal uncles: the dukes of Burgundy and Orléans. Having long been battered by invading English armies and marauding mercenary companies, France now suffered the further torment of civil war. But England gained no immediate advantage from France's troubles. The duke of Burgundy was sufficiently strong to maintain military pressure against the English, and Richard II had no taste for large-scale campaigns in France.

Religious Ferment

The turmoil and pessimism of the later fourteenth century were accompanied by a surge of protest against the Church. Outcries against clerical wealth and spiritual hollowness were centuries old, but they grew more strident now. Plague and social upheaval created a mood of radicalism just when the Church was most vulnerable to pious condemnation.

Early in the century, the papacy had abandoned faction-ridden Rome for Avignon in what is today southern France. There it remained for seven decades, under the shadow of the French monarchy, devoting itself more and more to administration and to collecting its revenues with ever greater efficiency. Although at the time Avignon was a papal city, outside the jurisdiction of the king of France, to many the papacy seemed to have forfeited its international character, and its grasping fiscal policies were resented all the more. For the English, who were at war with France during much of the fourteenth century, having to pay taxes to a French pope aroused growing hostility. One contemporary grumbled that the pope was supposed to lead Christ's flock, not to fleece it. The situation worsened after 1378 when the Church split into two fragments—one led by a pope at Avignon, the other by a pope at Rome. This tragicomic schism persisted to the end of the fourteenth century and beyond.

Opposition to the papacy and the Church proceeded along several lines. The English Franciscan philosopher William of Ockham contended against not only the faith/reason synthesis of St. Thomas Aquinas but also against the complacency, greed, and corruption of the contemporary Church. An avowed enemy of papal authority, he argued that the Church should be governed and reformed through ecclesiastical councils, the selection of which ought to begin at the parish level. Some continental writers expressed similar and even more radical views. They suggested that the clergy should renounce its wealth or be deprived of it, and that the pope should withdraw from politics and restrict his attention to spiritual matters.

As confidence in the established ecclesiastical order waned, piety became more individualized. The later fourteenth century witnessed an upsurge of mysticism, for example, with works such as *The Revelations of Divine Love* by the hermit mystic Dame Julian of Norwich. The medieval Church had always found room for mystics but had never been entirely comfortable with them. Mysticism implies a direct relationship between the believer and God that—although rarely questioning the sacraments or the priesthood—seemed to bypass them and diminish their importance. The Church served its members as mediator between God and humanity, but mystics could potentially achieve an immediate link with God through the beatific vision.

The alienation of the ecclesiastical hierarchy from the individual believer is illustrated in quite different ways in the writings of two great literary figures of the late fourteenth century: William Langland and Geoffrey Chaucer. The works of these two men mark the emergence of the English language as a dominant literary vehicle after centuries of French linguistic supremacy. And both men disclose—each in his own manner—the growing popular hostility toward the ecclesiastical establishment.

Langland (d. after 1388), like the mystics of his time, had no great interest in the sacramental functions of the priesthood. But unlike the mystics, he was a moralist, not a contemplative: he loved the Church as it should be but despised it as it was. Perhaps one might more properly say that his love for the essential Church—the Body of Christ—prompted him to condemn the corrupt behavior of contemporary clergy all the more severely. Langland was neither a revolutionary nor a heretic. He revered the Church as the agent of human salvation and the vehicle of divine love. But he denounced the Franciscan and Dominican friars for their greed, the theologians for their complexity, and the papacy for its malign influence on simple Christian believers. More than anything else, Langland condemned the avarice and arrogance of the wealthy and the selfish cruelty of those in power, whether clergy or laity. To Langland, wealth hardened people's hearts and made them uncharitable, and the Church should therefore return to a condition of apostolic poverty. In his masterpiece, *Piers Plowman*, he wrote:

> Ah, well it may be with poverty, for he may pass untroubled,
> And in peace among the pillagers if patience follow him.
> Our prince, Jesus, and his apostles chose poverty together,
> And the longer they lived the less wealth they mastered....
> If possession is poison and makes imperfect orders,
> It would be well to dislodge them for the Church's profit
> And purge them of that poison before the peril is greater.

Not only the Church but all society was corrupted by wealth:

> As weeds run wild on ooze or on the dunghill,
> So riches spread upon riches give rise to all vices.
> The best wheat is bent before it ripens,
> On land overlaid with marl or the dungheap.
> And so are surely all such people.
> Overplenty feeds the pride which poverty conquers.

Langland was bitterly critical of his society, but like a Hebrew prophet, he softened his protests with a strain of hope—hope for a purified humanity moved by love rather than greed.

William Langland's morose moral sensitivity contrasts sharply with the mood of his genial and worldly-wise contemporary, Geoffrey Chaucer (c. 1343–1400). Chaucer's literary genius derived in part from his ability to portray with remarkable insight the personalities and motivations of his characters. He entered into their minds and displayed them for all to see, yet was able to remain personally aloof from them. He was neither a conscious reformer nor a prophet crying out against the sins of his age but an acute observer of human character. In that role, he was able to illuminate vividly the vices and virtues of contemporary clerics. The pilgrims depicted in his *Canterbury Tales* include the Parson—a compassionate and well-intentioned village priest—and the Oxford Clerk—absorbed in his disinterested devotion to scholarship. They also include less attractive ecclesiastical types: the superficial, mannered Prioress; the Pardoner, who was essentially a salesman of indulgences; the lecherous Summoner; the Monk, who was addicted to the pleasures of the hunt; and the corrupt Friar:

> Highly beloved and intimate was he
> With country folk wherever he might be,
> And worthy city women with possessions;
> For he was qualified to hear confessions,
> Or so he said, with more than priestly scope;
> He had a special license from the pope.
> Sweetly he heard his penitents at shrift
> With pleasant absolution, for a gift.[2]

---

[2] *The Canterbury Tales*, Nevill Coghill, tr. (Baltimore, 1952). Langland's *Piers Plowman* is translated into modern English by, among others, J. F. Goodridge (Baltimore, 1959).

Chaucer on Horseback
This illustration is taken from the Ellesmere manuscript, which was nearly contemporary with Chaucer. (The Mansell Collection)

Criticism and resentment of the contemporary Church also found expression at the political level. During the later thirteenth and early fourteenth centuries, the papacy considerably expanded its right of "provision"—of directly controlling the appointment of English clerics at all levels, from parish and canonry to archdiocese. The right of papal provision—which reflected the growing tendency toward ecclesiastical centralization—gave the papacy the power to appoint a large number of clergy in fourteenth-century England. Resentful of such extensive control of the English Church by the Avignon popes, Parliament gave its support in 1351 to the Statute of Provisors, which succeeded in limiting papal provisions—but only slightly. A second Statute of Provisors in 1390 was more effective, but the popes retained considerable influence on English ecclesiastical appointments for some time to come. In doing so, they ensured continuing resentment.

The old issue of appeals to the pope from the church courts of England remained acute throughout the fourteenth century. Statutes of the time attacked papal appeals as much as papal provisions. The first Statute of Praemunire (1353) sought to limit such appeals but actually had little effect on them. It was not until the third Statute of Praemunire in 1393 that the practice was seriously curtailed. Finally, an accelerating conflict over the pope's right to tax the English clergy further clouded Anglo-papal relations during the fourteenth century. The English protested vehemently against papal taxation in 1375 and 1376, and on two occasions Richard II refused it altogether. These struggles, although inconclusive, diminished the popes' hold on the English Church and constituted a political expression of the rising anticlericalism that affected society at all levels.

Fourteenth-century anticlericalism found its most eloquent spokesman in John Wycliffe (d. 1384), an Oxford philosopher of broad and deep learning.[3] Wycliffe's thought followed closely the tradition of medieval scholastic philosophy. It was also tinged with anticlerical protest like that already manifested in many ways—in popular opposition to ecclesiastical wealth and corruption, in hostility between the English government and the papacy, and in scholarly attacks on medieval theology and the church hierarchy by writers such as Ockham. The mystical doctrine of direct communion with God, short-circuiting the priestly sacramental system, also made a deep impact on Wycliffe. In addition, by the later fourteenth century the Church itself was noticeably weaker than it had been in the High Middle Ages. Its moral authority was declining, its monopoly on literacy and learning had been shattered long ago, and laymen now occupied high positions in the royal administration and judiciary that had once been the exclusive preserve of clerics. With the decline in land income brought about by the plague, the Church's revenue fell, and the clergy found themselves in bitter competition with the equally hard-pressed nobility and monarchy for the taxes of the English laity. Many people were prepared to listen respectfully to Wycliffe's reform proposals, and some were ready to follow him.

Wycliffe first attained repute as a gifted and fundamentally orthodox Oxford theologian. In the mid-1370s, he came under the protection of the most powerful magnate of the age, John of Gaunt, duke of Lancaster, a younger son of Edward III. Shielded by John of Gaunt's favor, he became active in politics and began to drift away from Catholic orthodoxy. After 1378, his heterodox doctrinal views prevented him from continuing his political career, and he devoted his final years to writing.

In these years, his opposition to the Church and to traditional Catholic doctrine deepened. He condemned the Church's vast landed wealth and suggested that the king had the right to seize it. He questioned the doctrine of the Eucharist as it was explained by previous Catholic philosophers. Influenced by the trend toward mysticism, he cast doubt on the entire priestly sacramental system. To Wycliffe, the organized Church was not the essential mediator between God and humanity. Rather, it was an agency responsible for guiding individual Christians on their spiritual quests.

---

[3] Anthony Kenny, *Wyclif* (Oxford, 1985), emphasizes the scholastic cast of Wycliffe's mind, downplays his radicalism, and shortens his name.

Indeed, the true Church was not limited to the clergy alone but included the entire body of believers.

Such, in brief, were John Wycliffe's new religious doctrines. Most of his English contemporaries, even though disenchanted with traditional Catholic Christianity, were not yet ready for them. William Langland's longing for a purification of the old order was more congenial to the mood of the times than Wycliffe's more fundamental objections. Yet Wycliffe's scholarly influence was great: hostility to the Church was growing, and there were some who adopted his views. His followers were known as Lollards (from the Middle English word *lollaerd*—mumblers [of prayers]). The Lollards included a handful of Oxford scholars, but most came from among the poor and outcast. To them, Wycliffe's religious views held appeal with their strong overtones of social revolution. Within a few years, Wycliffe's doctrines had spread to the Continent, where they influenced the views of the Bohemian reformer, John Hus. In 1415, the fathers of the Council of Constance burned John Hus at the stake (after luring Hus to the council on an imperial promise of safe conduct—a very clever gambit). But Hus's doctrines endured to influence the Protestant reformers of the sixteenth century.

England had not produced an influential heretic since the fifth century when Pelagius had so annoyed St. Augustine of Hippo. And Wycliffe appears to have caught the leaders of the English Church off guard. In time, however, they reacted against his teachings and had little difficulty in enlisting the support of the lay establishment. Wycliffe himself enjoyed John of Gaunt's protection to the end and therefore had the pleasure of dying a natural death in 1384. But the monarchy had already officially condemned his doctrines, and during the later part of Richard II's reign it became royal policy to hunt down Lollards. This policy of repression was strengthened by a statute of 1401 bearing the forthright title, the *Statute on the Burning of Heretics*. By the early fifteenth century the immediate crisis was over, but the seeds of religious protest had been planted and continued to germinate.

The Great Revolt of 1381

Ecclesiastical wealth evoked a powerful protest from all levels of society in the later fourteenth century. But as William Langland's poetry demonstrates, popular opposition was directed not only against wealthy prelates but against wealthy nobles as well:

> The poor may plead and pray in doorways,
> They may quake for cold and thirst and hunger.
> None receives them rightfully and relieves their suffering;
> They are hooted at like hounds and ordered away.

These words illustrate a profound sense of grievance that ripened into increasing social antagonism. In 1381, the tension burst in a bloody uprising of peasants, urban workers, and other laborers—a rebellion known traditionally (if not quite accurately) as the "Peasants' Revolt."[4] This tragic rebellion fed on the social and economic ills of the age. More specifically, it was a product of the growing conflict between landlord and tenant that arose from the Black Death, the falling population, and the shortage of labor. As the labor supply diminished, wages soared, and landlords, mostly from the smallholding gentry, faced an economic squeeze between rising labor costs and shrinking markets. Working through Commons, they obtained the legislation that they desired: an ordinance of 1349 that froze wages at pre-plague levels, followed in 1351 by the first of a series of Statutes of Laborers. These measures succeeded in limiting wage increases but failed to halt them altogether. Landlords often found themselves competing with one another for peasants' services, and a black market in labor resulted. Nevertheless, tenants and wage-earners felt wronged by this legislation and often held the opinion, not unfounded, that the ruling orders were conspiring against them.

This conviction received powerful confirmation from a series of poll taxes levied between 1377 and 1381. Traditionally, parliamentary grants had fallen primarily on the wealthy, but poll taxes were assessed on rich and poor alike, by head count. The Commons, hard-pressed by declining land revenues and convinced that the peasants and wage-laborers were having things too much their own way, seized on the idea of reducing their own tax burden at their workers' expense. The most severe poll tax, that of 1381, was intended to help fund military campaigns in the seemingly endless war with France. Laborers overwhelmingly refused to pay, however, and the government's heavy-handed efforts to enforce collection lit the fuse of the Great Revolt.

The uprising lasted scarcely a month—from late May 1381 to the end of June. In the end, the government suppressed the rebels and restored the old social order. The revolt was a hopeless endeavor, but for a brief time it shook society to its foundations, and for many years thereafter it was remembered with dread. A violent protest against the miserable conditions resulting from war, depression, grinding taxation, and plague, the event illustrates the deep hostilities that afflicted English society in the later Middle Ages.

The revolt began in Essex and spread to neighboring Kent. Its participants included not only peasants but malcontents from a wide spectrum of rural and urban society, including men of some wealth and experience in local affairs. Among its many leaders, the most prominent were the Kentishman Wat Tyler (whose family origins are quite unknown) and a former priest named John Ball, whose memorable couplet symbolizes the radical, Christian-based egalitarianism of the rebels:

---

[4] See E. B. Fryde, *The Great Revolt of 1381* (London, The Historical Association, 1981). Important contemporary documents are collected and translated in R. B. Dobson, ed., *The Peasants' Revolt of 1381* (London, 1970).

The Great Revolt of 1381 This illustration from the Chronicle of Jean Froissart shows John Ball preaching on social injustice. (The Mansell Collection)

> When Adam dug and Eve span,
> Who was then the gentleman?

Having terrorized and murdered a handful of nobles and gentry of their respective shires, the rebels converged on London in mid-June and ran wild in the city for two days, killing and burning. They murdered such notables as Simon Sudbury—archbishop of Canterbury and, as chancellor, head of the royal government—and Sir Robert Hales, the king's treasurer and prior of the wealthy crusading order of Knights Hospitalers in England. The remainder of the court—"marvelously discouraged" as one eyewitness aptly put it—took refuge in the Tower of London. Then, according to a contemporary observer, the rebel leaders proclaimed

> ... that anyone who could catch any Fleming or other alien of any nation might cut off his head, and so they did forthwith. Then they took the heads of the archbishop and of the others and put them on wooden poles and carried them before them in procession as far as the shrine of Westminster Abbey. ... Then they returned to London Bridge and set the head of the archbishop above the gate, with eight other heads of those they had murdered, so that all could see them who crossed over the bridge. Thereupon they went to the church of St. Martin's in the Vintry, and found within it thirty-five Flemings, whom they dragged out and beheaded in the street.

On that day there were beheaded about 140 or 160 people in all. Then they made their way to the houses of Lombards and other aliens and broke into their dwellings and robbed them of all their goods that they could lay hands on. This continued all that day and the night following, amidst hideous cries and horrid tumult.

Although hostile to the gentry, nobility, and foreign merchants, the rebels remained respectful of the monarchy. The terrified court, barricaded in the Tower, had no recourse but to send out the fourteen-year-old king, Richard II, to negotiate. There were parleys on two successive days between the young monarch and the rebel leaders, and contemporary accounts of these meetings disclose some of the diverse rebel goals. They demanded above all the abolition of villeinage—that is, the freeing of all peasants from the traditional work service on their lords' demesne fields. They further demanded a ceiling on rents—not to exceed fourpence per acre. Beyond these specific concessions, they sought a series of reforms that would have had no less drastic an effect than the overturning of the late medieval social order: equality of all men before the law, abolition of all lordship except the king's, confiscation and redistribution of all ecclesiastical property not essential to the direct sustenance of the clergy, and the elimination of all English bishoprics but one. More generally, the rebels demanded inclusion in the "community of the realm"—traditionally limited to magnates, prelates, wealthy burghers, and country gentry. They sought a voice in the kingdom's politics, a role in what one rebel leader called "the great society." Centuries thereafter, such hopes found wide support, but in 1381 they were wildly unrealistic.

Richard II, having no real choice, submitted to the rebels for the moment. At the first of his two parleys with them, he agreed to some of their demands, including total amnesty and freedom from villein status. The jubilant rebels spent the evening in wild celebration. On the following day, at the second parley, the rebel force was considerably reduced by widespread and very severe hangovers and by the desertion of many who thought that their cause was won. Their leader, Wat Tyler, for reasons unknown, threatened one of the king's followers by brandishing a dagger, and the Lord Mayor of London responded by seizing and mortally wounding him. Tyler's followers were quieted by the young king's alert offer to be their leader. He led them out of London and they then dispersed. Perhaps they believed that they had triumphed. In fact, however, once they withdrew from London, their revolt was doomed. Although they continued to terrorize the countryside for the next week or two—pillaging monasteries, burning manors, and plundering towns—the rebellion quickly lost its initial enthusiasm. By the end of June the rebel bands had been suppressed and the old social order restored. The concessions were of course forgotten, but the rebels had gained one thing: out of fear of another such uprising, the government dropped the idea of taxing the entire population. The plan was not revived until the late twentieth century under Prime Minister Margaret Thatcher in 1989–1990, and it was one of the causes of her being driven from office, not by peasants but by conservatives.

In 1381, however, Richard II remained in office and crushed the Peasants' Rebellion:

> Afterwards the king sent out his messengers into divers parts to capture the evildoers and put them to death. And many were taken and hanged in London, and they set up many gallows around the city of London and in other cities and boroughs of the south country. At length, as it pleased God, the king saw that too many of his faithful subjects would be undone, and too much blood spilled, and he took pity in his heart and granted them full pardon, on condition that they should never rise again, under penalty of death or mutilation, and that each of them should get his charter of pardon, and pay the king, as a fee for sealing the charter, twenty shillings for his enrichment. And so finished this wicked war.

The Great Revolt had no real chance to overturn fourteenth-century society. Yet some of its goals were realized in the next few decades through the operation of basic economic forces. The old demesne economy was no longer paying its way, and English villeinage was rapidly disappearing of its own accord. A villein was essentially one who was bound to perform work services for his lord, and as demesne lands were divided more and more into tenants' plots, work service became unnecessary. By the early fifteenth century, the old manorial regime was all but dead, and villeinage was dying with it.

As the fourteenth century closed, the age of crisis was drawing to an end. The following century, although socially divided and deeply troubled, witnessed no repetition of the Great Revolt and produced no heretic of Wycliffe's stature. Aristocratic warfare reached a new level of intensity, but basic social and ecclesiastical institutions stood unchallenged. The epoch of transition from medieval to modern England was far from over, but the first great social and cultural upheaval had passed.

The Reign of Richard II (1377–1399)

Richard II owed his succession to the fact that his father, Edward the Black Prince, was Edward III's eldest son. The Black Prince died in 1376, Edward III died in 1377, and Richard II was thereupon raised to the throne at the age of ten (see the chart on page 267).[5] In the kingdom he inherited, the political-economic balance among crown, magnates, and gentry had shifted substantially since the days of Edward I. The ongoing expenses of war had forced the crown long ago to turn to Parliament for help, and in the course of Edward III's reign Commons had come to demand an ever greater voice in royal policy in return for its subsidies. The expansion and consolidation of

---

[5] On Richard II, see R. H. Jones, *The Royal Policy of Richard II: Absolutism in the Latter Middle Ages* (Oxford, 1968), a short, perceptive interpretation of the reign. See also Gervase Mathew, *The Court of Richard II* (London, 1968), and Anthony Tuck, *Richard II and the English Nobility* (London, 1973). There are some excellent special studies in F. R. H. DuBoulay and C. M. Barron, eds., *The Reign of Richard II: Essays in Honour of May McKisack* (London, 1971).

baronial estates and the growth of private armies had raised a handful of magnates to positions of formidable power and wealth. Parliament's efforts to control the royal council had culminated, during the Good Parliament of 1376, in the development of a process by which the Commons could remove unpopular royal ministers by impeachment. And Edward II's fall back in 1327 had demonstrated that, as a last resort, Parliament might formally depose the king.

Throughout his reign, Richard II strove to revive royal power and to restore the monarchy to what he believed was its rightful position of authority over the realm. His goal was to establish a regime of royal absolutism, but in pursuing that goal he so alienated a powerful group of magnates that he himself was deposed. It took the English monarchy a century to recover from the catastrophe. Although Richard II has sometimes been viewed as an unsuccessful precursor of the Tudors, his policies can be regarded more accurately as the last hurrah of Norman and Angevin royal power—as a final effort to re-create the powerful monarchy of the twelfth century and bring it to fruition.

Richard himself possessed courage and determination, as his behavior during the Peasants' Revolt makes clear. He was small in stature and perhaps slightly hunchbacked; his portraits disclose a sensitive, anxious face. Thoughtful and moody, he was a connoisseur of the arts who lacked keen intelligence and political acumen. And he was devoted to the cult of sacred kingship. Particularly during his last years, he preoccupied himself with the symbols and ceremonies of monarchy: he stressed the sacred qualities of the royal anointment, displayed the sun on his banners, and turned ordinary court procedures into elaborate and colorful pageants. In these and other ways, he gave visible expression to his lofty notions of royal absolutism. No monarch had ever surrounded himself with so much regal display as Richard. And none had pursued a royalist policy under such unfavorable circumstances.

In 1380 Parliament dismissed the regency council that had ruled during the opening years of Richard's reign. In the years just following, Richard surrounded himself with loyal friends, thereby creating a "court party" faithful to the crown. He favored these friends with earldoms, duchies, and high offices at court, and with their advice and support, he embarked on his policy of absolutism—heedless of the opinions of magnates and gentry outside his inner circle. The more successful of the Norman and early Angevin kings would never have made such a mistake.

The barons were in no sense a monolithic force. If anything they were even more faction-ridden than ever. They were at odds not only with one another but also with the gentry and townspeople, who now exercised considerable power in the Commons. But all classes found the young Richard's independent course alarming, and his position was rendered all the more insecure by a continuing series of military reverses abroad. Rumors circulated that some of Richard's court favorites were pocketing revenues intended for warfare and were plotting with foreign enemies. In 1381 and 1382 members of Parliament unsuccessfully demanded investigations of the king's household expenses. In 1384 two royal favorites were accused of financial irregularities. Richard, showing none of Edward III's pliancy, charged the accusers with defamation of character and punished them harshly. In 1385 Parliament requested an annual review of the household accounts, and although the king permitted the drawing up of an ordinance to that effect he never implemented it. Instead, he continued his hazardous policy of isolating his court and household from the meddling of the community.

In 1386 Parliament's dissatisfaction intensified. Thus far relations between crown and community had been tempered by the moderating influence of John of Gaunt, duke of Lancaster and younger son of Edward III. As uncle of the king, John of Gaunt had a foothold in court, and as England's wealthiest magnate—master of the immense Lancastrian inheritance through marriage—he was a political figure of commanding influence. But in 1386 he departed for a military adventure in Spain, and in his absence both court and community acted with less restraint. The Parliament of autumn 1386 demanded the dismissal of Richard's chancellor, Michael de la Pole. Richard responded that he would not dismiss even one of his kitchen scullions at Parliament's request. Thereupon, Parliament reminded him that if a king refused to govern with the assent of his people, a clear precedent existed "for deposing the king himself from the throne and elevating some close relative of the royal line." Abashed, Richard gave in, and Commons impeached Michael de la Pole on charges of graft and maladministration—misdeeds of which de la Pole was by no means entirely innocent.[6] Even more important, Parliament appointed a new royal council to govern for a year and authorized it to control revenues, supervise household expenses, and reform the royal government.

Early in 1387 Richard departed from Westminster—where the new council was sitting—taking with him his household and court favorites, including de la Pole. Ruling once again through his inner circle, he ignored the parliament-appointed council and did not return to Westminster until its year of power had almost expired. Meanwhile, he placed a series of constitutional questions before a group of England's chief justices, and they answered exactly as the king wished: they judged that the parliament-appointed council offended the royal prerogative and was therefore illegal, and that those who had forced it on the king should be punished as traitors (the customary penalty for treason was death). The judges proclaimed further that it was treason to hinder in any way the king's exercise of his royal power, that Parliament had no right to make demands on the king before granting him requested subsidies, and that the king was empowered to dissolve any parliament at his pleasure. Finally, they stated that no parliament could lawfully impeach any minister of the king without royal con-

---

6 See J. S. Roskell's meticulous analysis, *The Impeachement of Michael de la Pole, Earl of Suffolk, in 1386 in the Context of the Reign of Richard II* (Manchester, England, 1984).

sent, and that it was an act of treason to view Edward II's deposition as a legal precedent.

These judgments represented an unqualified assertion of the royal prerogative—a firm statement of the philosophy of royal absolutism that Richard cherished. According to this view, the king's counselors were to be chosen by the king alone and were responsible to the king alone. Parliament too was to be a royal tool, summoned and dismissed at the king's will. And anyone who acted contrary to these rules was subject to condemnation for treason. King Edward I would have nodded in his tomb.

But the judges' rulings had no effect on the king's enemies. Indeed, Richard's defiance united opposition against him. In November 1387, a group of magnates approached the king at Westminster and brought charges of treason against several of his favorites. Richard promised to arrest those accused and hold them until the next parliament, when the "appeal" of treason would be judged. In reality he was merely playing for time, and he permitted his accused favorites to remain at liberty. But in February 1388, the dissident magnates routed a royalist army at Radcot Bridge in Oxfordshire, leaving Richard with no adequate means of defending himself. Lacking the necessary military power, he submitted to the magnates and accepted their "appeals" against his favorites.

The so-called Merciless Parliament met in 1388 to hear the appeals of five great magnates. These "lords appellant" entered the assembly with almost unbelievable pomposity, "arm in arm, clad in cloth of gold," to prosecute their case. Dominated by them and their supporters, the Merciless Parliament convicted the accused counselors and executed several others as well. Michael de la Pole was sentenced to hang, but he had already fled to France, never to return. Richard's court circle disintegrated, and for the king there now remained no choice but to cooperate with his magnates and his parliaments. The barons appointed a new royal council whose members swore to support all acts of Parliament. And the five lords appellant requested and received £20,000 for their efforts and expenses "in procuring the salvation of the realm and the destruction of the traitors."

The Merciless Parliament stands as the central political event of Richard II's reign. It marks the zenith of parliamentary power and the nadir of the royal prerogative in fourteenth-century England. The lords appellant themselves justified their actions on legal and constitutional grounds, but their behavior betrays cruelty and vindictiveness. Like so many victorious magnates before them, they went too far. The magnitude of their triumph evoked venomous factionalism and widespread dissent. Moreover, England's wars abroad fared no better under the new government than before. The French campaigns remained hopelessly bogged down, and in 1388 an invading Scottish army inflicted a crushing defeat on the English. In 1389 John of Gaunt returned from Spain, and in the years that followed, Richard II enjoyed his tacit support. With events thus turning in his favor, Richard was able in 1389 to dismiss his baronial council and rule once more through counselors of his own choosing. The baronial council withdrew without protest, and Richard was again the master of his court.

For the next eight years the king mended his fences. In the style of Edward III, he cooperated with barons and Parliament in governing his realm. He did not abandon his dreams of royal absolutism, but he pursued them more cautiously than before. Gritting his teeth, he showed honor and favor even toward the lords appellant. And slowly he succeeded in building around him a new circle of trustworthy supporters. Meanwhile he tried to free himself from total financial dependence on Parliament by ending the war with France. A definitive peace eluded him, but he did succeed in arranging a truce that was to last for twenty-eight years. He sealed it by taking as his royal bride the princess Isabella, eldest daughter of the half-mad king of France, Charles VI. Isabella was a girl of six, but Richard himself was still in his twenties and could seemingly afford to wait some years for an heir. And Isabella brought with her a dowry of 800,000 francs.

Accordingly, when Richard returned to England with his child-bride late in 1396 his financial position was vastly improved. The dowry helped, and the freedom from war expenses helped still more. No longer did he have to go begging to Parliament or to permit parliamentary subsidies to hamper his exercise of the royal prerogative. Working through his sheriffs and other local administrators, he packed the spring Parliament of 1397 with his own supporters and overawed it with his military retainers. When a member of Commons demanded that royal household expenses be reduced, he was arraigned for treason and convicted. And the lords in Parliament ratified the king's declaration that anyone who "shall move or excite the Commons of Parliament or any other person to make remedy of any matter which touches our person, our government, or our regality, shall be considered a traitor."

With the situation so encouraging, Richard took his long-awaited vengeance on the lords appellant. The autumn parliament of 1397, again packed with royalists, moved savagely against all the king's former enemies—depriving them of their lands and liberty, forcing some into exile and executing others. Three of the lords appellant now suffered the irony of being themselves "appealed" in Parliament for treason. One of the three was murdered, a second legally executed, and a third banished from the realm. Richard II confiscated lands on an immense scale and redistributed them among a new group of magnates, some of them close friends of the king. A parliament of 1398 formally revoked all the acts of the Merciless Parliament, and everyone involved in antiroyalist activity during 1387 and 1388 was obliged to sue (that is, pay) for the royal pardon. The royalist opinions of the 1387 judges were now resurrected and, with Parliament's assent, declared to be the law of the realm. And Richard, anxious to secure still greater independence from annual parliamentary grants, demanded and received a lifetime privilege of collecting the subsidies on wool. Financially and constitutionally, the English throne had never stood higher. But standing so high, it was unstable.

Intoxicated by these triumphs, Richard lost all restraint. He forced huge loans from the burghers and assessed heavy fines on a number of shires for failing to support him in his struggle against the lords appellant ten years before. In autumn 1398, he banished the two remaining lords appellant, one of whom was Henry Bolingbroke, son and heir of the wealthy and aged John of Gaunt, duke of Lancaster. When Gaunt died early in 1399, the king refused to consider the claims of the banished heir. Henry Bolingbroke's sentence of exile was extended from ten years to life, and Richard seized the vast Lancastrian lands.

Henry Bolingbroke had been a very considerable landholder in his own right. At the time of his exile, he held the title Duke of Hereford. The addition of the Lancastrian patrimony would have made him a magnate of almost kingly wealth, and it is understandable that Richard would fear the concentration of such prodigious resources in the hands of any single magnate—particularly one who had formerly opposed him. Nevertheless, the king's seizure of the Lancastrian inheritance kindled the fear of the landholding aristocracy. Security of inheritance had always been of vital concern to the great noble families, and they now found themselves ruled by a king who flaunted the rights of noble heirs. Richard's throne had never seemed as secure as it was in early 1399, yet in fact the king could count on little support outside his immediate circle. He had sown hostility among all the articulate classes in the land. Supremely confident, he led an expedition into Ireland in the summer of 1399. While he was away, Henry Bolingbroke returned to England to claim his Lancastrian inheritance by force.

As a son of John of Gaunt and a grandson of Edward III, Henry Bolingbroke possessed the necessary royal blood, and when he landed in Yorkshire and moved southward, one magnate after another rallied to him. The aim of the rebels was not merely to install Bolingbroke in his Lancastrian estates but to make him king of England in Richard's stead. Richard returned from Ireland to find his cause abandoned. In August 1399, he negotiated with Henry's supporters and agreed to restore the Lancastrian patrimony. On his departure from the meeting, Richard was ambushed, forced to abdicate, and hauled off to a prison room in the Tower of London. Parliament received his abdication in September and recognized Henry Bolingbroke as King Henry IV of England. Richard died in captivity early in 1400—he was probably murdered—and the new Lancastrian dynasty stood unchallenged. But Richard II's deposition, which reinforced the precedent of Edward II's, left the Lancastrians an uncertain legacy and a tottering throne.

Whereas Edward II had been deposed because of his weakness, Richard fell because of his strength. He had pitted himself against a long and potent trend toward shared power between crown and community—a trend that by the late fourteenth century had progressed too far to be easily reversed. The magnates were by then extremely powerful, and the burghers and gentry had become politically articulate. None of them could be ignored. In his final years, Richard tried to control them by fear and failed. A century thereafter, when the Tudors succeeded at last in rebuilding royal authority, they did so on a sturdy foundation of popular support. That idea does not seem to have occurred to Richard II.

The Capture of Richard II
From a manuscript of Jean
Froissart's *Chronicles of France
and England* (c. 1460–1480).
(Reproduced with permission
of the British Library)

Conclusion

The fall of Richard II marks an appropriate end to a century of violence and
turmoil, a fundamental turning point in English politics. A king had been
deposed in 1327 but was succeeded by his eldest son and unquestioned heir.
With Richard II's forced resignation in 1399, the very concept of hereditary
succession was thrown into doubt. For Richard was the last of the Plantagenet kings. He had no son. The succession was irregular for the first time
in 200 years. Because legitimate succession was basic to the politics of the
High Middle Ages, the compromising of that principle in 1399 rocked the
political order. For the next century rival families contended for the throne,
afflicting England with misrule and civil war. Not until the establishment
and consolidation of the Tudor dynasty generations later was the destruc-
tive work of 1399 repaired.

The transition from medieval to modern England was far from complete in 1399. The English continued to suffer from recurring plagues, social
unrest, and political confusion. In emphasizing a change in dynasty, one
must not be misled into ignoring more subtle changes that were still in

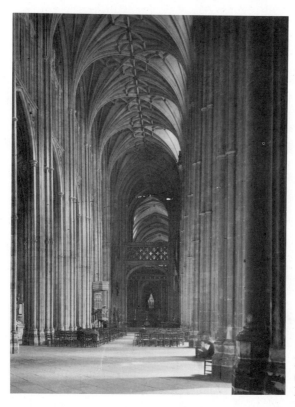

**Canterbury Cathedral
Nave (1379–1405)**
(National Monuments
Record)

process and would remain so for generations. As the period closed, England's population continued to fall, its struggle with France remained unresolved, its economy was spotty, its commitment to the Roman Church was slowly dissolving, and its countryside was turbulent. Yet for all that, England in 1399 was not a society in decline but a society in transition. There was anxiety and suffering, but there was also tremendous creativity. People such as Chaucer, Langland, and Wycliffe displayed originality of a degree that would ornament any age. More than that, all three demonstrated a heightened sense of national identity. Chaucer and Langland were crucial figures in the development of English as an important literary vehicle. Wycliffe dreamed of an English translation of the Bible and accorded the king a central position in the governance of the English Church. Richard II's reign was also a great creative age in the evolution of Perpendicular Gothic architecture—witness the naves of Canterbury and Winchester and the choir of York. The new architectural style was not only impressive in itself but also less continental, more distinctly English, than earlier Gothic styles had been. At this same time English merchants, who had once allowed their foreign rivals to dominate English trade, were creating lucrative new markets for themselves across northern Europe.

As the fourteenth century closed, all Europe was slipping gradually from medieval Catholic universalism toward modern nationalism. England was still a kingdom, not yet a nation. But it was becoming increasingly English as time went on—moving perceptibly toward the England of the Tudors and the Stuarts. In many respects the transition required a rejection of things medieval: feudalism, scholasticism, Christian universalism. But in other respects, modern England was built on medieval foundations: king, council, household, Parliament, the university, the tradition of scientific scholarship, the conquest of fields from forest and marsh, and the common law. More basic still was the growing awareness among the English that they were a single people—a conviction that began with Augustine of Canterbury, Bede, and Theodore of Tarsus and grew as the Middle Ages progressed. Many of the fundamental ingredients of modern English society and culture were clearly in evidence by 1399. They illustrate the essential medieval contribution to the making of England.

Appendix

The English Kings from Alfred to Henry IV

The Anglo-Saxon Kings

Alfred   871–899
Edward the Elder   899–924
Athelstan   924–939
Edmund   939–946
Eadred   946–955
Eadwig   955–959
Edgar the Peaceable   959–975
Edward the Martyr   975–978

Ethelred the Unready   978–1016
Edmund Ironside   1016
Canute   1016–1035
Harold Harefoot   1035–1040
Harthacanute   1040–1042
Edward the Confessor   1042–1066
Harold Godwinson   1066

The Norman Kings

William I (the Conqueror)   1066–1087
William II (Rufus)   1087–1100

Henry I   1100–1135
Stephen   1135–1154

The Angevin (Plantagenet) Kings

Henry II   1154–1189
Richard I (Lion-Hearted)   1189–1199
John   1199–1216
Henry III   1216–1272

Edward I   1272–1307
Edward II   1307–1327
Edward III   1327–1377
Richard II   1377–1399

The Lancastrian Kings

Henry IV   1399–1413

Bibliography

Bibliographies

Altschul, Michael. *Anglo-Norman England, 1066–1154.* Conference on British Studies Bibliographical Handbooks. Cambridge, 1969.

Bates, David. *A Bibliography of Domesday Book.* 1986.

Berger, Sidney E. *Medieval English Drama: An Annotated Bibliography of Recent Criticism.* 1990.

Bonser, Wilfrid. *An Anglo-Saxon and Celtic Bibliography (450–1087).* 2 vols. 1957.

_____. *A Romano-British Bibliography, 55 B.C.–A.D. 449.* 1964.

Boyce, Gray C. *Literature of Medieval History, 1930–1975.* 5 vols. 1981.

Elton, Sir Geoffrey, and others, eds. *Royal Historical Society: Annual Bibliography of British and Irish History.* 1976 ff. (Annual volumes for 1975 ff.)

Graves, Edgar B. *A Bibliography of English History to 1485.* 1975.

Guth, DeLloyd J. *Late Medieval England, 1377–1485.* Conference on British Studies Bibliographical Handbooks. Cambridge, 1976.

Keynes, Simon. *Anglo-Saxon History: A Select Bibliography.* 1987.

Mullins, E. L. C. *A Guide to the Historical and Archaeological Publications of Societies in England and Wales, 1901–1933.* 1968.

_____. *Texts and Calendars, I: An Analytical Guide to Serial Publications.* Royal Historical Society. 1958.

_____. *Texts and Calendars, II: An Analytical Guide to Serial Publications, 1957–1982.* Royal Historical Society. 1983.

Rosenthal, Joel T. *Anglo-Saxon History: An Annotated Bibliography, 450–1066.* 1985.

Royal Historical Society. *Writings on British History, 1901–1933.* Vol. II, *The Middle Ages, 450–1485.* 1968. The Royal Historical Society published annual supplements for each of the years 1934–1939.

Royal Historical Society. *Writings on British History, 1940–1945.* 2 vols. Vol. I, 1960. See further volumes in this series, published under the auspices of the University of London Institute of Historical Research, for 1946–1948, 1949–1951, 1952–1954, 1955–1957, 1958–1959, 1960–1961, etc.

Wilkinson, Bertie. *The High Middle Ages in England, 1154–1377.* Conference on British Studies Bibliographical Handbooks. 1978.

Reference Works

Cokayne, George E. *The Complete Peerage of England, Scotland, Ireland, Great Britain, and the United Kingdom.* Ed. by Vicary Gibbs et al. 13 vols. 1910–1959 (reprinted 1984).

Fryde, E. B., D. E. Greenway, S. Porter, and I. Roy, eds. *Handbook of British Chronology.* 3rd ed. Royal Historical Society. 1986.

Knowles, David, C. N. L. Brooke, and Vera London, eds. *The Heads of Religious Houses, England and Wales, 940–1216.* 1972.

Knowles, David, and R. N. Hadcock. *Medieval Religious Houses: England and Wales.* 2nd ed. 1971.

Manley, John. *Atlas of Prehistoric Britain.* 1989.

Sanders, I. J. *English Baronies: A Study of their Origin and Descent, 1086–1327.* 1960.

Spufford, Peter, with Wendy Wilkinson and Sarah Tolley. *Handbook of Medieval Exchange.* Royal Historical Society. 1986.

Stephen, Leslie, and Sidney Lee, eds. *The Dictionary of National Biography from the Earliest Times to 1900.* 22 vols. 1921–1922.

Woodcock, Thomas, and John Martin Robinson. *The Oxford Guide to Heraldry.* 1988.

General and Political History

General Medieval

Barrow, G. W. S. *Feudal Britain: The Completion of the Medieval Kingdoms, 1066–1314.* Paperback ed. 1972.

Bartlett, Robert, and Angus Mackay, eds. *Medieval Frontier Societies.* 1990.

Black, E. L. *Royal Brides: Queens of England in the Middle Ages.* 1987.

Bloch, Marc. *The Royal Touch: Sacred Monarchy and Scrofula in England and France.* 1973.

Brooke, Christopher. *From Alfred to Henry III, 871–1272.* 1961.

———. *The Saxon and Norman Kings,* rev. ed. 1978.

Brown, R. Allen, H. M. Colvin, and A. J. Taylor. *A History of the King's Works.* Vols. I and II, *The Middle Ages.* London, 1963.

Clanchy, Michael T. *England and its Rulers, 1066–1272: Foreign Lordship and National Identity.* 1983.

———. *From Memory to Written Record: England, 1066–1307.* 1979.

Davies, R. R. *Conquest, Coexistence, and Change: Wales, 1063–1415.* 1987.

———. *Domination and Conquest: The Experience of Ireland, Scotland and Wales, 1100–1300.* 1990.

Davies, Wendy. *Patterns of Power in Early Wales.* 1990.

———. *Wales in the Early Middle Ages.* 1982.

Dickinson, W. C. *Scotland from the Earliest Times to 1603.* 3rd ed. 1977.

Douglas, D. C. and George Greenaway, eds. and trs. *English Historical Documents.* Vol. II, *1066–1189.* 2nd ed. 1981.

Duncan, Archibald A. M. *Scotland: The Making of the Kingdom.* 1975.

Frame, Robin. *The Political Development of the British Isles, 1100–1400.* 1990.

Galbraith, V. H. *Kings and Chroniclers: Essays in English Medieval History.* 1982.

Given Wilson, Chris, and Alice Curteis. *The Royal Bastards of Medieval England.* 1984.

Jones, Michael, and Malcolm Vale. *England and Her Neighbors, 1066–1453: Essays in Honour of Pierre Chaplais.* 1989.

King, Edmund. *Medieval England, 1066–1485.* 1988.

Lloyd, J. E. A. *A History of Wales from the Earliest Times to the Edwardian Conquest.* 3rd ed. 2 vols. 1967.

Loyn, Henry. *The Middle Ages: A Concise Encyclopedia.* 1989.

Myers, A. R., ed. and tr. *English Historical Documents.* Vol. IV, *1327–1485.* 1969.

Owen, D. Huw, ed. *Settlement and Society in Wales.* 1989.

Reeves, A. C. *The Marcher Lords. A New History of Wales.* 1983.

Richardson, H. G. *The English Jewry under the Angevin Kings.* 1960.

Roth, Cecil. *A History of the Jews in England.* 3rd ed. 1964.

Rothwell, Harry, ed. and tr. *English Historical Documents.* Vol. III, *1189–1327.* 1975.

Sayles, G. O. *The Functions of the Medieval Parliament of England.* 1988.

Southern, R. W. *Medieval Humanism and Other Studies.* 1970.

Walker, David. *The Norman Conquerors. A New History of Wales.* 1977.

Whitelock, Dorothy, ed. and tr. *English Historical Documents.* Vol. I, *c. 500–1042.* 2nd ed. 1979.

Roman and Anglo-Saxon

An outstanding annual publication, *Anglo-Saxon England,* Cambridge, 1972 ff., is devoted to the history, archaeology, literature, and culture of this era.

Alcock, Leslie. *Arthur's Britain: History and Archaeology,* A.D. *367–634.* 1971.

Arnold, C. J. *Roman Britain to Saxon England.* 1984.

Barlow, Frank. *Edward the Confessor.* 1970.

Bassett, Steven, ed. *The Origins of Anglo-Saxon Kingdoms.* Studies in the Early History of Britain. 1989.

Blair, Peter Hunter. *Anglo-Saxon Northumbria.* 1984.

————. *An Introduction to Anglo-Saxon England.* 2nd ed. 1977.

————. *Northumbria in the Days of Bede.* 1976.

Brown, P. David, *Anglo-Saxon England.* 1978.

Burrell, Roy E. C. *The Romans in Britain.* 1971.

Campbell, James, ed. *The Anglo-Saxons.* 1982.

————. *Essays in Anglo-Saxon History.* 1986.

Chadwick, Nora K., ed. *Celt and Saxon: Studies in the Early British Border.* 1963.

————. ed. *Studies in Early British History.* 1954.

Chaney, William A. *The Cult of Kingship in Anglo-Saxon England.* 1970.

Clemoes, Peter, and Kathleen Hughes, eds. *England Before the Conquest: Studies in Primary Sources Presented to Dorothy Whitelock.* 1971.

Collingwood, R. G., and I. A. Richmond. *The Archaeology of Roman Britain.* Rev. ed. 1969.

Crossley-Holland, Kevin, ed. *The Anglo-Saxon World.* 1982.

Davies, Wendy. *Patterns of Power in Early Wales.* 1990.

————. *Wales in the Early Middle Ages.* 1982.

Driscoll, Stephen T., and Margaret R. Nieke, eds. *Power and Politics in Early Medieval Britain and Ireland.* 1988.

Dudley, Donald R., and Graham Webster. *The Roman Conquest of Britain,* A.D. *43–57.* British Battle Series. 1965.

Dumville, David, and Gillian Jondorf. *France and Britain in the Early Middle Ages.* 1990.

Dumville, David, and Michael Lapidge. *Gildas: New Approaches.* 1984.

Esmonde Cleary, A. S. *The Ending of Roman Britain.* 1990.

Evison, Vera I. *The Fifth-Century Invasions South of the Thames.* 1965.

Farmer, D. H., ed. *The Age of Bede.* Rev. ed. 1983.

Fisher, D. J. V. *The Anglo-Saxon Age, c. 400–1042.* 1973.

Fleming, Robin. *Kings and Lords in Conquest England.* 1991.

Frere, Sheppard S. *Britannia: A History of Roman Britain.* 3rd ed. 1987.

Harrison, David. *England Before the Norman Conquest.* 1978.

Hill, David. *An Atlas of Anglo-Saxon England.* 1981.

Hodges, Richard. *The Anglo-Saxon Achievement: Archaeology and the Beginnings of English Society.* 1989.

John, Eric. *Orbis Britanniae and Other Studies.* 1966.

Johnson, Stephen. *Later Roman Britain.* 1980.

Jones, Martin. *England Before Domesday.* 1986.

Keynes, Simon, and Michael Lapidge, eds. and trs. *Alfred the Great: Asser's Life of King Alfred and Other Contemporary Sources.* 1983.

Laing, Lloyd. *Celtic Britain.* 1979.

——, and Jennifer Laing. *Anglo-Saxon England.* 1979.

Larson, Laurence, M. *Canute the Great 995–1035 and the Rise of Danish Imperialism during the Viking Age.* 1912.

Levison, Wilhelm. *England and the Continent in the Eighth Century.* 1946.

Loyn, Henry R. *The Vikings in Britain.* 1977.

Morris, John. *The Age of Arthur, a History of the British Isles from 350 to 650.* 1973.

Myres, J. N. L. *The English Settlements.* The Oxford History of England. 1986.

Nash-Williams, Victor E. *The Roman Frontier in Wales.* 2nd ed. 1969.

Pollington, Stephen. *The Warrior's Way: England in the Viking Age.* 1989.

Richmond, I. A., ed. *Roman and Native in North Britain.* 1958.

——, ed. *Roman Britain.* Rev. ed. 1964.

Ritchie, R. L. Graeme. *The Normans in England Before Edward the Confessor.* 1948.

Ronay, Gabriel. *The Lost King of England: The East European Adventures of Edward the Exile.* 1990.

Salway, Peter H. *Roman Britain.* 1981.

Sawyer, Peter H. *From Roman Britain to Norman England.* 1978.

——. *Kings and Vikings.* 1982.

Smith, L. *The Making of Britain: The Dark Ages.* 1984.

Smyth, A. P. *Scandinavian Kings in the British Isles, 850–880.* 1977.

Somerset Fry, Plantagenet. *Roman Britain.* 1984.

Stafford, Pauline. *Unification and Conquest: A Political and Social History of England in the Tenth and Eleventh Centuries.* 1989.

Stanley, E. G., ed. *British Academy Papers on Anglo-Saxon England.* 1990.

Stenton, F. M. *Anglo-Saxon England.* 3rd ed. Oxford History of England. 1971.

——. *Preparatory to Anglo-Saxon England,* ed. Doris M. Stenton. 1970.

Thompson, E. A. *St. Germanus of Auxerre and the End of Roman Britain.* 1984.

Todd, Malcolm. *Roman Britain, 55 B.C.–A.D. 400.* 1981.

Webster, Graham. *Boudica: The British Revolt Against Rome* A.D. *160.* 1978.

_____, ed. *Fortress into City: The Consolidation of Roman Britain, First Century* A.D. 1988.

_____. *The Roman Invasion of Britain.* 1980.

Whittock, Martyn J. *The Origins of England, 410–600.* 1986.

Wilson, David. *The Anglo-Saxons.* 3rd ed. 1981.

Woods, J. Douglas, and David A. E. Pelteret, eds. and trs. *The Anglo-Saxons: Synthesis and Achievement.* 1985.

Wormald, Patrick, with Donald Bullough and Roger Collins, eds. *Ideal and Reality in Frankish and Anglo-Saxon Society: Studies Presented to J. M. Wallace-Hadrill.* 1983.

Norman Conquest to Magna Carta

Two excellent annual periodicals focus on the history and culture of the Anglo-Norman world and its neighbors: *Anglo-Norman Studies* (Woodbridge, Suffolk, 1979 ff.) and *The Haskins Society Journal: Studies in Medieval History,* ed. Robert B. Patterson (London, 1989 ff.).

Appleby, John T. *England Without Richard, 1189–1199.* 1965.

_____. *John, King of England.* 1960.

_____. *The Troubled Reign of King Stephen.* 1970.

Barlow, Frank. *The Feudal Kingdom of England, 1042–1216.* 4th ed. 1988.

_____. *The Norman Conquest and Beyond.* 1983.

_____. *William I and the Norman Conquest.* 1965.

_____. *William Rufus.* 1983.

Bates, David. *William the Conqueror.* 1989.

Bernstein, David J. *The Mystery of the Bayeux Tapestry.* 1986.

Brown, R. Allen. *Castles, Conquest, and Charters: Collected Papers.* 1989.

_____. *The Norman Conquest, Documents of Medieval History.* 1984.

_____. *The Normans.* 1984.

_____. *The Normans and the Norman Conquest.* 2nd ed. 1985.

Brundage, James A. *Richard Lion Heart: A Biography.* 1974.

Cassady, Richard F. *The Norman Achievement.* 1986.

Chibnall, Marjorie. *Anglo-Norman England, 1066–1166.* 1987.

Cronne, H. A. *The Reign of Stephen, 1135–54: Anarchy in England.* 1970.

Crouch, David. *The Beaumont Twins: The Roots and Branches of Power in the Twelfth Century.* 1986.

_____. *William Marshall: Court, Career, and Chivalry in the Angevin Empire, 1147–1219.* 1990.

David, C. W. *Robert Curthose, Duke of Normandy.* 1920.

Davis, R. H. C. *King Stephen, 1135–1154.* 3rd ed. 1990.

Douglas, David C. *The Norman Achievement, 1050–1100.* 1969.

_____. *The Norman Fate, 1100–1154.* 1976.

_____. *William the Conqueror: The Norman Impact upon England.* 1964.

Flanagan, Marie Therese. *Irish Society, Anglo-Norman Settlers, Angevin Kingship: Interactions in Ireland in the Late Twelfth Century.* 1990.

Freeman, Edward A. *The History of the Norman Conquest of England.* 6 vols. 1867–1879.

——. *The Reign of William Rufus and the Accession of Henry I.* 2 vols. 1882.

Gibbs-Smith, Charles H. *The Bayeux Tapestry.* 1973.

Gillingham, John. *The Angevin Empire.* 1984.

——. *Richard the Lionheart.* 2nd ed. 1989.

Harper-Bill, Christopher, Christopher J. Holdsworth, and Janet L. Nelson. *Studies in Medieval History Presented to R. Allen Brown.* 1989.

Hollister, C. Warren, ed. *The Impact of the Norman Conquest.* 1969.

——. *Monarchy, Magnates, and Institutions in the Anglo-Norman World.* 1986.

Holt, J. C. *The Northerners: A Study in the Reign of King John.* 1961.

Kapelle, William E. *The Norman Conquest of the North: The Region and its Transformation, 1000–1135.* 1979.

Kelly, Amy. *Eleanor of Aquitaine and the Four Kings.* 1950.

Kibler, William W., ed. *Eleanor of Aquitaine: Patron and Politician.* 1976.

Le Patourel, John. *Feudal Empires, Norman and Plantagenet.* 1984.

——. *The Norman Empire.* 1976.

Loyn, Henry R. *The Norman Conquest.* 3rd ed. 1982.

Matthew, D. J. A. *The Norman Conquest.* 1966.

Maund, K. L. *Ireland, Wales and England in the Eleventh Century.* 1990.

Nelson, Lynn H. *The Normans in South Wales, 1070–1171.* 1966.

Newman, Charlotte. *The Anglo-Norman Nobility in the Reign of Henry I: The Second Generation.* 1988.

Norgate, Kate. *England under the Angevin Kings.* 2 vols. 1887.

Painter, Sidney. *The Reign of King John.* 1949.

Pernoud, Rigine. *Eleanor of Aquitaine.* 1968.

Poole, Austin Lane. *From Domesday Book to Magna Carta, 1087–1216.* 2nd ed. Oxford History of England, 1955.

Powicke, F. M. *The Loss of Normandy, 1189–1204.* 2nd ed. 1961.

Ritchie, R. L. Graeme. *The Normans in Scotland.* 1954.

Round, John Horace. *The Commune of London and Other Studies.* 1899.

——. *Geoffrey de Mandeville, A Study of the Anarchy.* 1892.

Searle, Eleanor. *Predatory Kinship and the Creation of Norman Power, 840–1066.* 1988.

Thorpe, Lewis, ed. *The Bayeux Tapestry and the Norman Invasion.* 1973.

Turner, Ralph V. *Men Raised from the Dust: Administrative Service and Upward Mobility in Angevin England.* 1988.

Warren, W. L. *The Governance of Norman and Angevin England, 1086–1272.* 1987.

——. *Henry II.* 1973.

——. *King John.* 1978 (first published in 1961).

Whitelock, Dorothy, et al. *The Norman Conquest: Its Setting and Impact.* 1966.

Wilkinson, Donald, and John Cantrell, eds. *The Normans in Britain.* 1987.

Wilson, David M. *The Bayeux Tapestry: The Complete Tapestry in Colour.* 1985.

Thirteenth Century

Carpenter, D. A. *The Minority of Henry III.* 1990.

Chancellor, John. *The Life and Times of Edward I.* 1981.

Clifford, E. R. A. *A Knight of Great Renown: The Life and Times of Othon de Grandson.* 1961.

Coss, P. R., and S. D. Lloyd, eds. *Thirteenth-Century England, 2, Proceedings of the Newcastle-upon-Tyne Conference, 1987.* Woodbridge, Suffolk, 1988.

Cuttino, George P. *English Diplomatic Administration, 1259–1339.* 2nd ed. 1971.

_____. *English Medieval Diplomacy.* 1985.

Denholm-Young, N. *Richard of Cornwall.* 1947.

Galbraith, V. H. *Roger Wendover and Matthew Paris.* 1944.

Given, James. *State and Society in Medieval Europe: Gwynedd and Languedoc under Outside Rule.* 1990.

Herbert, Trevor, and Gareth Elwyn Jones. *Edward I and Wales.* 1988.

Labarge, Margaret Wade. *Simon de Montfort.* 1962.

Lloyd, S. D. *English Society and the Crusades, 1216–1307.* 1988.

Ormond, Mark, ed. *England in the Thirteenth Century: Proceedings of the 1984 Harlaxton Symposium.* Woodbridge, Suffolk, 1986.

Painter, Sidney. *William Marshal.* 1933.

Powicke, F. M. *King Henry III and the Lord Edward: The Community of the Realm in the Thirteenth Century.* 2nd ed. 2 vols. 1947.

_____. *The Thirteenth Century, 1216–1307.* 2nd ed. Oxford History of England. 1962.

Prestwich, Michael. *Edward I.* 1988.

_____. *War, Politics, and Finance under Edward I.* 1972.

Salzman, L. F. *Edward I.* 1968.

Stacey, Robert C. *Politics, Policy, and Finance Under Henry III, 1216–1245.* 1987.

Treharne, R. F. *The Baronial Plan of Reform, 1258–1263.* Rev. ed. 1971.

_____. *Simon de Montfort and Baronial Reform: Thirteenth-Century Essays.* E. B. Fryde, ed. 1986.

Fourteenth Century

Allmand, C. T. *The Hundred Years War: England and France at War, c. 1300–c. 1450.* 1988.

Barber, Richard. *Edward, Prince of Wales and Aquitaine: A Biography of the Black Prince.* 1978.

Barrow, G. W. S. *Robert Bruce and the Community of the Realm of Scotland.* 3rd ed. 1988.

Brown, Alfred L. *The Governance of Late-Medieval England, 1272–1461.* 1989.

Bruce, Marie Louise. *The Usurper King: Henry of Bolingbroke, 1366–1399.* 1986.

Denton, Jeffrey H., and John P. Dooley. *Representatives of the Lower Clergy in Parliament, 1295–1340.* 1987.

DuBoulay, F. R. H., and C. M. Barron, eds. *The Reign of Richard II: Essays in Honour of May McKisack.* 1971.

Fowler, Kenneth. *The Age of Plantagenet and Valois: The Struggle for Supremacy, 1328–1498.* 1967.

_____, ed. *The Hundred Years War.* 1971.

_____. *The King's Lieutenant: Henry of Grosmont, First Duke of Lancaster, 1310–1361.* 1969.

Fryde, Natalie. *The Tyranny and Fall of Edward II, 1321–1326.* 1979.

Given-Wilson, Chris. *The English Nobility in the Late Middle Ages: The Fourteenth Century Political Community.* 1987.

Hallam, Elizabeth M. *The Itinerary of Edward II and His Household, 1307–1328.* 1984.

Hamilton, J. S. *Piers Gaveston, Earl of Cornwall, 1307– 1312: Politics and Patronage in the Reign of Edward II.* 1988.

Holmes, G. A. *The Later Middle Ages, 1272–1485.* 1962.

Jones, R. H. *The Royal Policy of Richard II: Absolutism in the Later Middle Ages.* 1968.

Kaeuper, Richard W. *War, Justice, and Public Order: England and France in the Later Middle Ages.* 1988.

Keen, M. H. *England in the Later Middle Ages.* 1973.

Landen, J. R. *The Limitations of English Monarchy in the Later Middle Ages.* 1989.

McKisack, May. *The Fourteenth Century, 1307–1399.* Oxford History of England. 1959.

Maddicott, J. R. *The English Peasantry and the Demands of the Crown, 1294–1341.* 1975.

——. *Law and Lordship: Royal Justices as Retainers in Thirteenth- and Fourteenth-Century England.* 1978.

——. *Thomas of Lancaster, 1307–1322.* 1970.

Mathew, Gervase. *The Court of Richard II.* 1968.

Nicholson, Ranald. *Edward III and the Scots: The Formative Years of a Military Career, 1327–1335.* London, 1965.

Packe, Michael. *King Edward III.* L. C. B. Seaman, ed. 1983.

Palmer, J. J. N. *England, France, and Christendom, 1377–1399.* 1972.

Perroy, Edouard. *The Hundred Years War.* W. B. Wells, tr. 1951.

Phillips, J. R. S. *Aymer de Valence: Earl of Pembroke, 1307–1324.* 1972.

Prestwich, Michael. *The Three Edwards: War and State in England, 1272–1377.* 1981.

Roskell, I. S. *The Impeachment and Trial of Michael de la Pole, Earl of Suffolk, in 1386 in the Context of the Reign of Richard II.* 1984.

Russell, P. E. *The English Intervention in Spain and Portugal in the Time of Edward III and Richard II.* 1955.

Senior, Michael. *The Life and Times of Richard II.* 1981.

Taylor, John, and Wendy Childs. *Politics and Crisis in Fourteenth-Century England.* 1990.

Tout, T. F. *The Place of the Reign of Edward II in English History.* 2nd ed. 1936.

Tuck, Anthony. *Crown and Nobility, 1272–1461: Political Conflict in Late-Medieval England.* 1985.

——. *Richard II and the English Nobility.* 1974.

Vale, Juliet. *Edward III and Chivalry: Chivalric Society and its Context, 1270–1350.* 1982.

Vale, M. G. A. *The Angevin Legacy: The Hundred Years' War, 1250–1340.* 1990.

Walker, Simon. *The Lancastrian Affinity, 1361–1399.* 1990.

Waugh, Scott L. *England in the Reign of Edward III.* 1991.

Wilkinson, Bertie. *The Later Middle Ages in England, 1216–1485.* 1969.

Local and Regional Studies

An extremely valuable series of regional histories of England is being published by Longman, London and New York (1985 ff.) under the general editorship of Barry Cunliffe and David Hey. The volumes already published at this writing are: J. V. Beckett, *The East Midlands from AD 1000*; J. H. Betty, *Wessex from AD 1000*; Peter Brandon and Brian Short, *The South East from AD 1000*; Peter Drewett, David Rudling, and Mark Gardiner, *The South East to AD 1000*; David Hey, *Yorkshire from AD 1000*; Nick Higham, *The Northern Counties to AD 1000*; Marie B. Rowlands, *The West Midlands from AD 1000*; and Malcolm Todd, *The South West to AD 1000*. Other valuable local and regional studies are:

Biddick, Kathleen. *The Other Economy: Pastoral Husbandry on a Medieval Estate.* 1989.

Biddle, Martin. *Crafts and Industries of Medieval Winchester: Objects of Medieval Winchester.* 2 vols. 1990.

____. ed. *Winchester in the Early Middle Ages: An Edition and Discussion of the Winton Domesday.* 1976.

Brooke, Christopher, with Gillian Kier. *London, 800–1216: The Shaping of a City.* 1975.

Crawford, Barbara E. *Scandinavian Scotland: Scotland in the Early Middle Ages* 2. 1987.

Coleman, M. Clare. *Downham-in-the-Isles: A Study of an Ecclesiastical Manor in the Thirteenth and Fourteenth Centuries.* 1984.

Douglas, David C. *The Social Structure of Medieval East Anglia.* 1927.

DuBoulay, F. R. H. *The Lordship of Canterbury: An Essay on Medieval Society.* 1966.

Dyer, Christopher. *Lords and Peasants in a Changing Society: The Estates of the Bishopric of Worcester, 680–1540.* 1980.

Everitt, Alan. *Continuity and Colonization: The Evolution of Kentish Settlement.* 1986.

Finberg, H. P. R. *Tavestock Abbey: A Study in the Social and Economic History of Devon.* 2nd ed. 1969.

Harvey, Barbara. *Westminster Abbey and its Estates in the Middle Ages.* 1977.

Hill, J. W. F. *Medieval Lincoln.* 1948.

Hinton, David A. *Alfred's Kingdom: Wessex and the South, 800–1500.* 1977.

Keene, Derek. *Survey of Medieval Winchester.* 2 vols. 1985.

Miller, Edward. *The Abbey and Bishopric of Ely: The Social History of an Ecclesiastical Estate from the Tenth Century to the Early Fourteenth Century.* 1951.

Raftis, J. Ambrose. *The Estates of Ramsey Abbey: A Study in Economic Growth and Organization.* 1957.

____. *Warboys: Two Hundred Years in the Life of an English Medieval Village.* 1964.

Razi, Zvi. *Life, Marriage and Death in a Medieval Parish: Economy, Society and Demography in Halesowen, 1270–1400.* 1980.

Rosser, Gervaise. *Medieval Westminster, 1200–1540.* 1989.

Rubin, Miri. *Charity and Community in Medieval Cambridge.* 1987.
Searle, Eleanor. *Lordship and Community: Battle Abbey and its Banlieu, 1066–1538.* 1974.
Walker, David. *Medieval Wales.* 1990.
Williams, Gwyn A. *Medieval London: From Commune to Capital.* 1963.

Legal, Constitutional, and Governmental History

General Medieval

Baker, John Hamilton. *An Introduction to English Legal History.* 1990.
Bean, J. M. W. *The Decline of English Feudalism, 1215–1540.* 1968.
———. *From Lord to Patron: Lordship in Late Medieval England.* 1989.
Bellamy, John G. *Bastard Feudalism and the Law.* 1989.
Butt, Ronald. *A History of Parliament: The Middle Ages.* 1989.
Cam, Helen Maud. *Law-Finders and Law-Makers in Medieval England.* 1962.
———. *Liberties and Communities in Medieval England.* 1944.
Chaplais, Pierre. *Essays in Medieval Diplomacy and Administration.* 1981.
Chrimes, S. B. *An Introduction to the Administrative History of Medieval England.* 3rd ed. 1980.
Cockburn, J. S., and Thomas A. Green, eds. *Twelve Good Men and True: The Criminal Trial Jury in England, 1200–1800.* 1988.
Davies, Wendy, and Paul Fouracre, eds. *The Settlement of Disputes in Early Medieval Europe.* 1986.
Denholm-Young, N. *Seignorial Administration in England.* 1937.
Edwards, J. G. *Historians and the Medieval English Parliament.* 1960.
———. *The Second Century of the English Parliament.* 1979.
Fryde, E. B., and Edward Miller, eds. and trs. *Historical Studies of the English Parliament. Vol. I, Origins to 1399.* 1970.
Harriss, G. L. *King, Parliament and Public Finance in Medieval England to 1369.* 1975.
Haskins, George L. *The Growth of England Representative Government.* 1948.
Hearder, H., and Henry R. Loyn, eds. *British Government and Administration: Studies Presented to S. B. Chrimes.* 1974.
Helmholz, Richard H. *Canon Law and the Law of England.* 1987.
Howell Margaret. *Regalian Right in Medieval England.* 1962.
Hoyt, Robert S. *The Royal Demesne in English Constitutional History, 1066–1272.* 1950.
Hunnisett, R. F. *The Medieval Coroner.* 1961.
Jewell, Helen M. *English Local Administration in the Middle Ages.* 1972.
Jolliffe, J. E. A. *The Constitutional History of Medieval England from the English Settlement to 1485.* 4th ed. 1961.
Keeney, Barnaby C. *Judgment by Peers.* 1949.
Lyon, Bryce. *A Constitutional and Legal History of Medieval England.* 2nd ed. 1980.
———. *From Fief to Indenture.* 1957.
Milsom, S. F. C. *Studies in the History of the Common Law.* 1985.
Mitchell, Sydney Knox. *Taxation in Medieval England.* 1951.

Morris, William A. *The Medieval English Sheriff to 1300*. 1927.

Palmer, Robert C. *The County Courts of Medieval England, 1150–1350*. 1982.

Petit-Dutaillis, Charles, and Georges Lefebvre. *Studies and Notes Supplementary to Stubbs' Constitutional History*. 1930.

Plucknett, T. F. T. *Early English Legal Literature*. 1958.

____. *Studies in English Legal History*. 1983.

Pollock, Frederick, and Frederic William Maitland. *The History of English Law Before the Time of Edward I*. Rev. reissue of 2nd ed. 2 vols. 1968.

Poole, Austin Lane. *Obligations of Society in the XII and XIII Centuries*. 1946.

Ramsay, J. H. *A History of the Revenues of the Kings of England, 1066–1399*. 2 vols. 1925.

Richardson, H. G., and G. O. Sayles. *The English Parliament in the Middle Ages*. 1981.

____. *Parliaments and Great Councils in Medieval England*. 1961.

Sayers, Jane E. *Law and Records in Medieval England: Studies on the Medieval Papacy, Monasteries and Records*. 1988.

Sayles, G. O. *The King's Parliament of England*. 1974.

____. *Scripta Diversa*. 1982.

Schramm, Percy E. *A History of the English Coronation*. 1937.

Stubbs, William A. *The Constitutional History of England*. 6th ed. 3 vols. Oxford, 1897; abridged ed., Chicago, 1979.

Thorne, Samuel E. *Essays in English Legal History*. 1985.

Tout, T. F. *Chapters in the Administrative History of Medieval England*. 6 vols. 1920–1933.

Wolffe, B. P. *The Royal Demesne in English History: The Crown Estate in the Governance of the Realm from the Conquest to 1509*. 1971.

Young, Charles R. *The English Borough and Royal Administration, 1130–1307*. 1961.

____. *The Royal Forests of Medieval England*. 1979.

Roman and Anglo-Saxon

Abels, Richard. *Lordship and Military Obligation in Anglo-Saxon England*. 1988.

Chadwick, H. M. *Studies on Anglo-Saxon Institutions*. 1905.

Harmer, Florence E. *Anglo-Saxon Writs*. 1952.

Hollister, C. Warren. *Anglo-Saxon Military Institutions on the Eve of the Norman Conquest*. 1962.

John, Eric. *Land Tenure in Early England: A Discussion of Some Problems*. 1960.

Keynes, Simon. *The Diplomas of King Aethelred "The Unready' 978–1016: A Study in their Use as Historical Evidence*. 1980.

Loyn, H. R. *The Governance of Anglo-Saxon England, 500–1087*. 1984.

Oleson, Tryggvi J. *The Witenagemot in the Reign of Edward the Confessor*. 1955.

Norman Conquest to Magna Carta

Alexander, James W. *Ranulf of Chester: A Relic of the Conquest*. 1983.

Brown, R. Allen. *Origins of English Feudalism*. 1973.

Cheney, C. R. *Hubert Walter* 1967.

Galbraith, V. H. *Domesday Book: Its Place in Administrative History.* 1974.

——. *The Making of Domesday Book.* 1961.

Green, Judith A. *The Government of England under Henry I.* 1986.

Hallam, Elizabeth M. *Domesday Book through Nine Centuries.* 1986.

Hinde, Thomas. *The Domesday Book: England's Heritage, Then and Now.* 1985.

Hindley, Geoffrey. *The Book of Magna Carta.* 1990.

Holdsworth, Christopher, ed. *Domesday Essays.* Exeter Studies in History, no. 14. 1986.

Hollister, C. Warren. *The Military Organization of Norman England.* 1965.

Holt, J. C., ed. *Domesday Studies: Papers Read at the Novocentenary Conference of the Royal Historical Society and the Institute of British Geographers, Winchester, 1986.* 1987.

——. *Magna Carta.* 1965.

——, ed. *Magna Carta and the Idea of Liberty.* 1972.

——. *Magna Carta and Medieval Government.* 1985.

——. *The Northerners: A Study in the Reign of King John.* 1961.

Jolliffe, J. E. A. *Angevin Kingship.* 2nd ed. 1963.

Kealey, Edward J. *Roger of Salisbury, Viceroy of England.* 1972.

Keefe, Thomas K. *Feudal Assessments and the Political Community Under Henry II and His Sons.* 1983.

Keeton, George W. *The Norman Conquest and the Common Law.* 1966.

Poole, Reginald Lane. *The Exchequer in the Twelfth Century.* 1912.

Richardson, H. G., and G. O. Sayles. *The Governance of Mediaeval England from the Conquest to Magna Carta.* 1963.

——. *Law and Legislation from Aethelberht to Magna Carta.* 1966.

Round, John Horace. *Feudal England.* 1895.

Sawyer, Peter, ed. *Domesday Book: A Reassessment.* 1985.

Stenton, Doris M. *English Justice between the Norman Conquest and the Great Charter, 1066–1215.* 1964.

Stenton, F. M. *The First Century of English Feudalism, 1066–1166.* 2nd ed. 1961.

Sutherland, Donald W. *The Assize of Novel Disseisin.* 1973.

Turner, Ralph V. *The English Judiciary in the Age of Glanvill and Brackton, c. 1176–1239.* 1985.

——. *The King and His Courts: The Role of John and Henry III in the Administration of Justice, 1199–1240.* 1968.

——. *Men Raised from the Dust: Administrative Service and Upward Mobility in Angevin England.* 1988.

Van Caenegem, R. C. *The Birth of the English Common Law.* 2nd ed. 1988.

——. *Royal Writs from the Conquest to Glanvill.* 1959.

West, Francis J. *The Justiciarship in England, 1066–1232.* 1966.

Young, Charles R. *Hubert Walter, Lord of Canterbury and Lord of England.* 1968.

Thirteenth Century

Cam, Helen Maud. *Studies in the Hundred Rolls.* 1921.

Ellis, Clarence. *Hubert de Burgh.* 1952.

Hyams, Paul R. *Kings, Lords, and Peasants in Medieval England: The Common Law of Villeinage in the Twelfth and Thirteenth Centuries.* 1980.

Meekings, C. A. F. *Studies in Thirteenth-Century Justice and Administration.* 1981.

Milsom, S. F. C. *The Legal Framework of English Feudalism.* 1976.

Plucknett, T. F. T. *Edward I and Criminal Law.* 1960.

———. *The Legislation of Edward I.* 1949.

Powicke, Michael. *Military Obligation in Medieval England: A Study in Liberty and Duty.* 1962.

Waugh, Scott. *The Lordship of England: Royal Wardships and Marriages in English Society and Politics, 1217–1327.* 1988.

Fourteenth Century

Bellamy, J. G. *The Law of Treason in England in the Later Middle Ages.* 1970.

Booth, P. H. W. *The Financial Administration of the Lordship and County of Chester, 1272–1377.* 1981.

Buck, Mark. *Politics, Finance, and the Church in the Reign of Edward II: Walter Stapeldon, Treasurer of England.* 1983.

Edwards, J. G. *The Commons in Medieval English Parliaments.* 1958.

———. *The Second Century of the English Parliament.* 1979.

Given-Wilson, Chris. *The Royal Household and the King's Affinity: Service, Politics and Finance in England, 1360–1413.* 1986.

Hewitt, Herbert I. *The Organization of War under Edward III, 1338–1362.* 1966.

Holmes, George. *The Good Parliament.* 1975.

Lapsley, G. T. *Crown, Community, and Parliament in the Later Middle Ages: Studies in English Constitutional History.* Helen Maud Cam and Geoffrey Barraclough, eds. 1951.

Mackenzie, Kenneth R. *The English Parliament.* Rev. ed. 1959.

Palmer, Robert C. *The Whilton Dispute, 1264–1380: A Social-Legal Study of Dispute Settlement in Medieval England.* 1984.

Powell, J. Enoch, and Keith Wallis. *The House of Lords in the Middle Ages: A History of the English House of Lords to 1540.* 1968.

Raban, Sandra. *Mortmain Legislation and the English Church, 1279–1500.* 1983.

Roskell, J. S. *The Commons and their Speakers in English Parliaments, 1376–1523.* 1965.

Willard, J. F. et al., eds. *The English Government at Work, 1327–1336.* 3 vols. 1940–1950.

Economic and Social History

General Medieval

Arnold, Ralph. *A Social History of England, 55 B.C. to A.D. 1215.* 1967.

Aston, Michael, David Austin, and Christopher Dyer, eds. *The Rural Settlements of Medieval England: Studies Dedicated to Maurice Beresford and John Hurst.* 1989.

Aston, T. H., ed. *Landlords, Peasants, and Politics in Medieval England.* 1987.

Ault, Warren O. *Open Field Farming in Medieval England: A Study of Village By-Laws.* 1972.

Baker, A. R. H., and R. A. Butlin, eds. *Studies of Field Systems in the British Isles.* 1973.

Baker, Timothy. *Medieval London.* 1970.

Barraclough, Geoffrey. *Social Life in Early England.* 1960.

Bennett, Judith M. *Women in the Medieval English Countryside: Gender and Household in Brigstock Before the Plague.* 1987.

Beresford, Maurice. *The Lost Villages of England.* 1954.

———. *New Towns of the Middle Ages: Town Plantation in England, Wales and Gascony.* 1967.

———, and John Hurst, eds. *Deserted Medieval Villages.* 1989.

———, and J. K. S. St. Joseph. *Medieval England: An Aerial Survey.* 2nd ed. 1979.

Bolton, J. L. *The Medieval English Economy, 1150–1500.* 1980.

Brooke, Christopher, with Gillian Keir. *London, 800–1216: The Shaping of a City.* 1975.

Brooke, George C. *English Coins from the Seventh Century to the Present Day.* 3rd ed. 1950.

Bush, M. L. *The English Aristocracy: A Comparative Synthesis.* 1984.

Cantor, Leonard, ed. *The English Medieval Landscape.* 1982.

Carter, John Marshall. *Rape in Medieval England: An Historical and Sociological Study.* 1985.

Cornfield, Penelope J., and Derek Keene. *Work in Towns, 850–1850.* 1990.

Hallam, H. E. *Rural England, 1066–1348.* 1981.

Hanawalt, Barbara A. *The Ties that Bound: Peasant Families in Medieval England.* 1986.

Harding, Alan. *A Social History of English Law.* 1966.

Harvey, P. D. A., ed. *The Peasant Land Market in Medieval England.* 1984.

Hilton, R. H. *Class Conflict and the Crisis of Feudalism: Essays in Medieval Social History.* 1985.

Hinton, David A. *Archaeology, Economy and Society: England from the Fifth to the Fifteenth Century.* 1990.

Holt, J. C. *Robin Hood.* Rev. ed. 1989.

Holt, Richard, ed. *The Medieval Town: A Reader in English Urban History, 1200–1540.* 1990.

Kanner, Barbara, ed. *The Women of England from Anglo-Saxon Times to the Present.* 1979.

Keen, Maurice. *Chivalry.* 1984.

———. *The Outlaws of Medieval England.* Rev. ed. 1977.

King, Edmund. *England, 1175–1425.* 1979.

———. *Peterborough Abbey, 1086–1310: A Study in the Medieval Land Market.* 1973.

Langdon, John, *Horses, Oxen and Technological Innovation: The Use of Draught Animals in English Farming from 1066 to 1500.* 1986.

Lloyd, T. H. *Alien Merchants in England in the High Middle Ages.* 1982.

Longworth, Ian, and John Cherry, eds. *Archaeology in Britain since 1945: New Directions.* 1986.

Lucas, Angela M. *Women in the Middle Ages: Religion, Marriage, and Letters.* 1983.

Lunt, William E. *Financial Relations of the Papacy with England to 1327.* 1939.

——. *Financial Relations of the Papacy with England, 1327–1534.* 1962.

Miller, Edward, and John Hatcher. *Medieval England: Rural Society and Economic Change, 1086–1348.* 1978.

Moore, Ellen. *The Fairs of Medieval England: An Introductory Study.* 1985.

Orwin, Charles S., and Christabel S. Orwin. *The Open Fields.* 3rd ed. 1967.

Platt, Colin. *The Castle in Medieval England and Wales.* 1982.

——. *The English Medieval Town.* 1976.

——. *Medieval England: A Social History and Archaeology from the Conquest to 1600.* 1978.

Pollard, S., and D. W. Crossley. *The Wealth of Britain, 1085–1966.* 1968.

Postan, M. M. *Essays on Medieval Agriculture and General Problems of the Medieval Economy.* 1973.

——. *The Medieval Economy and Society: An Economic History of Britain, 1100–1500.* 1972.

——. *Medieval Trade and Finance.* 1973.

Power, Eileen. *Medieval Women.* M. M. Postan, ed. 1975.

——. *The Wool Trade in English Medieval History.* Oxford, 1941.

Pugh, Ralph B. *Imprisonment in Medieval England.* 1968.

Raftis, J. Ambrose. *Tenure and Mobility: Studies in the Social History of the Medieval English Village.* 1964.

Reynolds, Susan. *An Introduction to the History of English Medieval Towns.* 1977.

——. *Kingdoms and Communities in Western Europe, 900–1300.* 1984.

Roberts, Brian K. *The Making of the English Village: A Study in Historical Geography.* 1987.

——. *Rural Settlements in Britain.* 1977.

Rodwell, Warwick. *The Archaeology of Religious Places: Churches and Cemetaries in Britain.* Rev. ed. 1990.

Rosenthal, Joel, and Colin Richmond. *People, Politics and Community in the Later Middle Ages.* 1987.

Sawyer, P. H., ed. *English Medieval Settlement.* 1979.

Seebohm, Frederic. *The English Village Community.* 4th ed. 1890.

Stenton, Doris M. *English Society in the Early Middle Ages (1066–1307).* 4th ed. 1965.

——. *The English Woman in History.* 1957.

Tait, James. *The Medieval English Borough.* 1936.

Vinogradoff, Paul. *The Growth of the Manor.* 3rd ed. 1920.

——. *Villainage in England.* 1892.

Roman and Anglo-Saxon

Alcock, Leslie. *Economy, Society, and Warfare Among the Britons and Saxons.* 1987.

Birley, Anthony Richard. *Life in Roman Britain.* New ed. 1981.
——. *The People of Roman Britain.* 1980.
Blackburn, Mark, ed. *Anglo-Saxon Monetary History: Essays in Memory of Michael Dolley.* 1986.
Blunt, C. E., B. H. I. H. Stewart, and C. S. S. Lyon. *Coinage in Tenth-Century England: From Edward the Elder to Edgar's Reform.* 1989.
Dolley, R. H. M., ed. *Anglo-Saxon Coins: Studies Presented to Sir Frank Stenton.* 1961.
——. *Anglo-Saxon Pennies.* 1964.
Edwards, Nancy. *The Archaeology of Early Medieval Ireland.* 1990.
Fell, Christine, with Cecily Clark and Elizabeth Williams. *Women in Anglo-Saxon England and the Impact of 1066.* 1986.
Finberg, H. P. R., ed. *The Agrarian History of England and Wales.* Vol. I, pt. 2 (A.D. 43–1042). 1972.
Hanley, Robin. *Villages in Roman Britain.* 1987.
Hingley, Richard. *Rural Settlement in Roman Britain.* 1989.
Home, G. C. *Roman London,* A.D. *43–457.* 2nd ed. 1948.
Hooke, Della, ed. *Anglo-Saxon Settlements.* 1988.
Jackson, Kenneth. *Language and History in Early Britain: A Chronological Survey of the Brittonic Languages, First to Twelfth Century* A.D. 1953.
Liversidge, Joan. *Britain in the Roman Empire.* 1968.
Loyn, Henry R. *Anglo-Saxon England and the Norman Conquest.* 1962.
Maitland, Frederic W. *Domesday Book and Beyond.* 1897.
Margary, I. D. *Roman Roads in Britain.* 3rd ed. 1973.
Merrifield, Ralph. *The Archaeology of Ritual and Magic.* 1988.
——. *London, City of the Romans.* 1983.
Whitelock, Dorothy. *The Beginnings of English Society.* 1952.

Norman Conquest to Magna Carta

Darby, H. C. *Domesday England.* 1977.
Dolley, R. H. M. *The Norman Conquest and the English Coinage.* 1966.
Finn, R. Welldon. *Domesday Book: A Guide.* 1973.
——. *The Domesday Inquest and the Making of Domesday Book.* 1961.
——. *The Norman Conquest and its Effects on the Economy, 1066–86.* 1971.
Kealey, Edward J. *Harvesting the Air: Windmill Pioneers in Twelfth-Century England.* 1987.
——. *Medieval Medicus: A Social History of Anglo-Norman Medicine.* 1981.
Lennard, Reginald V. *Rural England, 1086–1135: A Study of Social and Agrarian Conditions.* 1959.
McDonald, John, and G. D. Snooks. *Domesday Economy: A New Approach to Anglo-Norman History.* 1986.
Painter, Sidney. *Studies in the History of the English Feudal Barony.* 1943. Reprinted 1980.
Rowley, Trevor. *The Norman Heritage, 1055–1200.* 1983.

Thirteenth Century

Altschul, Michael. *A Baronial Family in Medieval England: The Clares, 1217–1314.* 1965.

Given, James B. *Society and Homicide in Thirteenth-Century England.* 1977.

Hilton, R. H. *A Medieval Society: The West Midlands at the End of the Thirteenth Century.* 1966.

Homans, George C. *English Villagers of the Thirteenth Century.* 1941.

Kaeuper, Richard W. *Bankers to the Crown: The Riccardi of Lucca and Edward I.* 1973.

Lloyd, S. D. *English Society and the Crusades, 1216–1307.* 1988.

Titow, J. Z. *English Rural Society, 1200–1350.* 1969.

Treharne, R. F. *Essays on Thirteenth-Century England.* 1971.

Fourteenth Century

Barnie, John. *War in Medieval English Society: Social Values in the Hundred Years War, 1337–99.* 1974.

Bellamy, John. *Crime and Public Order in England in the Later Middle Ages.* 1973.

Bird, Brian. *Rebel Before His Time: The Story of John Ball and the Peasants' Revolt.* 1987.

Bird, Ruth. *The Turbulent London of Richard II.* 1949.

Bridbury, A. R. *Economic Growth: England in the Later Middle Ages.* Rev. ed. 1975.

Dobson, R. B. *The Peasants' Revolt of 1381.* 2nd ed. 1983.

DuBoulay, F. R. H. *An Age of Ambition: English Society in the Late Middle Ages.* 1970.

Dyer, Christopher. *Standards of Living in the Later Middle Ages: Social Change in England, c. 1200–1520.* 1989.

Fryde, E. B. *The Great Revolt of 1381.* The Historical Association. 1981.

Gottfried, Robert S. *Bury St-Edmunds and the Urban Crisis, 1290–1359.* 1982.

Hanawalt, Barbara A. *Crime and Conflict in English Communities, 1300–1348.* 1979.

Hilton, R. H. *Bond Men Made Free: Medieval Peasant Movements and the English Rising of 1381.* 1973.

———. *The Decline of Serfdom in Medieval England.* 2nd ed. 1983.

———. *The English Peasantry in the Later Middle Ages.* 1975.

———, and T. H. Aston, eds. *The English Rising of 1381.* 1984.

Holmes, G. A. *The Estates of the Higher Nobility in Fourteenth-Century England.* 1957.

Hybel, Nils. *Crisis or Change: The Concept of Crisis in the Light of Agrarian Structural Reorganization in Late-Medieval England.* 1989.

Keen, M. H. *English Society in the Late Middle Ages, 1348–1500.* 1991.

Logan, F. Donald, ed. *Norman London* (the description by William Fitz Stephen). 1990.

Maddicott, J. R. *The English Peasantry and the Demands of the Crown, 1294–1341.* Past and Present Supplements. 1975.

McFarlane, K. B. *The Nobility of Later Medieval England.* 1973.
Shrewsbury, J. F. D. *A History of Bubonic Plague in the British Isles.* 1970.
Thrupp, Sylvia. *The Merchant Class of Medieval London, 1300–1500.* 1948.
Ziegler, Philip. *The Black Death.* 1969.

Ecclesiastical History

General Medieval

Bettey, J. H. *Church and Community: The Parish Church in English Life.* 1979.
Blair, John, ed. *Minsters and Parish Churches: The Local Church in Transition, 950–1200.* 1988.
Butler, Lionel. *Medieval Monasteries of Great Britain.* 1987.
Colvin, H. M. *The White Canons in England.* 1951.
Dickinson, John C. *An Ecclesiastical History of England: The Later Middle Ages, From the Norman Conquest to the Reformation.* 1979.
———. *Monastic Life in Medieval England.* 1961.
Finucane, Ronald C. *Miracles and Pilgrims: Popular Beliefs in Medieval England.* 1977.
Harvey, Barbara F. *Monastic Dress in the Middle Ages: Precept and Practice.* 1988.
Hirsh, John C. *The Revelations of Margery Kemp: Paramystical Practices in Late Medieval England.* 1989.
Kemp, E. W. *An Introduction to Canon Law in the Church of England.* 1957.
Knowles, David. *The English Mystical Tradition.* 1961.
———. *The Monastic Order in England, 940–1216.* 2nd ed. 1963.
———. *The Religious Orders in England.* 3 vols. 1948–1959.
———. *Saints and Scholars: Twenty-Five Medieval Portraits.* 1962.
Lawrence, C. H., ed. *The English Church and the Papacy in the Middle Ages.* 1965.
———. *Medieval Monasticism: Forms of Religious Life in Western Europe in the Middle Ages.* 2nd ed. 1989.
Moorman, J. R. H. *The Grey Friars in Cambridge, 1225–1538.* 1952.
Rodes, Robert E., Jr. *Ecclesiastical Administration in Medieval England: The Anglo-Saxons to the Reformation.* 1977.
Roth, Francis. *The English Austin Friars, 1249–1538.* Vol. I. *History.* 1966.
Southern, R. W. *Western Society and the Church in the Middle Ages.* 1970.
Tyerman, Chrisotpher. *England and the Crusades, 1095–1588.* 1988.
Warren, Ann K. *Anchorites and their Patrons in Medieval England.* 1985.

Roman and Anglo-Saxon

Barley, M. W., and R. P. C. Hanson, eds. *Christianity in Britain, 300–700.* 1968.
Barlow, Frank. *The English Church, 1000–1066.* 2nd ed. 1979.
Brooks, Nicholas. *The Early History of the Church of Canterbury: Christ Church from 597 to 1066.* 1984.
Chadwick, Nora. *The Age of the Saints in the Early Celtic Church.* 1961.
Clayton, Mary. *The Cult of the Virgin Mary in Anglo-Saxon England.* 1990.

Dales, Douglas. *Dunstan: Saint and Statesman.* 1988.

Deanesly, Margaret. *The Pre-Conquest Church in England.* 2nd ed. 1963.

＿＿. *Sidelights on the Anglo-Saxon Church.* 1962.

Godfrey, John. *The Church in Anglo-Saxon England.* 1962.

Henig, Martin. *Religion in Roman Britain.* 1984.

Mayr-Harting, Henry. *The Coming of Christianity to Anglo-Saxon England.* 3rd ed. 1991.

Owen, Gail R. *Rites and Religions of the Anglo-Saxons.* 1981.

Ridyard, Susan J. *The Royal Saints of Anglo-Saxon England: A Study of West Saxon and East Anglian Cults.* 1988.

Rollason, D. W. *Saints and Relics in Anglo-Saxon England.* 1989.

Thomas, Charles. *Christianity in Roman Britain to A.D. 500.* 1981.

Webster, Graham. *Celtic Religion in Roman Britain.* 1987.

Whitelock, Dorothy, Martin Brett, and C. N. L. Brooke, eds. *Councils and Synods with Other Documents Relating to the English Church.* Vol. I, A.D. *871–1204,* Part 1, *871–1066.* 1981.

Norman Conquest to Magna Carta

Barlow, Frank. *The English Church, 1066–1154: A History of the Anglo-Norman Church.* 1979.

＿＿. *Thomas Becket.* 1986.

＿＿. *Thomas Becket and his Clerks.* 1987.

Brooke, Z. N. *The English Church and the Papacy from the Conquest to the Reign of King John.* 1931; reprinted with a new forward by C. N. L. Brooke, 1989.

Cheney, C. R. *English Bishops' Chanceries, 1100–1250.* 1950.

＿＿. *From Becket to Langton: English Church Government, 1170–1213.* 1956.

Cheney, Mary G. *Roger, Bishop of Worcester, 1164–1179.* 1980.

Chibnall, Marjorie. *The World of Orderic Vitalis.* 1984.

Dickinson, J. C. *The Origins of the Austin Canons and their Introduction into England.* 1950.

Elkins, Sharon K. *Holy Women of Twelfth-Century England.* 1988.

Gibson, Margaret. *Lanfranc of Bec.* 1978.

Hill, Bennett D. *English Cistercian Monasteries and their Patrons in the Twelfth Century.* 1968.

Jones, Thomas M. *The Becket Controversy.* 1970.

Knowles, David. *The Episcopal Colleagues of Archbishop Thomas Becket.* 1951.

＿＿. *Thomas Becket.* 1970.

Macdonald, A. J. *Lanfranc.* 2nd ed. 1944.

Matthew, D. J. A. *The Norman Monasteries and their English Possessions.* 1962.

Morey, Adrian, and C. N. L. Brooke. *Gilbert Foliot and His Letters.* 2 vols. 1965.

Nicholl, Donald. *Thurstan, Archbishop of York (1114–1140).* 1964.

Powicke, F. M. *Stephen Langton.* 1928.

Saltman, Avrom. *Theobald, Archbishop of Canterbury.* 1956.

Scammell, G. V. *Hugh du Puiset, Bishop of Durham.* 1956.

Smalley, Beryl. *The Becket Conflict and the Schools: A Study of Intellectuals in Politics in the Twelfth Century.* 1973.

Southern, R. W. *Saint Anselm and his Biographer: A Study in Monastic Life and Thought, 1059–c. 1130.* 1963.
———. *St. Anselm: A Portrait in a Landscape.* 1990.
Squire, Aelred. *Aelred of Rievaulx: A Study.* 1969.
Vaughn, Sally N. *The Abbey of Bec and the Anglo-Norman State, 1034–1136.* 1981.
———. *Anselm of Bec and Robert of Meulan: The Innocence of the Dove and the Wisdom of the Serpent.* 1987.
Whitelock, Dorothy, Martin Brett, and C. N. R. Brooke, eds. *Councils and Synods with Other Documents Relating to the English Church.* Vol. I, A.D. *871–1204,* Part II. *1066–1204.* 1981.
Wilks, Michael, ed. *The World of John of Salisbury.* Studies in Church History, Subsidia 3. 1984.

Thirteenth Century

Brentano, Robert J. *Two Churches: England and Italy in the Thirteenth Century.* 1968; new ed. with an additional essay by the author, 1988.
———. *York Metropolitan Jurisdiction and Papal Judges Delegate, 1279–1296.* 1959.
Denton, J. H. *Robert Winchelsey and the Crown, 1294–1313: A Study in the Defence of Ecclesiastical Liberty.* 1980.
Douie, D. L. *Archbishop Pecham.* 1952.
Hinnebusch, W. A. *The Early English Friars Preachers.* 1951.
Moorman, J. R. H. *Church Life in England in the Thirteenth Century.* Reprint with corrections. 1955.
Parker, Thomas W. *The Knights Templars in England.* 1963.
Sayres, Jane E. *Papal Government in England during the Pontificate of Honorius III (1216–1227).* 1984.
Wood, Susan. *English Monasteries and their Patrons in the Thirteenth Century.* 1955.

Fourteenth Century

Aston, Margaret. *England's Iconoclasts.* Vol. I: *Laws Against Images.* 1988.
———. *Lollards and Reformers: Images and Literacy in Late-Medieval Religion.* 1984.
———. *Thomas Arundel: A Study of Church Life in the Reign of Richard II.* 1967.
Dahmus, Joseph H. *William Courtenay, Archbishop of Canterbury, 1381–1396.* 1966.
Haines, Roy Martin. *Archbishop John Stratford: Political Revolutionary and Champion of the Liberties of the English Church, ca. 1275/80–1348.* 1986.
———. *The Church and Politics in Fourteenth-Century England: The Career of Adam Orleton, c. 1275–1345.* 1978.
Hudson, Anne. *Lollards and Their Books.* 1985.
———. *The Premature Reformation: Wycliffite Texts and Lollard History.* 1988.
———, and Michael Wilks, eds. *From Ockham to Wyclif.* Studies in Church History; Subsidia; 5. 1987.
McFarlane, K. B. *John Wycliffe and the Beginnings of English Nonconformity.* 1952.

Pantin, W. A. *The English Church in the Fourteenth Century.* 1955.

Robson, J. A. *Wyclif and the Oxford Schools.* 1961.

Thompson, A. Hamilton. *The English Clergy and their Organization in the Later Middle Ages.* 2nd ed. 1966.

Wright, J. Robert. *The Church and the English Crown, 1305–1334.* 1980.

Intellectual and Cultural History

General Medieval

Archer, Michael, Sarah Crewe, and Peter Cormack. *English Heritage in Stained Glass: Oxford.* 1988.

Bannon, W. R. J. *English Medieval Romance.* 1987.

Brewer, Derek, ed. *Studies in Medieval English Romances: Some New Approaches.* 1988.

Catto, J. I., ed. *The History of the University of Oxford.* Vol. I, *The Early Oxford Schools.* 1984.

Clifton-Taylor, Alec. *The Cathedrals of England.* 1970.

Clucas, Philip. *England's Churches.* 1984.

Cobban, Alan B. *The Medieval English Universities: Oxford and Cambridge to c. 1500.* 1988.

Coote, Stephen. *English Literature of the Middle Ages.* 1988.

Craig, Hardin. *English Religious Drama of the Middle Ages.* Rev. ed. 1964.

Crewe, Sarah. *Stained Glass in England, c. 1180–c. 1540.* 1987.

Denvir, Bernard. *From the Middle Ages to the Stewarts: Art Design and Society Before 1689.* 1988.

Gardner, Arthur. *English Medieval Sculpture.* Rev. ed. 1951.

Gransden, Antonia. *Historical Writing in England c. 550 to c. 1307.* 1974.

———. *Historical Writing in England c. 1307 to the Early Sixteenth Century.* 1982.

Harrison, F. L. *Music in Medieval Britain.* 1958.

Hoffmann, Thomas J. *Sacred Biography: Saints and Their Biographers in the Middle Ages.* 1988.

Jack, Ronald D. S. *Patterns of Divine Comedy: A Study of Medieval English Drama.* 1989.

Leader, Damian R. *A History of the University of Cambridge.* Vol. I: *The University to 1546.* 1988.

Oakeshott, Walter F. *The Sequence of English Medieval Art.* 1950.

Orme, Nicholas. *Education and Society in Medieval and Renaissance England.* 1989.

———. *English Schools in the Middle Ages.* 1973.

———. *From Childhood to Chivalry: The Education of the English Kings and Aristocracy, 1066–1530.* 1984.

Patterson, Lee. *Negotiating the Past: The Historical Understanding of Medieval Literature.* 1987.

Rickert, Margaret J. *Painting in Britain: The Middle Ages.* 2nd ed. 1965.

Salter, Elizabeth. *English and International: Studies in the Literature, Art, and Patronage of Medieval England*, Derek Pearsall and Nicolette Zeeman, eds. 1988.

Stone, Lawrence. *Sculpture in Britain: The Middle Ages.* 2nd ed. 1972.

Swanton, Michael James. *English Literature Before Chaucer.* 1987.

Talbot, Charles H. *Medicine in Medieval England.* 1967.

Webb, Geoffrey. *Architecture in Britain: The Middle Ages.* 1956.

Williamson, Paul. *Medieval Sculpture and Works of Art.* 1987.

Woodforde, Christopher. *English Stained and Painted Glass.* 1954.

Roman and Anglo-Saxon

Brooks, Nicholas. *Latin and the Vernacular Languages in Early Medieval Britain.* 1982.

Brown, George Hardin. *Bede the Venerable.* 1987.

Clapham, A. W. *English Romanesque Architecture Before the Conquest.* 1930.

Damico, Helen, and Alexandra Hennessy Olsen, eds. *New Readings on Women in Old English Literature.* 1990.

Duckett, Eleanor S. *Alcuin, Friend of Charlemagne.* 1951.

——. *Anglo-Saxon Saints and Scholars.* 1947.

Greenfield, Stanley, B. *A Critical History of Old English Literature.* 1965.

——. *Hero and Exile: The Art of Old English Poetry.* George H. Brown, ed. 1989.

Hanning, Robert W. *The Vision of History in Early Britain: From Gildas to Geoffrey of Monmouth.* 1966.

Henderson, George, *From Durrow to Kells: The Insular Gosple-Books, 650–800.* 1987.

Kennedy, Charles W. *The Earliest English Poetry: A Critical Survey of the Poetry Written before the Norman Conquest.* 1943.

Lapidge, Michael, and H. Gneuss. *Learning and Literature in Anglo-Saxon England.* 1985.

Nordenfalk, Carl. *Celtic and Anglo-Saxon Painting: Book Illumination in the British Isles, 600–800.* 1977.

Rice, D. Talbot. *English Art, 871–1100.* 1952.

Stanley, E. G., ed. *Continuations and Beginnings: Studies in Old English Literature.* 1966.

Stoll, Robert. *Architecture and Sculpture in Early Britain: Celtic, Saxon, Norman.* 1967.

Toynbee, J. M. C. *Art in Britain under the Romans.* 1964.

Whitelock, Dorothy. *From Bede to Alfred: Studies in Early Anglo-Saxon Literature and History.* 1980.

Norman Conquest to Magna Carta

Boase, T. S. R. *English Art, 1100–1216.* 1953.

Clapham, A. W. *English Romanesque Architecture after the Conquest.* 1934.

Darlington, R. R. *Anglo-Norman Historians.* 1947.

Evans, Gillian R. *Anselm. Outstanding Christian Thinkers.* 1989.

_____. *Anselm and a New Generation.* 1980.

Forde, Helen. *Domesday Preserved.* 1986.

Henry, Desmond P. *The Logic of St. Anselm.* 1967.

Legge, M. Dominica. *Anglo-Norman in the Cloisters: The Influence of the Orders upon Anglo-Norman Literature.* 1950.

_____. *Anglo-Norman Literature and Its Background.* 1963.

Liebeschiltz, Hans. *Medieval Humanism in the Life and Writings of John of Salisbury.* 1950.

Partner, Nancy F. *Serious Entertainments: The Writing of History in Twelfth-Century England.* 1977.

Tatlock, J. S. P. *The Legendary History of Britain.* 1950.

Williams, G. H. *The Norman Anonymous of 1100 A.D.* 1951.

Zarnecki, George. *Later English Romanesque Sculpture, 1140–1210.* 1953.

Thirteenth Century

Bony, Jean. *The English Decorated Style: Gothic Architecture Transformed, 1250–1350.* 1979.

Brieger, Peter H. *English Art, 1216–1307.* 1957.

Callus, D. A. P., ed. *Robert Grosseteste, Scholar and Bishop.* 1955.

Crombie, A. C. *Robert Grosseteste and the Origins of Experimental Science, 1100–1700.* 1953.

Hunt, Tony. *Popular Medicine in Thirteenth-Century England.* 1990.

Leff, Gordon. *Paris and Oxford Universities in the Thirteenth and Fourteenth Centuries: An Institutional and Intellectual History.* 1968.

McEvoy, James. *The Philosophy of Robert Grosseteste.* 1982.

Southern, Sir Richard. *Robert Grosseteste: The Growth of an English Mind in Medieval Europe.* 1985.

Swanson, Jenny. *John of Wales: A Study of the Works and Ideas of A Thirteenth-Century Friar.* 1989.

Vaughan, Richard. *Matthew Paris.* 1958.

Fourteenth Century

Aers, David, *Community, Gender, and Individual Identity: English Writing: 1360–1430.* 1988.

Brewer, Derek S. *Chaucer.* 3rd ed. 1973.

Bullock-Davies, Constance. *Register of Royal and Baronial Domestic Minstrels, 1272–1327.* 1986.

Courtenay, William J. *Schools and Scholars in Fourteenth-Century England.* 1987.

Evans, Joan. *English Art, 1307–1461.* 1949.

Hussey, S. S. *Chaucer: An Introduction.* 2nd ed., 1981.

Kenny, Anthony. *Wyclif.* 1985.

Leff, Gordon. *Bradwardine and the Pelagians.* 1957.

Morse, Ruth, and Barry Windeatt, eds. *Chaucer Traditions: Studies in Honor of Derek Brewer.* 1990.

Norton-Smith, John. *Geoffrey Chaucer.* 1974.

Phillips, Helen, ed. *Langland, the Mystics, and the Medieval English Religious Tradition: Essays in Honour of S.S. Hussey.* 1990.

Robbins, Rossell H. *Historical Poems of the Fourteenth and Fifteenth Centuries.* 1959.

Taylor, John. *English Historical Literature in the Fourteenth Century.* 1987.

Military History

Beeler, John. *Warfare in England, 1066–1189.* 1966.

Birley, Eric B. *Roman Britain and the Roman Army.* 1953.

Breeze, David John. *Roman Forts in Britain.* 1983.

Brown, R. Allen. *Castles from the Air.* 1989.

——. *English Castles.* 3rd ed. 1976.

Burne, A. H. *The Agincourt War: A Military History of the Latter Part of the Hundred Years War from 1369 to 1453.* 1956.

——. *The Crecy War: A Military History of the Hundred Years War from 1337 to the Peace of Bretigny, 1360.* 1955.

Carpenter, David. *The Battles of Lewes and Evesham, 1264/65.* 1987.

Davidson, H. R. E. *The Sword in Anglo-Saxon England.* 1962.

Hewitt, Herbert J. *The Black Prince's Expedition of 1355–1357.* 1958.

Humphries, P. H. *Castles of Edward I in Wales.* 1983.

Kenyon, John R., and Richard Avent, eds. *Castles in Wales and the Marches: Essays in Honour of D. J. Cathcart King.* 1987.

King, David James Cathcart. *The Castle in England and Wales: An Interpretive History.* 1988.

Marcus, Geoffrey J. *A Naval History of England.* Vol. I, *The Formative Centuries.* 1961.

Morgan, Philip. *War and Society in Medieval Cheshire, 1277–1403.* 1987.

Oakeshott, Ewart. *Records of the Medieval Sword.* 1990.

Platt, Colin. *The Castle in Medieval England and Wales.* 1982.

Renn, Derek F. *Norman Castles in Britain.* 2nd ed. 1973.

Seward, D. *The Hundred Years War.* 1982.

Simpson, W. Douglas. *Castles in England and Wales.* 1969.

——. *Hermitage Castle.* 3rd ed. 1987.

Index